HADRAT ALI,
THE FOURTH CALIPH

Encyclopaedia of Islam Series

HADRAT ALI
The Fourth Caliph

Editor-in-Chief

Dr. (Mufti) M. Mukarram Ahmed

ANMOL PUBLICATIONS PVT. LTD.

NEW DELHI - 110 002 (INDIA)

ANMOL PUBLICATIONS PVT. LTD.
4374/4B, Ansari Road, Daryaganj
New Delhi - 110 002
Ph.: 23261597, 23278000
Visit us at: www.anmolpublications.com

Hadrat Ali, The Fourth Caliph

First Published, 2006

ISBN 81-261-2393-1

PRINTED IN INDIA

Published by J.L. Kumar for Anmol Publications Pvt. Ltd., New Delhi and Printed at Mehra Offset Press, Delhi.

HADRAT ALI,
THE FOURTH CALIPH

CONTENTS

PREFACE

Islam stands for peace—peace for all, not for the Muslims, alone. In fact, Islam, when defined, incorporates in its fold, safety and security for the whole mankind. Holy Quran, the divine scripture addresses all humanbeings, not only the Muslims. Prophet of Islam, Hadrat Muhammad (peace be upon him) is known as the benefactor of mankind. Thus, Islam's message is for the whole universe and Allah (God) is the Lord of all the worlds. Islam is universal in its nature, essence, belief, philosophy, ideology approach and practice.

Surprisingly, Islam—despite being the most progressive, logical and scientific religion, on this planet—is also the most misunderstood religion. This confusion about Islam has recently increased, due to certain eventual reasons. Militant struggles by groups of staunch followers of Islam, against oppressive regimes in their respective lands—Palestine, Iraq, Russia, China, Philippines and an ongoing conflict in Sudan, to name a few—and to top all of these, the attack on World Trade Centre of New York, and inspite of subsequent fall of the Taliban, the still existing resistance in Afghanistan—have collectively contributed in deteriorating the situation, further. But, there is always a blessing in disguise. Resultantly, the said misunderstandings have instantly diverted the minds of people towards it and resulted into a deep interest in knowing Islam. Now, more and more people want to know about Islam, the religion, which has once again stirred the world community. Islam however, from its early days, advocates non-violence, peace and fraternity, but ironically, today it has been made known merely for militancy and terrorism. Islam which, on the very first day had raised the banner of reasoning and enlightenment in a dark age, on the one hand and humanity, equality and fundamental rights on the other, is today termed as an orthodox and autocratic faith. But, again, it has increased the anxiety and quest for awareness about this wonderful religion, among educated people, from all walks of life, the world over, in general and the West in particular.

Ironically, one prefers to ignore millions of Muslims, living in harmonious and peaceful (multi-racial) societies like India, Malaysia, Lebanon, South Africa and Mauritius and on the contrary, he or she loves to frequently talk about Muslim militant forces at war with various regimes. They symbolise Islam with dogmatism and terrorism.

The need of the hour is to correct the situation and to eradicate this feeling and tendency, prevailing all over and to depict the true picture of Islam. Hence, this bold and courageous endeavour, to bind the whole world of Islam in the form of a series, spanning over 101 books and titled as **Encyclopaedia of Islam**. This study also explores the relevance of Islam in the contemporary world.

One may believe it or not, today Islam is the fastest developing religion, which is spreading—through voluntary preaching and invitation—in the whole world and in West, including USA at a faster pace, than ever. Over the past few years, the popularity of Holy Quran and other authentic Islamic books has touched new heights. Islam is perhaps seen as the last bastion of spirituality, morality tradition and religious values, leading to real salvation.

For a comprehensive study of Islam, one intelligent reader requires exclusive, authentic and exhaustive books to satisfy their urge, answer their quest and convince them on all counts. This voluminous study is aimed at the same goal. These 101 books are in fact a grand treasure of knowledge and awareness about Islam and as well as a window, leading to Islamic wisdom. Further, it ascertains the honourable status of Islam as a perfect social and political system in the new world order.

No doubt, interpretations and explanations are essential for making any subject comprehensive for the readers—students and scholars alike. But original sources always form the best material to quench the thirst of a seeker of knowledge and convince a questioning brain. That's why, the Compilers and Editors of these volumes have banked upon the scriptures, original interpretations and old authentic classics. We have simply reproduced the authenticated texts, with introductory and linking notes and paragraphs, in order to make the text-matter easier to understand. We have not tempered with any material, it is either reproduced or presented in compact form. That's all. To support the matter, authentic extracts have been taken from Holy Quran and certified Traditions only. All efforts for maintaining utmost objectivity, have been made. In order to evade any possible controversy, all disputed matters have been avoided.

The honest intention of the Editors and Compilers is focused on projecting Islam in totality and in nutshell—bringing the whole world of Islam in the fold of one voluminous book. Peculiarly, every volume of this vast study is a comprehensive book in itself and covers a particular aspect or dimension of Islam. To make it straight, all the 101 volume make one exhaustive huge book on one hand and each volume is a separate book on the other. Hopefully, this research-based work would fill the vacuum, for a book of knowledge on Islam and prove to be a source of information and reference for all scholars, researchers and general readers, coming from amongst the Muslims, Non-Muslims, orientalists and of course those Western scholars and researchers, who may require a good source in an international language. For knowing Islam in totality and for discovering the treasures of Islamic wisdom and knowledge, they may easily refer to this multi-volume.

—Editors

One

HISTORICAL BACKGROUND

The Dark Age

Merely, a look at the map of the ancient World would convince the reader that the peninsula known as Arabia occupies a unique position with regard to the continents of Asia, Africa and Europe. It is situated in Asia, yet nothing but the narrow Red Sea divides it from Africa, whilst one has only to cross the Suez Canal to be in the Mediterranean Sea and Europe. It is thus almost the centre of the three continents and yet stands apart from all of them. It is surrounded by water on all sides except a narrow strip of land on the north. It has the Red Sea in the west, the Indian Ocean in the south and the south-east, the Persian Gulf and the Euphrates in the north-east. The Arabs call it Jazirat ul-Arab which literally means the Arabian Island. Yet this land surrounded by water on all sides except the north has no rivers of its own. It has an area of 120,000 square miles, or more, but its produce is not sufficient to support its scanty population.

Ancient empires and civilizations flourished in Persia, Egypt and Rome but they could never conquer the whole of Arabia. The cause for this comparative independence of Arabia lies in the fact that excepting for the province of Yemen which has some fertile land, the rest of Arabia consists of barren hills, deserts and valleys in which there is no cultivation, or only such cultivation which can last as long as there is rain water collected in the hollows of the land. When this water, due to lack of further rain, dries up, and which happens often, the population has to shift to new pastures. The greater part of the population lives in tents and is nomadic, and the camel is its ship of the desert. It is a land in which the production of the means of livelihood is entirely dependent on rain water.

The country, known as Arabia is, has been, and will always continue to be a country of caravans. Yet in this very desert of a land, God has built for ever the spiritual home of all mankind, viz., the Kaaba at Mecca — the centre of attraction, the centre of self-sacrifice, the centre of love, the centre of the union of the human and the Divine Soul.

Regions and Deserts of Arabia : The best-known regions of Arabia were Hijaz, Yemen, Najd, Hadramaut, Umman, Najran, Asir, Yamama, Khaibar, Hijr and Al-Ahqaf. Of the deserts, the largest in size is called Ad-Dahna or Ar-Rub ul-Khali. But the whole country is a desert in one sense.

Mesopotamia and Syria were once considered to be parts of Arabia but are no longer counted as such. Most of the provinces which have been named above lie on the fringe of the country, the centre being desert. Starting with the Persian Gulf and going round as does the clock we find first Bahrain on the shores of the Persian Gulf, the town of Kweit lies to the north of Bahrain. We then pass through Amman with the famous town of Muscat as its capital. Further round is the vast territory of Hadramaut with Mukkala as its port. To the north-west of Hadramaut is Al- Ahqaf, once the country of Ad. Further round and to the south- west of Arabia is the fertile land of Yemen. Aden, Hudaida, Sana and Mecca (famous for its coffee) are situated in Yemen. Further north is Al-Hijaz on the coast of the Red Sea with Mecca, Medina, Jeddah, Taif and Yanbu as its chief towns.

Between Yemen and Al-Hijaz is the small province of Al-Asir. To the north-east of Medina is the territory of Khaibar. North of Medina on the way to Sham or Syria is Hijr, the town of the Prophet Saleh and his people Thamud. Further north is Tabuk. West of Hijr is Madyan, the place of the Prophet Shoaib. In the centre or rather in the centre of southern Arabia is the great desert of Ad-Dahna and to its north is Najd with Riyad as its capital. Ibn Saud the present ruler of Hijaz comes from Riyad.

Climate and the Characteristics : The climate of Arabia is extremely dry except in some coastal towns and watered valleys. Dates are the chief production but Taif and some other places produce a number of fruits. The people are very hardy and individualistic, loving liberty and freedom from restraint. If the English are a nation of shop- keepers, the Arabs might be called a nation of traders and this is especially true of the people of Mecca whose sole means of livelihood is trade fostered by the pilgrimage to Mecca.

The Language : But the thing that distinguishes Arabia from all other countries in the world is Arabic. Latin, Greek and Sanskrit are highly infexional lanaguages. The Arabic language, however, is not only inflexional but has another peculiarity of its own not possessed by any Aryan or Mongolian tongue. In Arabic, all words, excepting particles, proper names and names of birds and animals and things for which there can only be one word, are dervied from roots which can be moulded to express every kind of meaning which the root is capable of expressing. In this way, Arabic is capable of immense expansion without any increase of its roots. And it can express in one word what other languages do in two, three or four words. It appears as if the Arabs, having little agriculture to attend to and less building to erect, have spent all their skill and all their energy in the building and cultivation of their language. Very few historians of Arabia have paid attention to the enormous influence of the Arabic language on the lives of the people of Arabia, but it is a factor which is of the greatest importance in all matters concerning the Arab people.

The Arabs are the descendants of Nuh. Historians have divided Arabs into three categories:

(1) Arab Baida, or Aboriginal Arabs,

(2) Arab Ariba, or those who made Arabia their home and adopted Arabic as their language,

(3) Arab Mustariba, or settlers.

Arab Baida : Arab Baida were all descendants of Laz, son of Sam, son of Nuh. They have been divided into tribes, the names of which are:-

(1) Ad

(2) Thamud

(3) Abail

(4) Amalaqa

(5) Tasam

(6) Judais

(7) Umaim

(8) Jurham

(9) Hadramaut

(10) Hadhud

(11) Abd Zakham, and others.

Of these Ad and Thamud are repeatedly mentioned in the Quran. Prophet Hud was sent to Ad and Saleh to Thamud.

Ad and Thamud : The following passages in the Quran show that they were both powerful peoples worshipping idols and building stone temples and houses on rocks and out of rocks.

Says Hud to Ad:

> Do you build on every height a sign for no use at all?
> And you make strongholds as if you were not going to die.
> And when you lay hold (on people).
> You lay hold tyrannically.
> Therefore reverence God and obey me
> And reverence Him Who has provided you with what you know.
> He has provided you with cattle and sons,
> And gardens and springs.
>
> (Quran, 26: 128 to 134.)

But Ad would not believe and though the prophet warned them of a coming storm, they would not listen to him and were destroyed. Another passage in the Quran refers to Ad in the following words:

> Hast thou not seen how thy Lord did with Ad
> (And) the people of Eram possessors of lofty columns,
> Such as have not been made in any other cities?
>
> (Quran, 89: 6 to 8.)

> The people of the prophet Saleh called Thamud lived in Hijr:
> And Thamud who hewed out huge rocks in the valley?
>
> (Quran, 89:9.)

And Saleh said to Thamud:

> Are you going to be left in the state in which you are in this life, secure?
> In gardens and springs
> And fields (of corn) and palm trees with tender spadices?
> And you hew out houses out of mountains with great show.
> Therefore reverence God and obey me,
> And obey not the command of those who are unrestrained:
> Who do evil in the land and do not do good.
>
> (Quran, 26: 146 to 152.)

But they would not believe and though the prophet warned them of a coming thunder and earthquake, they would not follow him and were destroyed.

It is stated that Ad was a very powerful and tall race the like of which did not exist anywhere else.

Arab Ariba : It appears that at some ancient date, another family of the children of Sam, son of Nuh, migrated into Arabia and adopted the language of the land, viz., Arabic. This latter family is said to have been the descendants of Qahtan or Yuqtan. Yuqtan was the son of Abar son of Shalikh son of Arfakhs had son of Sam son of Nuh.

Yarab conquered or destroyed all the descendants of Laz son of Sam son of Nuh and settled on the land. The language of the forefathers of Ya'rab was not Arabic but Arabic seems to have conquered the conquerors who gave up their original tongue in favour of Arabic. Some say that Ya'rab and Yemen are synonymous terms and there cannot be any doubt that Yemen was the home of Ya'rab and his immediate successors. Yemen is the only part of Arabia where there is sufficient rain water all the year round for the foundation of a kingdom. Saba was the capital of the Queen of Sheeba as mentioned in the Quran. One tribe of this family ruled over Yemen and Hadramaut. Another tribe called Azd conquered Medina and settled there. Another tribe called Khuz'a defeated Jurham and conquered Mecca. Nasr the son of Azd conquered Yamama. Umran the son of Khuza conquered Amman.

It will be seen that the provinces of Arabia are named after the names of the conquerors and it is certain that at the time of Muhammad's birth the children of Qahtan were the most powerful tribes in Arabia and that even now the greater part of the population of Arabia is descended from them. How the ancestors of Prophet Muhammad are connected with these Arab Ariba will be explained in the next section.

Arab Mustariba : About four thousand years ago there was a prosperous kingdom in the land now called Mesopotamia. The language spoken there was not Arabic but some form of ancient Persian and the people worshipped idols and heavenly bodies. In that land, and at that time, there was born a child called Ibrahim or Abraham. He was also a descendant from Nuh. His father called Adhar was a carpenter or sculptor engaged in making images for the idol-worshippers. The son, however, was a searcher of the Truth and doubted the veracity of the faith of his forefathers. He would not worship the stars, the moon or the Sun, because they were themselves subject to some superior power who ordered their rising and their setting. He would not worship the idols as these could not speak, eat, or help themselves in any way. God had destined him to be the Patriarch of the True Religion. What are now called Judaism, Christianity and Muhammadanism are mere names. The true religion or faith is the Faith of Abraham and its eternal name is

Islam — Submission to God and peace amongst all Mankind. The Quran preaches the faith of Abraham. In fact, there is no other faith and Muhammad came (as we shall see later) not to found a new religion but to convert the idol worshippers to the faith of Abraham and to unite the Christians and the Jews under the banner of Islam — the faith of Abraham.

> And they say, "Be Jews or Christians, you will find the path."
> Say, "Not so, the faith (is the faith) of Abraham the single-minded."
> And he was not of the pagans.
>
> (Quran, 2:135.)

> And who turns away from the faith of Abraham
> Save one who makes a fool of himself?
>
> (Quran, 2:130.)

> And when his Lord taught Abraham certain words,
> Then he carried them out:
> Said He: "I am surely going to make thee a leader of men."
>
> (Quran, 2:124.)

So that, the life of Muhammad is, according to the Quran, nothing but the continuation of the life-work of Abraham.

How did Abraham Come to Arabia?

He was driven out of his land by his father and his father's companions.

> And remember Abraham in the Book.
> He was truthful (also a) prophet.
> When he said to his father: "O my father! why dost thou worship that which hears not, and sees not and cannot avail thee aught?
> O my father! surely as to me, knowledge has been given to me which has not been given to thee,
> Therefore follow me, I will guide thee on the perfect path.
> O my father! worship not the evil one. Surely the evil one is disobedient to Arrahman (the most Merciful).
> O my fahter! I am surely afraid that a suffering from Arrahman (the most Merciful) will touch thee,
> Then thou shalt be an ally of the evil one."
> He replied: "Art thou turned away from my deities, O Abraham?

> Surely if thou desist not I will stone thee to death,
>
> And get away from me for a long long time."
>
> (Quran, 19:41 to 46.)

So Abraham left his father and his country, but not before he had taught them a lesson as described in Chapter 21 of the Quran, v.v. 51 to 75. One day, when they had gone out to a fair, Abraham entered their temple and broke all the idols into pieces except the principal one. When people came back and found the idols broken, they were enraged; and Abraham was put on his trial:

> They said: "O Abraham! Is it thee who hast done this to our deities?"
>
> He said: "Nay, he did it (who did it),
>
> Here is their chief, ask them then if they can speak."
>
> (Quran, 21:62-63.)

But idols don't speak and so the prosecutors and judges were made to hang down their heads in disgrace and were made to say out of their own mouths what Abraham had intended them to say:

> Surely thou knowest that these speak not.
>
> (Quran, 21:65.)

> "Why do you worship such things then?" was Abraham's retort. They wanted to burn him but God saved him and he left with his followers and settled in Palestine. Here he remained for a long time and was very prosperous but his mission took him to Egypt where he went accompanied by his wife Sarah.

He was well received by the king of Egypt who gave him many presents, including a girl named Hajirah. Abraham returned to Palestine from Egypt. He was getting on but had no children from Sarah as she was barren. He, therefore, married Hajirah and God gave him his first son called Ismail or Ishmael. Ishmael grew up to be a knowing, wise and faithful son, and when he had become a most comely youth, Abraham saw in a dream that he was sacrificing his only son to God. The dreams of the prophets being forebodings of the truth, Abraham with the consent of Ishmael prepared to carry it out, but God who intended to show the world how a faithful servant is prepared to sacrifice everything for the sake of God substituted a sheep in place of Ishmael and this event is annually commemorated by the sacrifice of a suitable animal by Muslims all over the world on the tenth day of the 12th month of the Muslim year.

This happened in Palestine. Sometime afterwards, Abraham, by God's order, took his son Ishmael and his second wife Hajirah to Mecca and settled them there. At this time Ishmael was about fifteen years of age. Abraham himself returned to Palestine. Ishmael's mother died soon after this. Ishmael learnt Arabic from the descendants of the tribe of Jurham and soon afterwards married Umara daughter of Saida son of Asama son of Aqil of the tribe of Amalaqa.

Shortly after this marriage, Abraham returned to Mecca and Ishmael having divorced Umara married another girl named Saida daughter of Madad son of Amar of the tribe of Jurham.

This marriage met with the approval of Abraham and Muhammad is a direct descendant of Ishmael by this second marriage. Muhammad thus inherited Persian blood through Abraham, Egyptian blood through Hajirah the second wife of Abraham, and pure Arabic blood through Saida wife of Ishmael.

> Sometime after this marriage, God ordained Abraham and Ishmael to rebuild the Kaaba at Mecca. The story of the building of the Kaaba is described in Chapter 2, v.v. 124 to 129 and references to Kaaba, Mecca, Hajj or pilgrimage and the importance of Hajj to all Muslims, nay to the whole mankind, uniting them in the service of one God with the Kaaba as its spiritual centre are made in many parts of the Quran. When Abraham and Ishmael were building the Kaaba, they prayed to God for the acceptance of their service and for the continuation amongst their offspring of a people who would be obedient to God and finally for the raising amongst their offspring of a Messenger or Prophet of God who would recite God's signs to them and teach them the Book and the Wisdom and who would purify their souls.
>
> (Quran, 2:127 to 129.)
>
> It was in fulfilment of this prayer that Muhammad was sent to the Arabs and through them to the whole world to teach mankind God's Word and the Wisdom and to purify their souls
>
> (Quran, 2:151, 3:163 and 62:2).
>
> It is said that in obedience to God's commandment Abraham made the yearly pilgrimage to Mecca as long as he lived. He, and not Muhammad is, therefore, under God's order the founder of the Hajj.
>
> (Quran, 22:26 to 33.)

Muhammad's Ancestors : ISHMAEL had twelve sons and one of them was named Qaidar, one of whose descendants was Adnan. Muhammad's pedigree is traced to Adnan in this way:

Muhammad (Pbuh) was the son of

(1) Abdullah	the son of
(2) Abdul-Muttalib	" " "
(3) Hashim	" " "
(4) Abd-Manaf	" " "
(5) Qusai	" " "
(6) Kilab	" " "
(7) Marah	" " "
(8) Kaab	" " "
(9) Luwai	" " "
(10) Ghalib	" " "
(11) Fihr	" " "
(12) Malik	" " "
(13) Nadr	" " "
(14) Kanana	" " "
(15) Khuzaima	" " "
(16) Mudrika	" " "
(17) Yas	" " "
(18) Mudar	" " "
(19) Nizar	" " "
(20) Muid	" " "
(21) Adnan	" " "

The fifth son of Malik above mentioned was also called Quraish and hence all his descendants are called Quraish after him.

It has already been related above that the tribe of Khuz'a conquered Mecca and dispersed the descendants of Adnan who were scattered in various parts of Arabia.

Qusai : In the 5th century of the Christian era, Qusai, the fifth ancestor of Muhammad, joined all the tribes of the Quraish and took possession of Hijaz and the custody of the Kaaba which had been wrested from their forefathers.

Dar un Nadwa : He rebuilt the Kaaba. He also built a palace for himself (near the Kaaba) in which a special room called Dar un Nadwa was set apart as an office and an assembly house for carrying on the government of Hijaz. The chiefs of the Quraish used to assemble there and under Qusai's guidance it was decided that the Quraish should feed the pilgrims for three days during the period of pilgrimage.

Abd ud Dar : After Qusai's death, his son Abd ud Dar was recognised as ruler in his father's place and when Abd ud Dar died there was a dispute between his grandsons and his brother Abd Manaf's sons as to the government of Hijaz but after the intervention of the influential people of the Quraish it was decided that Abd Shams, the son of Abd Manaf, should be in charge of the water supply of the pilgrims and the collection of taxes and the feeding of the pilgrims.

Abd ud-Dar's grandsons were to look after the fighting forces of the Quraish, to take care of the Kaaba and the Assembly House (Dar un-Nadwa). The government of Hijaz and more specially of Mecca, was thus divided into two departments - Revenue and Military. The Revenue was to be in the hands of Abd-Shams and the Military were to be under the control of the grandsons of Abd ud-Dar.

Hashim : But not long after this arrangement, Abd-Shams gave up his duties to his younger brother Hashim the great grandfather of Prophet Muhammad.

In this way, the fulfilment of Abraham's prayer was nearing its end.

Hashim was the wisest and the most generous amongst the Arabs. It was he who organised the merchandise of the Quraish, and every year caravans went south to Yemen and came back laden with its produce. Caravans also travelled north to Syria or Sham and brought back dried fruits, silk and other merchandise of the most valuable kind to Mecca.

Caravans also travelled east to Najd and Mesopotamia and west to the sea-coast; and Mecca thus became the great market of Arabia. Moreover, the annual assemblage of pilgrimage who came to worship their gods set up inside and outside the Kaaba and the Great Fair held at Mena on the occasion made Mecca the most important and the richest town in Arabia. Hashim's bravery and generosity made him the beloved of all Arabia.

Umayyah : But jealousy, like hope, always springs afresh in the human breast and Umayyah, the son of Abd-Shams, became jealous of his uncle's good fortune and great power. He tried hard to win over the government of the revenue of Mecca into his hands but remained unsuccessful.

At last, he could refrain himself no longer and threw out an open challenge to Hashim as to who was the better man. A public meeting was called and judges were appointed to decide the issue. The loser was to forfeit fifty head of camel and to be banished from Arabia for ten years.

Each candidate delivered addresses as to his qualifications, virtues and rights. The judges decided in favour of Hashim and Umayyah had to forfeit fifty camels and to leave the country for ten years. He went away to Syria or Sham. Hashim made a grand feast and distributed the flesh of the fifty camels amongst Meccans.

Abd ul-Muttalib : Hashim married a noble lady of Medina and had a son from her named Shabih. When Hashim died, his brother Muttalib went and fetched Shabih from Medina or Yathrib as it was then called. The people thought that Shabih was Muttalib's slave and by mistake called Shabih Abd ul-Muttalib (the servant or slave of Muttalib) and he is now known as Abd ul-Muttalib only.

When Abd ul-Muttalib grew up he was as famous as his father in bravery, generosity and fairmindedness. He was the grandfather and later the guardian of Muhammad.

Harb : Harb, the son of Umayyah challenged Abd ul-Muttalib and again the judges decided in favour of Abd ul-Muttalib and against Harb. Thus, there sprang up a great ill-feeling between the houses of Umayyah and Hashim in which the Umayyads were certainly in the wrong but they had some excuse, because, if their ancestor Abd-Shams had not abdicated his authority in favour of Hashim they would have been the rulers of Mecca. The antagonism has had the most serious consequences in the history of Islam. It arose about half a century before the birth of Muhammad. He and the first two Caliphs did their best to wipe it out but there are some things beyond the control of human power and this antagonism has been one of such affairs. But it is wholly and solely a political matter and has nothing to do with religion. Those who have imported religion into the controversy have prostituted their faith.

Abd ul-Muttalib and Zam-Zam : To continue our story of the descent of Muhammad:

When Abraham settled Hajirah and Ishmael at Mecca, there was a spring of drinkable water near their abode called Zam-Zam. But this spring had, during the course of centuries, been covered up with the debris of buildings and its exact situation had been lost. When Abd ul-Muttalib had the charge of supplying water to the pilgrims he naturally searched for the situation of this old spring. He and his eldest son Harith looked for it for a long time but in vain. None of the Quraish helped them. On the other hand, they made fun of them.

One night, Abd ul-Muttalib dreamt that the Zam-Zam was situtated at the place occupied by two idols, Asaf and Naila. Father and son started removing the idols and digging the ground. Their kinsmen objected to this but they continued in their search for this old spring. In the Quran, water is likened to God's spiritual blessing. Thus, Mecca was on the eve of the discovery of Zam-Zam, its healing water, and the birth of Muhammad its spiritual Healer.

Abd ul-Muttalib's Vow : When Abd ul-Muttalib felt his loneliness, he made a vow that if God (the Meccans even then believed in Allah or God as the Supreme Deity) gave him ten sons and made him the discoverer of Zam-Zam. He would sacrifice one son in God's name. Strange to say, he was successful in rediscovering the spring of Zam-Zam and in due time God gave him ten sons.

The discovery of Zam-Zam made Abd ul-Muttalib the most revered amongst the people of Mecca. When his sons came of age, he wished to carry out his vow of sacrificing one son in God's name.

He took all his sons to the Kaaba and drew lots. The name drawn was that of his youngest son Abdullah (the servant of God) whom he loved most.

Abd ul-Muttalib took his son and wanted to slaughter him (as Abraham tried to do about two thousand five hundred years before). He loved his youngest son most as did the people. They tried to dissuade him from his dreadful purpose.

Abdullah : After much argument and discussion, it was decided to refer the matter to the decision of a wizard or astrologer called Shiya. Shiya decided that ten camels being the blood-money for one man, Abd ul-Muttalib should put ten camels on one side and Abdullah's name on the other and draw lots. If Abdullah's name was drawn, the number of camels was to be increased by ten till the camels were drawn and when that happened the camels were to be slaughtered in God's name instead of Abdullah.

This was accordingly done and it was not till the number of camels had been increased to one hundred that the camels were drawn. The hundred camels were slaughtered and from that day one hundred camels were fixed as the ransom for the loss of one human life.

Abd ul-Muttalib had altogether thirteen sons born to him and six daughters.

Abraha's Invasion of Mecca : Whilst, Abd ul-Muttalib was in charge of the government of the Kaaba, and the care of the pilgrims, Abraha the Christian chief of Yemen built a shrine at Sana intending to make it the centre of attraction and of trade for the Arabs but he could not accomplish his object as long as Mecca retained its sacred position in the eyes of the Arabs.

Abraha, therefore, invaded Mecca in the year of the Prophet's birth but God destroyed his army; and Mecca was saved. The event is thus referred to in the Quran:

Hast thou not seen how thy Lord did with the companions of the elephant?

Did He not cause their stratagem to be lost?

And He sent against them flocks of birds

Throwing them stones of baked clay,

And He made them like stubble eaten away.

(Quran, Ch. 105.)

This was in the 40th year of the reign of Kisra Naushirwan of Persia, also called the first year of the elephant, also the year of Muhammad's birth and 570 or 571 of the Christian era.

Abdullah's Marriage with Amina : Abdullah, the youngest son of Abd ul-Muttalib, was married to Amina, daughter of Wahab son of Abd-Manaf son of Zuhrah, the chief of Bani-Zuhrah. Abdullah was twenty years of age and Abd ul-Muttalib was about seventy but so vigorous was the old man that the same day he married the daughter of his own uncle named Halah, who gave birth to Hamza the Prophet's uncle and later known as the Lion of Islam. Abdullah remained three days in the bride's house and then brought her home. Sometime after this, Abdullah went to exchange merchandise in Syria and left Amina pregnant. On his way back from Syria, he stopped at Medina with his friends where he became sick and died whilst Muhammad was still in his mother's womb. Abd ul-Muttalib on hearing of Abdullah's sickness had sent his eldest son Harith to bring him back but he brought the sad news of Abdullah's death to the old man's sorrow and Amina's grief.

Social Conditions

Political Status : The true history of Arabia begins with Islam. There was nothing but chaos before Muhammad made it a powerful country under his guidance. Nowhere in the whole peninsula was there any state or authority which could enforce law and order. At the beginning of the sixth century the Kindites (descendants of Qahtan through Ya'rab) had attempted to form a kingdom in central Arabia, but they soon fell a prey to the general disorder in the country and about the time of the Prophet's birth (571 A.C), anarchy reigned amongst the nomad tribes of al-Hijaz and Najd.

In the rest of the country, the Arabs had not even the semblance of power left to them. The Jews who had been driven out of Palestine by the Christians had built forts from the frontiers of Palestine to Khaibar and were the richest, most powerful and influential people in the land between Medina and Palestine but they were not organised under any one ruler, and judging by later events, one cannot say that they were at all capable of doing any good to themselves or to their adopted country. The best-known colonies of these Jews were the Banu-Nazir, the Banu-Quraiza and the Banu-Qainuqa.

In the rest of Arabia, the antagonism which at that time existed between Byzantium and Ctesiphon kept Ghassanids in Hauran were under Greek (or Roman) suzerainty whilst the Lakhmids in Hira and Anbar were under the Persian empire.

In the south, the Abyssinians had overthrown the Himyarites (the remnants of the ancient Sabeans) in about 571 A.C. but they were themselves overthrown by a native prince acting under the influence of the Persian Emperor and his agents.

Politically, therefore, Arabia in the sixth century was in the worst possible state that could be imagined. Having no ruler or king of its own, it was torn into pieces by the rivalries of its own unruly tribes and by the intrigues and rivalries of its neighbouring foreign states and by the greed and rapacity of its Jewish colonists.

The Religion : The life of the pre-Islamic Arabs, especially in Hijaz depended on trade and they made a trade of their religion as well. Taking advantage of the House built by Abraham and Ishmael at Mecca, or Becca as it was called in ancient times, they made it a house of the deities of all the Arabs so that people might come and worship their deities and bring them trade and money. About four hundred years before the birth of Muhammad one Amr bin Lahya bin Harath bin Amr ul-Qais bin Thalaba bin Azd bin Khalan bin Babalyun bin Saba, a descendant of Qahtan and king of Hijaz, had put an idol called *Hebal* on the roof of the Kaaba. This was one of the chief deities of the Quraish before Islam. It is said that there were altogether three hundred and sixty idols in and about the Kaaba and that each tribe had its own deity.

Not only had they idols and deities in the Kaaba but they had them also in other cities, some of which to Mecca he put up a stone or an image in his own town and made the circuit round it.

The shapes and figures of the idols were also made according to the fancy of the worshippers. Thus Wadd was shaped like a man, Naila like a woman, so was Suwa. Yaghuth was made in the shape of a lion, Yauq like a horse and Nasr like a vulture.

The tribe called Kalb worshiped Wadd; Huzail worshipped Suwa; the people of Yemen worshipped Nasr; Hamdan, Yauq; Bani-Thaqif of Taif Lat; Bani Kanana Uzza; Aus and Khazraj Manat; and so on and so forth.

Besides Hebal, there was another idol called Shams placed on the roof of the Kaaba.

There were also pictures of Abraham, Ishmael, Jesus and Mary placed inside the Kaaba..

The blood of the sacrificed animals brought by the pilgrims was offered to the deities in the Kaaba and sometimes even human beings were sacrificed and offered to the gods.

The tribe of Ghatfan had an imitation Kaaba made which they called Laith. Pilgrims went there also. Similarly, Bani-Khasham had a place called Zul-Khalsa. Near the hill called Uhud there was a place of worship called *Saida*. The tribe Rabia' had a place of worship called Zul-Kabat. Najran had a domed house called the Kaaba of the Najran.

In fact, there were as many deities as there were priests who wanted to make money out of their deities. Of true religion or true religious worship there was nothing at all. They believed neither in a day of judgment nor in rewards or punishments, or a life hereafter.

Besides idol-worship, they also worshipped the stars, the sun and the moon. It is difficult to say how starworship was introduced into Arabia or by whom. But astrology and astronomy are the oldest of human acquistions and there are people even today who believe that the stars and other heavenly bodies have an influence over human affairs; and ignorant people are always ready to worship anything that they regard as a guardian of mankind or any thing that may do good or harm to them according to their theories.

Mention of Idol-worship in the Quran : Idol-Worship is so old and so persistent that even Nuh found it impossible to uproot it and this cry to God is:

> Nuh said: "My Lord! surely they have disobeyed me and followed one whose wealth and children increase him in nothing but loss.
>
> And they have planned a great plan.
>
> And they say: "Forsake not your deities and forsake neither Wadd nor Suwa'; neither Yaghuth, nor Yauq, nor Nasr.
>
> (Quran, 71:21 to 23)

Abraham bewailed the same thing when he said:

> And (remember) when Abraham said: "My Lord!
>
> Make this town peaceful and save me and my children from worshipping idols.
>
> My Lord, surely they have caused a large number of men to be lost...
>
> (Quran 14: 35-36)

With reference to the three special deities of the Meccans, says God:

> Have you then considered al-Lat and al-'Uzza

> And Manat, the third, the last?
>
> Are there males for you and for Him females?
>
> A most unfair division that!
>
> They are nothing but names which you have given them, you and your forefathers;
>
> No authority has God sent down for them, They (the unbelievers) follow nothing but a guess and what their souls desire..
>
> (Quran, 53: 19-23)

The Meccans also believed in the Supreme Being Allah but they fancied that He could not be approached except through some minor deity or through the angels whom they called "the daughters of Allah".

> And those who take protectors besides Him (say):
>
> "We worship not these but in order that they may bring us nearer to God in position..."
>
> (Quran, 39:3.)
>
> But "Devotion," says God "is exclusively due to him."
>
> (Quran, 39:3.)

It is this joining gods with God that is called *Shirk* in the Quran, and which is the unpardonable sin of mankind and in which the Quraish were engrossed at the time of Muhammad's birth so much that their very livelihood depended upon this worship. It has been so in all countries and in all ages. The guardians of temples and the priests thereof are the spiritual robbers of mankind.

The Status of Women

Killing of Daughters: Amongst Bani Tamim and the Quraish, daughters were regarded as a nuisance and some fathers prided themselves on their feats of murdering their daughters.

When a daughter grew up to the age of five or six, the father dug a deep pit in the desert, took his daughter to the pit, pushed her into it and in spite of her cries buried her alive.

A man called Qais bin Asim buried ten daughters of his in this way. All the Arabs were not equally addicted to this cruelty but very few tribes were free from this atrocious custom. Some killed their children for fear of poverty as stated in the Quran:

> And kill ye not your children for fear of poverty
> We provide them with livelihood and you also;
> Surely killing them is a heinous sin.
>
> (Quran, 17:31)

Marrying Widows: When a person died and left a widow or widows, the nearest male relation had to cover her or them with his mantle and they became his wives.

Even a son, in this way, took his step-mother as his wife. This most heinous custom was abolished by the Quran:

> And marry not those women whom your fathers have married,
> But what is past (is past)
> Surely (such marrying) is an indecency and a heinous affair;
> And an evil way.
>
> (Quran, 4: 22.)

All this was possible because there was no authority to enforce any laws in Arabia except tribal customs and because women were regarded as mere chattels

Fornication and Adultery: The relations amongst men and women in pre-Islamic days were such as were not and could not be controlled by any laws. The women were as lawless as the men and that may have provided some excuse to fathers who killed their own daughters. Women put on their best ornaments and clothes and went out singly, in twos, and in parties, to the outskirts of the desert to satisfy their desires. There they met young men. Neither the men nor the women were ashamed to indulge in the most lustful deeds and the most indecent talk by means of which the males enjoyed themselves and the females satisfied their desires. Fornication was not considered a crime or a sin.

In the battle of Uhud, Hind, the wife of Abu-Sufyan son of Harb son of Umayyah, excited the passions of the Quraish warriors against Muhammad by the following song:-

> If you advance, we will embrace you and we will prepare for you beds of sexual intercourse;
>
> But if you go back we will leave you the leaving without a Joy.

Some women, when they gave birth to a child and did not know, or could not say, who the father was, were not ashamed to assign the child to the man who most resembled it.

Polygamy and Divorce: There were no laws regulating marriage and divorce. A man married as many wives as he liked and divorced as he wished. A man had to say to his wife, " Thou art to me as the back of my mother" and she was divorced but could not marry another. So great was the force of this unjust custom that in the early days of the Prophet's mission even he did not know how to deal with it till God abolished it. The matter is explained in chapter 58 of the Quran

Gambling and Drunkenness : Drunkenness, gambling and fornication went hand-in-hand and those who were not addicted to these vices could be counted on one's fingers. Those who were not so addicted were considered mean, stingy and unsociable. "And when I die mary not one who is humble, weak or who does not gamble, and avoids his people." This is the will left by a Pre-Islamic poet to his widow.

There were hundreds of names for wines and every corner of a street had its prominent wine shop. Trade and wine-selling had become synonyms.

It seems that those Arabs who became Christians were the main cause of the introduction of Syrian wines into Arabia. Drinking is an essential part of the lives of Christian nations; and America has been forced back to wine drinking after having vainly tried to go "dry" for ten years.

Bani-Taghlab were a Christian people and their chief poet (addressing a female) says:

Heigh-ho! get-up with thy cup of wine,

And give me the morning drink,

And leave not a single wine of the wines of Indrina. Indrina was a town in Syria.

Wines which when mixed with hot water smell like roses.

Parties of drunkards met at one another's house; camels were slaughtered; dancing and singing girls were invited and when all became thoroughly drunk they indulged in sexual intercourse to their heart's content.

A poet of their own time thus describes the beauty and the pleasure of these parties:

The companions of my drinks

Are bright like the stars;

And as the evening comes,

So does the singing girl

Robed in saffron Southern clothes;

Her chest is open wide,

Embraced by many braves:

And when we say to her
"Do sing";
With a slow and rhythmic motion,
She advances to our feet,
And with the help of drinking wines
And with my pleasures deep
And with my spending of the wealth
Do I pass the life I lead.
And were it not for pleasures
Which delight a noble youth,
I swear by thee I'd gladly die.

And the poet goes on to explain in several more couplets what those pleasures were:

> The first was to disregard the advice of wise people and to indulge in drinking red and black wines which bubble up when mixed with hot water.

The second was to have a dark cloudy day — and what a lovely day that would be! and be engaged with a female beauty in a tent so that the day's duration was cut short and time passed quickly.

The third was to slaughter a fat she-camel pregnant with a young one and to have the young one roasted with the fatty hump of her mother and being served by young maids.

And it did not matter to these revellers whether the camel was their own or belonged to some one else. The more helpless the owner the more pleasant for them.

Stories of drunken orgies are so numerous that a book might easily be compiled to contain all these. This state of affairs lasted till drinking and gambling were entirely forbidden by the Quran.

Gambling was practised by means of arrows. As the greater part of the wealth of the Arabs consisted of camels, the stakes were also camels. Camels were slaughtered and the flesh divided into ten parts.

Lots were then drawn by means of ten arrows mixed together and placed in the hands of a third party. The arrows were either marked with one, two or three notches or were unmarked. Those who drew the blank arrows got nothing, those who drew the marked arrows got as many portions of the flesh as were the marks on the arrows.

The flesh was then given to the winners according to their shares and distributed by them to the poor and the needy or to their friends. Those who did not gamble were considered mean and uncharitable.

Usury : The Arabs were also given to lending money on heavy rates of interest, and when the money lent was not paid at the stipulated time, interest was added to the capital and further interest charged on the whole as is done by money-lenders all over the world. But the Arab usurers sometimes not only added interest to the capital but increased the latter also. If the loans were not paid the creditor sometimes took possession of the borrower's wife and children, or sometimes the wife and children themselves became the subject of a mortgage.

Tribal Wars : The Pre-Islamic Arabs were ferocious warriors. It did not matter what the cause was. Every tribe had its feuds and unless a tribe or an individual who considered himself wronged had its or his revenge there was no peace. But then the other side considered itself wronged and so the feuds went on.

For forty or fifty years before Islam there had been about one hundred and thirty two battles called Ayyam ul-Arab (lit.. the days of Arabs)

One of these feuds arose amongst the tribes of Abbas and Zabyan in this way. They each had a famous horse respectively called Dahas and Ghabra. A race was run and one side was guilty of some infringement of the rules of racing. This led to a feud which lasted for forty years.

Another feud is called "The War of Basus". Basus was a woman who had a she-camel. This camel by accident trespassed into the pasturing ground of another tribe. The camel was wounded. The tribes (Bakar and Taghlab) got inflamed and had a bloody war. Aus and Khazraj, two tribes of Medina, were engaged in a most bloody war in which they lost a good many of their chief men. This war was terminated by the Prophet when he emigrated to Medina.

The evil of these fights was not the mere destruction of the lives and wealth of the people. When one tribe conquered another, they took possession of the females of the conquered and committed acts of indecency either in the open field or wherever they pleased. When peace was made and these women were returned they were taken back as a matter of course.

Cruelty and Plunder : The Arabs of Pre-Islamic days, semi-barbarous as they were cut off live flesh from the backs of camels and the tails of fat sheep which they roasted and enjoyed eating. They were given to mutilating their captives (both men and women).

Women were sometimes tied to the tails of horses which were then made to gallop so that the poor victims were crushed to death. This was the pastime of the nobles.

Sometimes a man was locked up in a cabin till he died of hunger and thirst.

Camels were, similarly, tied at the tombs of deceased persons till they died for lack of food.

Belief in Ghosts, Devils and Evil Spirits : In common with all pagans and semi-civilised or semi-barbarous peoples, the Pre-Islamic Arabs believed in all kinds of invisible beings collectively called jin (something hidden and invisible).

Those jins that were supposed to live in jungles and deserts and ruins and misled people were called ghoul. They were supposed to be both male and female. It is difficult to say whether all the supposed jins were really considered to be invisible, or whether some of them were really not invisible but men living in the desert whom these Arabs called jin. It is said that these jins mixed with the Beduins of the desert and when the latter lighted fires in the desert in winter the jins came and warmed themselves at these fires but refused to join in eating. They had various names. Those who lived with men were called Amar those that annoyed children were called Ruh. Those who were wicked were called Shaitan. Those who were still more wicked were called Ifrit. A man called Khurafa is said to have been carried away by them and on his return after a long time he is reported to have spoken strange things.

All this kidnapping and other stories about the jins joining Beduins in warming themselves before the fires would show that the jins or at least some of them were wild men of the desert who spoke some aboriginal language which the Arabs did not understand.

Soothsayers and Fortune-tellers : There was no lack of wizards, soothsayers and fortune-tellers in Arabia. But in this the Arabs were not alone. Even now the world is not rid of these social pests. Each soothsayer was supposed to be possessed by some jin who gave him information about the past or the future. They accused the Prophet also of being a kahin or one possessed. But God cleared him of these accusations. When ignorant people are incapable of understanding something which is beyond their ken they explain it by something known to them howsoever absurd the explanation may be. And the disbelieving Arabs called Muhammad a poet, a mad man, or a sorcerer. To them he possessed supernatural powers which, according to their knowledge, could only be explained by such names as mentioned above.

The Kahins or fortune-tellers lived in temples and were both men and women. When they were asked about the future, they excited themselves into a state of hysteria and predicted the future. They received valuable presents. Some of them who afterwards became Muslims acknowledged their fraudulent practices.

Even poets were considered to be possessed and on this theory when once the Prophet was unwell for two or three days and did not go to say his prayers in the Kaaba, the wife of Abu Lahab came and said to him.

"I hope that thy devil has left thee."

She was a poor unfortunate woman who was engrossed in her superstition. How could she understand the higher spiritual elevation of Muhammad?

One poet boasts of his own devil.
I and every poet of men,
Each has his devil
But whilst others have females,
Mine is a male..

Poets and Poetry : The Pre-Islamic Arabs were not a literary race. Very few of them could read or write. In fact, the art of writing was still in its infancy. The written documents or engravings that are still preserved are of the most primitive type. In spite of this, the majority of the Arabs-men, women and children-were steeped in poetry. The language lent itself to poetic forms and it had been cultivated as no other language had ever been cultivated before. The Arabs were Arabs (i.e., those who speak fluently and intelligently). The rest of the world, according to them, were Ajami (deaf and dumb, the very opposite of fluent and intelligent).

But their poetry consisted mostly of personal or tribal boasting of the love of women and wine of their fondness for gambling and drunkenness.

It was also the handmaid of warriors for exciting their passions and a poet was considered to be the equal of a hundred soldiers.

Odes and poems were recited on the occasion of the pilgrimage and the best ones were said to be hung in the Kaaba. Saba-Muallaqat which are still extant were such seven selected poems. But it is possible that the world Muallaqat may only mean "Selected and pearled together "and not literally "hung up". If so, they would mean the seven classical poems. These poems are still studied by all Arabic scholars. They are the most difficult pieces of Arabic literature to understand on account of the numerous allusions to Arabic customs, names and peculiarities of the life of the Arabs.

Allied to poetry was the art of love-making. And both individuals and tribes boasted of their superiority in this art. The more obscene and vulgar their exploits the greater was their boasting. To them it was the life-blood of their chivalry.

Imra ul-Qais was the Shakespeare of the Arabs. In addition, he was a prince and a ruler. He committed the most unmentionable indecencies with his own cousin sister (his father's sister's daughter) and other women. These indecencies have been the subject of a most famous poem composed by him called Qasida-Lamia. In spite of these indecencies the ode was on everybody's tongue both old and young.

These poets are thus referred to in the Quran:

And as to the poets, the deviators follow them.

Dost thou not see them wandering in every valley?

And that they say what they do not do?

(Quran, 26: 224 to 226.)

Pre-Islamic poetry, instead of elevating the human soul, degraded it to its lowest depths. But its eloquence cannot be denied. It represented the Arab character to perfection.

The Virtues : No people, howsoever wild or barbarous, can exist for long without some virtues. The Arabs were wild but not sophisticated as the Jews were, whom Jesus came to reform.

Frankness: The quotations from Arabic poetry, already given, prove that though the Arabs boasted of their vices they did not hide their sins under the cloak of religious hypocrisy as did the Jews at Khaibar. And in their wars with Muhammad, which will be described later on, the Arabs tried their best to kill Muhammad and his companions and to turn them back to the oldways of worship but they never poisoned him or his companions as did a Jewish lady at Khaibar. The disbelieving Arabs were bitter in their hatred of Muhammad but they were open enemies and in their heart of heart as they believed Muhammad to be a perfectly honest and noble man. Their opposition to him was based on the fact that Muhammad's preaching was certain to ruin their livelihood. They did not and could not foresee that he came to unite and to make them a prosperous nation. When in the end they did see that, their support of Muhammad was as great as their previous antagonism.

Love for Independence: The Arabs were as a whole a free people. They were free-booters but still they had not been with the servility which is inseparable from foreign yoke. There may have been political intrigues due to the influence of the rival empires of Persia and Byzantine but the people as a whole were not subjugated to any ruler. The very fact that each tribe and each family had to fight for its existence made them love liberty. In fact, the love of liberty had become the love of unruliness, but still it was there. It was not easy for any ambitious ruler to make them the slaves of his wishes.

Bravery and Hunting: The greatest insult that could be given to an Arab was to insinuate that he was a coward. The Arabs had no fear. They loved adventures involving danger. Not only men but women were brave to the extreme. They accompanied their males to the battlefield knowing full well the danger they exposed themselves to. Trade and hunting were almost the only lawful occupations they had. And there is no better training than hunting for the cultivation of bravery. To kill or to be killed is the underlying principle of hunting and the practice of this occupation stood the Arabs in great stead. Under such a rigorous method of living, only the fittest could survive. The weak and the cowardly had no chance of success in life.

Hospitality and Generosity: The hospitality of the Arabs is renowned all over the world and is inherited from Abraham. The guest was honoured by the Arabs as if he was one of God. They would slaughter a camel or a sheep for him. They would protect him from all harm at the cost of their own lives as long as he was within their protection. The rich would make themselves poor by slaughtering their camels and distributing the flesh thereof to their friends and the poor. This generosity went so far in the time of Ignorance that even the chastity of women was considered second to the pleasures of the guest. Story books are full of anecdotes of Arabic generosity and Arabic hospitality. There may be exaggeration in the majority of these stories but that they are based on facts is not denied by anyone.

Memory and Intelligence: Never in the history of mankind has there ever been a race of men who cultivated their memory as did the Arabs. And memory we know is one of the greatest pillars of brain power. Every Arab knew his genealogy by heart for ten to twenty generations back. They all could recite poems.. The classical poems were the inheritance of the whole people. So great was their power of memorising and recollection that men like Ali, Abu Bakr and Umar had merely to listen to long verses of the Quran to remember them. And once learnt they never forgot them. Even toady there are Arabs who not only know the Quran by heart but also thousands of traditions of the Prophet whit the names of all the reporters in correct order. To this they add all the famous poems, all the proverbs and witty sayings of their forefathers.

The Arabs were prodigies of intellect and it did not take them long after Islam to master all the sciences of the Greeks, Indians and Romans and to add to them. In Algebra, in Astronomy, in Philosophy, in Grammar, in Poetry, in History, in Chemistry, in Navigation, in Eloquence and in all the arts the world is indebted to their labours and without this Arab Intelligence there could have been no modern Civilization.

Religious and Moral Condition of Others : Jews: The Jews under Moses were God's favoured people but they annoyed Moses as long as he lived. They rose to great eminence under David and Solomon but when Jesus appeared amongst them they were entirely subject to the Romans. This was not their only misfortune, they had become hard-hearted, formal and sophisticated. They loved controversy and dispute, the breaking of all the laws whilst pretending to keep their form. More than half of the historical portions of the Quran relate to the doings or misdoings of the Jews. They were told not to fish on the Sabbath day, but to get out of this difficulty they erected dams and locks in their rivers and when fish came there on the Sabbath day they closed these locks and captured the fish afterwards. They were forbidden to practise usury but they could not live without it, and so they broke all the laws. Jesus came to reform them but they persecuted him. Every reformer that was sent to them was persecuted or killed, and Muhammad met with no better fate. He was persecuted by them and poisoned by one of their females, the effects of which remained. The Prophet is stated to have said that his last fatal illness was due to this poison. Greedy, selfish, quarrelsome and revengeful-these were the traits that distinguished the Jews. It is a thousand pities that a race who had the largest number of prophets amongst their forefathers should have degenerated to such an extent.

Before the time of Muhammad's birth the Jews had been expelled from the Holy Land by the Christians and had setteld in Northern Arabia but their treachery was destined to drive them away from Arabia as well.

The wrong-doings of the Jews towards their own prophets, towards Christians in the days of Christ, towards Muhammad and his followers in Arabia, make a painful reading and enough of it will be related in the pages of this book in due course.

Christians: If the condition of the Jews in the sixth century of the Christian era was bad, that of the Christians was worse.

Jesus was one of the five major prophets mentioned in the Quran, viz.

Nuh, Abraham, Moses, Jesus and Muhammad (PBUH) : Jesus, as is apparent by his teachings had come to confirm the Law and the Torah and it was his mission to expound the reality underlying the principles of the Old Testament as against the formalism and ritualism of the Jews.

But Paul, who followed him was not content with this simple truth. He was for converting the Greeks and other heathens. He incorporated the mythology of the Greeks into the spiritualism of Christ and Christianity henceforth became tainted with heathenism. The doctrine of trinity belonged to Greek or Egyptian mythology but Paul introduced it into Christianity and since then the Christians have never been able to get rid of the curse of worshiping deities of their own making.

> And the Jews say: "Azra is the son of God,"
> Whilst the Christians say: "The Messiah is the son of God."
> These are their sayings with their mouths;

They copy the saying of those who disbelieved before (them).
God's displeasure be upon them!
How do they turn away?
They have adopted their learned men and their monks as lords besides God,
And (also) the Messiah son of Mary.
And they were ordered to worship none but one God;
There is no deity but He.
Gloried be He, away from what they join.

(Quran, 9: 30-31.)

Eastern Roman Empire : About 325 A.C. (After Christ) the Roman Empire was divided into two; and Constantine, the Emperor of the Eastern Roman Empire, adopted Christianity as his state religion. This made the Christians worse than ever before. They began to fight amongst themselves on doctrines of their inventions and from that day to this there is no stoppage of the foundation of new sects amongst them. In Arabia, the Christians worshipped Mary as one of the members of the holy trinity-the others being Jesus and God. Jesus taught the service of God and the brotherhood of mankind. But each Christian sect has its own definition of Godhead and its own views on the brotherhood of mankind. No two of them can agree together and at the time of Muhammad's birth they had nothing left of the spirit of Christianity except amongst some solitary holy divines and God-loving people as there must always be some amongst each people.

They are not all on a level.

(Quran , 3:112.)

And of those who call themselves Christians

We (also) took their covenant,

They also forget a portion of what they were reminded of,

Wherefore We feed them with enmity and hatred amongst themselves to the day of the Awakening...

(Quran, 5:14.)

It is really most shameful that the followers of the Prince of Peace should be at each other's throats. As these lines are being written (3rd January 1936), Reuter is wiring all over the world that the Italians have destroyed the Swedish Red Cross Hospital in

Abyssinia. Italy has been declared the aggressor and yet goes on piling up aggression upon aggression in the face of the whole world-Christians and non-Christians put together. This was the spirit of the Christianity of the Eastern Roman Empire. This was also the spirit of the Christianity of the Roman Catholics in Spain after the Muslims had been brutally murdered there in the fifteenth century. But whoever, be he nominally a Muslim, a Christian or a Jew, is cruel towards mankind is God's enemy.

> For this reason have We prescribed for the children of Israel
> That he who kills a person without the latter being guilty of killing of another
> Or of doing evil in the land,
> Then his action is such as if he had killed all mankind.
> And he who saves one life is
> As if he had saved all mankind...
>
> (Quran, 5 : 32.)

But with the Christians of the sixth century killing of their opponents was a plesure. The Emperor Julian is reported to have said:

> "No wild beasts are so hostile to men as Christian sects in general are to one another."

> "The condition of Constantinople under Justinian, the Christian and glorified legislator, is the best index to the demoralised and degraded state of society all over Christendom. Public or private virtue had no recognition in the social conceptions; a harlot sat on the throne of the Caesars, and shared with the Emperor the honours of state. Theodora had publicly plied her trade in the city of Constantine and her name was a byword amongst its dissolute inhabitants. And now she was adored as a queen in the same city by 'grave magistrates, orthodox bishops, victorious generals and captive monarchs'. The empire was disgraced by her cruelties, which recognised no religious or moral restraint. Seditions, outbreak, and sanguinary tumults, in which the priesthood always took the most prominent part, were the order of the day. On these occasions, every law, human or divine was trampled under foot; churches and altars were polluted by atrocious murders; no place was safe or sacred from depredations; the bonds of society were rent asunder, and revolting outrages were perpetrated in broad day light.......

> "Humanity revolts from the accounts of crime which sully the annals of Christian Constantinople. Whilst the Prophet of Islam was yet an infant, one

of the most virtuous emperors who ever ascended the throne of Byzantine was massacred, with his children and wife, with fearful tortures at the instance of a Christian monarch. The emperor was dragged from his sanctuary, and his five sons were successively murdered under his eyes; and this tragic scene closed with the execution of the emperor himself. The empress and her daughters were subjected to merciless cruelties and then beheaded on the very ground which had been stained with the blood of poor Emperor Maurice. The ruthless treatment meted out to the friends, companions and partisans of the imperial victim, serves as an index to the morality of the Byzantine Christians. Their eyes were pierced, their tongues were torn from the root, their hands and feet were amputated; some expired under the lash, others in flames, others again were transfixed with arrows."

> And if God were to seize mankind on account of their wrongdoing,
>
> Not a living thing would He leave thereupon (i.e.., on the earth),
>
> But He postpones them to a fixed term... (Quran, 16:61.)

But when the time for God's punishment comes (whether it be here or hereafter) no one can put it back. Mankind do not realize that in spite of the liberty given to them the kingdom of the heavens and the earths is in the hands of God.

> Evil has appeared on land and sea for what the hands of mankind have earned that He may cause them to taste some of what they have done in order that they may return.
>
> (Quran, 30:41.)

The Persians : Where the Persians any better than the Christians. Yes and no. Yes, because the Persians were not so cruel as the Christians, and no, because they were equally depraved.

The nominal faith of Persia was Zoroastrianism which laid down that all the good in the world was due to Ormuzd and all the evil to Ahriman but Ormuzd always succeeded. They worshipped Ormuzd. The Persians were, however, a fighting race and when they subjugated alien races their faith became corrupt. Old Magism or the worship of the elements of nature, was revived and Zoroastrianism was mixed with old Sabaeism of the Medes and Chaldeans.

The Persian of the sixth century recognised no law of marriage or divorce except his own will. He could marry his nearest kindred and do as he pleased.

"The worship of true God had given place to a Chaldeo-Magian cult and the fierce intolerance with which Ardeshir and his-successors persecuted rival creeds, failed to achieve its purpose.

"The Persian empire, under the later Sasanides, only rivalled in the turmoil of its sects and the licentiousness of its sovereigns, in the degeneration of its aristocracy and the overweening pride of its priesthood, the empire of the Byzantines. The kings were gods; they were absolute masters over the person and property of their subjects, who possessed no rights, and were virtual serfs....

"All these evils betokened a complete depravity of moral life, and foreshadowed the speedy extinction of the nation in its own iniquities. This doom though staved off for a time by the personal character of Kisra nushirwan, became inevitable after his death. But a Master had already appeared destined to change the whole aspect of World."

Indians and Chinese : What about India and China? These lands are the guardians of ancient philosophy and ancient literature. Were they morally any better than the Christians of Europe and the Mago-Zoroastrians of Persia?

India has no authortative history of the land before the Muslims conquered it. There can be no doubt, however, that India had philosophers and learned men long before the world knew anything about philosophy and learning.

The Upanishads and the Bhagavad Gita are the immortal productions of Indian learning. Though there is much inter-mixture of ideas in these two works, they are also full of passages which are the nearest approach to monotheism in any ancient religion.

But later Hinduism has degenerated this high conception of godhead into a degraded form of pantheism against which the Arya and the Brahmo Samajists are rebelling.

The introduction and perversion of caste-system has also reduced Hinduism to the level of human worship. Idol-worship has now thrived in India for thousands of years and Buddhism which once tried to free men from the worship of all gods has itself fallen a victim to idol-worship.

However grand the theories and ideas of Hindu philosophers about God and religion may be, religion in actual practice amongst the Hindus is and has been for many centuries nothing but the "worship of priests, the manes and the Vedic gods". Trees, stones and other natural objects were and are the subjects of popular adoration. Female infanticide was not uncommon and the burning alive of the widows with their husbands' corpses was considered an act of merit.

All this was due to the fact that women were considered as the property of the males and as having no rights of their own.

A woman was not allowed to study the Vedas or to take part in the ablutions of the manes or in the sacrifices to the gods.

"Women, says Manu, have impure appetites, they show weak flexibility and bad conduct. Day and night must they be kept in subjection.

"As regards the Sudras, he declared, almost in the words of the Pandeets that the Creator had made them slaves and that a man belonging to that caste, even when he is emancipated by his master, cannot be free; for bondage being natural to him, who can deliver him from it.

Such in brief was the religious and social condition among the people of one of the most gifted sections of the Aryan race at the time when the Prophet of Islam brought his Message to the world."

It is not necessary to go deeply into the history of the moral and religious status of the Chinese. That gifted nation has always been a practical people.. They have been worshipping the souls of their forefathers for generations; and religious theories which afflict the Arab, the Jew, the Christian and the Hindu are no concern of theirs.

They have always been a race of hard-working peasants, pedants, robbers, great legislators and artisans. Slavery, concubinage and gambling have been in their blood and no one has been able to free them from these national vices.

Love of God, belief in Heaven or Hell or in God's Messengers was unknown to the Chinese. They were materialists pure and simple.

Two

LIFE OF A BRAVE MAN

Early Life

Family Background : Hadrat Ali was the son of Abu Talib, a prominent Quraish chief and custodian of the Holy Kaaba Abu Talib was so called because he was the father of "Talib", the eldest brother of Hadrat Ali. The real name of Abu Talib was Abd Manaf. He was, however, more popularly known by his title than by his real name. Abu Talib was the son of Abdul Muttalib. Abdul Muttalib was also a surname, his real name being Shaybah. Abdul Muttalib was the son of Hashim. Hashim was a great man of the line and his descendants came to be known as Hashimites.

The mother of Hadrat Ali was Fatima. She was the daughter of Asad who was a son of Hashim. Fatima was a cousin of Abu Talib. Thus both the father and mother of Hadrat Ali were Hashimites and that was a great honour.

Ancestral Relationship with Holy Prophet : The Holy Prophet was the son of Abdullah who was the son of. Abdul Muttalib. Abdullah and Abu Talib were real brothers. Abu Talib was thus the real paternal uncle of the Holy Prophet of Islam. Hadrat Ali was the first cousin of the Holy Prophet. The Holy Prophet and Hadrat Ali had a common grandfather—Abdul Muttalib.

Abdul Muttalib was the son of Hashim, who was the son of Abd Manaf, who was the son of Qussay, who was the son of Murrah, who was the sort of Kaab who was the son of Luayy, who was the son of Ghalib, who was the son of Fihr, who was the son of Malik, who was the son of Nadr, who was the son of Kananah. Beyond Kananah the ancestry extended to Hadrat Ismail and Hadrat Ibrahim who flourished some 2500 years earlier.

The Birth : The exact date of birth of Hadrat Ali is not known with any degree of certainty. According to traditions, Hadrat Ali was born on the thirteenth of "Rajab" in the 28th year of the Elephant Era. The Elephant Era according to the annals of Arabia, commenced when Abraham the Christian Viceroy of Yemen, invaded Mecca with the intention of destroying the Kaaba and shifting the centre of pilgrimage to Yemen. The invasion failed and the Christian army had to beat a retreat without achieving its object. That marked the retreat of Christianity from the heartland of Arabia and paved the way for the rise of Islam. The Holy Prophet of Islam was born in the Year of the Elephant. According to scholars, the Year of the Elephant corresponds to the year 571 of the Christian Era. On this basis the year of the birth of Hadrat Ali would have to be placed around 599 or 600 C. E. Anyhow Hadrat Ali was at the junction of the two centuries, the sixth and the seventh.

Hadrat Ali was born under unusual circumstances. On the thirteenth of the holy month of "Rajab" Fatima, the mother of Hadrat Ali, visited the Kaaba for performing the pilgrimage. During the course of the pilgrimage while circumambulating the Kaaba, Fatima felt the pangs of child birth. She retired to a secluded place in the precincts of the Holy Kaaba and there Hadrat Ali was born. Hadrat Ali had thus the unique honour of being born in the House of God. This unparalleled honour has endowed Hadrat Ali with a halo of sanctity which has become the subject of many legends. A hundred years later, Zain-ul-Abidin, a grandson of Ali (son of Hadrat Hussain) met an Arab woman at Najaf who told him that her grandmother had helped Fatima on the occasion of the birth of Hadrat Ali. She narrated that according to the account of her grandmother, the child was beautiful a smile played on his lips, it did not cry like other children and its birth did not cause any pain to his mother.

The Name : Fatima wanted to name the child "Asad" after the name of her father. Abu Talib wanted to name him Zaid. When the mother and the child came home, the Holy Prophet and Hadrat Khadija came to see the new-born child. Since his birth the child had not opened his eyes and that worried Fatima and Abu Talib. As the Holy Prophet took the child in his lap he opened his eyes. The first person that Hadrat Ali saw after his birth was the Holy Prophet. When the Holy Prophet was asked whether he approved of the child being named as Asad or Zaid, he said that as the child was born in the House of God, he should be named Ali, the word Ali being a derivative of Allah. Hadrat Ali had thus the distinction of being named after Allah. No person before him had ever been so named. The name acquired further sanctity as it was proposed by the Holy Prophet.

The Childhood : Hadrat Ali's first cousin, the Holy Prophet was a posthumous child as he was born after the death of his father Abdullah. He lost his mother Aamina when he was hardly six years old. Thereafter he became a ward of his grandfather Abdul Muttalib. He lost his grandfather when he was nine years old. The Holy Prophet next lived with his uncle Abu Talib who was a real brother of his father. In the house of Abu Talib, the Holy Prophet was well cared for. Abu Talib loved the Holy Prophet more than his own sons. Fatima, the wife of Abu Talib gave the Holy Prophet the love of a mother. The Holy Prophet accompanied Abu Talib on his trade journeys. It was under the loving care of Abu Talib and Fatima that the Holy Prophet grew into manhood. At the age of twenty-five, some time around 596 C. E. the Holy Prophet married a rich lady, Hadrat Khadija and shifted to her house. There was not much distance between the two houses and the two families visited each other frequently. The Holy Prophet could never forget the love that Abu Talib and Fatima had borne for him. Even after his marriage the Holy Prophet regarded himself as a member of the family of Abu Talib. In this context it is probable that the Holy Prophet and Hadrat Khadija would have rejoiced at the birth of Hadrat Ali and would have held some function to celebrate the occasion.

Life in the Desert : No detailed account of the early years of the childhood of Hadrat Ali is available and where the source books are silent, the story has been reconstructed on the basis of the laws of plausibility and probability. It was the custom of the Quraish of Mecca that they entrusted their new-born sons to the care of foster parents belonging to the tribes of the desert and it was in the open air of the desert that the young sons of the Quraish were bred during the first few years of their childhood. We know that the Holy Prophet spent the first five years of his childhood with his foster parents in the desert. We do not know who were the foster parents of Hadrat Ali. Hadrat Ali had a strong constitution and after the Holy Prophet he was the most eloquent person among the Quraish. This provides evidence to the effect that like the Holy Prophet, Hadrat Ali spent the first few years of his childhood in the desert. It appears that the necessary arrangements in this behalf were made by the Holy Prophet and he paid for the maintenance of Hadrat Ali in the desert.

Induction as a Member of the Family by Holy Prophet : As the Holy Prophet had arranged for the stay of Hadrat Ali in the desert, it appears that on return from the desert the young Ali was brought to the house of the Holy Prophet and he arranged some function to mark the occasion which was attended by Abu Talib and his family and other close relatives. The Holy Prophet had looked after the young Ali since his birth and he developed a great liking for him. It was against this background that the Holy Prophet requested. Abu Talib that. Ali be entrusted to his care and be allowed to live with him as a member of his family. Abu Talib agreed as he felt that the Holy Prophet would look after. Ali in a much better way than he could.

Most of the writers have expressed the view that the Holy Prophet took over the responsibility for the maintenance of Hadrat Ali to provide financial relief to Abu Talib whose financial position had grown weak. It is difficult to accept this view. Abu Talib was a Quraish chief and he enjoyed reputation as such and commanded great influence. Like other Quraish he undertook trading activities. There is no evidence to the effect that he was involved in any financial difficulties. If Abu Talib had really any financial difficulty, the Holy Prophet who was in affluent circumstances could have supplemented the financial resources of Abu Talib by providing financial assistance as a son would help a father in old age. The truth of the matter is that Hadrat Ali was entrusted to the Holy Prophet not because of any financial consideration but because the Holy Prophet had developed a liking for the child and wanted to have him by his side.

In entrusting Ali to the care of the Holy Prophet, Abu Talib did not part from Ali. Ali visited the house of his parents everyday and he was as much a member of the house of Abu Talib as that of the Holy Prophet. Indeed the house of the Holy Prophet was an extension to the house of Abu Talib and the young Ali lived with the Holy Prophet as a younger brother would live with an elder brother without any break with the paternal house.

Umayyads versus Hashimites : It appears that most of the accounts of the period were written when the Umayyads had wrested power from the Hashimites. Because of the rivalry between the Umayyads and the Hashimites most of the writers during the Umayyad period tried to create the impression that the Hashimites were not good managers and that the financial position of Abu Talib had deteriorated because of his inefficiency. This view is uncharitable. The Muslims are under great obligation to Abu Talib for his guardianship of the Holy Prophet and for his support of Islam and such views which cast an indirect aspersion on Abu Talib have to be rejected because of the bias on the part of the writers.

As Ward of the Holy Prophet : Hadrat Ali became the ward of the Holy Prophet at the age of five. No account is available from the source books about the life of Hadrat Ali during this period. As Hadrat Ali came to be attached to the Holy Prophet during this period, we can derive help from the life of the Holy Prophet in order to undertake a biographical study of Hadrat Ali. There are three turning points in the life of the Holy Prophet. The first turning point was his marriage with Hadrat Khadija in 596 C. E. when he was twenty-five years old. The second turning point was the call to prophethood in 611 C. E. when he was forty years old. The third turning point was the migration to Yathrib in 622 C. E. when he was fifty-one years old. The life of the Holy Prophet is thus divisible into four periods. The first period of 25 years extends from 571 to 596 C. E. The second period of 15 years extends from 596 to 611 C. E. The third period of 11 years extends from 611 to 622 C. E. The fourth and the last period covering ten years extending from 622 to 632 C. E. We have sufficient details about the third and fourth periods. A few details are available about the first period, but there are practically no details in any source book pertaining to the period from 596 to 611. These were the formative years preliminary to the call to prophethood and in order to get a complete picture of the life of the Holy Prophet we will have to reconstruct the life story of the Holy Prophet during this period on the basis of further research. The law of plausibility and probability will also have to be pressed into service to set the narrative in proper perspective. As Hadrat Ali became the ward of the Holy Prophet during this period, we cannot reproduce an account of the life of Hadrat Ali during this period from any source book. We will have to undertake an exercise in the reconstruction of the biography of Hadrat Ali during this period.

House of the Holy Prophet : When Hadrat Ali came to live with the Holy Prophet that was some time in the year 604 C. E. By this time eight years had passed since the marriage of the Holy Prophet and Hadrat Khadija. At the time the Holy Prophet was thirty-three years and Hadrat Khadija was forty-eight years old. During these eight years, Hadrat Khadija had given birth to seven children. Out of these three were sons and four were daughters. All the three boys died during infancy. The girls survived. These were Zainab, Ruqayya, Umm Kulthum and Fatima. There were no more births thereafter. All the source books that have come down to us are silent as to the activities of the Holy Prophet during this period. We know that Hadrat Khadija was a rich lady and when the record is silent about any business activity of the Holy Prophet that tends to create the impression that the Holy Prophet depended on the wealth of his wife. The Holy Prophet being the greatest of all men of all times and a personification of perfection in all spheres of human activity could not be supposed as living on the wealth of anybody else howsoever close. Years later in verse of the Holy Quran, Allah said: "Were thee not poor, and did. We not enrich thee?". A person who depends on the wealth of another person cannot be regarded as a rich man. The test of richness is that such richness should be on his own account and because of his own efforts. We know that the Holy Prophet was skilful Manager and a man endowed with such qualities could not be expected to sit idle. We know that the Holy Prophet was known as "Amin". This means that he was a banker and a person who practiced banking must necessarily be a rich man. The Holy Prophet undertook some trade journeys before his marriage and such journeys proved to be profitable from the business point of view. There appears to be no ground to believe that the Holy Prophet stopped all business activity after marriage. On the other hand the plausibility is that he undertook such activities on a still bigger scale. It appears that during this period the Holy Prophet headed a trade organisation whereof his wife and some other friends were partners. We can thus conclude, that when Hadrat Ali came to live with the Holy Prophet, he found in the house of the Holy Prophet all the comforts that are found in the house of a rich man.

Education : As the Holy Prophet was rich, it is certain that on taking over the responsibility for the maintenance of Hadrat Ali, the Holy Prophet made the best possible arrangements for his education. Later in life, Hadrat Ali came to enjoy reputation of being the most learned man of his age in Arabia. This points to the fact that the Holy Prophet took particular care in educating Hadrat Ali. Hadrat Ali was a precocious child. At an early age he came to master knowledge, which others could hardly understand.

Trade Journeys : Though there is no record to show that the Holy Prophet undertook any trade journeys during this period, there are strong plausible grounds to hold that the Holy Prophet was very active in business enterprises and that he undertook at least one or two journeys every year. These journeys were generally undertaken to Yemen and Syria. There are indications that the Holy Prophet undertook some sea voyages as well and visited Egypt and Abyssinia. We know that when the Holy Prophet was child he accompanied his uncle Abu Talib on trade journeys. Against this background, we would not be far from the truth to hold that the young. Ali often accompanied the Holy Prophet on such trade journeys. These journeys were highly educative and contributed a good deal to the broadening of the outlook of Hadrat Ali

Born at Kaaba : Hadrat Ali knew that he was born in the Kaaba. He had therefore, a fond attachment for the Kaaba, sometime in 605 C. E. the Quraish reconstructed the Kaaba. A dispute arose about the placing of the Holy Stone as each section of the Quraish wanted to have this honour for itself. It was ultimately decided that on the appointed day whosoever was the first to enter the Kaaba should decide as to how the dispute was to be resolved. On the appointed day the Holy Prophet was the first to enter the Kaaba. He decided that the Holy Stone should be placed in a mantle and this mantle should be upheld by a representative of each section of the Quraish. The stone was carried in this way to the place where it was to be fixed in the wall. There the Holy Prophet lifted the stone from the mantle and fixed it at the appropriate place in the wall. Young Ali was present in the Kaaba on this occasion and he watched the proceedings with great interest. Hadrat Ali felt a sense of pride at the association of his family with the Kaaba. He himself was born in the Kaaba and his guardian had presided at the ceremony of laying down the Holy stone. The Kaaba was verily the House of God, but he wondered why it was studded with over three hundred and sixty idols made of stone. The people worshipped these idols and sacrificed animals at their altar. The young Ali wondered why these deaf and dumb idols were worshipped and propitiated when they were not capable of conferring any benefit or inflicting any wrong on the people.

Relations with Holy Prophet : At this impressionable period of his life, the young Ali was most impressed with the personality and character of the Holy Prophet. The Holy Prophet was the paragon of virtues and the personification of human perfection. The Holy Prophet, Hadrat Abu Bakr and some other friends often met at the house of the Holy Prophet. The young Ali listened attentively to such talks. From these talks the young Ali gathered that the Holy Prophet was in quest of a new order of things. Ali resolved in his young mind that in any adventure in the discovery of a new order of things, he would stand by the side of Muhammad (peace be on him). He came to know from Abu Talib how a Christian monk in Syria had prophesied many years ago that Muhammad (peace be on him) was destined to be a prophet of God. He heard from Hadrat Khadija that her dreams signified that great destiny awaited Muhammad (peace be on him) and that he was to be the greatest leader of men and the saviour of humanity. The young Ali anxiously longed to see the day when such dreams would be realised. He was moved by a strong determination that as and when Muhammad (peace be on him) was lifted to the status of prophethood. He, as the ward of the Holy Prophet, would play his part in promoting the mission of the Holy Prophet. Hadrat Ali regarded the Holy Prophet not merely as a brother or a guardian, but as his guide and preceptor. Availing of the company of the Holy Prophet, the young Ali took pains to acquire most of the attributes which were the distinguishing features of the character of the Holy Prophet. It was a result of this training received because of close association with the Holy Prophet that Hadrat Ali in due course grew to be the alter ego of the Holy Prophet.

The Youngest Convert

Turning Point in History : The year 611 C. E. was a turning point in the life of Hadrat Muhammad (peace be on him) for it was in this year that he was commissioned as a prophet of God to communicate the message of Islam to mankind. It was a turning point in the life of Hadrat Ali for in this year he was converted to Islam. This was a turning point in the history of Islam. In fact it was a turning point in the history of mankind. It marked the end of the age of ignorance and the dawn of a new era of enlightenment.

Call to Prophethood : Just as the clouds appear before the rain, thus Hadrat Muhammad (peace be on him) had some indications beforehand of the things to come. He had frequent dreams. In some dreams he saw himself flying to the heavens in the great void of space. In some dreams he saw the stars bow to him. In some dreams he heard the trees, the rocks and the other inanimate objects calling to him. In some dreams he saw himself standing at the summit of a mountain and calling to the people assembled below the valley. These dreams foretelling of some great thing to come motivated Hadrat Muhammad (peace be on him) to contemplate and mediate. To seek enlightenment through contemplation and meditation, Hadrat Muhammad (peace be on him) sought the solitude of a cave in Mount Hira, some distance away from the city of Mecca. Hadrat Muhammad (peace be on him) spent long hours in the cave absorbed in thought and meditation. When the stay in the cave extended to a long time. Hadrat Ali brought food for Hadrat Muhammad in the cave. Hadrat Ali kept watch on the cave and patrolled the neighbourhood. One day in the year 611, the angel Gabriel appeared in the cave and gave Hadrat Muhammad (peace be on him) the tidings that God had commissioned him as a prophet and charged him to communicated the message of God to the people. The visitation of the angel, an unusual occurrence, was a novel experience which upset Muhammad (peace be on him) and made him highly nervous.

Converts to Islam : When the Holy Prophet returned home he was highly agitated and most nervous. He told of the occurrence in the cave to his wife Hadrat Khadija. She consulted her cousin Waraqa b Naufal who was versed in religious lore. Waraqa said that the angel who had appeared before Muhammad (peace be on him) was the same angel who had appeared before. Abraham, Moses and other prophets. Waraqa added that the visitation of the angel was a great event and she should rejoice that her husband had been chosen by the Almighty God as His Messenger. When Khadija told Muhammad (peace be on him) what Waraqa had said, Hadrat Muhammad (peace be on him) said that the burden of prophethood would be too heavy for him to bear and he did not know who would accept conversion to the new faith at his hand. Hadrat Khadija consoled him and said that the Almighty Who had chosen him as His Messenger would Himself guide him in fulfilling His mission of prophethood. Hadrat Khadija offered herself as the first person to owe allegiance to Muhammad (peace be on him) as the prophet of God. When Hadrat Ali came to know of the conversion of Hadrat Khadija he hastened to offer his allegiance to the Holy Prophet. Hadrat Ali was the first among the youth to be converted to Islam. In some books it is written that when Hadrat Muhammad (peace be on him) invited Hadrat Ali to the new faith, he showed some hesitation and said that he would consult Abu Talib in the first instance. This version of what happened is far from the truth. There was no hesitation on the part of Hadrat Ali in accepting the truth. Hadrat Ali had indeed been longing for the day when the call from the Almighty would come and when the call came he was so much overwhelmed with joy that there could be no question of any hesitation. The acceptance of the new faith on the part of Hadrat Ali was spontaneous and without any hesitation for Hadrat Ali had the firm conviction that Hadrat Muhammad (peace be on him) was the true prophet of God.

Early Years of Islam : During the first three years, Islam remained a private affair and no attempt was made to proclaim Islam publicly. The message of Islam was during this period conveyed privately to his friends by the Holy Prophet. Among the persons outside the family of the Holy Prophet, Hadrat Abu Bakr was the first to be converted to Islam. Abu Bakr in turn brought some of his friends to the fold of Islam. Those who accepted Islam persuaded their friends to accept Islam. In this way the chain came to be extended and the progress of Islam, though not spectacular was quite satisfactory. The early Muslims prayed in secluded glens or other solitary places. On one occasion Abu Talib happened to see the Muslims praying behind the Holy Prophet in a glen outside Mecca. Hadrat Ali was one of the congregations. Abu Talib asked Hadrat Ali as to whom they were praying and what was the religion they had adopted Hadrat Ali told his father that they were praying to Allah, the Lord of the world and the universe. There was no god but Allah and Muhammad (peace be on him) was His prophet. Abu Talib pondered for a while and said "If Muhammad has become the prophet, hold fast to him for he cannot but be right. I know that his elevation to prophethood was expected many years ago". When the Holy Prophet and Hadrat Ali visited the house of Abu Talib, they had a more detailed discussion about the new faith. Abu Talib was sympathetic but as he was one of the tribal chiefs he could not abandon the faith of his forefathers. He warned the Holy Prophet that he would have to face the opposition of the Quraish. He promised that though he would not accept the new faith he would stand by him through thick and thin and he would enjoy his full support. Fatima, the wife of Abu Talib, was more sympathetic. She said that she had mothered Muhammad and Muhammad (peace be on him) was not the man to make a false claim. She observed that it was yet too early for her to make a decision whether she was going to accept Islam or not Jafar a brother of Ali, put a few questions to the Holy Prophet who answered them satisfactorily. Jafar wanted some more time to consider over the matter.

Invitation to Banu Hashim : After three years of the call to prophethood the Holy Prophet received the command of God that he should publicly proclaim the message of Islam and that he could make a beginning with his relatives, belonging to the house of Banu Hashim. The Holy Prophet invited the Hashimites, about forty men to a feast. After the feast the Holy Prophet gave an account as to how he had been visited by the angel Gabriel who had conveyed to him the orders of Allah commissioning him as His prophet. He said that there was no god but Allah and that he was. His Messenger commissioned to call the people to the faith. He added that the members of the house of Hashim should feel proud that this honour had come to one of them Waxing eloquent. The Holy Prophet said that in the task of promoting the new faith he needed their support. He posed the question, "Who out of you would support me in this task"? A silence fell on the guests and no one uttered a word. Young Ali thereupon rose to say, "Holy Prophet, I will be your support"? The Holy Prophet looked approvingly at young Ali and thanked him for his support. The Holy Prophet posed the same question for the second and third time but no one out of the guests promised any support. Each time the young Ali rose to offer his support in unequivocal terms. Abu Talib had already assured the Holy Prophet of his protection and he did not consider it advisable to make a public declaration of his support or protection at that stage. He, however, felt happy at the courage shown by the young Ali. He felt that there was something extraordinary in the new faith which had motivated young Ali to the demonstration of such courage in public. Abu Lahab, a step uncle of the Holy Prophet, took a hostile attitude. He ridiculed the new faith and felt sorry that his nephew had lost his senses and was suffering from some hallucination. He wanted the guests to disperse. The Holy Prophet felt very unhappy at his failure to win the support of the Banu Hashim.

Course of Truth : Though disappointed, the Holy Prophet was not daunted. He knew that the course of the Truth could not be anything but rough and that in order to fulfil his mission he should prepare himself to face difficulties. After his disappointment with the Banu Hashim the Holy Prophet decided to make a public declaration of his faith. One day he mounted the hillock Mt. Safa and called the people to come and listen to him. Hadrat Ali was by the side of the Holy Prophet. In response to the call a large crowd gathered at the foot of the hill to listen to the Holy Prophet. Addressing the people, the Holy Prophet said: "O people, if I tell you that on the other side of this hill there were the forces of an enemy coming to attack you, would you believe me"? They said, "yes we would believe you, for you are known to be truthful". Thereupon the Holy Prophet said, "if I tell you that there is no god but Allah and I am His prophet, would you believe me". The people made no reply and the crowd dispersed. The people, steeped deep in ignorance, were not yet in the mood to know the Truth. As the Holy Prophet and Hadrat Ali came down from the hill they felt that they would have to carry a great struggle in the cause of their mission before any results could be achieved.

Battle between Truth and Falsehood : The public proclamation of Islam by the Holy Prophet led to a great crisis. The people were not prepared to accept any change in their age-long beliefs and the Holy Prophet was not inclined to relax or spare any effort in the fulfilment of the great mission that had been entrusted to him by God. Thus began a battle between truth and falsehood. It was an extraordinary battle in the annals of mankind. In this battle, waged under the command of the Holy Prophet, Hadrat Ali was the right-hand man of the Holy Prophet and was always in the forefront of the struggle. As in the subsequent battles fought between the Muslims and the pagans in the conventional style, Hadrat Ali proved to be warrior of extraordinary valour whose sword put hundreds of the unbelievers to death. It appears that at this stage during the second decade of seventh century when the stage was set for a conflict between truth and falsehood, Hadrat Ali received some sort of military training which stood him in great stead in the following years of his life, marked by open warfare between the Muslims and the pagans.

Muslim Community : In spite of the fact that at the feast held by the Holy Prophet in the honour of the men belonging to the house of Banu Hashim, no one had responded to his call, some members of the family were attracted to the new faith. These included Jafar, his wife. Asma and Hamza Jafar was a brother of Hadrat Ali and Hamza was an uncle of the Holy Prophet and Hadrat Ali. It appears that Hadrat Ali played an important part in the conversion of Jafar and his wife who were particularly attached to Hadrat Ali. When the Holy Prophet gave the call at Mt. Safa and invited the people to the new faith, they had refused to listen to him. In spite of that, some persons were attracted by the new faith and they offered allegiance to the Holy Prophet regardless of what the other people said. By 615 C.E. despite untoward circumstances and unfavourable conditions about one hundred persons, men and women had joined the fold of Islam and the Muslim community had come to acquire particular identity of their own.

Quraish in Action : The growing strength of the Muslim community stirred the Quraish to action. They launched a vilification campaign against the Holy Prophet, Islam and the Muslims. In objectionable verses the Quraish poets ridiculed the Holy Prophet and his faith. Hadrat Ali was poet and it appears that he composed some verses highlighting the truth about Islam.

The Quraish made a crude and undignified attempt towards the character assassination of the Holy Prophet. Some said that he had gone mad and had lost his senses. Some said that he was the victim of some hallucination. There were others who said that he was wizard or a "Kahin" Some said that he was the victim of some 'Jinn'.

When all attempts of vilification and character assassination failed, the Quraish made preposterous demands as a proof for the veracity of the Holy Prophet. They demonded that if the angel appeared to him he should show them the angel. They said that if he was the beloved of God, he should ask God to turn the rocks of Mecca into gold. They wanted him to show them some miracle. He should get the desert of, Arabia converted into oasis. Some said that if he was prophet and knew of things not known to others, he should show them the spots where treasure was buried under the earth. The Holy Prophet maintained that the Holy Quran was his miracle and he challenged the unbelievers to produce anything like that.

When all the tactics of the Quraish proved abortive they resorted to physical force. They persecuted the Muslims and subjected them to great hardships. When the persecutions of the Quraish became unbearable, the Holy Prophet ordered his followers to migrate to Abyssinia. About eighty Muslims including women migrated to Abyssinia. About two dozen Muslims including. Abu Bakr and Hadrat Ali were left in Mecca and this included the Holy Prophet and the members of his family. Thus to all intents and purposes the Muslims evacuated Mecca.

Migration to Abyssinia : The source books that have come down to us do not throw sufficient light on the wisdom of migration to Abyssinia. It was the year 615 C. E. and by this time Hadrat Ali had come of age. Hadrat Ali was an embodiment of courage and bravery. When the Quraish subjected the poorer sections of the Muslims to hardships, Hadrat Ali asked the permission of the Holy Prophet to retaliate and fight against the Quraish who used force against the Muslims. There were some other young men among the Muslims who were of the same view as Hadrat Ali and who were prepared to fight against the Quraish and die for the defence of Islam. The Holy Prophet felt that with such a meager number of Muslims, any headlong-armed conflict between the Muslims and the Quraish was likely to be against their interests. The migration to Abyssinia was undertaken not because of the fear of the Quraish but it was undertaken to restraining the Muslims from open war with the Quraish. The Prophet also felt that if the Muslims established a settlement outside. Arabia that would help in the promotion of Islam in other parts of the world. A Muslim settlement along the borders of Arabia was likely to be a source of strength to the Muslims in. Arabia. The Muslims who migrated to Abyssinia were likely to have better opportunities for economic betterment and that would work to the advantage of the Muslim community as a whole. That would also help the Muslims in Arabia strengthen their trade relations with Abyssinia. The Quraish were alive to these advantages that were likely to accrue to them as a result of the migration of a batch of the Muslims to Abyssinia. Accordingly, the Quraish sent a delegation to Abyssinia to prevail on the Negus of Abyssinia to expel the Muslims from his country. The Negus invited the Muslims to his court and asked them to explain what was the faith they had adopted Jafar, the brother of Hadrat Ali, acting as the spokesman of the Muslims presented such a splendid picture of Islam that the Negus was much impressed and he refused to oblige the Quraish.

Great Setback : The discomfiture of the Quraish mission to Abyssinia gave a great setback to the cause of the Quraish. They had failed to convince the Negus of the genuineness of their cause. On the other hand the Muslims had succeeded in impressing the Negus and he had agreed to patronise them. Thus in the first round of the battle between the truth and falsehood, falsehood suffered defeat while the truth scored a victory. Although we are not very definite as to what role Hadrat Ali played in the battle but there are strong grounds to believe that he played an important part in winning the battle.

Social Boycott of Banu Hashim : Exasperated at the failure of their mission in Abyssinia, the Quraish stepped up their opposition to the Holy Prophet and his mission. The Holy Quran served as shield for the Muslims, and in order to break up this line of defence of the Muslims, the Quraish launched an attack against the Holy Quran. They levied the charge that the Holy Quran was not a revealed book, it owed its authorship to a Christian Jabir. Allah Himself refuted the charge by pointing out that Jabir was not an Arab and he was not proficient in the Arabic language. A challenge was given to the Quraish that if they maintained that the Quran was a work of human authorship, they should produce something like that. The Quraish were unable to accept the challenge and thus attack on the Quran failed.

Miracles of the Holy Quran : In the meantime the Holy Quran showed its miraculous aspect in many ways and came to the help of the Muslims when things had become difficult for them. One day Umar, a fiery youth among the Quraish and an inveterate enemy of the Muslims, girded his sword and came out of his house with the intention of putting an end to the life of the Holy Prophet. In the way he met a friend who advised him to take care of his sister and her husband first who had become Muslims. At the house of his sister, Umar heard some verses of the Holy Quran which moved him to such an extent that he hastened to the house of the Holy Prophet not with a on intention of killing him, but to owe him allegiance. The conversion of Umar to Islam proved to be a matter of great assest to the Muslims and a setback for the Quraish.

Al Tufail b. Amr of the Daus tribe having heard of the Holy Prophet came to him at Mecca. Al Tufail was an eminent Arabic poet. The Quraish met Al Tufail and put pressure on him not to see Muhammad (peace be on him) as he was a wizard and a sorcerer. Al Tufail said that he was a poet and after hearing the verses of the Holy Quran he would be in the position to judge how far the Quran was genuine or otherwise. He saw the Holy Prophet, heard some verses of the Holy Quran and was so much impressed that he lost no time in conversion to Islam.

A delegation of a dozen Christians from the interior of Arabia, having heard of the advent of the Holy Prophet, came to Mecca with a view to meeting the Holy Prophet. The Quraish tried to prevail upon them not to see the Holy Prophet as according to their assessment he was an imposter. The Christians said that they would be able to judge this issue for themselves after they had seen the Holy Prophet. They saw the Holy Prophet, heard the Holy Quran, were impressed and were converted to Islam.

Manoeuvres of the Quraish : The Quraish failed miserably in their attack on the Holy Quran. In view of their defeat on this front, the Quraish changed their strategy and adopted new manoeuvres. They whipped up their persecution campaign on the one hand and offered inducements to the Holy Prophet on the other hand. They offered him the crown of Mecca in case he desisted from his activities. The Prophet was neither daunted by the persecution campaign of the Quraish nor was he attracted by their inducements. He declared that even if all the wealth of the world was offered to him, he would not falter in the fulfilments of the mission entrusted to him by God. By 616 the Quraish felt the ground slipping under their feet. Their mission to Abyssinia had failed. Their attack on the Holy Quran had failed. Their campaign of persecution had failed to overawe the Holy Prophet. Their inducements had been turned down scornfully by the Holy Prophet. The Quraish failed to prevail any Muslim to return to his previous faith. On the other hand some remarkable conversions had been made to Islam. Islam had spread outside Mecca and pockets of the Muslims had come to be established in other parts of Arabia.

Social Boycott : Because of their repeated failures, the Quraish became desperate. They felt that now the only way before them was to kill Muhammad (peace be on him). The Holy Prophet enjoyed the protection of his tribe Abu Hashim and as long as such protection was there Muhammad (peace be on him) could not be killed according to the tribal code, for any such murder would have precipitated tribal warfare. The Quraish approached Abu Talib, the head of the Banu Hashim to prevail upon Muhammad (peace be on him) to desist from his teachings. Abu Talib consulted the Holy Prophet whether he could accommodate the Quraish in any way. The Holy Prophet expressed his resolution in strong terms that he would not fail or falter in the performance of the mission that had been entrusted to him by God. Thereupon the Quraish asked Abu Talib to withdraw the protection of Banu Hashim from Muhammad (peace be on him). Abu Talib consulted the Holy Prophet again and tried to prevail upon him to compromise with the Quraish in some way which could avert the crisis. The Prophet told his uncle that he could withdraw his protection from him if he liked but he could not compromise in any way in the matter of the mission entrusted to him by God. Abu Talib felt unhappy on the growing rift between the Muslims and the Quraish, but he assured him that he would not abandon him whatever might come. Abu Talib accordingly told the Quraish that he could not withdraw his protection from Muhammad (peace be on him). Thereupon the Quraish decided to enforce social boycott against Banu Hashim. An agreement was drawn up which was signed by the Banu Hashim. The agreement provided that the Quraish would neither marry their daughters to the Banu Hashim nor marry the daughters of Banu Hashim. It was also provided that they would neither sell anything to nor buy anything from the Banu Hashim. The document was hung on the Kaaba. The Holy Prophet and the Banu Hashim moved to a glen outside Mecca and there remained in a state of semi-captivity for a period of two to three years. Thereafter the social boycott was lifted and the Banu Hashim returned to their homes in Mecca.

The Consequences : The accounts of the social boycott available in the source books that have come down to us are incomplete and do not present a true picture of the actual state of affairs. We know that during this period the Banu Hashim lived in a glen outside Mecca. The point to be determined is whether the Banu Hashim were driven to this glen by the Quraish or did the Banu Hashim move there out of their own accord. In the boycott instrument the Quraish were not required to drive the Banu Hashim out of their homes in Mecca. It appears that the Banu Hashim shifted to the glen which belonged to Abu Talib out of their accord for reasons of safety and with a view to living together in a time of crisis. The boycott was only against Banu Hashim. Abu Lahab and his wife who were Banu Hashim did not join the other members of the Banu Hashim. It appears that all other families of the Banu Hashim sided with the Holy Prophet even though they had not accepted Islam. An important issue in this connection is whether Abu Talib had become a Muslim by the time the boycott was enforced. In the biography of the Holy Prophet, Ibn Ishaq quotes some verses composed by Abu Talib with reference to the boycott. A translation of these verses is available in Guillaume's Life of Muhammad. Addressing the Quraish,. Abu Talib says:

> "Did you not know that we have found Muhammad a prophet like Moses described in the oldest books."

When the boycott was lifted and the boycott document was torn, Abu Talib composed some more verses which provided:

> "The deed was torn up and all that was against God's wish was destroyed."

A person giving expression to such thoughts as these could not be anyone other than a Muslim. It appears that Abu Talib would have accepted the new faith but he could not make an open declaration because he felt that people would say Abu Talib has professed Islam out of the fear of death.

Most of the writers refer to this event as a siege. It is doubtful whether this was in fact a siege. According to the agreement of boycott there was no stipulation for siege. The ban was only on marriage and purchase or sale of goods This did not include any siege. This did not restrict the movements of Banu Hashim either. According to most of the accounts that come down to us the impression is created that the Banu Hashim in the glen were starved and they were forced to subsist on the leaved of trees. This is not the correct presentation of facts. The boycott was enforced against Banu Hashim alone. Many Muslims still lived in proper Mecca and there were no restriction on their purchase or sale of goods. If the Muslims of Mecca purchased provisions from the market and supplied them to the Banu Hashim in the glen, they could do so for there was no term in the agreement of boycott that no one was to be allowed to supply any article of food and drink. Hardship was certainly involved in the segregation of the Banu Hashim in the glen outside Mecca. But the Holy Prophet being a great man was resourceful enough to overcome such hardships. In any proper account of Islamic history the emphasis should not be on the hardships inflicted by the enemies of Islam, the emphasis should be as to how the Muslims overcame such hardships and defeated the enemy and his own game. Under the leadership of the Holy Prophet the Banu Hashim met the ordeal of the social boycott successfully. The social boycott failed to achieve the purpose for which it was intended and once again in the battle between the truth and falsehood, the Quraish met a reverse and the Muslims scored a victory.

Hadrat Ali on the Scene : In the accounts of this period that have come down to us, there is no mention of Hadrat Ali. By this time Hadrat Ali had come of age. He was well educated, highly intelligent, most enterprising and brave. It is difficult to believe that if the accounts make no mention of Ali, the inference is that he was idle and had nothing to do. When Abu Talib decided to espouse the cause of Muhammad (peace be on him), Hadrat Ali most probably played an important part in prevailing upon Abu Talib to take the decision he did. We know that when the Holy Prophet migrated to Yathrib he entrusted the responsibility for winding up the business in Mecca to Hadrat Ali. In the accounts that have come down to us the Holy Prophet is shown as a good manager and businessman, but in the accounts of the post-prophethood period there is no account of any business activity on the part of the Prophet. The writers of the period apparently harboured the delusion that any business undertaking was repugnant to prophethood. An impression is tried to be created that in the post-prophethood period the Holy Prophet undertook no business and depended on the wealth of his followers—Hadrat Abu Bakr, Hadrat Uthman and others. This is an erroneous presentation, for Islam is not a religion for the next world alone, it is a religion for this world as well. To abstain from business may be the Christian or the Buddhist concept of piety but that is not the Islamic concept of prophethood. The Holy Prophet is the greatest man of all times and such a man perfect in every way cannot be without independent sources of income. It appears that when Hadrat came of age, the Holy Prophet entrusted the responsibility for running the business to Hadrat Ali. It appears that during the period of the social boycott Hadrat Ali continued to run the business of the Holy Prophet (SAW). The boycott agreement merely restricted the sale or purchase by the Quraish, it did not and could not apply to business transactions elsewhere. It appears that Hadrat Ali undertook business journeys during this period and the necessary provisions procured from outside Mecca were duly supplied to the Banu Hashim in the glen.

Holy Prophet and Quraish : The troubles of the Holy Prophet and the Muslims did not come to an end with the end of the social boycott. Frustrated at the failure of the boycott, the Quraish were in a sullen and hostile mood and they began to think of the adoption of more stringent measures which could bring the Muslims to their knees. In the meantime Abu Talib fell sick. He was already eighty years old and the strain of the confinement during the boycott had proved too heavy for him and had undermined his health. The malady grew worse and when no hope was left of his survival, a deputation of the Quraish visited him at his deathbed. They said that as he was going to depart from the world, out of regard for him they were inclined to offer terms of peace to Muhammad. Abu Talib summoned the Holy Prophet to his presence and the Quraish were asked to name their terms. They said that if Muhammad desisted form maligning their faith and criticising their gods, they would let him alone to have his own way without any interference by the Quraish. The Holy Prophet said that the way of the Quraish was the way of many gods, while his way was the way of the Oneness of God whereunder there is no god but Allah and all other gods are false. As the two ways crossed each other no agreement could be reached between the parties. The Quraish, thus foiled, began to prepare for another major offensive against the Holy Prophet and the Muslims to be launched after the death of Abu Talib.

Bequest of Abu Talib : Before his death, Abu Talib recorded a bequest and had it hung in the Kaaba. According to "Rauza-tu's-Safa" this bequest reads as follows:

> "O thou people of Quraish' Thou art the chosen race of God, and the best in the world. In my dying behest I will ask you to be kind and well disposed towards Muhammad because he is a trustee from among the Quraish and most truthful from amongst the whole population of Arabia. He has in his person all those things which compel me to leave a will in his favour. He has tidings to reveal which your heart accepts although for fear your lips do not respond to confirm the call of your heart. I find that the half-barbarians of the Arabian desert, in contrast to you, respond to the call and obey his orders and verily these are the people who will be exalted in this world and the hereafter mark me when I say that your chiefs will be dishonoured and stiff necked though they now are, they will soon be humbled. I see the entire country has sincerity and enthusiasm for his message and the people have widened their hearts to receive that love. In short, they are willing to follow and obey him. O thou Quraish'. It is high time that you should befriend him, support him and follow him in the path that he treads. I swear by God that only those who desist to follow him who are not destined to reform and only those will follow in his footsteps who are destined to be great, pious and noble. If their is some respite or delay in my death and I survive a few more days I will support his cause. As far as it lies within my power I will protect him from the evils of the enemy."

This bequest was written by Hadrat Ali and was dictated by Abu Talib.

Banu Hashim's Boycott

Seventh to the Tenth Year of the Mission : From the tenth month of the 7th Year of Muhammad's mission till the tenth year, for a period of close upon three years, Muhammad and the whole of Banu-Hashim were shut up in a pass away from the population of Mecca. The rest of the Quraish would neither buy anything from them nor sell them anything and all social intercourse was cut off.

The Muslims at this period numbering four hundred or (hereabouts were thus divided:

(1) About 80 males with a number of women and children living in Abyssinia.

(2) A number of Muslims of the Banu-Hashim living besieged with Muhammad and the rest of the Banu-Hashim in the Pass.

(3) Various other individuals and families spread over Mecca and other parts of Arabia but not belonging to Banu Hashim, who though not actually ex-communicated were also being persecuted by the unbelievers.

The small body of Muslims was thus scattered and cut off from their guide Muhammad. Under such circumstances, according to the Quraish, the annihilation of the Muslims and the disappearance of Islam was only a question of time. And it would have been so but for the unshakable courage and conviction of the Muslims and the help of God which is always theirs.

Muhammad was not daunted by this adversity. During the sacred months, he would come out of his refuge, for, then, according to Arab custom, all war was stopped. Muhammad would then go and preach Islam amongst the pilgrims at Ukaz, Majannah and Dhull- Majaz. But Abu-Lahab, the curse of the Quraish, would follow Muhammad wherever the latter went: whilst Muhammad preached the Unity of God and love of mankind, Abu-Lahab yelled, "don't listen to this man, he is a liar."

Muhammad, hungry and famished, would bear all this and a great deal more of abuse and persecution, but say nothing in reply. He knew that the Word of God was taking root in the hearts of men outside Mecca and the help of God was near.

But during the latter half of the siege so, great was the distress amongst Banu-Hashim that they were reduced to eating leaves of trees and the boiled leather of their shoes. The children cried for milk and food but nothing was to be had. Their parents had become skeletons and cries of the hungry children echoed all over the hills of Mecca.

Abu-Jahl, Abu-Lahab and the other hard-hearted amongst the Quraish were jubilant. The end of Muhammad, they thought, had come. But whatever the faults, follies and sins of the Arabs of this period, they were not all so utterly depraved. There were brave men amongst them still alive, and though unbelievers, they could not see this state of affairs last long. A nation who regarded the feeding of the guest as a great honour could not see their own kith and kin starved to death in such a brutal manner. But what could they do? The cheifs were against them. At first a few kind-hearted souls began to smuggle food for the children of the besieged and one of them, Hisham bin Amr, was so moved by the pitiable condition of the besieged that he went to Zuhair bin Abi-Umayyah. The latter's mother Atikah was one of the daughters of Abd ul-Muttalib.

Hisham said to Zuhair, "O Zuhair, you eat food, you wear clothes, enjoy the company of women and we know where and how your uncles are in the siege. Are you pleased with such a state of affairs? They are starving for lack of food and there is no social intercourse between them and us. I swear by God that if they were my uncles and I was asked to do what you have been asked to do, I would never consent."

Zuhair felt the sting of cowardice implied in this mild taunt of Hisham and agreed with him that the agreement excommunicating Banu- Hashim must be cancelled. They consulted their friends and three others, to wit: Mutim bin Adi, Abul-Bakhtarim Ibn Hisham and Zamah bin Aswad joined them. And the five of them covenanted to stand together till the writing excommunicating Banu-Hashim was cancelled.

On the morrow, according to their secret arrangement, Zuhair went to the Kaaba, performed his Tawaf, or circumambulating of the Kaaba seven times and cried out to men:

> "O ye people of Mecca! O ye people of Mecca!"

The people gathered there to listen to him when he addressed them thus:

> "Shall we eat our food and put on our clothes and let Banu-Hashim die? We neither buy from them nor sell them anything. I swear by God I will not sit down till this cruel and unjust document is torn into pieces."

As soon as Abu-Jahl heard this, he cried:

> "Thou art a liar, by God thou shall not tear this document."

Zamah, Abul-Bakhtari, Hisham bin Amr and many others told Abu Jahl that he was the liar, not they, and that all the people present were on their side. Abu-Jahl shook with anger and terror and knowing that the people were against him, took to his heels.

Mutim then got up to tear the document into pieces, but it is said that on his handling it, he found that with the exception of the words :

> "In thy Name of God!" the rest of the document had been eaten up by white ants or had been decomposed by earth.

Muhammad Comes out of the Siege and Begins to Preach again Inside and Outside Mecca.

Muhammad and his companions in the Pass were now free to come out and they did, but otherwise the enmity of the unbelievers remained as severe as hithertofore. Muhammad's enemies were bent on uprooting his religion by force as well as by guile.

The persecution of Muhammad and his fellow-believers was re-doubled and he was unable to help them against the unbelievers. Only in the sacred months was there really any liberty of speech and even then it was interrupted.

Death of Abu Talib and Khadijah : Muhammad had not been free for many months when his uncle Abu- Talib who was now eighty years of age (Tenth year of Muhammad's mission) fell sick. When the Quraish knew that Abu-Talib's end was near, they gathered round him and said:

> "O Abu-Talib, thou art amongst us as thou well knowest, and thou art in a state which thou canst see for thyself and we are certainly afraid on thy account. And thou knowest what has happened between us and thy nephew (Muhammad). Call him and make him agree with us and we will agree with him that he hold back his hand from us and we will hold back our hands from him and that he let us and our religion alone and we will let him and his religion alone."

But God had forewarned Muhammad:

> Therefore yield not to those who declare (the truth) to be a lie.
>
> They wish that thou shouldn't be slack so that they might be slack.
>
> (Quran, 68: 8-9)

Muhammad was called, or came, when the people were present at Abu-Talib's bed of sickness. When Muhammad was told what they had come for, he said:

> "I have only one thing to say and it will make you kings of Arabia and rulers of foreign countries."

Said Abu-Jahl: "Alright, by thy father, let it be ten words."

Said Muhammad: "Say, 'God is One, we leave worship of all beside Him'."

They all left him and what they said is thus described in the Quran:

> And say the unbelievers: "This (man) is an enchanter (and) a great liar.
> Has he converted (lit. made) all the deities into One God?
> Most surely this is a wonderful thing."
> And the chiefs from among them break away, saying:
> "Go away and persevere with regard to your deities.
> Most surely there is some object in this (new) thing?"
>
> (Quran, 38:4 to 6.)

Nothing was or could be settled between the unbelievers and Muhammad. Abu-Talib died; and a few days after him Khadijah also breathed her last.

State of Prophet's : The state of Muhammad's mind cannot be imagined: Grief overtook him as it had never overtaken him before. He used to say that of all earthly calamities the death of Abu-Talib was the greatest. Muhammad loved Abu-Talib more than any man ever loved his father and Abu-Talib had been more than a father to him. He was his best friend and protector on this earth.

The death of Khadijah made matters still worse. She who had loved him so dearly and comforted him in his physical and mental troubles was no more.

Prophet's Renewed Efforts for the Propagation of Islam : Whatever his griefs, Muhammad was now full 50 years of age. His wisdom and experience were a match for a thousand men and his courage and perseverance were unparelled to any body.

The unbelievers increased their persecutions. One day when Muhammad was passing through the streets of Mecca a wicked man amongst the Quraish threw mud over his head. Muhammad did not say a word but went home and his daughter Fatima washed the mud from his holy person. As she did so, she cried: The grief of her mother's recent death and the enmity of the unbelievers towards her father made her burst with tears. Muhammad, who loved her as dearly as he loved Khadijah, was also deeply moved but not a word passed his lips against his enemies. He checked himself as he always did and simply said, "My daughter, don't cry. God will protect thy father."

Abu-Bakr Beaten : Either at this time or some time previous, whilst the Prophet was praying at the Kaaba one Uqba bin Abi-Muit put his cloth round the Prophet's neck and tried to strangle him to death. Abu-Bakr came running there and asked them to desist saying to them, "Will you kill a man because he says 'God (Allah) is my Lord'." They fell upon Abu-Bakr and gave him very severe beating.

Once again, the dirty entrails of the animals sacrificed to the deities of Mecca were thrown on the Prophet's back whilst he was praying. The unbelievers laughed but the Prophet was so absorbed in his prayers that he did not notice anything. His daughter Fatima removed the refuse from his back.

Abu-Bakr's Intended Emigration : Matters became so serious that even Abu-Bakr, the Prophet's dearest friend, thought of leaving Mecca. With this intention and probably with a view to searching for a safe refuge, he left Mecca and reached a place called Birk-Alghamid; there he met Ibn ul-Dughnah, the chief of the tribe of Qarah. Ibn ul-Dughnah asked Abu-Bakr as to where he was going and was informed that he was tired of being persecuted by the unbelievers of Mecca and was intending to emigrate somewhere else. Ibn ul-Dughnah, knowing the position and character of Abu-Bakr, could not bear this and accompanied him back to Mecca and told the cheifs of Mecca that Abu-Bakr was under his protection and that they were not to molest him. The unbelievers agreed on one condition , viz., that Abu-Bakr should not recite the Quran loud enough for their children and womenfolk to hear. Abu-Bakr at first consented to this but he could not help reciting the Quran aloud. The unbelievers complained to Ibn ul- Dughnah who demonstrated with Abu-Bakr but the latter refused to agree to the condition of the Quraish; and in this way the recital of the Quran and persecution of the Quraish went together. The Muslims not willing to be cowed down and the unbelievers determined to put them down by all means at their disposal.

Muhammad's Journey to Taif : Muhammad now thought of nothing but of carrying out the message of God. He was certain of success and every injury that he met within the course of his mission was an incentive to further work. He was willing to die but unwilling to be idle. He told Abu-Jahl that the latter's days were numbered and he told the Quraish generally that they would soon enter the faith which they now ridiculed. As to himself he had no care. God was looking after him. The Message must go forward. Not only Mecca but the whole of Arabia must hear the Word of God.

Accompanied by his adopted son Zaid, be went on foot to Taif, about sixty miles away from Mecca. This was the tenth month of the Tenth year of the Prophet's mission. On the way to Taif he went to preach to the tribe of Banu-Bakr and found them as hard-hearted as the unbelievers at Mecca. He then visited the descendants of Qahtan. They were also equally stubborn and refused to listen to Muhammad. The Prophet might have guessed what sort of welcome he would get from the people of Taif. He, however, thought only of his duty and not of the immediate consequences of his visit. At Taif there was a big temple for the worship of the deity called Al-Lat. The Prophet went there and saw the chiefs of Taif and invited them to the service of One God. Banu-Thaqif were the influential people of Taif and three brothers of this tribe named (1) Abd Yalii bin Arm- bin Umayr, (2) Masud (3) Habib were their leaders. Muhammad invited them towards God. They were extremely proud. One of them said to him:

> "If thou wast the Messenger of God, He would not let thee wander on foot in this way."

The second said: "Was there no one else left to God to make His messenger?"

The third said: " It is dangerous to speak to thee if thou art true; and unfitting if thou art a liar!'

Muhammad left them but they set the wicked people of Taif and the children and the young men upon Muhammad and his only companion. Brickbats were thrown at him till Muhammad bled profusely. There was nothing left for Muhammad but to go back to Mecca. Even then the crowd pursued him for three miles pelting him with stones till his shoes were full of blood. About this pelting the Prophet has related, 'I fled for three miles from Taif, but so sore and unconscious was I that I did not know whence I was running or whither."

At last he reached the plantation of one Utba bin Rabia and the crowd left him. He took shelter there.

Muhammad's Prayer to God : If there was any just occasion for any man to curse his enemies, it was now for Muhammad to do so with regard to the people of Taif He was bleeding and his heart was almost broken at the cruel treatment he had so unjustly received. He might have said, " O God! destroy these people who are so wicked and not one of them has any sense of fairness." He did nothing of the kind. This is how he prayed to God:

> "O God! I bring to thee the plaint of the weakness of my power, the poverty of my means and the contempt of the people against me.
>
> "O most Merciful of the merciful!
>
> "Thou art the Maintainer of the weak and Thou art my Maintainer. In whose hands has Thou put me? He who is a stranger and sour- faced, or he who is my enemy?
>
> "But if Thou art not angry with me, I care not for him because Thy comfort is vast enough for me. O Lord! I seek refuge in the Light of Thy face which illumines all darkness and which sets right all the affairs of this world and of the next from thine own wrath and from Thine own displeasure. I seek nothing but Thy pleasure, and I have no power to do any good or to prevent any evil except with Thy help."

The above is a literal translation of Muhammad's prayer but the delicacy of feeling and the humility of heart breathed in these words can only be felt in the original. The Prophet does not complain of the treatment he has received but only of his own weakness and poverty. He is afraid of nothing except God's anger which he avoids by his heart to heart communication with God. To prayers like this God replies:

Therefore persevere thou a noble persevering.

> They see it far,
> But We see it near. (Quran, 70 : 5 to 7.)

Muhammad was certain in his own soul that the Quraish would one day believe in him and was patient against all outward unfavourable portents.

He was now sitting in the plantation of the sons of Rabia who served him with a plateful of grapes brought by their slave Addas. Addas was a Christian and when he heard Muhammad say "With the Name of God" before he ate his grapes he wondered how an Arab could say that and on his being told that his guest Muhammad was a prophet, Addas at once believed in him.

Muhammad was now in a most perilous state. He had no protector amongst the Quraish to save him from actual death if his enemies chose to kill him.

He sent his messengers to various notables of the Quraish for protection, but none would undertake it except Mutim bin Adi, whose sons took Muhammad home and told the Quraish that he was under their father's protection.

Muhammad's Message to Various Tribes : The Quraish (or rather the unbelieving Quraish) now knew full well that Muhammad had no powerful friend left. Mutim bin Adi himself was an unbeliever and his protection was not of much weight in the eyes of the Quraish. They knew of Muhammad's failure to convert the people of Taif and other tribes of the Arabs. But Muhammad was never defeated. After his return to Mecca, he visited the dwellings of Banu-Kindah, Banu-Kalb, Banu- Hanifah and Banu-Amir. Not a single one of them listened to his voice. They all rejected, him and some with great arrogance.

Banu-Amir wanted to help him on condition that if he succeeded they should have the command of affairs. And when Muhammad told them that was in the hands of God, they rejected him with contumely.

Muhammad's Engagement to Aishah and Marriage with Saudah : In the Tenth year of his mission, Muhammad, in order to cement his friendship with Abu-Bakr who had been a tower of strength to all Muslims, was engaged to Aishah binte Abu-Bakr, but the consummation of this marriage did not take place till some years afterwards at Medina.

Later on , Muhammad married Saudah, a widow of one of those early Muslims who had emigrated to Abyssinia and then returned to Mecca where her husband had died with no one to look after her. Up to this time the law about Muslim marriage had not been revealed to the Prophet and in fact it was not revealed till long after the Hijrah or emigration to Medina.

Last Phase at Mecca

Abu-Bakr, Muhammad's life-long friend and Chief Minister, was the first to confirm his faith in Muhammad's Vision and was hence styled As-Siddique, the truthful. But the unbelievers and the wavers were up against him more than ever. There was one thing remarkable about the Meccan unbelievers. They were not hypocrites. Their opposition to Muhammad and his fellow-believers was open and unconcealed. They again began to beat and torture the Muslims.

Conversion of Abu-Dhar Ghiffari : Muhammad's fame and the principles of Islam had now spread over Arabia. The deputation of 20 converts from Christianity was inculcating Islam in their own territory and Tufail who was a learned man and a leader of Yemen was converting his own people to Islam in Yemen.

But the most fruitful ground for the spread of Islam and its cultivation was being prepared in Medina. This was due entirely to Muhammad's preachings to pilgrims and traders during the holy months. The spiritual sun of Islam (Muhammad) was having his Satellites of faith.

A man named Abu-Dhar of the tribe of Ghifar living at Medina (as yet called Yathrib) was drawn towards the Truth. He sent his brother Amis to see Muhammad and find out the truth about him. Amis returned and reported that Muhammad preached the doing of good and the prevention of evil. Abu-Dhar was not quite satisfied, and so he set out in person to find out the exact truth about Muhammad. When he reached Mecca he would not declare who he was and wanted to investigate the matter secretly for himself. He met Ali bin Abu-Talib by chance and was led into the presence of the Prophet. Abu-Dhar asked the prophet to explain to him what Islam was, and immediately believed. His enthusiasm was so great that he returned to the Kaaba and declared his Islam there. The unbelievers began to beat him and might have killed him but for his being recognised by Abbas the uncle of the Prophet who told the unbelievers that Abu-Dhar belonged to the tribe of Ghifar with whom they had frequent dealings. They then released Abu-Dhar but he again declared his faith and was again going to be beaten when Abbas had him rescued and sent back to Medina.

Conversion of Swaid bin Sabit : Swaid bin Samit was a resident of Medina and was named "the perfect" amongst his people. He heard of Muhammad and came to Mecca. When he met Muhammad he said to the Prophet, " I also have the like of what you have."

"What is that?" asked Muhammad.

"The wise sayings of Luqman was the reply. The Prophet heard his sayings and appreciated their value. Then the Prophet recited the Quran. Swaid at once acknowledged his faith.

Conversion of Ayas bin Madh : About this time Aus and Khazraj, the two chief tribes of Medina, were having quarrels amongst themselves and a deputation of the later under the leadership of Ans bin Rafi came to Mecca to get supporters from the Quraish. With him were a number of young men including one Ayas bin Madh. Muhammad heard of this deputation and preached Islam and its beauties to them. Ayas at once believed but Ans became angry. It mattered little. The seed was sown. Ayas returned to Medina and died there declaring his faith.

Conversion of Damad : Damad was an inhabitant of Yemen and an enchanter. He had heard that Muhammad was one possessed of a jinn. He came boasting to the Quraish and said, "I can cure Muhammad of his malady."

He went, or was taken to the Prophet. He said to the Prophet, "Will you listen to my charms?" The Prophet said, "You had better listen to mine first" and he recited:

> All praise belongs to God,
>
> We praise Him and ask His help.
>
> He whom God guides no one can misguide,
>
> And he whom God causes to be lost has no guide.
>
> And I bear witness that there is no deity but God (Allah)
>
> One without a partner.
>
> And I bear witness that Muhammad is His Servant and Messenger, etc.

These are the opening words of the address in each Friday prayers and Muhammad was going to recite further but Damad stopped him and asked him to repeat these words three times and when that had been done, he said, " It is enough. I have heard poets, enchanters and Kahins but never heard such a thing before. These words are as deep in their meaning as is the sea. I am a Muslim."

War of Buath : After the return of Ans bin Rafi to Medina an extremely bloody war called Buath took place between Aus and Khazraj in which a great many of both sides were killed. The Khazraj won at first and then the Aus came back and fought so furiously that the Khazraj lost heavily. As in Harb ul-Fijar near Mecca, both sides lost heavily and both were decimated. The only people who gained thereby were the Jews in and around Medina.

Jews Expecting a Prophet in their Favour : The Jews who had been driven out of their homes by the Christians were expecting a prophet to come and help them. The ruin of both Aus and Khazraj made them boast that they would soon capture Medina and the rest of Arabia and destroy the idol-worshippers and Adand Irm had been destroyed before. "That Prophet will come and conquer you," they said to Aus and Khazraj, who were now both reduced to great straits. Aus and Khazraj jointly appointed Abdullah bin Muhammad as their chief to reorganize themselves but events were shaping themselves independently of these two tribes or of the boasting of the Jews.

First Pledge at Uqaba : Uqaba is a place between mount Hira and Mina near Mecca. In the eleventh year of the Prophet's mission, he met six men of Medina at this place on the occasion of the Hajj and preached Islam to them. The names of this party are given as follows:-

(1) Abu Imama Asad bin Zararah

(2) Auf bin Harith

(3) Rafi bin Malik

(4) Qutbah bin Amir bin Hudaida

(5) Aqaba bin Amir bin Nabi

(6) Saad bin Rabi

These people spread the news of Muhammad's mission at Medina and next year (twelfth of Muhammad's mission) a bigger and more representative party of Aus and Khazraj came to Hajj. Muhammad met them again at Aqaba and preached Islam to them. Twelve of them represented their party. They became Muslims and made the following pledge at the hands of Muhammad:

(1) We will join no one (and nothing) in the worship (or service) of God.

(2) We will not commit adultery or fornication.

(3) We will not commit theft.

(4) We will not kill our children.

(5) We will not bring false charges.

(6) We will obey the Prophet of God (Muhammad) in all that is good.

When they had taken the oath or pledge Muhammad said: "He who carries it out has paradise for his reward and he who neglects anything of it, his affair is with God. He may forgive or He may not."

And Muhammad sent Musab bin Umayr to teach them the Quran and Islam and to make them understand the principles of the faith.

Musab went and preached Islam at Medina where it spread most rapidly.

Conversion of Usaid and Saad bin Madh : Musab put up with one Asad bin Zararah at Medina. One day, Musab and Asad bin Zararah and some other Muslims held a meeting at a certain well in order to do something to convert the tribes of Banu Abd ul-Ashhal and Banu Zafar.

Saad bin Madh and Usaid bin Hudair were the respective leaders of these two tribes. They got wind of this meeting of Musab and went there to prevent the meeting having any effect.

Sad told Usaid: "How careless you are? These two men (meaning Musab and Asad) are misleading the foolish people amongst us. You better go and tell them to desist from doing so and avoid coming to our quarters. I would go and do it myself but for the fact that Asad is my aunt's son."

Usaid bin Hudair put on his armour and went to Musab and began to abuse him and call him names without sitting down.

Musab replied: "I wish you would come and sit down and listen to me. If I say anything that is not proper you may reject it." "All Right," said Usaid and sat down. Musab then explained to him what Islam meant and read out portions of the Quran. Usaid believed and after making himself clean, acknowledged his faith and said two Rakats of prayers.

Meanwhile, Saad bin Madh was anxiously waiting for Usaid. When the latter returned, Saad asked him what had happened. Usaid replied: "I have told them all about it and they say they will not do anything without consulting you but you are wanted there very badly yourself." Saad went and what happened to Usaid happened to him.

Conversion of Banu Abd ul-Ashhal : But Saad like Umar bin Khattab was a man of action. He put on his armour, called all his people together the same day and said:

"O Banu Abd ul-Ashhal : What do you think of me?"

"You are our leader and chief man. Your advice and your views are always the best and the noblest" said they.

"In that case," said Saad, "I will not speak to any man or woman amongst you until you believe in God and His Messenger (Muhammad)," and, before evening fell, they were all Muslims.

News of the happenings at Medina were reaching Muhammad and he was digesting it all and making his own plans. Muhammad was always all eyes and ears for the good of Muslims. Nothing escaped his notice and every news that he heard was carefully registered in the vast chambers of his spacious mind.

Second Oath at Uqaba : Musab's preaching was highly successful at Medina and one result of it was that in the next year (thirteenth of Muhammad's mission) 73 men and 2 women were deputed by the Muslims of Medina to meet the Prophet and to induce him to come to Medina. This was the Hajj or pilgrim season, and, by appointment, Muhammad met them again at Aqaba. This was Muhammad's third meeting with the Medinites. His uncle, Abbas bin Abd ul-Muttalib, who was not as yet a convert to Islam accompanied Muhammad. Abbas Knew as well as Muhammad that the unbelievers amongst the Quraish were after Muhammad's life and whoever sided with Muhammad would have to fight them. He was the first to speak and he said:

> "O ye people of Khazraj! Muhammad has a position amongst us which you know and we have protected him from our people as much as we could and as you have seen, he is one of the most respected amongst his people and a power in his town. He refused to join any one except you. If you think you can carry out what you promise in calling him to you and if you can defend him against his enemies then the burden of your undertaking is upon you. But if you are going to surrender him and abandon him after having taken him with you, you better leave him alone."

The Medinites replied:

> "We have heard thee and now we want to hear the Prophet of God."

Muhammad read out the Quran and invited them to Islam and then said:

> "Do you pledge that you will defend me as you will defend your women and children?"

Bara bin Marur, their chief, stretched out his hand and said:

> "We pledge, O Prophet of God. We are, by God, the children of war and we have inherited fighting from our forefathers."

Then Abul-Hathim bin Taihan said: "O Prophet of God! between us and the Jews there are connections which might be broken. If that happens, it may be that thy God will make it appear to thee to return to thy people and leave us."

Muhammad smiled and said:

> "Nay, in life and death I am with you and you are with me. I will fight whom you fight and I will make peace with whom you make peace."

The people were then ready to take the pledge but Abbas bin Ubadah stopped them saying:

> "O ye people of Khazraj! do you know the significance of the pledge you are making with this man? You are pledging him on a red and black (meaning most sanguinary) war against the people (meaning Quraish — enemies of Muhammad). If you think that when your property is plunged into danger and your nobles into death you are going to surrender this man, you had better leave him now. Because if you do so, it will be a shame for you in this world and the next. But if you think you can carry out what you are called upon to do in spite of the loss of wealth and the death of your nobles then take him because it will be for your good both here and hereafter." And the people accepted Muhammad in spite of loss of wealth and the death of their nobles.

"What shall be for us, O Prophet of God, if we remain firm in our pledge? "they asked.

"Paradise" was the reply.

Then they all stretched out their hands and took the pledge which was as follows:

> "We pledge that we will hear and obey in times of our distress and in times of our plenty and in what befalls us of happiness and of anguish and that we will speak the truth wherever we be, not fearing the censure of the censurers on the path of God."

And Muhammad appointed twelve men to teach them Islam at Medina and told them that he had appointed twelve disciples to preach Islam. There were nine men of the tribe of Khazraj, namely,

(1) Asad bin Zararah

(2) Rafi bin Malik

(3) Ubadah bin Samit

(All these three had pledged themselves in the first oath at Aqaba also).

(4) Saad bin Rabi

(5) Mandhar bin Amr

(6) Abdullah bin Rwaha

(7) Braa bin Marur

(8) Abdullah bin Amr

(9) Saad bin Ubadah

and three men of Aus named:

(10) Usaid bin Hudair

(11) Saad bin Khuthimah

(12) Abul-Hathim bin Taihan

Muhammad and his companions were happy that the whole affair had been accomplished without trouble and without the Quraish being aware of their secrets. Suddenly they heard a voice yelling:

> "O ye Quraish! Muhammad and the young men with him have met to fight you."

The Medinites were ready to fight the Quraish but Muhammad told them that those were not his orders and asked them to return to their tents and sleeping places. On the morrow, the Quraish visited the tents of the Medinites and asked them why they had pledged themselves to Muhammad but they got no reply. The Muslims kept quiet. The Quraish returned uncertain of the situation and the Medinites had time to pack and go back to Medina.

Then the Quraish found out more about the pledge and pursued the Medinites but did not succeed in catching any except Saad bin Ubadah, the ninth disciple of Muhammad above named. They beat him and tortured him till he was rescued by Jubair bin Mutim and Harith Umayyah with whom he had trade relations and whom he had given shelter before.

Most Critical Time : As the days passed and Quraish, the enemies of Muhammad, learnt more and more about the pledge of Aus and Khazraj at Aqaba they grew more and more violent. The unbelievers and the Muslims could not exist together. The raging fire of disbelief and idolworship must fight the Light of Islam and put it out if it could. Muhammad knew all this beforehand and hence his precautions in the pledge he took at Aqaba. Before the Quraish could kill his followers he ordered them to emigrate to Medina.

Migration to Medina

The Holy Prophet's ascension to the Heavens proved to be a turning point in the life of the Holy Prophet and as such in the history of Islam. It had its repercussions on the life of Hadrat Ali. After this momentous event in the annals of mankind, the clouds began to settle and things became easier for the Holy Prophet and for that matter for the Muslims. The tribes around Mecca who had heretofore refused to listen to the Holy Prophet, now came to be divided among themselves and some persons out of them accepted the new faith. To overcome the grief and the irreparable loss because of the death of Hadrat Khadija, the Holy Prophet married an elderly lady Hadrat Sauda. She was a good housewife, she looked after the house of the Holy Prophet with proper care. She looked after the young daughters of the Holy Prophet with great affection and consoled them in their grief at the loss of their mother. In 621 C. E. a delegation from Yathrib came to Mecca and they accepted Islam. The Jews of Yathrib observed that according to their scriptures, that was the time for the advent of a new prophet. After the end of the social boycott, the Muslims stepped up trading activities. It appears that at this time while the Holy Prophet devoted his attention to religious affairs, Hadrat Ali concentrated his attention at the management of the business affairs. The traditional accounts of the period that have come down to us create the impression that by this time the economic resources of the Holy Prophet had dried up and neither he nor Hadrat Ali had any source of income This view cannot be accepted for an ideal prophet could not neglect this aspect of his activity. In the conduct of business the Holy Prophet entrusted this responsibility to Hadrat Ali and he discharged this responsibility with due diligence. Heretofore the Holy Prophet had avoided any armed conflict with the Quraish. A state akin to cold war prevailed between the Quraish and the Muslims for a period of over ten years. In 622 C. E. the people of Yathrib invited the Holy Prophet and his followers to migrate to Yathirb and live in their midst. They promised their full support to the Holy Prophet and his followers. The Holy Prophet directed his followers to migrate in batches to Yathrib. By the beginning of the month of September in 622 C. E. all male members of the Muslim families had left Mecca for Medina except the Holy Prophet, Hadrat. Abu Bakr and Hadrat Ali.

Quraish's Plot to Assassinate Holy Prophet : The migration of the Muslims to Yathrib caused a great stir in the Quraish camp. They felt that if the Muslims gained strength in Yathrib, they would be a source of great danger for the Quraish. The Quraish held a council of war under the leadership of Abu Sufyan and Abu Jahl. The Quraish felt that as long as Muhammad lived, be it in Mecca or elsewhere he would continue to be a great challenge for the Quraish. The Quraish took cognizance of the fact that in spite of their hostility, Islam was fast spreading in various parts of Arabia. They viewed the process of the growth of Islam with great concern and alarm. They held that in the circumstances their safety lay in the assassination of Muhammad (peace be on him). The Quraish resolved that Muhammad (peace be on him) should be assassinated before he could proceed to Yathirb. The council of war decided that the young men belonging to all sections should surround the house of Muhammad at night and assassinate him when he came out of his house in the morning by falling on him and putting an end to him with the blows of their daggers.

Frustration of the Plot : The Holy Prophet was forewarned of the Quraish plot by

Allah. It was revealed that if the unbelievers plotted Allah could frustrate their plot and Allah was the best planner. The Holy Prophet asked Hadrat Ali to sleep on his bed that night. Thereafter he was to wind up business in Mecca and come to Yathrib. After the departure of other Muslims to Yathrib, Hadrat Abu Bakr had sought the permission of the Holy Prophet to migrate to Yathrib Hadrat Muhammad (peace be on him) had asked him to wait for it was possible that he might have a good companion for the journey to Yathrib Hadrat. Abu Bakr was, however, asked to keep ready for the call to migrate might come any moment. That day before the Quraish youth could come to besiege his house the Holy Prophet left for the house of Hadrat. Abu Bakr gave him the tidings that the time for their migration to Yathrib had arrived. At night in the cover of darkness the Holy Prophet and Hadrat. Abu Bakr left Mecca for Yathrib. They did not take the direct road to Yathrib. They moved in the opposite direction and took refuge in a cave in the mount. Their some five miles south of Mecca In the house of the Holy Prophet at Mecca, Hadrat Ali locked the doors from inside and lay on the bed of Holy Prophet. He covered himself with the mantle which was the cover of the Holy Prophet. At night the youth of the Quraish surrounded the house according to plan. Peeping inside the house, they saw the bed occupied and felt satisfied that the Holy Prophet was sleeping there as usual. The Quraish youth kept the vigil throughout the night and they felt assured that during the night no one entered the house, nor went out of it. When the day dawned and the door of the house was opened, it was Hadrat Ali and not the Holy Prophet who had to face the brunt of the fury of the Quraish at the frustration of their plan "Where is Muhammad" asked the Quraish, and Hadrat Ali replied that he had left for Yathrib. When their plan was thus thwarted, the Quraish youth were very furious but Hadrat Ali faced them boldly without showing any sign of fear. In utter disgust and disappointment the Quraish youth dispersed to carry the tale of the failure of their plan to their leaders, Abu Sufyan and, Abu Jahl. Once again in the battle between the truth and falsehood, the truth triumphed. That was the closing scene of the drama that had been played at Mecca during the period 611 -622 C. E. During this period of eleven years all the manoeuvres that the Quraish had adopted ended in their failure and defeat. Hadrat Ali remained in Mecca for a few days and when he had settled all accounts and wound up business he took farewell of Mecca and took the road to Yathrib. It was not a flight as some writers tried to present, it was a march on the road to the fulfilment of destiny. With the migration of the Muslims from Mecca the war between the Quraish and the Muslims was not over. It meant that such war was now to be carried on a wider front to the increasing advantage of the Muslims and the ultimate surrender of the Quraish

Analysis of the Events : When we objectively assess and analyse the events that took place during the three years covering the period 620-622, we notice certain facts which have not been given due coverage in the traditional accounts that have come down to us. The event of the Holy Prophet's ascension to the. Heavens was too novel and strange to be believable even by the Muslims. The way success came to the Muslims immediately after the ascension established the truth of the extraordinary event. The plan chalked out by the Quraish to assassinate the Holy Prophet was a close secret and the way the plan came to naught shows that the Holy Prophet enjoyed the protection of God. The way Hadrat Ali offered his life for the sake of the Holy Prophet shows his great love and devotion to the Holy Prophet. How he faced the Quraish youth thwarted in their plan shows his unusual courage and strength of character. A question may be asked that when the Holy Prophet had already escaped from his house where was the need of Hadrat Ali lying on the bed of the Holy Prophet and risking his life. This was necessary to prevent the pursuit of the Holy Prophet. If the Quraish had come to know that night that the Holy Prophet had left Mecca for Yathrib, an immediate pursuit by the Quraish would have been dangerous for the Holy Prophet. By a delay of twelve hours in the pursuit the Quraish lost the track of the Holy Prophet and could not catch him. In the traditional accounts that have come down to us, an impression is created that the entire project was financed by Hadrat. Abu Bakr and that the Holy Prophet was penniless at the time of migration. This impression is erroneous for evidence is available to the effect that out of the two camels that Hadrat. Abu Bakr had purchased for the journey, the Holy Prophet actually paid for the cost of one camels. The way Hadrat Ali was left in Mecca to settle accounts shows that the Holy Prophet had some business undertaking in Mecca which was managed by Hadrat Ali. This shows that at the time of migration neither the Holy Prophet nor Hadrat Ali were resourceless. In some accounts it is stated that Hadrat Ali travelled from Mecca to Yathrib on foot obviously because he had little money This is not correct. There was no monetary difficulty either in the case of the Holy Prophet or Hadrat Ali.

Settlement in Medina : Hadrat Ali arrived in Yathrib renamed as Medina-tun-Nabi or Medina in the honour of the Holy Prophet towards the close of September in the year 622 C. E. The Holy Prophet welcomed him to Medina and appreciated his services for risking his life for him at Mecca in facing the fury of the Quraish. The Holy Prophet was glad to note that the task allotted to Hadrat Ali at Mecca had been properly and satisfactorily done by him

The world of Medina was quite different from the world of Mecca. At Mecca the Muslims were a persecuted people, at Medina they were the masters of their destiny. At Mecca they were surrounded by enemies and at Medina they were in the midst of friends. The life at Medina marked a break with the past. The days of trials, tribulations and tortures were over, the Muslims were now set on the path of fulfilment. The Muslims were now to build a new society and a new commonwealth

The climate of Mecca was dry, but the climate of Medina was damp. The landscape of Mecca was marked by barren rocks and stony wastes, the landscape of Medina was marked by agricultural fields, gardens and groves of date palms. The change in the physical scene affected the health of the emigrees and some of them including Hadrat. Abu Bakr fell sick. Hadrat Ali withstood the climatic change without being affected in health. He spent most of his time in nursing the sick and helping them in adjusting themselves to the new environments

The Brotherhood : The Medinites felt honoured to have the Holy Prophet and his companions in their midst and in order to ensure the comfort and well-being of their friends from Mecca they were prepared to undergo any sacrifice themselves. Under the electrifying influence of Islam, the Medinites came to develop such traits of character which are unique and without a parallel in the annals of mankind.

The emigrants from Mecca were not to adjust themselves to the changed physical environments alone, they had to adjust themselves to changed social environments as well. To bring about such adjustment and rehabilitation the Holy Prophet established a fraternity among the Muslims from Mecca and those of Medina whereunder each emigrant was paired with a resident of Medina of the corresponding status. For their selflessness and help in the rehabilitation of the emigrants from Mecca in the society of Medina, the Medinites came to be known as "Ansars"—helpers. The brotherhood that was established in Medina during this period shows to what heights men can rise when they are motivated by some noble purpose. The bonds established as a consequence of this brotherhood surpassed the ties of blood relationship.

According to the accounts that have come down to us the Holy Prophet paired all emigrants except Hadrat Ali with the Ansars. According to some traditions quoted by Arman Sarhadi in his book Ali Abu Talib, Hadrat Ali felt great disappointment in being passed over in the process of pairing. It is stated that Hadrat Ali went weeping in his house where he was consoled by his wife Hadrat Fatima. Later the Holy Prophet paired Hadrat Ali with himself declaring that Hadrat Ali was to him what Haroon was to the prophet Moses.

It is difficult to believe in the veracity of this tradition. By this time Hadrat Ali was still unmarried and it is prima facie untrue that his wife Fatima consoled him. Hadrat Ali was a man of great courage who could face any ordeal and he was not the man to weep because he was not paired with any Ansar. At his time Hadrat Ali was a member of the family of the Holy Prophet. Hadrat Ali had not acquired an independent identity of his own so far apart from being a member of the family of the Holy Prophet and the question of pairing him with any Ansar did not arise.

Implications of the Pairing : The pairing of the Holy Prophet and Hadrat Ali was a matter of great significance and it had deep implications and repercussions. In the various source books that have come down to us, nc light is thrown on such implications. We will, therefore, have to undertake an exercise on our own account in spelling out the underlying implications. In the process of brotherhood-formation every emigrant from Mecca was paired with an Ansar of Medina. The Holy Prophet was himself an emigrant from Mecca and the question that arises for consideration is why did the Holy Prophet not pair himself with any Ansar of Medina? To be paired with the Holy Prophet was a great honour and many Ansars coveted this honour. If the Holy Prophet had shown preference for some particular. Ansar that would have been a cause for jealousy on the part of the other. Ansars who equally coveted the honour In Medina the status of the Holy Prophet was that of a ruler and if he had shown preference for some particular Ansar, that would have been a cause of heart burning for the other Ansars. The Holy Prophet did not pair himself with any Ansar because of his impartiality.

A consequence of the pairing of the emigrants and the Ansars was that the emigrants shared with the Ansars their income and property. If the Holy Prophet did not pair with particular Ansar the question is what was the source of income of the Holy Prophet in Medina'?. When the Holy Prophet, in order to maintain his impartiality did not choose to have a share in the income and property of a particular Ansar, it implies that he had his share in the income and property of all Ansars. It is a common practice with religious fraternities that each person belonging to the fraternity contributes a certain percentage of his income to the common fund of the fraternity which is placed at the disposal of the head of the fraternity. It appears that the Ansars of Medina constituted some common fund of similar nature and placed it at the disposal of the Holy Prophet. Presumably some property was also placed at the disposal of the Holy Prophet the income whereof could be utilised to meet his expenses as well as other common needs. The emigrants from Mecca were traders and in Medina as well they undertook trading activities. Indeed Medina offered more trading opportunities than Mecca. The Holy Prophet ran some sort of business at Mecca which was managed by Hadrat Ali. It appears that the same business was continued in Medina. As the Holy Prophet had to devote a good deal of his attention to the affairs of the State, the responsibility for running the business enterprise rested a good deal on Hadrat Ali. The Holy Prophet and Hadrat Ali were already cousins and the brotherhood constituted signified that the ties between the Holy Prophet and Hadrat Ali became still closer and stronger and they shared each other's property.

Masjid-i-Nabwi : In 623 C. E. the Holy Prophet decided to build a mosque in Medina which was to be a prayer house as well as a community centre. The Holy Prophet asked the Muslims to offer their services in labour as well as capital towards the construction of the mosque. Hadrat Ali was the first person to offer his services as labourer. He shovelled the earth when the foundations were being laid and later carried on baskets of brick and mortar which he passed on to the masons. Hadrat Ali composed some verses for the occasion and he recited them as he worked as a labourer. Some of these verses which have been preserved are:

> "Whoever builds a mosque
> And works whether sitting or standing
> Puts up with the pain of labour
> While others shirk work
> For fear of dust and pain
> Both of these verily cannot equal each other"

As the other Muslims laboured they chanted

> "There is no life but the life of the next world
> O God have mercy on the Muhajirin and the Ansar"

Within a few months the mosque was completed. It was square in share and each side measured fifty yards. The mosque faced towards the north and had three gates on each of the remaining three sides. Adjoining the mosque apartments were constructed for the household of the Holy Prophet. Hadrat Ali also had an apartment in the mosque. The mosque was monument of simplicity. The walls were made of mud bricks and the roofs were supported by trunks of palm trees. The apartments for the household were hung with blankets of camel hair as doors. The courtyard in each case was hardly six to seven paces in length, and the length of the rooms did not extend ten paces.

The First Battle : When the Muslims established themselves in Medina and succeeded in acquiring strength the Quraish of Mecca fumed and fretted at the success of the Muslims. Fearing lest Islam might be accepted by the tribes in the immediate neighbourhood of Medina, the Quraish heavily bribed these tribes not to be moved by any overtures by the Muslims. Some of the missionaries sent by the Holy Prophet to these tribes were murdered. The Jews of Medina had expected that the Prophet they were looking for would be a prophet of the Jews and would promote the Jewish faith, but when the Holy Prophet began to preach Islam which was an improvement on the Jewish faith, they became hostile to the Muslims. The Quraish of Mecca incited the Jews of Medina to create difficulties for the Muslims in Medina. In Mecca the Muslims were traders. In Medina the people who accepted Islam and came to be known as "Ansars" were agriculturists. All trade in Medina was in the hands of the Jews. When the Muslim emigrants tried to undertake trading activities in Medina, they had to face competition and hostility of the Jews. The Holy Prophet realised that in the circumstances the Muslims would have to wage a war against the Quraish and the Jews on the economic front. The caravan route from Mecca to Syria ran close to Medina. There were some danger points on the route where the caravans could be ambushed by a small force. The Holy Prophet decided that in order to break up the trade monopoly of the Quraish, their caravans should be ambushed by the Muslims at strategic points.

Quraish Caravans : In the winter of 623 C. E. Abu Sufyan, the Quraish leader, led a trading caravan to Syria This caravan was to return in the spring of 624 C. E. In the first week of March, Hadrat Ali and Zubayr b. Awwam were commissioned by the Holy Prophet to undertake a reconnoitenng exercise and bring intelligence about the movements of the caravan of the Quıaish Hadrat Ali and Zubayr brought the intelligence that the caravan was nearing Badr. The Holy Prophet held a council of war and after taking the pros and cons of the case into consideration, it was decided that the Muslims should make an attempt to ambush the caravan. A force of 313 persons was raised and they marched to Badr some eighty miles from Medina.

Abu Sufyan, the leader of the Quraish caravan, was an astute man. He apprehended that the Muslims would try to ambush the caravan. He accordingly sent a message to the Quraish of Mecca that they should send a force to escort the caravan. The Quraish raised a one thousand strong fully equipped force and they marched at great speed to meet the caravan.

When the Muslims reached Badr they found that the caravan of the Quraish had already crossed the danger point and could no longer be ambushed. The Muslims felt frustrated that their prey had eluded them God, however, assured the Holy Prophet that a better prize was in store for them.

The caravan of the Quraish marched to Mecca at great speed and they met in the way the force that had come to their assistance. Abu Sufyan desired that as the danger of the ambushing of the caravan by the Muslims was over the force should return with the caravan to Mecca. Abu Jahl who commanded the Quraish force said that it was a good opportunity for them to attack the Muslims and annihilate them. The caravan under. Abu Sufyan proceeded to Mecca and the Quraish force confident of their strength and superiority rushed forward for a clash with the Muslims.

The Battleground : When Abu Jahl came to know that the Muslims had assembled at Badr, he advanced to Badr. When the Muslim force came to know that the Quraish force was advancing to Badr they occupied the wells in the valley and encamped in the rocky part of the valley.

When the Quraish reached Badr they occupied that part of the valley which was plain. The Muslims had not come prepared for a full-fledged war, they had merely intended an ambush and minor showdown. Now a full-fledged battle was forced on them. That was to be the first armed conflict between the Muslims and the Quraish. There were heavy odds against the Muslims. The Quraish force was three times the force of the Muslims in strength. The Quraish force was fully equipped, while the Muslim force was ill equipped. The Quraish could fight on horseback while the Muslims had to fight on foot. A greater part of the night before the battle was spent by the Holy Prophet in prayers. The Holy Prophet prayed:

> "O Lord I beseech you to fulfil the promise that You have given to me O Lord, if you allow this band of the Muslims to perish, there will be none to worship You on the earth"

Hadrat Abu Bakr and Hadrat Ali kept watch over the Holy Prophet by turn. Allah assured the Holy Prophet that He would not allow the Muslims to perish, and that He would help them in their war against the unbelievers.

The Battle : When the day dawned, the two forces met in battle array. The Quraish raised boastful cries highlighting their superiority, skill and richer resources. The Muslims were in a humble mood and invoking the aid of God they raised the shouts "Allah-o-Akbar" (Allah is great). That was the first battle to be fought by the Muslims and they had no previous experience of war. The Holy Prophet, however, exhibited the qualities of a great military General. He marshalled the Muslim forces in a superb way and arrayed them in such manner that they could contend against the larger force of the enemy. The previous night it had rained. That worked to the advantage of the Muslims for the rocky ground under their feet became firmer, while the ground under the feet of the Quraish became muddy and slippery. The Holy Prophet divided the Muslim force in a number of commands, each under a Commander. One unit was placed under the command of Hadrat Ali and he was given the flag by the Holy Prophet.

As a prelude to the battle proper, three warriors—Utba, Shaiba, and Al—Walid stepped out of the ranks of the Quraish and challenged the Muslims to duel in single combat. In response to this challenge three Ansars stepped out of the ranks of the Muslims to fight the duel. The Quraish taunted the Muslim emigrants and wanted them to come forward to cross swords with them if they had any trait of chivalry about them. Thereupon Hadrat Ali was the first to step forward from the ranks of the Muslims to accept the challenge of the Quraish. He was followed by Hamza and Ubaida b Hanth. In the contest that followed Hadrat Ali killed. Al Walid and Hamza killed Shaiba. In the duel between Ubaida and Utba. Ubaida was mortally wounded Hadrat Ali and Hamza rushed to the help of Ubaida and cut off the head of Utba. Thereupon with a cry of rage three Meccans darted to assail Hadrat Ali and Hamza. All the three Meccans fell dead before the blows of the swords of Hadrat Ali and Hamza.

Exasperated at the death of its six warriors in single combat, the Quraish led the charge and tried to break through the ranks of the Muslims. The Muslims stood fast at their posts and when the fury of the Quraish force was spent, the Muslims launched a counter-attack and forced the Quraish to fall back. The ground was muddy and slippery and in the confusion that followed many Quraish slipped in the mud when the Muslims availing of the advantage thrust their swords in their bodies. Miraculously the battle ended in the favour of the Muslims. Over seventy persons from among the Quraish fell dead on the battlefield. All the leaders of the Quraish who held the command were killed. Over seventy persons were taken prisoners. A large booty fell into the hands of the Muslims. Hadrat Ali was not conspicuous in performing prodigies of valour. According to tradition he killed twenty-one persons—two brothers of Hadrat Ali—Talib and Aqueel fought on the side of the Quraish Out of these Talib was killed and. Aqueel was taken prisoner. When the booty was distributed Hadrat Ali got an armour, a sword and a camel.

Significance of the Battle : In its dimensions the battle of Badr was one of the most insignificant battles, but in its significance it proved to be one of the most momentous battles in the history of mankind. The battle became a turning point in the history of Islam. If the Muslims had lost the battle, that would have been the end of Islam as the Holy Prophet himself feared. The Muslims victory in the battle established the truth of Islam. The battle humbled the pride of the Quraish. It cast a pall of mourning over Mecca for almost every family among the Quraish lost some dear one in the battle. The Quraish who had persecuted the Muslims for over eleven years had now to lick their own wounds. The battle marked the beginning of the end of paganism in Arabia. The tribes who were under the influence of the Quraish refused to listen to the message of Islam now felt the need of winning the favour of the Muslims. With the defeat of their allies, the Jews of Medina were forced to rethink of their relationship with the Muslims. Because of the booty that the Muslims recieved at the battle the economic conditions of the Muslims in Medina improved. The battle adversely affected the economic conditions of the Quraish firstly because of the loss that they suffered at the battle and secondly because trade route to Syria became unsafe for them. The great significance of the battle was that it assured the Muslims that a great destiny awaited him. The Holy Prophet felt happy that God had kept His promise with him. The battle proved to be a landmark in the life of Hadrat Ali for thereafter he came to be acclaimed as the greatest and the bravest warrior among the Muslims. Because of his bravery in the battle of Badr, Hadrat Ali won from the Holy Prophet the title of "Haider-i-Karrar" (the warrior whom nobody could beat).

Three

POST-MIGRATION PERIOD

Married Life

When the Holy Prophet migrated to Yathrib he left his family at Mecca. As soon as the Muslims settled in Yathrib the Holy Prophet and the other Muslims called their families to Medina. At the time of migration Sauda, an elderly lady, was the only wife of the Holy Prophet whom he had married after the death of Hadrat Khadija. About a year after his arrival in Medina the Holy Prophet married Hadrat Aishah, a daughter of Hadrat Abu Bakr.

Married to Hadrat Fatima : By this time, Hadrat Fatima, the youngest daughter of the Holy Prophet, had come of marriageable age and the Holy Prophet had to consider the question of her marriage Hadrat. Abu Bakr waited on the Holy Prophet and asked for the hand of Hadrat Fatima. The Holy Prophet made no answer. Thereafter Hadrat Umar asked for the hand of Hadrat Fatima and the Holy Prophet maintained silence. In the Arabian society of the day the disparity in the age of the bride and the bridegroom did not matter. The Holy Prophet married Hadrat Khadija when he was twenty-five and she was forty, fifteen years older than him Later the Holy Prophet when over fifty married Hadrat. Aishah yet within her teens. When the Holy Prophet did not respond to the requests of Hadrat. Abu Bakr or Hadrat Umar, he was not bothered about the age question, his silence was due to the fact that he had to wait for the guidance of God which was meant to get in all matters of importance affecting his person.

After the battle of Badr, Hadrat Ali made his suit. The Holy Prophet told Hadrat

Ali that he would give his reply after consulting Hadrat Fatima. The Holy Prophet consulted Hadrat Fatima and she maintained silence signifying her assent. In the meantime the Holy Prophet received the revelation that God approved of the marriage of Hadrat Fatima with Hadrat Ali. When Fatima, the mother of Hadrat Ali, called on the Holy Prophet to press the suit on behalf of Hadrat Ali, the Holy Prophet was pleased to announce his acceptance.

Preparation for Marriage : According to the accounts available in the source books, Hadrat Ali had no money to meet the expenses of the marriage. He had to sell his armour to raise the necessary funds. Hadrat Uthman who enjoyed reputation for his wealth agreed to purchase the armour for five hundred dirhams. After the transaction had been completed and the amount had been paid, Hadrat Uthman presented the armour to Hadrat Ali as a marriage gift saying that the armour would be more useful for a warrior like Hadrat Ali than for a trader like him. Hadrat Ali was reluctant to accept the gift, but Hadrat Uthman prevailed to accept it in the name of God, for thereby it would serve the cause of Islam in fighting against its enemies. That made Hadrat Ali accept the gift with many thanks. When Hadrat Ali told of the transaction to the Holy Prophet, the Holy Prophet praised the conduct of Hadrat Uthman and prayed for him.

The Marriage Khutba : On the day fixed for the marriage, the Muslims assembled in the mosque and the Holy Prophet delivered the Khutba solemnising the marriage. The Holy Prophet said that all praise was due to God who should be extolled for His various bounties, Who should be worshipped for His power and majesty, and Who should be obeyed for. His omnipotence. The Holy Prophet observed that it behovest the people to seek refuge in God for fear of. His wrath Dwelling on the might of God, the Holy Prophet said that. His are the ordinances which prevail in. Heaven and Earth. He is the one who by His might ordained the existence of all creation through His commandments. He gave us the power of discrimination. He honoured us giving His religion and commissioning Muhammad as His Prophet Referring to the importance of marriages in human society the Holy Prophet said that undoubtedly the Almighty Lord made matrimonial alliances as the means of a fresh relationship which is a fundamental necessity and a just affair which is made incumbent on all and sundry, and through which creation is linked. The Holy Prophet observed that verily Allah is He Who has created human beings from a drop of blood for this end. He has created the relations of the in-laws. Surely God is omnipotent. His decrees are enforced according to. His decisions. His judgements decree the fate and every fate is governed by an appointed time. Every appointed time is predetermined. Over and above this, God can obliterate or keep intact whatever. He likes. The original record of all this is with Him. After these introductory remarks the Holy Prophet declared:

> "Now in obedience to the Will of God I perform the marriage ceremony of Fatima with Ali and ask you to bear witness that I have given Fatima in marriage to Ali against a dowery of 400 pieces of silver coin. May God create love between the pair bless them, purify their offspring make their progeny a mine of wisdom and a source of God's blessings and solace to the believers in faith."

The Holy Prophet ended the Khutba by asking for the forgiveness of God for himself and for the Muslims.

An Ideal Marriage : According to all accounts that have come down to us, the marriage of Hadrat Ali and Hadrat Fatima was an ideal marriage. It was a union of two great souls. Hadrat Hafsa a daughter of Hadrat Umar and later a wife of the Holy Prophet wrote some verses highlighting the greatness of the pair. She said:

> Fatima is superior to womankind in the world,
>
> She is the lady whose face shines as the full moon
>
> She is the bride whose groom
>
> Excels all in scholarship.

According to some authors Hadrat Ali was twenty-one years old at the time of marriage, while Hadrat Fatima was sixteen years old. According to other researches the date of the birth of Hadrat Ali is to be placed around 599 C. E. and on this basis he was 24/25 years old at the time of marriage. Hadrat Fatima was born around 604 C. E. and on this basis she was 19/20 years old at the time of marriage. There appears to be a tendency with the old writers to underestimate the ages of persons particularly women. In most of the books, for example, it is said that at the time of her marriage with the Holy Prophet Hadrat Aishah was a child barely nine years old. Hadrat Aishah was more or less of the same age as Hadrat Fatima or very nearly so and was well within her teens at the time of her marriage.

Undoubtedly the marriage of Hadrat Ali and Hadrat Fatima was an ideal marriage. As the marriage was performed by the Holy Prophet in accordance with the Will of God, it could not be anything but an ideal marriage. As an ideal marriage it should have been a happy marriage. In this context there are two aspects of the case need special consideration. One is the economic factor and the other is the temperamental factor.

Economic Aspects : The economic aspect of the matter is that all writers of old are unanimous on the point that Hadrat Ali was very poor in his book Ali, the Superman, Dr. Ata Mohiuddin observes that Hadrat Ali was extremely poor and the young couple were obliged from the first day to live from hand to mouth. It is observed that often days passed without any fire being lit in their hearth. It is further observed that his bedsheet was so small that if he covered his head, his legs remained uncovered and if he covered his legs his head was exposed. The account provided that Hadrat Fatima had to work too hard. She did not have the wherewithal to wash her clothes which were blackened and soiled on account of dust and dirt. The shoulder on which she carried pitchers of water from the well was swollen and the hands with which she worked the handmill to grind corn were often covered with blisters. There is a story that she requested the Holy Prophet to give her a maid slave to assist her, but he turned down the request. According to another story Hadrat Ali hired himself as an ordinary manual labourer. One day he hired himself as a labourer to draw water from the well for a date per bucket. He drew sixteen buckets when his hands were blistered. He was given sixteen dates which he took to the Holy Prophet and both of them had their meal of these dates. I have long pondered over the question of the poverty of Hadrat Ali and even the Holy Prophet. It appears to me that such accounts are highly exaggerated and remote from the truth. I have prayed to God to show me light whereby I could ascertain the truth that Islam is not a religion for the next world alone it is a religion for this world as well Islam does not favour accumulation of riches and the hoarding of wealth, but it does not command poverty either. It stands for the middle course marked neither by richness nor by poverty.

The Holy Prophet being an ideal Prophet had to set an example in this respect. As such while the Holy Prophet could not be very rich, he could not be poor either. Islam stands for simplicity and austerity but simplicity and austerity are not another name for poverty How could Allah permit his beloved to starve. When the Muslims migrated to Medina, Ansars shared all their resources with the Muslims. Under the circumstances how could the. Ansars permit Hadrat Ali and Hadrat Fatima, the beloved daughter of the Holy Prophet, to live from hand to mouth on the verge of starvation. Hadrat Ali and Hadrat Fatima were after all human beings and how could they be happy when they had to starve for days. When selecting husbands for their daughter even ordinary persons take steps to ensure that their daughter is married in a family which is quite well off. This is a parental obligation and it is unbelievable that the Holy Prophet would have married this beloved daughter to a person who had no source of income. The Holy Prophet married his two daughters to Hadrat Uthman, one after the other, and Hadrat Uthman was the richest person among the Quraish. The Holy Prophet could not discriminate between his daughters by marrying two daughters to a very rich man, and marrying the daughter whom he loved most to a man who was extremely poor. Hadrat Ali was the greatest warrior of the age. He was also the greatest jurists, grammarian and scholar of the age. When the Muslims set up a polity at Medina it was an obligation on the part of the State to provide means of sustenance for Muslims according to their qualification and utilise their services in the interest of the State. Under the circumstances the accounts that Hadrat Ali was very poor are not correct.

Temperamental Differences : It appears that there were some temperamental differences between the husband and wife. Hadrat Ali is said to be hot tempered while Hadrat Fatima was cool headed. It is related that one day Hadrat Ali picked up a quarrel with Hadrat Fatima. Hadrat Fatima felt aggrieved and she went to the Holy Prophet to complain of the conduct of Hadrat Ali. Hadrat Ali followed her and hid himself behind a wall to listen what transpired between the Holy Prophet and Hadrat Fatima. The Holy Prophet advised Hadrat Fatima to have patience and submit to her husband. When Hadrat Ali saw the Holy Prophet later, the Holy Prophet counselled him to be kind to his wife. Due to the wise counsels of the Holy Prophet, both Hadrat Ali and Hadrat Fatima succeeded in making adjustments which ensured mutual happiness. Hassan, their first child, was born in 625 C. E. and Hussain, the second child, was born in 626 C. E. The Holy Prophet had great love for Hassan and Hussain and he treated them as his own sons.

Jews in Medina : When the Holy Prophet and the Muslims migrated to Yathrib there was considerable number of Jews in the city. Some time in the first century of the Christian era, the Romans expelled the Jews from Palestine and some of the tribes of the Jews found refuge in Yathrib. The Jews were money lenders. They lent money to the people of Yathrib at exhorbitant rates of interest. Because of their wealth the Jews dominated the economic scene in Yathrib. The indigenous people of Yathrib belonged to two main tribes, the Aus and the Khazraj. The two tribes fought among themselves and they had also to contend against the growing influence of the Jews. It was with a view to counter balancing the influence of the Jews that the people of Yathrib invited the Holy Prophet and the Muslims to come and live in their midst.

When the Holy Prophet proclaimed his prophethood in Mecca and the news travelled to Yathrib, Jews confirmed that according to their sacred books that was the time for the advent of a prophet. When the Holy Prophet came to Yathrib, the Jews found in him all the signs of prophethood that had been foretold in their books. The Jews regarded themselves as the chosen people of God and that made them think that all prophets must necessarily belong to their race. When Jesus Christ who was not a Jew proclaimed his prophethood, the Jews denied his prophethood and had him executed. The Jews of Yathrib had thought that the Prophet of Arabia would be subservient to them. When the Holy Prophet adopted an independent policy and declared that Islam was an improvement on the Jewish faith, the Jews developed an attitude of an animosity to Islam

Animosity of the Jews : The Holy Prophet followed with regard to the Jews the policy of 'live and let live'. He promulgated a charter of rights whereunder the Jews were guaranteed freedom to worship without any interference. It was undertaken that the two communities would live on terms of mutual friendship. In any attack on the Muslims, the Jews were to help the Muslims. When the Holy Prophet established a polity and the Muslims acquired strength, the Jews came to regard the growing strength of the Muslims as a menace to their influence. They accordingly launched a campaign of vilification against Islam. A Jewish lady Asma wrote pungent verses ridiculing and vilifying Islam and the Holy Prophet. She was warned by the Muslims to refrain from her nefarious activity, but when she persisted, a Muslim stabbed her to death. Abu Afaq, another Jewish poet wrote venomous satires and lampoons ridiculing Islam. He met the same fate as Asma and was assassinated by a Muslim young man. The Jews perverted the verses of the Holy Quran and gave them ominous meanings. The Prophet enjoined the Muslims to spend in the way of Allah. The amounts thus were to be a loan against. Allah Who would repay it many times the original amount Islam forbade the charging of interest. That adversely affected the interets of the Jews. Most of the Quraish emigrees who were traders in Mecca undertook trading activities in Medina as well. That broke the monopoly of the Jews in trade Finhas, a Jewish rabbi, held out that the God of the Muslims was poor who asked of loan from the people, but the God of the Jews was rich Who needed no loan and Who had made the Jews rich. He maintained that they did not need God, but God needed them. He observed that the dependence of God on the Jews was manifest from the fact that He had given interest to the Jews but had denied it to the Muslims. The rabbi came across Hadrat Abu Bakr who took him to task for his sacrilege Hadrat. Abu Bakr slapped the rabbi on the face and said that were it not for the treaty between the Muslims and the Jews, he would have cut off the head of Finhas, the enemy of Allah. During this period many verses of the Holy Quran were revealed exposing the perfidy of the Jews. It was pointed out that the Jews had gone on rejecting the signs of God and slaying. His messengers and they were transgressors.

Hadrat Ali and the Jews : In the original accounts that have come down to us there is no mention of the activities of Hadrat Ali with reference to the Jews. The silence of the authorities in this respect does not mean that Hadrat Ali was inactive and he took no part in the cold war that prevailed between the Muslims and the Jews. The Jews boasted of at their superior knowledge and argues that as Muhammad (peace be on him) was illiterate, he could not be a prophet of God. Hadrat Ali was the most learned scholar among the Muslims and it appears very probable that Hadrat Ali met the arguments of the Jews at intellectual level and exposed their perfidies and transgressions during the course of history Hadrat Ali was prominent poet as well and we will not be far from the truth when we say that Hadrat Ali composed verses vindicating Islam. Islam is a missionary religion and when the Muslims had established a polity at Medina they took steps to convert the unbelievers and the people of the Book to Islam. As Hadrat Ali was the most eloquent person among the Muslims, excepting the Holy Prophet, it appears that Hadrat Ali played a prominent role in propagating the message of Islam. In spite of the general hostility of the Jews to the Muslims, Hadrat Ali succeeded in converting some of the Jews to Islam. The Holy Prophet as the Head of the State, had to adjudicate on disputes among the people, including the Jews. Because of his great learning and vast legal knowledge, Hadrat Ali assisted the Holy Prophet in setting the disputes. Certain persons in Medina had accepted Islam for consideration of self-interest and expediency. Such persons led by Abdullah b Ubay owed nominal allegiance to Islam. These hypocrites and dissemblers aimed at the subversion of Islam from within. The Holy Prophet made Hadrat Ali responsible for keeping a watch on the activities of the hypocrites. The Jews aided and patronised the hypocrites in violation of the terms of the agreement between the Muslim and the Jews.

Bani Qainuqa : The Jews of the Bani Qainuqa tribe were the first to violate the terms of their agreement with the Muslims. These Jews had a walled stronghold outside Medina. When the Holy Prophet called upon these Jews to respect their agreement with the Muslims their leader adopted a defiant attitude and said:

> "O Muhammad ' Do you take us to be akin to the Quraish whom you can defeat. We are a different and a tougher people. If you cross arms with us, you will know for yourself what we are."

In spite of the offense given by the Qainuqa Jews, the Holy Prophet kept quiet and decided to bide his time for an actual confrontation. A crisis developed soon after the battle of Badr. A Muslim lady visited a goldsmith's shop in the Banu Qainuqa quarters. A Jew rogue crept up behind her and pinned her skirt to her bodice. When the lady after the disposal of her business in the shop walked unwittingly into the street, her skirt fell exposing her nakedness. Some Jews collected and began to jeer at the Muslim lady. A Muslim came that way and he fell upon the Jews with his sword. He killed the rogue who had done the mischief. He was on the point of killing another Jew when he himself was killed.

When the Holy Prophet came to know of the happening, he asked the Bani Qainuqa to pay compensation for the wrong done by them and give adequate assurance of good conduct in the future. Banu Qainuqa defied the warning and prepared for war. This exhausted the patience of the Holy Prophet and he ordered punitive action against Banu Qainuqa. The Holy Prophet gave the flag to Hadrat Ali and a Muslim force led by Hadrat Ali marched to the quarters of Bani Qainuqa. The Jews shut themselves in their stronghold and the Muslims besieged the strongholds. Hadrat Ali blocked all routes from where any help could come to Bani Qainuqa from outside. Thereafter the Muslims tightened the siege. Despairing of any help from without the

Bani Qainuqa surrendered after a fortnight. Under the Jewish law all males among the Bani Qainuqa could be beheaded and their females and children could be sold as slaves. The Holy Prophet took a lenient view and merely ordered their expulsion from Medina. The property of Banu Qainuqa was confiscated. As a gesture of good will to the "Muhajirin", the Ansars decided to forego their share. The confiscated properties were distributed among the "Muhajirin" including Hadrat Ali. Even if it is held that the financial position of Hadrat Ali was weak in anyway, his financial position definitely improved after the operation against Bani Qainuqa, for as a result of this battle he came to own a good deal of property. It was the first battle to be fought under the independent command of Hadrat Ali. In this battle Hadrat Ali gave a good account of his generalship.

The Battle of Uhud : The battle of Uhud was an extension of the battle of Badr. Smarting under the ignominy of their defeat at Badr, the Quraish of Mecca assembled a large army of 3,000 persons and marched to Medina to avenge their defeat at Badr. The force was led by Abu Sufyan. The force included every adult among the Quraish. The force was fully equipped with war weapons. The force was accompanied by a considerable number of women. They sang songs to inspire the warriors. They said that if the Quraish won the battle, they would throw open their arms to embrace them, but in case they were defeated, their women would turn away from them. The Quraish were confident that this time they would win and teach the Muslims a lesson.

Holy Prophet's Preparations : When the Holy Prophet came to know of the intentions of the Quraish of Mecca, he held a council of war. He was personally of the view that in view of the strength of the enemy the proper course for the Muslims was to remain in Medina and let the enemy besiege the city. The idea was that if the enemy besieged the city, its force would have to be dispersed in a number of sectors and the Muslims could strike a blow at the enemy where the enemy's concentration was the weakest. The younger element among the Muslims, however, insisted that the battle should be fought in the open at some distance away from Medina. Their argument was that the enemy should not be allowed to approach Medina at any cost. Though the Holy Prophet believed that the defensive strategy proposed by him was the best in the circumstances yet in deference to the enthusiasm for the young men to keep the enemy away from Medina he agreed to meet the enemy in the open outside Medina. The Muslims could assemble a force of one thousand persons only. When the Holy Prophet gave the order for the march to the battlefield, three hundred hypocrites led by Abdullah b Ubbay withdrew and went to their homes. The Holy Prophet was thus left with 700 persons only and this was one fourth of the strength of the enemy.

The Battlefield : Uhud, a few miles from Medina, was a great stretch of barren rock rising out of the desert without any growth of vegetation. The Holy Prophet commanded the Muslim warriors to take up their position at Uhud on the rising ground. A band of archers took up position on an adjoining mound behind the main position. The archers were commanded not to abandon their posts under any circumstances, without the approval of the Holy Prophet.

The Duel : As usual the battle began with a duel Talha bin. Abu Talha, the standard-bearer of the Quraish, stepped forward and challenged the Muslims to a single combat Hadrat Ali, the standard bearer of the Muslims, stepped forward to accept the challenge Talha b. Abu. Talha was an expert swordsman among the Quraish and it was the common belief that nobody could beat him. As Talha stepped forward he boasted of his prowess. Talha was the first to attack Hadrat Ali. Hadrat Ali warded off the attack on his shield Talha was wearing a coat of arms. Hadrat Ali aimed his blows at the legs of Talha. The legs were severed and Talha fell dead. Then another brother of Talha Abu Shaiba stepped forward to seek a duel with a Muslim warrior. He was done to death by Hadrat Hamza. Thereafter the third brother, Said b. Abu Talha, rushed waving his sword and seeking vengeance for his two brothers. He was killed by Saad b. Abu Waqqas. The murder of the three brothers one after the other made the Quraish furious. Their flag was next held by Irtas b Sharjeel, a formidable man. He challenged the Muslims saying that he who coveted death should step forward to measure swords with him. Hadrat Ali met the challenge and killed Irtas. Thereupon Asama b Zaid dashed at Hadrat Ali, with a view to striking a blow at him, before he could adjust himself after killing Irtas Hadrat Ali moved his sword right and left and struck a mortal blow on his assailant who reeled and fell down dead. After the death of six warriors from among the Quraish one after the other, no other warriors of the Quraish could dare challenge a duel with the Muslims.

The Battle : After the duels, the battle began. The Quraish charged with great force, but the Muslims held fast. Then in a counter-attack the Muslims broke the enemy's line and the Quraish fell back. At this stage, the contingent of the Muslim archers, contrary to the instructions of the Holy Prophet left their position in order to plunder the camp of the retreating Quraish Khalid b Walid who was still a non-Muslim and was commanding a contingent of the Quraish cavalry rushed with his contingent and occupied the position vacated by the Muslim archers. That exposed the Muslims to an attack from the rear as well as from the front. That changed the course of the battle. The defences of the Muslims were broken and in the confusion that followed many Muslims were martyred. Hamza, an uncle of the Holy Prophet, fell fighting. His dead body was desecrated by the Quraish as a mark of their fury against the Muslims. Hinda, the wife of Abu Sufyan, the leader of the Quraish ripped the dead body, took out his liver and chewed it. It was such a barbarity which an unscrupulous woman like Hinda alone could practise. Among the Muslims who were martyred was Masab b Umayr. He bore some physical resemblance to the Holy Prophet and seeing his dead body the Quraish shouted that Muhammad (peace be on him) had been killed In the confusion that followed, the Holy Prophet was wounded and he fell in a pit over the dead bodies of his followers Hadrat Ali charged the Quraish with unprecedented fury and killed many men of the enemy. He received no less than sixty-one wounds. When the Quraish continued shouting that the Holy Prophet had been killed and Hadrat Ali could no longer see the Holy Prophet where he was stationed, he rushed to the spot where the Holy Prophet lay wounded. He took the Holy Prophet out of the pit and with aid of other companions including Hadrat. Abu Bakr and Hadrat Umar escorted the Holy Prophet to a safer place Hadrat Ali fetched water in his shield and dressed the wounds of the Holy Prophet taking no heed of the wounds that he himself had received in the battle. As in the meantime the Quraish continued shouting that the Holy Prophet had been killed, and no contradiction was made from the Muslim camp the Muslim warriors engaged in combat with the Quraish were demoralised. They felt that if the Holy Prophet had been killed there was no point in fighting the battle. At this juncture at the instance of the Holy Prophet, Hadrat Umar shouted back at the Quraish to say that the Holy Prophet was very much alive On regaining consciousness, the Holy Prophet charged Hadrat Ali to launch a counter attack against the Quraish Hadrat Ali rallied the Muslims, exhorted them to fight for the glory of Islam and fell upon the enemy with the ferocity of a lion. Hadrat Ali broke into the lines of the enemy and caused great havoc in the ranks of the enemy. So great was the slaughter caused by Hadrat Ali in the ranks of the enemy that his sword broke down. Thereupon the Holy Prophet sent Hadrat Ali his own sword, and with this sword Hadrat Ali caused further havoc among the ranks of the Quraish. He held the flag in his right hand and when his right hand was wounded he held the flag in his left hand Hadrat Ali drove back the enemy Because of the prodigies of valour performed by Hadrat Ali, the Quraish could not take advantage of the victory that they had won at an earlier stage of the battle. Abu Sufyan accordingly commanded the Quraish to return to Mecca. He, however, shouted in a boastful mood that the Quraish had taken the revenge for their defeat in the battle of Badr. Abu Sufyan declared that the Quraish would soon have another confrontation, when the Muslims would be annihilated. When after the battle Hadrat Ali returned to the camp, his entire body was covered with so many wounds that Umm Salim and Umm Atiya, the Muslim nurses did not know how to dress the wounds of Hadrat Ali. The Holy Prophet washed and dressed the wounds of Hadrat Ali himself and said that God in Whose cause Hadrat Ali had received the wounds would heal them. Hadrat Ali said, "May God grant me the patience to bear this suffering. It was indeed a favour of God that He gave me the courage to stand and fight in spite of these wounds and not to leave the field " For his marvellous bravery, the Holy Prophet conferred on Hadrat Ali the appellation "Asad Allah," the lion of God

Assessment of the Battle : The battle of Uhud is an important battle in the annals of Islam. In the early stage the battle went in favour of the Muslims, but because of a practical mistake made by the archers, the tide of the battle was reversed and the Quraish came to have the upper hand. The Muslims were thoroughly demoralised and practically lost the will to fight. It was at this stage that Hadrat Ali took the command and prevented the Quraish from taking advantage of the victory that they had won earlier. The battle that would have otherwise ended in the annihilation of the Muslims concluded as a drawn battle. The Quraish could gain no booty; they could not make any Muslim a captive. True, many Muslims died as martyrs, but the casualties in the ranks of the Quraish were larger still.

Hadrat Ali played the role of hero in the battle. His services were highly appreciated by the Holy Prophet and the Companion. Some Muslim poets composed verses in the honour of Hadrat Ali. Extolling his bravery one of the poets said:

> "There is no sword better than the sword of Ali;
>
> And there is no young man superior to Ali.

There is some controversy about the number of unbelievers killed by Hadrat Ali at the battle of Uhud. According to some accounts the number was about two hundred. According to more conservative accounts the number was about two dozen. We need not enter into any controversy about the number of persons killed. The basic point is that Hadrat Ali played the role of a great hero at the battle of Uhud and he succeeded in averting a crisis which was fraught with great danger for the Muslims.

Campaign against Jews

Banu Nadeer : Banu Nadeer were a Jewish tribe who had their settlement outside Medina. The Holy Prophet had given them a charter of freedom and they were expected to be loyal to the Muslims. They, however, indulged in activities prejudicial to the interests of the Muslims. Kaab b. Ashraf, a notorious poet of the tribe, composed lampoons satiring Islam and the Holy Prophet. He visited Mecca and wrote elegies commemorating the death of the Quraish who had fallen in the battle of Badr. Kaab was killed by a Muslim young man and the Jews felt bitter at his death. Another Jew of Banu Nadeer. Abu Raafi' Sallam incited the Arab tribes of Sulaim and Ghatfan to rise against the Muslims.

Tragedy of Bin Maunah : In 625 C. E., one of the chiefs of the tribe of Kilab, Abu Basra Aamir, requested the Holy Prophet to send Muslim missionaries to propagate Islam among the tribe. The Holy Prophet sent seventy Muslim missionaries with the chief. The party halted at a place Bin Maunah and sent a Muslim, Haram b Mathan, along with the letter of the Holy Prophet to Aamir b Tufail, the principal chief of the tribe of Kilab. Aamir b Tufail killed Haram and marched with an army to Bin Maunah. He assassinated all the Muslim missionaries except one. Amr b. Umayyah by name. Aamir b Tufail released. Amr b Umayyah according to his mother's vow to free a slave. On his way back to Medina, Amr b Umayyah killed two persons belonging to the tribe of Banu. Amar considering them to be enemies. As a matter of fact the Holy Prophet had given the tribe amnesty. When the case was brought to the notice of Holy Prophet he agreed to pay indemnity to the tribe for its murdered persons.

Holy Prophet's Visit : According to the terms of the treay that the Muslims had made with Banu Nadeer, they had to pay a share of the indemnity In order to collect such share, the Holy Prophet with ten companions including Hadrat. Abu Bakr, Hadrat Umar and Hadrat Ali went to the settlement of Banu Nadeer. The Jews received the Holy Prophet with due courtesy and asked him to sit while they would bring their contribution. The Jews secretly contrived one of them to climb the wall and from there throw a big stone on the Holy Prophet. The Holy Prophet perceived their game. He got up from the place and returned to Medina without bothering to collect the share due from Banu Nadeer.

The Expedition : At the treacherous conduct of Banu Nadeer, the Holy Prophet sent an ultimatum to them that as they had violated their agreement with the Muslims, they should evacuate their settlement within ten days. The Banu Nadeer were incited by other Jewish tribes and the hypocrites in Medina to accept the challenge of the Muslims and give them a fight. After the expiry of the period of ultimatum Holy Prophet led a force to the Jewish settlement. The Jews shut themselves in their citadel and the Muslims camp was set up outside the fort. The Jew archers shot arrows which struck the Holy Prophet's camp. The camp was shifted to a safer place and the safety arrangements were tightened by Muslims. The Holy Prophet appointed Hadrat Ali on intelligence duty. One day Hadrat Ali received the intelligence that a party of the Jews led by Urwa b. Anis, a renowned warrior among the Jews, was to fall on the Muslims that night. Their plan was to steal into the Holy Prophet's camp and pierce him with arrows Hadrat Ali kept watch hidden in a safe place. When at nightfall the party appeared Hadrat Ali fell on them and sliced off Urwa's head Hadrat Ali, thereafter fought single handed with the followers of Urwa till some warriors from the Muslim camp joined him and all Jews were exterminated Under the orders of the Holy Prophet the severed heads of Urwa and his followers were hung outside the citadel of the Jews

The Banu Nadeer had expected help from other Jews and the hypocrites of Medina. The Holy Prophet blocked all ways from which any help could reach the beleaguered Jews. The siege dragged on for eleven days and when no help came from outside, the Banu Nadeer lost heart and surrendered. According to the Jewish law, all male members of the Jews could be killed and their women and children could be enslaved. The Holy Prophet took a lenient view. They were required to evacuate the settlement and migrate to Syria or elsewhere. They could carry movable property with them except arms. The Jews accepted these terms and they migrated to Syria. The immovable property left by them was distributed among the Muhajirs In the operations against the Banu Nadeer, Hadrat Ali played a conspicuous role. It was his action against Urwa and his followers that demoralised the Jews and led to the ultimate victory of the Muslims.

Battle of the Ditch : The Battle of the Ditch was an extension of the battle of Uhud as the battle of Uhud was an extension of the battle of Badr. The Quraish suffered defeat at the battle of Badr. The battle of Uhud was fought by the Quraish to take revenge of their defeat at the battle of Badr. The battle of Uhud proved to be indecisive. The Quraish were, therefore, still suffering from the ignominy of their defeat at the battle of Badr. The Quraish allied themselves with some Arab tribes of the desert and succeeded in mustering a force ten thousand strong.

Defence of Medina : When the Holy Prophet came to know of the war preparations of the Quraish, he held a council of war. It was felt that in view of the large strength of the forces of the enemy it would not be possible for the Muslims to face the enemy in the open. The Muslims had a bitter experience of the battle of Uhud and it was not proper to repeat the mistake. It was accordingly necessary to adopt a new strategy to face the enemy. Salman Farsi, a companion who hailed from Persia, suggested that a ditch be dug around Medina for the purposes of defence. This advice was accepted by the Holy Prophet and it was decided that in the impending battle the Muslims should remain on the defensive.

The Ditch : Medina had natural defences on three sides. Only the fourth side was vulnerable to attack. It was decided that a ditch should be dug on this side. The site for the ditch was demarcated by the Holy Prophet. All male adults of the Muslim community in Medina were mobilised to dig the ditch. The labour force was divided into batches and each batch had a leader. Each batch was required to dig a ditch ten yards long Hadrat Ali led one batch. The Holy Prophet, Hadrat Ali and all other companions worked day and night as labourers to dig the ditch. The Muslims laboured to the rhythm of a war song. They sang

> "By God, had not Allah guided us,
> We would not have been on the right path
> We would not have given any Sadaqa
> Nor offered prayer
> May Allah bestow on us
> Confidence and calmness of mind

May He make our steps firm
To face the enemy
The enemy has risen against us,
And seeks our destruction
Allah, we seek Your protection
There is no welfare except
That in the next world,
Allah, shower Your Grace
On the. Ansars and the Muhajirs"

These verses were composed by Hadrat Ali. These verses inspired the Muslims to action and the entire stretch of the ditch was completely dug within twenty days. The ditch was five yards deep and five yards broad. Each batch of the Muslims who had dug the ditch was required to stand guaid over the ditch in their part of the sector. In each sector there were archers who shot arrows to keep the enemy away from the ditch

The Battle : The forces of the Quraish and the Arab tribes arrived beating drums and raising shouts boasting of their strength and invincibility. When they reached Medina and found that a ditch intervened between them and Medina they were confused as the Arabs were not used to ditch warfare. They set up their camps at some distance from the ditch. Thus began the siege of Medina. The enemy made several attamets to cross the ditch but the Muslim archers kept them at bay. The enemy approached the Jews of Banu Quraiza in Medina to help them in crossing the ditch. The Banu Quraiza were heavily bribed. They threw some dead animals in that part of the ditch where the Muslims defence was not very strong. Due to the treachery of the Banu Quraiza, some warriors of the Quraish led by Amr b. Abd would managed to cross the ditch. Brandishing his sword Amr challenged the Muslims to a duel in single combat. Amr was a formidable man who enjoyed the reputation of being equal to a thousand men in physical strength. Hadrat Ali rose to accept the challenge. The Holy Prophet bade him sit down. Amr repeated his challenge for the second time and Hadrat Ali rose up once again to accept the challenge. The Holy Prophet once again asked Hadrat Ali to sit down. Amr gave the challenge for the third time and Hadrat Ali stood up again to accept the challenge This time the Holy Prophet let Hadrat Ali accept the challenge. When the duel began, Hadrat Ali appeared to be no match for Amr. Amr confident of his physical strength said to Hadrat Ali that he did not want to kill him Hadrat Ali retorted that he intended to kill him. Amr succeeded in inflicting some wounds on Hadrat Ali, but each time Hadrat Ali aimed a blow, Amr successfully avoided the blows. When it appeared that the end of Hadrat Ali was imminent, something miraculous happened. Amr imagined that someone was going to stab him in the rear. He turned his head. It was for a moment, but Hadrat Ali took full advantage of the opportunity and with a blow of this sword cut off the feet of Amr. Amr fell down and Hadrat Ali stabbed him to death. Thereupon Usl, the son of Amr, fell upon Hadrat Ali. Hadrat Ali was now as ferocious as a lion. He killed Usl with one stroke of his sword. Thereafter Naufal attacked Hadrat Ali. Hadrat Ali charged with full force and while retreating Naufal fell into the ditch. Hadrat Ali jumped after him in the ditch and killed him there. Ikrama b. Abu Jahl who had crossed the ditch along with Amr did not dare face Hadrat Ali. He along with all other men who had crossed the ditch withdrew and recrossing the ditch found refuge in their camp. Hadrat Ali was the hero of the day. It came to be felt that if Ali could overthrow Amr who was believed to be equivalent to ten thousand men. Ali would be a man equivalent to the thousand men. When the sister of Amr came to know that her brother had been killed she enquired from the people as to who killed him and when she came to know that Hadrat Ali had killed him, she said that verily Hadrat Ali was the bravest man among the Quraish.

Flight of Quraish : The death of Amr at the hands of Hadrat Ali demoralised the Quraish and their allies. The men of the Banu Ghatfan came to feel that some supernatural power was helping the Muslims. The Holy Prophet sent his agents to work with the confederates and give them the message of Islam. The leader of Banu Ghatfan accepted Islam and defeat them. The Muslims under the command of the Holy Prophet did not fall into the trap. As the siege lengthened, the Arabs of the desert became weary of the prolonged struggle Under these circumstances more Arab tribes left for their homes. The confederates also began to suffer on account of the scarcity of food and fodder. It was nature that struck the final blow at the confederates. One midnight, a strong storm lashed the countryside. Rain and fast-blowing winds overturned the tents of the confederates and extinguished their fires. The Muslims were safe in their houses in Medina, but the confederates who had to bear the brunt of the fury of the storm rain and hail were unnerved. Losing all hope of victory Abu Sufyan, the Quraish leader, mounted his camel and ordered a retreat. Thus, miserably foiled, the great coalition which had appeared so invincible at the outset suffered a great reverse. The battle ended in the triumph of Islam. That raised the morale of the Muslims and they came to believe that Islam was the truth against which the forces of falsehood could not maintain a stand. The Muslim victory in the battle of the Ditch was due to the superior generalship and organisational skill of the Holy Prophet and the prodigies of valour on the part of Hadrat Ali. The battle of the Ditch struck the last nail in the coffin of the Quraish of Mecca. Thereafter the Quraish lost their initiative, which now passed on to the Muslims.

Campaign Against Banu Mistaliqs : In 627 C. E Jewish tribe of Mustaliq which had its settlement at some distance from Medina entered into an alliance with the tribe of

Banu Khuzaa and both agreed to make common cause against the Muslims. The Holy Prophet deputed an emissary to contact the Banu Mustaliq and report about the true state of affairs. The emissary reported that the Banu Mustaliq were in a hostile mood and were planning an invasion of Medina. The Holy Prophet thereupon led a Muslim force to the territory of Banu Mustaliq. Hadrat Ali bore the standard as usual

The Holy Prophet gave the Banu Mustaliq the option to submit but they chose to fight. The battle began with a duel between Qatada, the leader of Banu Mustaliq, and Hadrat Ali. In a few rounds Hadrat Ali killed Qattada. Thereafter another Jewish leader Malik confronted Hadrat Ali. Hadrat Ali killed him in no time. After the death of Malik his son crossed swords with Hadrat Ali with the intent to avenge the death of his father. He could not withstand the blows of the sword of Hadrat Ali and he met the same doom as his father. Thereafter the tribe lost the will to fight. They laid down arms and agreed to pay tribute

Hadrat Aishah's Necklace : While returning from the campaign against Banu Mustaliq an incident took place which cast its shadow on the future course of Islamic history. Each time the Holy Prophet went on a campaign, one or two of his wives accompanied him and the decision was always taken by the drawing of lots. On the Banu Mustaliq campaign Hadrat Aishah accompanied the Holy Prophet. She travelled on the back of a camel in a closed litter. On the way to Medina the returning army followed by its long procession of supplies, captives and thousands of beasts after travelling throughout the night broke camp at dawn Hadrat Aishah left her litter to satisfy a natural need and returned to her camel. Back in the litter she noticed that she had lost her necklace of Yemenite agates Returning in her footsteps she sought the necklace for some time, and at last finding it, returned to the caravan. But the spot was deserted and the caravan had been left. The camelman seeing the litter closed and thinking that it was occupied had placed it on the camel and departed with it Hadrat Aishah called aloud but no one responded to her call. She decided to lie there covering herself hoping that someone would come to fetch her. Soon she fell asleep "We belong to God and to Him we return" fell on the ears of Hadrat Aishah and she awoke with a start. A young man stood there holding a camel by its tether. The young man Safwan bin Muattal following the army in the rear noticed a young woman sleeping in the desert and upon approaching her recognised her as the wife of the Holy Prophet. Hadrat Aishah quickly covered herself with a veil, Safwan adjusted the camel's saddle-girth and made it kneel Hadrat. Aishah mounted the camel. Holding the beast by the bridle, Safwan took the road to Medina. After a long and tiring journey, Hadrat Aishah caught up with the army at noon. The arrival of Hadrat Aishah attended by a young man caused some rumours in the camp.

Back in Medina, the calumnies of the slanderers gained publicity. Safwan swore that in his lifetime he had never touched a woman Hadrat Aishah fell sick. She realised that the behaviour of the. Apostle of God towards her had changed. She went to the house of her father. Amidst sobs, Hadrat Aishah asked her mother, "Mother," what story are the people relating about me ". Her mother replied, "Do not be distressed by Allah, there is not handsome and noble woman whom her husband loves, but has other wives besides her, that such tales are bandied about" This did not console the young lady. She knew no rest, and her tears did not cease to flow. The Holy Prophet consulted his friends about divorcing Hadrat Aishah. Hadrat Umar said that he was certain that the hypocrites were speaking lies. He added, "By reason of God not allowing a fly to settle upon your blessed skirts, because it alights also on impure things, how then God would not preserve you and your name from a worse defilement". The other Companions advised the Holy Prophet to keep his exalted mind at ease, for they were certain that God would cause the innocence of the young lady to become manifest. Hadrat Ali was of the view that there was no dearth of women for the Holy Prophet and Hadrat. Aishah could be divorced even though she was innocent.

The Revelation : One day, Hadrat Aishah was sitting in the house of her parents and was weeping when the Holy Prophet appeared all of a sudden and after the usual salutation spoke to his wife, "O, Aishah if you are innocent, God will come to your help; if you are guilty repent, and ask forgiveness " Hadrat Aishah said that she had to wait till God cleared her of the insinuation for He alone was her witness. Before the Holy Prophet could leave that house of his father-in-law the signs of divine revelation manifested themselves on the Holy Prophet. His mother-in-law placed a cushion under his head and covered him with a Yameni cloak. When the revelation was over, drops of perspiration trickled down his face. He smiled and said, "Glad tiding to you. Aishah, God the Most High has exculpated you and borne witness to your innocence. Hadrat Aishah thereafter returned to the house of the Holy Prophet and those who had slandered were punished

Bitterness between Hadrat Aishah and Hadrat Ali : This incident led to some bitterness between Hadrat Aishah and Hadrat Ali. Hadrat Ali had not levied any charge against Hadrat Aishah. He had only said in a casual way that she could be divorced even if she was innocent. The grievance of Hadrat Aishah was that Hadrat Ali should have defended her like Hadrat Umar. The Holy Prophet had great love for Hadrat Aishah and that became a matter of some jealousy with others. It appears that even Hadrat Fatima had some grouse on this account. The Holy Prophet offered her the advice, "If your father loves a person, why should you not love that person as well."

Banu Quraizah : There were originally three settlements of the Jews in Medina namely those of Banu Qainuqa, Banu Nadeer, and Banu Quraizah. Every settlement was a stronghold. The Holy Prophet gave them a charter of freedom, whereunder they enjoyed autonomy in the administration of their affairs. The Jews entered into agreements of alliance with the Muslim community and undertook to help the Muslims in the event of any attack on Medina. The Jews, however, did not honour such agreements and the Muslims had to take punitive action against them. After battle of Badr, action had to be taken against the Banu Qainuqa. They were expelled from Medina and they migrated to Syria. After the battle of Uhud action had to be taken against Banu Nadeer. They were expelled from Medina and they migrated to Khyber.

The Only Jew Settlement : At the eve of the battle of the Ditch there was only one settlement of the Jews in Medina, namely that of Banu Quraizah. They assured the Muslims of their loyalty and entered into a fresh agreement whereunder they bound themselves to help the Muslims in the event of any attack on Medina. When the battle of the Ditch began they assured the Muslims that they would stand by them. They, however, avoided active assistance on one pretext or the other. In the course of the battle they acted treacherously. Huyayy b. Akhtab, the leader of Banu Nadeer who had been expelled by the Muslims from Medina approached Banu Quraizah and prevailed upon them to cast in their lot with the Quraish and their confederated who were fighting against Islam. Banu Quraizah were heavily bribed by the Quraish and they undertook to assist the confederates in their action against the Muslims. The Holy Prophet sent Saad b Muadh, the chief of the Aus tribe, to them to prevail upon them to abide by their agreement which they had made with the Muslims. Confident of the victory of the confederates, the Banu Quraizah adopted a hostile attitude and declared that they knew of no treaty with the Muslims. At the stage it was not possible for the Muslims to take any action against the Jews and the Holy Prophet chose to be quiet. It was because of the treachery of Banu Quraizah that some of the Quraish warriors were able to cross the Ditch and challenge the Muslims to duel. When Hadrat Ali killed Amr, the "Hazar Mard", in single combat and all the Quraish warriors who had crossed the Ditch were forced to retreat, the Holy Prophet decided to keep a close watch on the movements of the Banu Quraizah. When the battle of the Ditch began, the Holy Prophet shifted the women and children of Muslim families to safer quarters. The game of the Quraish was to have access to this quarter and carry away Muslim women and children as captives. Banu Quraizah undertook to help the Quraish. One day the Jews sent a spy to procure intelligence about the quarter where the Muslim women and children were lodged. Hadrat Safia, an aunt of the Holy Prophet, saw the spy. She stealthily stole behind the spy and struck a mortal blow on his head with a pole that she carried in her hand. Thereafter, the Muslims strengthened the guard at the quarter. The Muslims had expelled the Banu Nadeer from Medina after the battle of Uhud and their leader Huyayy b. Akhtab was a persona non-grata for the Muslims. Banu Quraizah gave asylum to Huyayy who was an arch enemy of the Muslims. During the course of the battle of the Ditch, Banu Quraizah at the instance of Huyayy created difficulties for the Muslims

Operation against Banu Quraizah : The Banu Quraizah had expected that the battle of the Ditch would end in the defeat of the Muslims and that they would be duly rewarded by the confederates for the services rendered to their cause. When the battle of the Ditch ended in the discomfiture of the Quraish and their allies, the Banu Quraizah felt themselves stranded and exposed to the wrath of the Muslims. Soon after the battle of the Ditch, the Holy Prophet sent a small force under the command of Hadrat Ali to the Jewish quarter. Hadrat Ali contacted the leader of the Jews, Kab b. Asad, and brought home to him the point that as they had violated the terms of their agreement with the Muslims and were guilty of high treason they could no longer be allowed to live in Medina. They were advised that they should lay down arms and migrate elsewhere. The Jews ridiculed the proposal and abused the Holy Prophet and Muslims. Hadrat Ali tried his best to make them see the light of reason and migrate elsewhere in their own interest. When Hadrat Ali did not succeed in prevailing upon the Jews to migrate from Medina on their own account, he reported the matter to the Holy Prophet. The Holy Prophet thereupon ordered a military operation against the Jews. The Holy Prophet handed the war banner to Hadrat Ali and the Muslim force marched to the quarter of the Jews under the command of Hadrat Ali. The Jews shut themselves in their citadel and the Muslim force besieged them. Banu Quraizah had expected that the Quraish and the Jews of Khyber would come to their assistance, but as the days passed on, no help came and the things became difficult for them with the prolongation of the siege. On the Sabbath Day, Kab b. Asad, the leader of the Banu Quraizah, told his people that things were getting difficult for them from day to day and that it would not be possible to withstand the siege for long. He placed three proposals before his people. The first proposal was that they should be converted to Islam and should accept Muhammad (peace be on him) as the Prophet of God. His people turned down the proposal and said that they would never accept Islam. Kab said that the next alternative was that they should kill their women and children and thereafter fall upon the Muslims and either kill them or be killed. His people said that they would not kill their women and children. Kab said that as it was the Sabbath Day the Muslims would not be expecting any attack from them. His third proposal was that they should attack the Muslims on the Sabbath Day. The Jews said that their ancestors who fought on the Sabbath Day were converted to apes and that therefore they would not fight on the Sabbath Day lest they might also be turned into apes

End of Banu Quraizah : The siege lasted for twenty-five days. On the last day Hadrat Ali carried the citadel by assault. All Jews were taken captive and Hadrat Ali offered his midnight prayer in the courtyard of the citadel. In spite of their defeat the Holy Prophet was inclined to offer the Jews easy terms, more or less the terms which had been previously offered to Banu Qainuqa and Banu Nadeer. The Jews, however, desired that

Saad b Muadh, the leader of the Banu, Aus be appointed as the arbitrator. The Holy Prophet accepted the proposal and Saad was asked to suggest terms that should be offered to the Jews Saad asked the Jews whether they would like the terms to be offered to them under the Islamic law or the Jewish law. They said that as they were Jews and not Muslims and they would like the Jewsih lay to be applied to their case. Saad consulted the Jewish rabbis and asked of them the question "If in a battle against the Muslims you would have won and taken the Muslim men and woman captive how would you have treated the captives under the Jewish law?'. They said that in that case they would have killed the men and sold the women and children as slaves. Thereupon Saad gave his verdict that all male adults of the Banu Quraizah should be killed and their women and children should be sold as slaves. On hearing this verdict, the Jews were stunned and a pall of mourning fell upon them. It was a harsh sentence, but for all that happened the Jews were themselves to blame. They were guilty of high treason and they had to face the consequences of their misconduct. Even then if they had thrown themselves on the mercy of the Holy Prophet, they would have escaped with a lighter punishment. Instead of asking for terms from the Holy Prophet they sought the verdict of an arbitrator of their own choice. Again they had opted for the Jewish law and the sentence awarded was in conformity with such laws. The verdict was carried into effect. Over two hundred male Jews were executed. The Holy Prophet commissioned Hadrat Ali to supervise the process of execution. About six hundred Jews comprising women and children were sold as slaves. The property of the Jews was confiscated and distributed among the Muslims. Details about such property are not available, but as the Jews were a rich people this property, both movable and immovable, must have been considerable and the share of each Muslim would have been sufficient to make him well to do. That would have considerably improved the financial position of Hadrat Ali and in this context, the oft-repeated accounts of the poverty of Hadrat Ali or the Holy Prophet cannot be accepted. As over six hundred Jews were sold as slaves, Hadrat Fatima would have got a slave girl to work for her. In the battle of the Ditch or in the military operations against Banu Quraizah, Hadrat Ali played the most important part. It was Hadrat Ali who killed the "Hazar Mard" of the Quraish in a duel. It was Hadrat Ali who carried the citadel of Banu Quraizah by assault. Details about the exploits of Hadrat Ali are not available in the accounts that have come down to us

Operation against Banu Saad : After the expulsion of the Jews of Bani Qainuqa and Banu Nadeer from Medina the policy of the Jews was to incite the Arab tribes to revolt against the Muslims. The Bedouin tribes of Banu Saad and Banu Bakr who lived in the neighbourhood of Khyber and Fidak were already hostile to the Muslims. The Jews incited them to attack Medina. They promised to provide them with arms and transport. Intelligence was brought to the Holy Prophet that these tribes were mustering a force and planned to attack Medina. The policy of the Holy Prophet was to strike before the enemy could strike and thus wrest the initiative from the enemy.

Hadrat Ali's Operations : Hadrat Ali was commissioned by the Holy Prophet to undertake an expedition against the Banu Saad and Banu Bakr. It was not to be a regular battle. It was to be a tactical raid to be carried with utmost secrecy, with a view to springing a surprise on the enemy. Hadrat Ali had a small force of a hundred persons with him. The force did not march in battle array, the party travelled as a caravan of traders in order to avoid suspicion. A series of forced marches conducted at night to conceal the movements brought the party in close proximity to Fidak, some distance from Khyber. Here they came across a scout of the enemy. He was taken captive. He volunteered to lead Hadrat Ali and his men to the camp of Banu Saad and Banu Bakr, provided he was given amnesty. Hadrat Ali gave him the amnesty, and the scout led Hadrat Ali and his men to Fidak where the forces of Banu Saad and Banu Bakr were camping oblivious of any danger. Hadrat Ali and his men made a surprise attack on the enemy. The attack was so unexpected, sudden and furious that the forces of the tribes could not take a stand and were scattered after suffering heavy losses. So intense was the slaughter that the tribes laid down arms and sought for terms. The tribes undertook to remain faithful to the Muslims and offered a tribute of 100 camels and 2000 goats. Hadrat Ali and his men returned triumphant to Medina where the Holy Prophet appreciated their services. One-fifth of the booty was placed at the disposal of the Holy Prophet as stage share and the rest of the animals were distributed among the men who had participated in the foray.

Some Points : In the various accounts that have come down to us, there is some confusion about this operation. In some accounts Banu Saad and Banu Bakr are stated to be Jews. This does not appear to be correct. They were Arab tribes who were pagans. In some accounts it is said that Fidak was conquered as a result of these operations. This is not correct. Fidak was conquered a year later after the conquest of Khyber. In the Atab annals this operation is referred to as Sayra-i-Fidak. The term Sarya is used to denote the operation in which the Holy Prophet did not participate in person. Such operations which were led by the Holy Prophet himself were known as Ghazwas. The Sayra-i-Fidak neutralised the Arab tribes of Banu Saad and Banu Bakr and paved the way to the Hudaibiya pact of the Muslims with the Quraish of Mecca.

Victory of Khyber

In 628 C. E. six years had passed since the Holy Prophet and his Companions left Mecca, the city of their birth. During this period of six years the Muslims had fought three battles against the Quraish, the battles of Badr, Uhud and Ditch. After the battle of the Ditch the Quraish had lost initiative which now came to rest with the Muslims In view of this changed position, the Holy Prophet decided to visit Mecca with a view to performing the Hajj. During the Hajj season, the Holy Prophet along with his Companions including Hadrat Ali started for Mecca to perform the Hajj. When the Quraish of Mecca came to know that the Muslims were coming to Mecca they sent Khalid b Walid and Ikrama b. Abu Jahl with two hundred horsemen to intercept the Muslims and prevent their entry into Mecca. The Muslims came to know of the intention of the Quraish at the early stages of the journey. The Holy Prophet consulted his Companions to decide whether they should return to Medina or continue their journey to Mecca. The consensus of opinion was that they should go ahead and if the Quraish chose to fight they would also fight, otherwise not. Instead of following the direct route to Mecca the Muslims followed a less frequented way full of rough rocks through the ravines of Mudniya. After a weary march the Muslim caravans comprising one thousand men reached Hudaibiya on the lower side of Mecca and within the sacred territory for the purposes of the pilgrimage.

The Pledge : The Muslims encamped at Hudaibiya and here Urwa b Masud, a son-in-law of Abu Sufyan, came to see the Muslims on behalf of the Quraish. He talked in diplomatic language and tried to impress that the Quraish were strong and would not allow the Muslims to visit Mecca. He also insinuated that at the time of crisis the followers of the Holy Prophet were likely to leave him. Thereupon Hadrat Abu Bakr flared up and said 'May God curse you, how dare you think that we will abandon the Holy Prophet Rest assured, we will stand by him, whatever the cost, and will fight for him to the last" While talking, Urwa in the usual Arab way pushed his hand too close to the beard of the Holy Prophet. A Companion who stood near warned him "Keep your hands away from the beard of the Holy Prophet for the hand that touches the sacred beard would be cut"

When Urwa returned to Mecca, the Holy Prophet sent Hadrat Uthman with him to assure the Quraish that the Muslims merely wanted to perform the Hajj and they had no intention of fighting against the Quraish. When Urwa returned to the Quraish, he gave his impressions about the Holy Prophet and the Muslims in the following terms.

> "O people of the Quraish' I have seen kings, but by God I have never seen any king as I have seen Muhammad amongst his Companions. If he makes his ablutions, they would not let the water fall on the ground, if a hair of his body falls they pick it up. They will not surrender him for anything in any case, do what you may"

Hadrat Uthman met the Quraish leaders, but they adopted delaying tactics. When Hadrat Uthman took long to come, a rumour got current in the Muslim camp that Uthman had been killed by the Quraish. Thereupon all the Muslims took the pledge that they would fight against the Quraish to seek revenge for the murder of Hadrat Uthman.

The Treaty : When the Muslims were poised to take up arms and attack Mecca, Hadrat Uthman returned to the Muslim camp with Suhail b. Amr, an eminent citizen of Mecca, whom the Quraish sent to negotiate a treaty with the Muslims. Suhail was notorious for his hostility to Islam. He was one of the principal persecutors when the Holy Prophet declared his mission. He had fought in the battle of Badr and had been taken captive. He was later ransomed. After a lengthy discussion, the Holy Prophet and Suhail came to terms and agreed to execute a treaty Hadrat Ali was commissioned to draft the treaty. The Holy Prophet dictated that it was a treaty between Muhammad, the Prophet of Allah, and the Quraish. Suhail objected to the preamble on the ground that the Quraish did not acknowledge him as the prophet of God and as such the reference to his apostlehood should be omitted. Hadrat Ali did not agree to omit the relevant words. Thereupon the Holy Prophet omitted these words himself. According to the treaty of Hudaibiya, truce was declared between the Muslims and the Quraish for ten years. If any tribe wished to enter into treaty with the Muslims it could do so and whoever wished to enter into a treaty with the Quraish was likewise free to do so. If anyone from the Quraish came to the Muslims and was converted to Islam he was to be returned to the Quraish. On the other hand if a Muslim sought refuge with the Quraish, he was not to be delivered to the Muslims. It was further stipulated that the Muslims would withdraw that year without performing the Hajj, but they would be free to perform the Hajj the following year when they could stay in Mecca for three days.

Muslim Reaction : Prima facie the pact was loaded in favour of the Quraish and most of the Muslims were critical of its terms. Hadrat Abu Bakr and Hadrat Ali, however, felt that the Holy Prophet knew things better than what his followers could comprehend and that what appeared to be disadvantageous to the Muslims might ultimately turn to their advantage. Hadrat Umar waited on the Holy Prophet and gave expression to his dissatisfaction with the terms of the treaty. The Holy Prophet assured him that whatever he had done was under the command of God and that the terms which appeared to be against the interests of the Muslims would turn out to their favour. While on the way back to Medina God sent a revelation that the treaty was victory for the Muslims as subsequent events showed this treaty was in fact a prelude to the conquest of Mecca. In later years someone asked Hadrat Ali as to how the treaty of Hudaibiya was a victory for the Muslims when the terms thereof were apparently in favour of the Quraish. Hadrat Ali pointed out that during the previous seventeen years the Quraish had been waging a war against the Muslims sometimes cold, sometimes hot. Their aim was to crush Islam. When by the treaty of Hudaibiya the Quraish agreed to a truce for a period of ten years, it amounted to a confession of their failure. Heretofore the Quraish had exercised a pressure on the tribes of the desert not to ally themselves with the Muslims. By the treaty both the Muslims and the Quraish could have allies from amongst the tribes. This was a subtle point fraught with grave consequences. As things took shape later, it was such alliances that paved the way for the conquest of Mecca by the Muslims. It was stipulated that a Muslim who sought refuge with the Quraish was not to be returned to the Muslims but someone from the Quraish who sought refuge with the Muslims was to be returned to the Quraish. Apparently the stipulation was against the Muslims, but it was really not so. When a Muslim was to seek refuge with the Quraish, it would obviously be a case of apostasy and there was no advantage in pressing for the return of a person who had ceased to be a Muslim. When a man from the Quraish sought refuge with the Muslims and was later returned to Quraish, there were two possibilities. If his faith in Islam was strong he would still remain a Muslim and was likely to cause the conversion of other people to Islam. If on the other hand his faith was not strong, it would be a good riddance for the Muslims. Moreover by this time the stage of the conversion of individuals was over. The Holy Prophet was now looking forward to mass conversions and in this context there were not likely to be many cases of individuals seeking shelter with the Muslims or the Muslims seeking shelter with the Quraish. The treaty of Hudaibiya indeed set the stage for the expansion of Islam to the peninsula of Arabia.

Battle of Khyber : About a hundred miles from Medina on the route to Syria was an important settlement of the Jews called the Khyber. Literally "Khyber" means a fort and the place was so named because it consisted of a series of forts. There were six or seven forts and each fort was occupied by a different section of the Jews. It was an oasis in the desert and was conspicuous for its fields and groves of date palms. It was an important market as well. After their expulsion from Medina, most of the Jews of Banu Qainuqa and Banu Nadeer took refuge in Khyber. In the battle of the Ditch, the Jews of Khyber had helped the Quraish. When after the battle of the Ditch, the Jews of Banu Quraizah were executed, the Jews of Khyber vowed vengeance and they planned an invasion of Medina on a large scale. They were seeking an alliance with the Quraish. In the meantime by the treaty of Hudaibiya, the Quraish had made a truce with the Muslims and were no longer free to join the Jews in an attack on Medina. That was the first advantage that accrued to the Muslims as a result of the treaty of Hudaibiya. After the neutralisation of the Quraish in any conflict between the Muslims and the Jews, the initiative now came to lie with Muslims. Taking full advantage of this favourable situation immediately on return from Mecca after signing the Hudaibiya pact, the Holy Prophet led a Muslim force to Khyber.

The Battle : The Jews were caught in surprise at the appearance of the Muslim forces. The Prophet asked them to submit. They ridiculed the offer and said that their forts were impregnable and that they would teach the Muslims bitter lessons. They shut themselves in their forts and the Muslims besieged them. The first battle took place on the fort called Nairn. The Muslim forces were commanded by Muhammad b Musailmah. The battle was fierce. The Muslim commander was martyred, but the fort was captured. In the following days they captured other small fortresses. The main fort of the Jews was Qamus and it was regarded as impregnable. The siege dragged on for twenty one days, but the Jews held out. The Holy Prophet sent a force under the command of Hadrat Abu Bakr to overpower the Jews, but the mission did not succeed. The Holy Prophet changed the commander everyday, but the fort proved to be a hard nut to crack. With the failure of successive missions the Holy Prophet said that the following day he would entrust the command to a person who was the beloved of Allah as well as His Prophet and who would conquer the fort. The following day when the Muslim forces assembled to lead the attack, all were anxious to know as to who was to have the honour of commanding the Muslim forces and winning the victory that day. The honour fell to the lot of Hadrat Ali. The Holy Prophet put the armour on Hadrat Ali with his own hands. He handed him the standard and after praying for the victory of the Muslims, the Holy Prophet commanded the Muslim forces to attack the fort in the name of God. As the Muslim forces came close to the fort the Jew warrior Marhab emerged out of the fort, and challenged Hadrat Ali to a duel Marhab, also known as Abu Ablit, and Antar enjoyed reputation as a great warrior equivalent to a thousand men. Marhab sang the battle song.

"I am Abu Ablit;
My name is Antar.
I am armed to the teeth.
My home is Khyber.
I am a lion
Whom none can face"

Hadrat Ali accepted the challenge with the battle song:

"I am Ali, the lion of God.
I fight in the name of God.
Be prepared for your doom.
Hell awaits you."

The day Hadrat Ali appeared to be endowed with unusual extraordinary power he killed Marhab in no time.

Thereafter another Jewish warrior Rabih b. Abu Aqiq stepped forward to challenge Hadrat Ali. Rabih charged at Hadrat Ali, but he missed the mark. Thereafter Hadrat Ali charged at his adversary with the speed of lightning and severed his head with the stroke of his sword.

Thereafter another Jew warrior stepped forward. He sang as he rushed at Hadrat Ali

"I am Yasir
I am a ferocious lion,
None can escape my claws"

In reply, Hadrat Ali said:

"O infidel, your death calls you
I invoke the aid of God
And strike the heads of those
Who come to oppose me"

Yasir aimed a blow at Hadrat Ali, but Hadrat Ali warded off the blow with great dexterity. Then Hadrat Ali attacked and Yasir fell dead

The death of three successive Jew warriors unnerved the Jews and they ran back to shut themselves in the fort. Before the Jews could shut the gate of the fort, Hadrat Ali struck at the gate and uprooted it. Thereafter the Muslim forces rushed inside the fort and massacred the Jews who resisted them Hadrat Ali performed prodigies of valour and killed a large number of the Jews. The Jews could not withstand the onslaught of the Muslims for long. Soon their resistance broke down, they laid down arms and sued for terms. Thus the fort which was regarded as impregnable fell before the might of Hadrat Ali. According to legend, Hadrat Ali exhibited supernatural strength that day and was most ferocious than the fiercest of lions. Verily, he was the "Lion of Allah."

Victor at Khyber : As Hadrat Ali returned to the Muslim camp, the Holy Prophet went forward to greet him and hailed him as the Victor of Khyber. There was great rejoicing in the Muslim camp at this great victory.

As a result of the victory, in accordance with the Jewish law, all male Jews could be executed. The Jews pleaded for mercy and undertook to pay one half of the produce of their lands to the Muslims as annual tribute. The Holy Prophet took a lenient view. He accepted the terms offered by the Jews and a treaty was executed accordingly. The Jews undertook to remain faithful to the Muslims and accepted their paramountcy.

A prominent Jew is lady, Zainab held a feast in the honour of the Holy Prophet and his Companions. At the dinner the Holy Prophet first took a morsel of meat and after chewing it, threw it aside saying that the meat was poisoned. A Companion Bashr ate a good deal of meat and he died on the spot. The feast ended in confusion. Zainab was put to explanation and she admitted her guilt. She pleaded that she had poisoned the meat thinking that if Muhammad (peace be on him) was a false prophet the world would get rid of him

Account differ about the fate of Zainab. According to one account she became a Muslim and was pardoned. According to another account she was executed.

Conquest of Fidak : After the conquest of Khyber, the Muslims marched to Fidak, another Jewish settlement, not far from Khyber. Having seen the fate of the people of Khyber, the people of Fidak did not choose to fight. They agreed to execute a treaty of peace with the Muslims on the same terms as had been agreed upon in the case of the Jews of Khyber. As Fidak had fallen without fight, the annual tribute therefrom was earmarked as the private purse of the Holy Prophet. After meeting the household expenses of the Holy Prophet, the proceeds were to be utilised for the welfare of the widows, the orphans, the needy, the distressed and the wayfarers.

Consequences of the Battle : The battle of Khyber was another turning point in the annals of Islam. It had far-reaching consequences. The Muslim rule was no longer confined to Medina and its immediate neighbouring areas, it came to be extended to other parts of Arabia and the Jews who had been so hostile to the Muslims had become the subjects of the Islamic state. The Quraish could no longer bank on the support of the Jews.

If we study the events that took place one after the other we can discern the Hand of God directing the course of things in favour of the Muslims. The Hudaibiya pact which was apparently unfavourable to the Muslims paved the way to the conquest of Khyber and the conquest of Khyber paved the way to the conquest of Mecca. Hadrat Ali was the victor of Khyber. The exploits of Hadrat Ali at Khyber have attained the dimensions of legends. History is however silent as to how Hadrat Ali was rewarded for his services. The amount of the tribute from Khyber was sufficiently large and Hadrat Ali as the Victor of Khyber must have got a lion's share thereof. Because of his fraternity with the Holy Prophet, Hadrat Ali had his share in the tribute from Fidak as well. All this made him sufficiently rich and all accounts that dilate on the poverty of Hadrat Ali appear to be far from the truth.

Mecca Conquered

According to the terms of the treaty of Hudaibiya, the Arab tribes had the option to be allied with the Quraish or the Muslims. In pursuance of this option, the Banu Bakr joined the Quraish and their enemies, the Banu Khuzaah, allied themselves with the Muslims. Incited by the Quraish, the Banu Bakr attacked the Khuzaah, looted their property and killed their men. Even when the Banu Khuzaah sought the sanctuary of the Kaaba, they were chased and put to death. The Banu Khuzaah sent a deputation to Medina and wanted the Muslims to come to their aid according to the terms of their treaty with them. The Holy Prophet assured the Banu Khazaah that the Muslims would fulfil their obligation to them. The Holy Prophet thereupon sent a message to the Quraish making three alternative demands. The first alternative was that the Banu Bakr and the Quraish should pay blood money for the victims of Banu Khuzaah. The second alternative was that the Quraish should terminate their alliance with Banu Bakr. The third alternative was that the treaty of Hudaibiya should be considered to have been abrogated. In a fit of arrogance, the Quraish replied that they would neither pay blood money, nor terminate their alliance with Banu Bakr and that in the circumstances they were prepared to consider that the Hudaibiya pact had been abrogated.

The Hudaibiya Pact : The life of Hudaibiya pact did not exceed two years. It was a short period, but nevertheless much had happened during this period which had added to the strength of the Muslims and correspondingly weakened the position of the Quraish. After the conquest of Khyber the material sources of the Muslims had considerably increased. After the discomfiture of the Jews, many Arab tribes joined the Muslims as their allies. The Muslims were now in a position to raise a sufficiently large army. The Quraish soon realised that they had imprudently abrogated the treaty of hudaibiya. Abu Sufyan, the chief of the Quraish, rushed to Medina to seek the renewal of the treaty of Hudaibiya. Umm Habiba, a daughter of Abu Sufyan, had accepted Islam and was a wife of the Holy Prophet. Abu Sufyan wanted his daughter to intercede with the Holy Prophet in his behalf. He sought the help of Hadrat. Abu Bakr, Hadrat Umar and Hadrat Ali as well. The Holy Prophet me. Abu Sufyan, with due courtesy and brought home to him the point that if the Quraish wanted peace they should accept the suzerainty of the Muslims as the Jews had done. Abu Sufyan was not agreeable to this and the negotiations failed. Abu Sufyan returned to Mecca as a disappointed man. During his stay in Medina he had come to realise that the Muslims had become a power and the position of the Quraish vis a vis the Muslims had become difficult.

March to Mecca : After Abu Sufyan had left Medina, the Holy Prophet ordered preparations to be made for a foray. The Holy Prophet mustered a force ten thousand strong men and took the road to Mecca. Having reached in the neighbourhood of Mecca, the Muslims encamped at Marr al Zahran. When at night fire was lit in the Muslim camp it appeared as if the whole of the desert was on fire. That alarmed the Quraish Abu Sufyan realised that it would be futile for the Quraish to resist the Muslims. He visited the Muslim camp and was converted to Islam. That was the end of the Quraish opposition. The following day the Muslim army marched triumphantly into Mecca. The various contingents of the Muslim army marched into Mecca through different gates. Hadrat Ali held the banner of Islam. The triumphant entry of the Muslims in Mecca marked the vindication of the truth of Islam. The city which eight years ago had treated the Muslims cruelly and driven them to seek refuge with strangers in Medina now lay at the feet of the Muslims. In the hour of triumph the Holy Prophet forgot every evil suffered and forgave every injury that had been inflicted on him. He granted general amnesty to the people of Mecca.

Destruction of the Idols : The triumph of the Muslims was the triumph of Allah and the defeat of the idols. The Holy Prophet visited the Kaaba along with his Companions. The Holy Prophet with the stroke of the stick held in his hand broke the idols which lay in the lower cavities of the walls. As the stone gods were destroyed one by one, the Quraish looked on aghast at the massacre of their gods, while the Holy Prophet recited the verse from the Quran:

> "Say, the Truth has come and falsehood gone Verily falsehood is ever vanishing"

The more important idols, including that of Hubal, the god of war, were placed higher up in the cavities of the walls beyond the reach of the hand or stick. The Holy Prophet asked Hadrat Ali to ascent on his shoulders and destroy the idols which were placed higher up. Hadrat Ali hesitated to ascend the shoulders of the Holy Prophet but when the Holy Prophet repeated the command, Hadrat Ali complied and destroyed all idols. According to legend, Hadrat Ali is reported to have said that while standing on the shoulders of the Holy Prophet he felt that his hand could reach to the heights of the Heaven

Address to the People : To the people assembled in the Kaaba who witnessed the destruction of the idols the Holy Prophet addressed as follows:

> "There is no god but Allah. He has no associate. He has today made good. His promise that He had held to his bondman and helped him in fulfilling his mission. With the triumph of truth every claim of privilege, whether that of blood or property, is abolished except that of the custody of the Kaaba and of supplying water to the pilgrims. Bear in mind that for anyone who is slain the blood wit is hundred camels. O people of Quraish, God has abolished from you all pride of the time of ignorance and all pride in your ancestry, because all persons are descended from Adam and Adam was made of clay."

Then the Holy Prophet, turning to the people said:

> "O ye Quraish, what do you think of the treatments that I should accord you'?". They said 'Mercy, O Prophet of Allah! "We expect nothing but good from you ". Thereupon the Holy Prophet declared I speak to you in the same

words as Joseph spoke to his brothers. This day there is no re-proof against you, go your way for you are free."

This announcement was received with great joy and applause.

Banu Jazima : Having destroyed the idols of the Kaaba, the Holy Prophet sent out small expedition to the neighbouring settlements to destroy the idols in the local temples. Thereafter a number of expeditions were sent to the neighbouring tribes to call them to Islam. The Holy Prophet issued instructions that the tribes who accepted the call were not to be harmed Khalid b Walid was sent to the tribe of Banu Jazima. The tribe accepted the call and declared themselves as Muslims, but Khalid b Walid who had an old feud with the tribe asked the men to lay down arms and then had them killed. When the Holy Prophet came to know of this he felt much annoyed. He raised his hands towards heaven and said "O Lord! I am not responsible for what Khalid has done". The Holy Prophet sent Hadrat Ali with a good deal of money to smooth the feelings of Banu Jazima. Hadrat Ali paid indemnity for the blood that had been shed. He treated them generously, expressed great regrets at what had happened and assured them of the good will of the Muslims. Hadrat Ali lived in the midst of the tribe for some time and educated them in the Islamic way of life. Hadrat Ali performed the mission entrusted to him with great credit and returned to Mecca when the Banu Jazima were fully satisfied.

The Battle of Hunain : After the fall of Mecca, the Holy Prophet sent a mission to the neighbouring tribes of Hawazin and Thaqueef inviting them to accept Islam. They rejected the invitation and chose the war path, boasting that they were not cowards like the Quraish of Mecca. The two tribes along with their allies mustered in considerable strength at Autas, a few miles to the east of Mecca on the way to Taif. The coalition was led by Malik b. Auf, a fiery commander of considerable skill.

The Pass : When the Holy Prophet came to know of the hostile intention of the tribes he decided to take action against them. On a cold day of February 630 C. E., the Muslim forces under the command of the Holy Prophet set out from Mecca. The Muslim army consisted of 12,000 men fully armed. Out of these, 10,000 men were from Medina, while 2000 were the Muslim converts of Mecca. It was a large force and some of the Muslims felt proud of their strength. In order to reach Autas, the Muslim army had to pass the narrow pass of Hunain, some ten miles north east of Mecca. It was narrow defile, leaving little room for the army to pass through except in single file. As the vanguard of the Muslim army entered the defile, a rain of arrows fell on it let loose by a group of archers of the hostile tribes who lay hidden in the precipitous rocks Taken unawares the advance guard of the Muslim army fled in panic. There was considerable confusion and the camels, horses and men ran into one another to seek cover. As the advance guard retreated precipitately from the pass, the rest of the army which had still to enter the pass fled in panic in various directions.

The Battle : The Holy Prophet stood firm at the place where he was at some distance from the mouth of the pass. Only a dozen companions stood by the side of the Holy Prophet, all other men fled for safety. The men who stood around the Holy Prophet included Hadrat Abu Bakr, Hadrat Umar and some members of the Hashimites. Seeing that the Holy Prophet having been abandoned by his men could easily be overcome the hostile tribesmen descended from the heights of the mountains and rushed towards the site where the Holy Prophet stood surrounded by a dozen persons. Under the instructions of the Holy Prophet, Hadrat Abbas shouted at the top of his voice "O Muslims, come to the Holy Prophet of Allah." The call was heard by the Muslims and they returned to fight. As the forces of the tribes advanced boasting of their initial victory and satirising the Muslims for their cowardice, the Holy Prophet throw a handful of dust against the enemy. The Holy Prophet exhorted his men to be stout hearted and not to get nervous. By the time the forces of the tribes arrived, most of the Muslims were ready for combat.

Out of the ranks of the enemy, Abu Nadhul, a giant of a man— very tall and well built—stepped forward and challenged the Muslims to a duel. Hadrat Ali accepted the challenge. With the speed of lightning Hadrat Ali struck at the camel on which Abu Nadhul was riding. Abu Nadhul fell from the beast and before he could recover from his fall Hadrat Ali was at his head, giving him blows after blows with his sword. Soon Abu Nadhul was killed. Thereafter the battle began. In the hand to hand fighting the tribes were no match for the Muslims. They lost ground and they had to retreat. It was now their turn to pass through the defile when the Muslims rained arrows at them. As many as seventy men of the enemy were killed while passing through the defile.

Confrontation at Autas : The Holy Prophet posted a contingent to guard the pass and led the main army to Autas on other side of the defile in pursuit of the enemy. In the confrontation at Autas, the tribes could not withstand the onslaught of the Muslims. Finding the resistance useless, the tribes broke the camp and retired to Taif. Immense booty fell in the hands of the Muslims. This included 24,000 camels and 400 Oqiyahs of silver. The number of persons taken captive exceeded six thousand.

Siege of Taif : From Autas, the Muslim forces set out for Taif. The people of Taif were proud with traditions of bravery. They were a rich people and considered themselves to be superior to all other tribes in Arabia. Sometime in 619/620 C. E. ., when the Holy Prophet was persecuted by the Quraish of Mecca he had visited Taif to seek refuge. The people of Taif had maltreated the Holy Prophet and had turned him out of their city. Now the tables were turned. The people shut themselves in the fort and could not face the Muslims in the open. The Holy Prophet decided to lay a siege to the city. The Muslim catapults began to throw stones in the fort but this did not lead to any tangible result. The Muslims tried the testudo device whereunder a group of soldiers shielded by a cover of cowhide advanced to set fire to the gate. The enemy threw red hot scraps of iron on the testudo which made it ineffecitve. The siege dragged on for two weeks but still there was no sign of the fall of the fort. The Holy Prophet had other business to attend and he could not afford to remain at Taif for long. The Holy Prophet raised the siege and returned to Mecca

Operations of Hadrat Ali : The Holy Prophet commissioned Hadrat Ali to undertake operations against the tribes in the neighbourhood of Taif who were feudatories to Taif. Hadrat Ali began his operations by destroying the idols in the temples in the neighbourhood of Taif. The principal god of the people was Allat and when Hadrat Ali destroyed this idol, he was involved in a skirmish with the men of Banu Khusham Shahab, the leader of Banu Khusham and a formidable man enjoying reputation as a great warrior challenged Hadrat Ali to a duel. Hadrat Ali killed Shahab. With the murder of their leader Shahab and the destruction of their god Allat, the men of Banu Khusham were unnerved. They laid down arms and accepted Islam. The other tribes in the neighbourhood of Taif were similarly subdued and converted to Islam

Conversions to Islam : With the conversion of the tribes around Taif to Islam, the position of the people of Taif became precarious. When Hadrat Ali advised them to accept Islam, they agreed to send a deputation to Mecca to wait on the Holy Prophet. The deputation agreed to accept Islam, but they wanted that a respite should be allowed to them to continue to worship their idols for some time. They begged for a respite for one year and reduced the period of grace to six months, three months and one month. The Holy Prophet rejected the demand outright on the ground that he who had accepted Islam could no longer worship the idols. The deputationists next asked for exemption from prayers. This demand was rejected on the ground that there could be no faith without prayers. Thereupon the deputationists urged, "Then, at least give us exemption from the payment of Zakat". The Holy Prophet rejected the demand on the ground that Zakat was a compulsory levy. The Holy Prophet made the deputationists bear in mind that Islam was a matter of faith, if one had faith in Islam he had to accept all that Islam had enjoined. There could be no compromise in the matter of the injunctions of Islam. The Holy Prophet made them realise that it was open to them not to be converted to Islam, but once they accepted Islam, they had to strictly follow all the commandments of Islam. The deputationists understood the position and accepted Islam for themselves and for the people of Taif who they represented

Return to Medina : With the conversion of the people of Taif to Islam, the mission of Mecca was completed. The Holy Prophet and his Companions performed the "Umrah", and thereafter returned to Medina. Eight years earlier the Muslims had escaped from Mecca an oppressed people, now they were the masters of Mecca, Medina and a greater part of Arabia. That was verily a positive proof of the truth of Islam. Thus God fulfilled all the promises that He had made with His Prophet.

Campaign against Banu Tay : Banu Tay came into prominence under their chief Hatim Tay Hatim Tay made a great name for himself for his generosity and munificence Poets and minstrels sang of his unprecedented exploits of generosity Many romantic tales got current in. Arabia highlighting his golden deeds. He acquired fame as a great hero of. Arabia, a veritable symbol of selflessness, charity and generosity Hatim was a contemporary of the Holy Prophet, but no occasion rose for Hatim to meet the Holy Prophet. According to the assessment of the Holy Prophet Hatim had the attributes of a Muslim and if Islam had been offered to him he would have accepted it Hatim died before Islam began to spread in. Arabia

Son of Hatim : Hatim was succeeded by his son. Adi. Adi tried to follow in the footsteps of his father. He tried to be generous and munificent but he could not attain that fame that had been earned by his father. Adi was very religious in his won way and was very particular in the worship of idols in the local temple. When Islam came to spread to the neighbouring tribes, Banu Tay showed a hostile attitude to Islam. Thereupon the Holy Prophet sent an expedition to Banu Tay under the command of Hadrat Ali

Flight of Adi : When Hadrat Ali reached the territory of Banu Tay, Adi could not make up his mind to face the Muslims in battle. He quietly escaped to Syria with a few followers, leaving his clansmen to their fate. Hadrat Ali overpowered the Banu Tay and returned to Medina carrying in his train a large number of men and women of Banu Tay as captives. These included Sufana, a daughter of Hatim. At Medina, the Holy Prophet set Sufana at liberty because of the consideration for her father, the illustrious Hatim Sufana had some attributes of her father. She said that she was the daughter of a man who ransomed prisoners, fed the poor and helped those in distress. As the daughter of such a man she could not accept her liberty unless her clansmen were also freed. The Holy Prophet out-hatimed Hatim, and set all prisoners of Banu Tay free. That impressed Sufana a good deal. She felt that the Holy Prophet was great man, and the religion that he preached was the true faith. She felt that to be generous to others and yet to worship idols who were incapable of doing any harm or good was inconsistent. One who professed to be generous should necessarily worship such Being who was Almighty, Omnipotent and Sustainer of all mankind. When Sufana left Medina she was already a Muslim at heart. Sufana proceeded to Syria and told her brother of the generous treatment that Banu Tay had met at the hands of the Holy Prophet. Adi visited Medina and accepted Islam. He had lessons in Islam from Hadrat Ali. Thereafter the entire tribe of Banu Tay accepted Islam.

Christians of Najran : When Islam began to spread there were some tribes which professed Christianity. After the expedition to Tabuk some Christian tribes were converted to Islam. Some Christian tribes chose not to change their faith, but they accepted the suzerainty of the Muslims and agreed to pay them an annual tribute.

There was a large Christian community in Najran and in 631 C. E. the Holy Prophet invited them to accept Islam. In response they challenged the Holy Prophet to a Mubahila. The Mubahila was an ancient way of ascertaining the truth. In a religious contest each of the disputing parties was required to take a solemn oath that they were right and true and called on God to wreak. His vengeance on them if they lied. It was believed that in such case the liar was visited by the wrath of God and was destroyed. The Holy Prophet accepted the challenges and asked the Christians of Najran to send a deputation to Medina.

Christian Deputation : A deputation of the Christian priests headed by their chief. Aqib accordingly arrived in Medina. They were dressed in fine silken robes and wore golden rings in their fingures. When dressed thus, they waited on the Holy Prophet in the mosque, the Holy Prophet did not pay any attention to them and did not even return their salutation. Greatly puzzled they left the mosque and meeting Hadrat Uthman complained to him that the Prophet of Islam had invited them to Medina, but he had paid no attention to them when they had visited him in the mosque. Hadrat Uthman took them to Hadrat Ali, Hadrat Ali told them that the indifference of the Holy Prophet was due to the fact that they were dressed in silk finery and were loaded with jewelry. He advised them to cast off their jewelry and be dressed in simple cotton robes. When they had changed their dress, Hadrat Ali took them to the Holy Prophet in the mosque.

Disputation with Christians : This time the Holy Prophet welcomed them and made them sit near him. He told them that when they had first come to him, he had turned his head away because Satan accompanied them with their finery and jewelry. Thereafter the Holy Prophet entered into a discourse with them and the talk centred round the personality of Jesus Christ. The Christians wanted to know what was his opinion about Jesus Christ. The Holy Prophet said that like other prophets he was a Prophet of God. The Christians next asked whether he regarded Jesus Christ as a son of God. The Holy Prophet said that God is far above having a wife or a son and as such Jesus was not a son of God. The Christians then posed the question if Jesus had no father and his mother Mary had not sinned what then is the status of Jesus if he is not the son of God. The Holy Prophet said that they would have their answer the following day. At night the Holy Prophet had a revelation about the true nature of Jesus Christ. When the Christians met the Holy Prophet the following day, he told them that the likeness of Jesus with Allah is as the likeness of Adam. Adam was born without a father and so was Jesus born without a father, but neither. Adam nor Jesus were the sons of God.

Mubahila : At this reply of the Holy Prophet, the Christian priests felt stranded, but to keep up appearances they desired that a Mubahila be held. The Christians named five priests who were to take part in the Mubahila. The Holy Prophet nominated five persons who were to take part in the Mubahila on behalf of the Muslims. These included the Holy Prophet himself, Hadrat Ali, Hadrat Fatima, Hassan and Hussain. The Holy Prophet did not nominate any of his wives in this behalf. The nomination was confined to such persons who had blood relation with him. The Holy Prophet declared that the Mubahila would be held the following day. At night the Christians could get no sleep. They felt that truth shone in the eyes of the Holy Prophet and to invoke the curse of God with people like him would invite destruction for the Christians. The following day when the Christian priests waited on the Holy Prophet they said that they had neither the conviction to profess Islam nor the strength to enter into any deputation or fight with the Muslims. They said that while maintaining their own faith, they would accept the paramountcy of the Muslims and pay an annual tribute. The Holy Prophet accepted the offer, entered into a treaty with them and allowed them to return to Najran. The way in which the Christians gave the challenges of Mubahila in the first instance and then backed out of it, was a confession of failure on the part of the Christians and their acknowledgement of the supremacy of Islam as a faith.

Banu Zabada : The Banu Zabada was an Arab tribe who had their settlement a few miles west of Medina. The tribe had accepted Islam and they had a mosque in their settlement. The chief of the tribe was Amar b Madi Kurb. Amar had a blood feud with Ushus Khusee, the chief of a neighbour tribe. The tribe of Ushus Khusee had also accepted Islam. In the days of ignorance Ushus Khusee had killed the father of Amar. Amar burnt with the urge to seek vengeance from Ushus for the murder of his father. As both the parties had accepted Islam the case was brought to the Holy Prophet for arbitration. After hearing the case, the Holy Prophet decided that after the acceptance of Islam the question of seeking vengeance in the case of any blood feud which had prevailed in the days of ignorance did not arise. The judgement hurt Amar. He and at his instance his tribe abjured Islam and raised the standard of revolt. In a rebellious mood,. Amar killed Harith b Kab, the chief of a tribe which had accepted Islam. The aggrieved tribe brought the high handedness on the part of Amar and Banu Zabada to the notice of the Holy Prophet.

Action against Banu Zabada : On receiving complaint against Banu Zabada, the Holy Prophet ordered punitive action. The Holy Prophet appointed Hadrat Ali as the commander of the expedition to be led against the rebellious tribe. Hadrat Ali led a Muslim force to meet the rebels. When the two forces confronted each other in battle array, Amr b Madi Kurb stepped forward from the ranks of Banu Zabada, boasted of his lineage and his skill as a warrior and challenged Hadrat Ali, the Commander of the Muslim forces to a single combat. Hadrat Ali stepped forward and raised the shout of Allah-o-Akbar. The shout of Hadrat Ali was more ferocious than the roar of a lion and it struck terror in the hearts of the enemy. When the duel began. Amar aimed blows at Hadrat Ali who skilfully avoided all blows. Then it was the turn of Hadrat Ali to strike at his adversary. The charge of Hadrat Ali was so forceful that Amar reeled under it and fell on the ground helpless. Hadrat Ali bade him rise up and take the sword. Amar rose from the ground but he was too nervous to fight. He took to his heels and fled from the battlefield. The bad performance of their leader demoralised the force of Banu Zabada and it laid down arms without fight. Hadrat Ali returned victorious to Medina and in his train followed a large number of captives. According to traditions the men of Banu Zabada said that as they faced the Muslims on the battlefield it appeared to them that some super natural power was aiding the Muslims. The men of Banu Zabada repented and were re-converted to Islam Later. Amar also appeared before the Holy Prophet, offered repentence and was reconverted to Islam.

FOUR

CENTRE OF POWER

GOVERNOR OF MEDINA

Wars between Byzantines and Persians : In the course of history, wars between the Byzantines and the Persians had been fought every now and then. In these wars sometimes the Persians had the upper hand and sometimes the Byzantines had. In the early years of the seventh century the Persians defeated the Byzantines. As the Christians were monotheists, the pagans of Arabia hailed the victory of the Persians over the Christian Byzantines. At that time the Holy Prophet prophesied that within ten years the tables would be turned and the Byzantines would defeat the Persians. This prophecy was fulfilled and in the later twenties of the seventh century the Byzantine emperor Hercules inflicted a crushing defeat on the Persians. It was at this stage of the Perso-Byzantine conflict that Islam rose into power. The Byzantines could not view the growing strength of Islam with favour. It was accordingly apprehended that after defeating the Persians the Byzantine emperor Hercules would invade Arabia. After the conquest of Mecca when Islam came to spread throughout Arabia, the invasion of Arabia by the Byzantines appeared to be imminent. It was rumoured that the Byzantine emperor was mustering a large army in Syria to invade Arabia.

Expedition to Tabuk : To forestall any invasion of Arabia by the Byzantines the Holy Prophet decided to undertake an expedition to Tabuk on the borders of Syria. The hot season had set in and the season was unfavourable to the undertaking of any expedition. It was the harvesting season and the people were generally loath to leave their homes and go to the war. In spite of these difficulties the Holy Prophet was able to raise an army of thirty thousand men. To finance the expedition, the Holy Prophet invited voluntary contributions and the Companions subscribed liberally to the cost of the war.

The Rumours : The expedition to Tabuk was led by the Holy Prophet himself. In his absence from Medina the Holy Prophet appointed Hadrat Ali as the Governor of Medina. As such Hadrat Ali did not participate in the expedition. The hypocrites spread the rumour that Hadrat Ali had been left at Medina because he did not have the courage to face the Byzantines. This cut Hadrat Ali to the quick and while the Muslim forces were still at Jorf, a few miles from Medina, Hadrat Ali visited camp and apprised the Holy Prophet of what the hypocrites were saying. The Holy Prophet told Hadrat Ali that he was to him what Haroon was to Hadrat Musa. Just as Hadrat Musa had appointed Haroon to look after his people during his absence, thus he had appointed Hadrat Ali to look after Medina during his absence. The Holy Prophet pointed out that as the hypocrites were liable to do any mischief he had to appoint a member of his household to look after his household during his absence. Trouble could be expected from the tribes and it was necessary that the administration of Medina was left in the hands of a person who could be a source of awe for the enemy. Fully satisfied Hadrat Ali returned to Medina. He summoned. Abdullah b Ubay and told him in plain words that if he or any of his followers tried to indulge in any mischief or spread any false rumour he would cut off their heads. That struck terror in the hearts of the hypocrites and they refrained from doing any mischief. Hadrat Ali maintained law and order with a stern hand. He looked after the needs of the household of the Holy Prophet effectively.

Tabuk Campaign : The Muslim army reached Tabuk after a weary march. Contrary to expectations, there was no Byzantine force at Tabuk to meet the Muslims. On coming to know of the advance of the Muslim army, the Byzantines withdrew their army well within Syria. The Muslims achieved their object without firing a shot. The strategy of the Muslims was purely defensive, aimed at keeping the Byzantine army away from the borders of Arabia. The Byzantines who had one time threatened to invade Arabia were no longer in the mood to measure swords with the Muslims. This was a moral victory for the Muslims and the tribes in the border region who had heretofore offered allegiance to the Byzantines transferred their allegiance to the Muslims.

Holy Prophet's Address : At Tabuk the Holy Prophet delivered a classical address which has passed into history. He said'

"Verily, the most veracious discourse is the Book of Allah.

The Most trustworthy stronghold is the word of piety.

The best of precedents is the precedent of Muhammad.

The noblest speech is the invocation of Allah.

The finest of the narratives is the Quran.

The best of the affairs is that which has been firmly resolved upon.

The worst in religion are those things which are created without sanction.

The best of the ways is the one bidden of prophets.

The noblest death is the death of a martyr.

The most miserable blindness is waywardness after guidance.

The best of the actions is that which is beneficent.

The best guidance is that which is put into practice.

The worst blindness is the blindness of the heart"

Return from Tabuk : On return from Tabuk, the Holy Prophet was glad to see that during his absence Hadrat Ali had maintained law and order satisfactorily and the hypocrites were in a chastened mood. The hypocrites had constructed a mosque and they asked the Holy Prophet to perform the opening ceremony of the mosque. The Holy Prophet consulted Hadrat Ali who was of the view that a separate mosque for any section of the Muslims should not be patronised. Later, the Holy Prophet had a revelation advising the Holy Prophet against the patronage of the mosque. The Holy Prophet ordered the demolition of the mosque. Hadrat Ali supervised the demolition of the mosque. Soon after Abdullah b Ubbay, the leader of the hypocrites died. Thereafter his followers repented and joined the fold of Islam as true Muslims. Hadrat Ali played an important part in suppressing the activities of the hypocrites.

Hadrat Abu Bakr as Amir ul Hajj : In 631 C. E. the Holy Prophet sent from Medina a delegation of three hundred Muslims to perform the Hajj. Hadrat Abu Bakr was appointed as the leader of the delegates. Hadrat Abu Bakr had thus the honour of being the first "Amir-ul-Hajj" in the history of Islam.

The Revelation : Sometime after Hadrat Abu Bakr and his party had left for the Hajj, the Holy Prophet recieved revelation about the regulation of the Hajj and the ordering of relationship between the Muslims and the infidels. It is related that when the revelation came someone suggested to the Holy Prophet that he should send news about the revelation to Hadrat. Abu Bakr. The Holy Prophet said only a man of his own house could proclaim the revelation.

The Proclamation : The Holy Prophet summoned Hadrat Ali and asked him to proclaim the revealed verses to the people on the day of sacrifice when they assembled at Mina. Hadrat Ali went forth on the Holy Prophet's slit-eared camel, and soon overtook Hadrat Abu Bakr and his party. When Hadrat Ali joined the party Hadrat. Abu Bakr wanted to know whether he had come to give orders or to convey them. Hadrat Ali said that he had not come to replace Hadrat. Abu Bakr as "Amir-ul-Hajj", and that his mission was merely to convey a special message to the people on behalf of the Holy Prophet.

Declaration of Discharge : At Mecca on the occasion of the Hajj, Hadrat. Abu Bakr presided at the Hajj ceremony while Hadrat Ali read the verses of the revelation which came to be known as the Declaration of Discharge. According to the Declaration it was provided that henceforward the Muslims were discharged of all obligations that they had undertaken with the non-Muslims. All treaties or agreements with them were to be no longer effective. Henceforward the non-Muslims were not be allowed to visit the Kaaba or perform the Hajj. New rules for the performance of the Hajj were proclaimed. No one was to circumambulate the Kaaba. Naked Polytheism was to be no longer tolerated. A grace period of four months was laid down and thereafter all agreement with the non-Muslims were to stand as abrogated.

Importance of the Declaration : The Declaration of Discharge was really the declaration of the victory of Islam, the victory of the truth over falsehood. The battle between the truth and falsehood began in 611 C. E., with the proclamation of the prophethood of the Holy Prophet. This battle was waged for twenty years in one form or the other. It came to an end with the Declaration of Discharge signifying the ultimate victory of Islam. From the day this proclamation was made, a new era dawned in. Arabia. Henceforward Islam alone was to be the faith of the Arabs.

Claim to the Caliphate : In some quarters, an argument is advanced to the effect that as on this occasion the Declaration of Discharge was read by Hadrat Ali, while Hadrat Abu Bakr was the. Amir ul Hajj. This established the precedence of Hadrat Ali over Hadrat. Abu Bakr, and as such when on the death of the Holy Prophet, Hadrat. Abu Bakr became the caliph in disregard of the claim of Hadrat Ali. We shall discuss this aspect of the matter in detail in the later part of the book. Here we may pause to consider two questions, firstly why was the proclamation read by Hadrat Ali when Hadrat. Abu Bakr was the Amir ul Hajj and secondly whether this established the precedence of Hadrat Ali over Hadrat. Abu Bakr and others in the matter of caliphate. The revelation emanating from God were particularly sacrosanct and these had to be proclaimed to the people either by the Holy Prophet himself or by some member of his house in whom he had particular confidence. The choice of Hadrat Ali to read the proclamation was not relevant to the question of succession. The question of succession had to be considered in the context of to other considerations This did not establish the precedence of Hadrat Ali over Hadrat. Abu Bakr for Hadrat Ali did not replace Hadrat. Abu Bakr as. Amir ul Hajj; Hadrat Ali's role was merely confined to the delivering of a special message. This established the precedence of Hadrat Ali over other Hashimites with whom the Holy

Prophet had blood relations. Hadrat Ali was the first among the Hashimites to profess Islam and among the Hashimites he remained closest to the Holy Prophet.

Banu Ramla : By 631 C. E. most of the tribes in the neighbourhood of Medina had accepted Islam. The people of the Banu Ramla tribe still held out against Islam and they had become a source of menace to the Muslims. They lived in a rugged country in the inaccessible defiles of the mountains at some distance from Medina. They waylaid caravans and after plundering them would retire to their strongholds in the mountains. They would even raid the city of Medina and after plundering the people sought shelter in the mountains.

Campaign against Banu Ramla : The Banu Ramla tribe created a law and order problem for Medina and in 631 C. E. the Holy Prophet decided to take punitive action against the tribe. The Holy Prophet sent an expedition against the tribe under the command of Hadrat. Abu Bakr. The Muslim army penetrated deep into the mountains without facing any resistance. One night as the Muslim soldiers lay asleep in their camp, the Banu Ramla people made surprise attack on the Muslim camp and killed many Muslims. The Muslim army had to withdraw in a state of confusion. Thereafter the Holy Prophet sent another expedition under the command of Hadrat Umar. This expedition fared no better and the Muslim army had to retreat after suffering losses. A third expedition under'. Amr b. Al Aas also failed in achieving its object.

Expedition under Hadrat Ali : After the failure of three expeditions, the Holy Prophet ordered the fourth expedition under the command of Hadrat Ali. In the earlier expeditions, the Muslim army had failed to reach the stronghold of the tribe and had to withdraw without actual confrontation with the tribe Hadrat Ali changed the tactics. Instead of following the established route, Hadrat Ali led the Muslim army along mountainous tracks where they hid themselves during the day and advanced during the night. Hadrat Ali succeeded in beating the Banu Ramla at their own game. After several nights march, the Muslim army reached the stronghold of the tribe and made a surprise attack on the enemy. The mountainous tribe could never imagine that the men of the plains could ever penetrate through the depth of the mountains and reach their stronghold. In the confrontation that followed many persons of the tribe were killed and they were ultimately forced to surrender. Hadrat Ali returned triumphant to Medina carrying an immense booty and a large number of prisoners. Heretofore all battles that the Muslims had fought had been fought in the plains. The battle against Banu Ramla was the first battle that the Muslims had to fight in mountainous terrain. The Muslims had no experience of fighting in hilly tracts and as such the first three expeditions undertaken by the Muslims against the people of the hills failed. The People of the hills were expert in guerilla warfare. They could hide in the mountain recesses and fall upon the Muslims in surprise at all odd hours. By these tactics the Banu Ramla warriors prevented the Muslims from reaching their main settlement in the hills. Hadrat Ali was the first Muslim General to score a victory in a mountainous territory. When Hadrat Ali returned triumphant to Medina, the Holy Prophet and the Muslims welcomed him a few miles outside the city. The Holy Prophet appreciated the services of Hadrat Ali in superlative terms. According to the Shute traditions, the Holy Prophet addressed Hadrat Ali on this occasion in the following terms:

> "O Ali' If I were not apprehensive that the Muslim community would exaggerate your deeds like the Christians who extolled the achievements of Jesus Christ by ascribing divinity to him, I would have narrated the superiority of your character today in such a way that wherever you went, the people would have worshipped the very dust of your feet."

Khalid b. Walid's Mission to Yemen : After the conquest of Mecca the tribes around Mecca and Medina accepted Islam. It was now the turn of the remoter parts of Arabia to be introduced to Islam. The Holy Prophet sent missions to various parts of Arabia. One of such mission under Khalid b Walid was sent to Yemen to invite the Yemenites to Islam. Khalid b Walid was a soldier and a swordsman, but not a scholar or a preacher. He was a late convert to Islam and in spite of his enthusiasm, he did not have that depth in the understanding of Islam which could attract others to Islam. The Yemenites were proud of their ancient civilization and culture and could not believe that anyone from the interior of Arabia, always regarded by them as a backward area, could be a source of enlightenment for them. The Jews and the Christians had their high-powered missions in Yemen. Some of the people of Yemen were Christians and some of them were Jews. The Christian priests and Jewish rabbis had a strong hold on the people of Yemen and in spite of his best efforts for over six months, Khalid b Walid was not able to make any headway in Yemen. The Holy Prophet recalled Khalid b Walid from Yemen.

The Mission of Hadrat Ali : The Holy Prophet thereafter commissioned Hadrat Ali to proceed to Yemen. A force of three hundred soldiers assembled at Quba outside Medina. The Holy Prophet tied the turban on the head of Hadrat Ali with his own hands and handed him the standard. The Holy Prophet prayed to God to enlighten the mind of Hadrat Ali, to make his tongue eloquent, to make his talk impressive and to make his conduct a source of attraction for others. Although Hadrat Ali proceeded to Yemen at the head of the force, he was commanded not to use force. The force was only meant for defence in the case of any attack. It was a voyage of enlightenment. People were to be converted to Islam not by an appeal to arms but by an appeal to their hearts.

Strategy of Hadrat Ali : On reaching Yemen, Hadrat Ali realised that the people of Yemen were very much under the influence of the Christian priests and Jewish rabbis and unless such priests and rabbis were effectively tackled, there was little likelihood of any success with the common men. The Christian priests and Jewish rabbis were proud of their religious knowledge. They challenged Hadrat Ali to a debate. Hadrat Ali was used to fighting duels with his adversaries in the case of battles, now he had to fight an intellectual duel. The first challenges came from a Christian priest renowned for his learning and piety. A public debate was held. The Christian priest advanced arguments in favour of the perfection of Christianity and of Jesus Christ being the son of God. It was observed that in such circumstances there could be no question of another faith. Hadrat Ali smashed these arguments one by one. He quoted from the Christian scriptures wherein Jesus Christ had himself spoken of the advent of a prophet after him Hadrat Ali took pains to explain that Islam acknowledged Jesus Christ as a prophet but did not regard him as a son of God. He maintained that Islam was a perfected form of all previous religions. The debate lasted for several days, and at last Kaab admitted the superiority of Islam and was converted to Islam. With his conversion many Christians were also converted to Islam.

The Jewish rabbis felt concerned at the success of Islam. They challenged Hadrat Ali to a public debate. This debate lasted for several days and ended in the victory for Islam. Some of the Jewish rabbis accepted Islam and following them many Jews accepted Islam. Thereafter Hadrat Ali spread his men throughout the length and breadth of Yemen to carry the message of Islam to the people. When the people came to know that their priests and rabbis had accepted Islam they lost the will to resist Islam and accepted the new faith willingly. Within a few months most of the people in Yemen were converted to Islam. These people came to look to Hadrat Ali as a great hero.

The Farewell Pilgrimage : Early in 632 C. E in the Hajj season, the Holy Prophet decided to proceed to Mecca to perform the Hajj. The pilgrimage was planned on a large scale. Messengers were sent to all parts of Arabia calling upon the Muslims to assemble at Medina for the purpose of the pilgrimage. In response to this call, over one lakh Muslims gathered at Medina to proceed to Mecca to perform the Hajj.

The Caravan : After all arrangements had been completed, a caravan of over one lakh Muslims fired with their enthusiasm for Islam started for Mecca to visit the House of God and offer their submission to God. It was a remarkable sight like which the people to Arabia had not seen before. The Holy Prophet rode at the head of the caravan. All his wives accompanied him. Hadrat Ali rode by his side. He was accompanied by Hadrat Fatima.

Dhul Hulaifa : At Dhul Hulaifa on the outskirts of Mecca, the Holy Prophet and all his followers put on the "Ihram"—the pilgrim's garb. The Holy Prophet gave the signal call "Labbayyak. Allah hummah Labbayyak" —here I am at your service O Lord, and this was repeated by all one lakh persons in the congregation. The entire valley came to ring with the sound, the Muslims calling on their Lord, submitting to Him and placing themselves at His disposal.

Mecca and Mina : The party reached Mecca on the fourth of Zul Hajj after a journey of nineteen days. After a stay of four days in Mecca the pilgrims left for Mina on the 8th of Zul Hajj and passed the night there. The following day the pilgrims proceeded to Arafat.

Farewell Address : After mid-day prayers on the 9th of Zul Hajj at Arafat, the Holy Prophet delivered the historic Hajj Khutba which has come to be known as the farewell address. After giving praise to God and thanking Him for the bounties that he had conferred on the Muslims and had crowned their efforts in the cause of the Truth with success, the Holy Prophet said:

> "O People, listen carefully to my words for I may not be among you next year, nor ever address you again from this spot O People, just as you regard this month as sacred, so regard the life and property of every Muslim as sacred Return the goods entrusted to you to their rightful owners. Hurt no one, so that no one may hurt you. Usury is forbidden. Satan has despiated in leading you astray in big things, so beware of his manoeuvres in tempting you in small things. Women have rights over you as you have rights over them. Be good to them. You may soon have to appear before. Allah and answer for your deeds. So beware Do not go astray after I am gone. O People, no prophet will come after me and no new faith will be born. Worship your Allah. Say your prayers. Keep fast during the month of Ramadan. Give of your wealth in charity. All Muslims, free or slaved, have the same rights and the same responsibilities. None is higher than the other unless he is higher in virtue. Feed your slaves as you feed yourself. Do not oppress them. Do not usurp their rights. All distinctions between the Arabs, the non-Arabs, the black and the white are abolished. All Muslims are brothers. Do good. Be faithful to your trusts. Be kind to the orphans. Remember God Know that while man being mortal is bound to die God being immortal will live forever."

Having spoken these words, the Holy Prophet turned his face to the Heaven and said "Be my witness O. Allah, that I have conveyed Your message to Your people ". Thereupon the people corroborated saying, "Yes, O Prophet of Allah, you have done so and done it magnificently"

The Revelation : After the Holy Prophet had delivered the address, Allah revealed to him the verses:

> "This Day have I perfected for you, your faith. And completed My blessings upon you. And have chosen for you Islam as religion "

All other prophets including Moses and Jesus Christ had to leave their unfulfilled mission to their successors. The Holy Prophet of Islam alone had the unique distinction of seeing the successful fruition of his mission during his lifetime.

Reaction of Companions : As the Companions including Hadrat Ali heard these verses about the perfection of the faith, they wept because they felt that the mission of the Holy Prophet having been completed, he was apt to depart to meet his Lord.

After the farewell address the party left Arafat in the evening and passed the night at Muzdalfa. The following day they went to Mina and sacrificed the animals. The Holy Prophet sacrificed 63 animals, one for each year of his life. These were shared by Hadrat Ali. The men then shaved their heads and the ceremony of the hajj was completed. Thereafter the pilgrims left for Medina. On the return journey while the Companions were happy that their faith had been perfected, they were overwhelmed with grief at the thought that such consummation implied that the Holy Prophet was soon to depart from their midst.

Khum Ghadir : On the way to Medina the caravan of those who had participated in the Farewell pilgrimage spread over several miles. When the Holy Prophet reached the valley of Khum some midway between Mecca and Medina, the Holy Prophet received the following revelation:

> "O Messenger of God, make known what has been revealed to you from your Lord, for if you do it not, you will not have conveyed His message. Allah will protect you from mankind. Lo,. Allah guided not the unbelieving folk."

Calling a halt near a pond Ghadir in the valley of Khum the Holy Prophet sent men to call all persons of the caravan who had gone ahead or lagged behind to assemble there to hear the command of the Holy Prophet.

Address of the Holy Prophet : When all people, over one lakh in number, had assembled at the pond in the Khum valley, the Holy Prophet addressed them. The exact text of the address is not available. There is a good deal of controversy about the contents of the address and both the Sunnis and the Shias have their own versions of the address.

According to the Sunni writers the Holy Prophet said that after him the Muslims would have to face hard times. He wanted them to remain united and to obey those in authority. He said that he was the last of the prophets and there was to be no prophet after him. He observed that God had given him superiority over all those who inhabit the world and they include all the past and future generations. The Holy Prophet observed that God had given him the keys of His treasures and He had asked him to confirm the solemn pledges which, He had made with them. God had confided. His secret to him and had given him help so that he had been enlightened. Thus he had made the beginning and thus he would set the final seal. He added that no one could derive power except from Allah. He wanted mankind to fear God. He exhorted the Muslims not to wage war except in the name of God and in the cause of Islam. He continued that after him there would be people who would accuse him of falsehood but ultimately the truth would prevail for he did not invite the people to anything else but towards God.

The Controversy : There is a good deal of controversy about the Holy Prophet's address at Khum Ghadir but the fact is that the sayings of the Holy Prophet are a continuation of his life-long message and struggle in the light of the teachings of the Holy Quran the final word of Allah. Whatever is compatible with it is only to be accepted.

Esteemed Counsellor

Illness of the Holy Prophet : A short time after returning from the Farewell pilgrimage the Holy Prophet fell sick. The poison which the Jewess had given to him at Khyber had slowly penetrated into his system and began to show its effect. The Holy Prophet felt that having fulfilled the mission entrusted to him by God, his earthly life was to end and he was to meet his Master. One night when he had some respite the Holy Prophet accompanied by Hadrat Ali went to the graveyard and there prayed for the souls of his companions who had fallen in the battle of Uhud. Then he returned to the apartment of his wife Maimuna. The exertion, because of the visit to the graveyard, had its effect and the fever became severe. The Holy Prophet assembled all his wives and told them that on account of his sickness it would not be possible for him to visit each wife in turn. He wanted their permission to stay in the apartment of Hadrat. Aishah till he recovered. All the wives agreed to the proposal and the Holy Prophet supported by Hadrat Ali and Hadrat. Abbas moved to the apartment of Hadrat. Aishah. The Holy Prophet directed that during his illness, Hadrat. Abu Bakr should lead the prayers.

The Last Address : A day later the fever subsided and the Holy Prophet took a bath. Refreshed by the bath he felt some relief and went to the mosque to offer the noonday prayer. At the conclusion of the prayer the Holy Prophet took his seat on the pulpit to address the congregation. The Holy Prophet said:

> "There is a servant whose Lord has given him the option between the life on this earth, and the life hereafter in nearness to his Lord and the servant has chosen the latter."

Thereupon tears rolled down from the eyes of the Companions and they said," Holy Prophet, how can we live without you."

The Holy Prophet continued :

> "O people' it has reached me that you are afraid of the approaching death of your prophet. Has any previous prophet lived forever among the people to whom he was sent? So that I should live forever among you. Behold I am about to go to mv Lord You too will go there sooner or later."

After the address, the Holy Prophet retired to the quarter of Hadrat. Aishah. The exertion had its effect and the fever became violent again. The night following the seventh of June 632 C. E. lay heavy on him. He was overheard praying constantly to Allah for His blessings, the morning of the eighth June brought some relief, when the fever pain somewhat subsided. Moving the curtain he saw the Muslims offering their prayers. The Holy Prophet supported by Hadrat Ali walked to the mosque. The people made way for him, opening their ranks as he stepped forward Hadrat. Abu Bakr stepped backward to vacate his seat for the Holy Prophet. The Holy Prophet told Hadrat. Abu Bakr by a motion of his hand to continue to lead the prayers.

After the conclusion of the prayers, the Holy Prophet took his seat on the pulpit. He said that he had heard that the people were objecting to send an expedition to the Syrian front under the command of Usama. He observed that their objection was not valid as Usama was fit to lead the expedition to avenge the death of his father. He exhorted the people to do what was lawful and to refrain from doing that which was unlawful. He said that he had not made lawful except that which God had declared lawful nor he had prohibited anything but that which God had forbidden.

Holy Prophet's Demise : The Muslims were happy to see the Holy Prophet in their midst. They felt that the Holy Prophet had recovered and that there was no danger to his life. Thereafter the Holy Prophet returned to the apartment of Hadrat. Aishah. The exertion had its effect. The condition of the Holy Prophet grew worse and within a few hours he passed away.

The faithful assembled in the mosque. There was an air of uneasiness in the atmosphere. There was a whispering that the Holy Prophet of Islam was dead. There were suppressed sobs and sighs. What would happen to the Muslims when the great prophet was to be no longer in their midst was the thought that disturbed everybody. All eyes were turned to the quarter of Hadrat. Aishah. The faithful had the fond hope that the door of the chamber would open any moment and the Holy Prophet would emerge with his face radiating divine light.

In the courtyard of the mosque, Hadrat Umar moved among the people and said:

> "Who says that the Holy Prophet is dead I testify that he is alive and has gone to Allah like Moses and would return to us after sometime "

Then Hadrat. Abu Bakr came and addressed the people saying.

> "Listen to me, ye people. Those of you who worshipped Muhammad know that he is dead like any other mortal. But those of you who worship the God of Muhammad know that He is alive and would live forever."

Thereafter Hadrat. Abu Bakr quoted the following verses from the Holy Quran:

> "Muhammad is but a Messenger,
> Messengers of God have passed away before him
> What, if he dies or is killed
> Will you turn back upon your heels?
> And whosoever turns back upon his heels
> Will by no means do harm to Allah,
> And Allah will reward the thankful"

The effect of the address of Hadrat. Abu Bakr was electrical. It appeared as if the people did not know of this verse of the Holy Quran until Hadrat. Abu Bakr had recited it.

According to the will of the Holy Prophet, Hadrat Ali and Hadrat. Abbas washed the body of the Holy Prophet and prepared it for burial. The Holy Prophet was buried in the chamber of Hadrat. Aishah where he had died

Hadrat Ali's elegy on the death of the Holy Prophet

Hadrat Ali was overwhelmed with grief at the death of the Holy Prophet. He expressed his grief in heart-rending verses. He said:

> "May my parents be sacrificed on you, O Messenger of God
> With your death things have come to an end
> Which could not end thus with the death of any other person
> The process of prophethood has come to an end
> News of the Unseen have ceased,
> Revelations from Almighty have ceased

You gave a message of hope to the people
You showed them the right path
You established a new order
You are the saviour of humanity
You established equality among the people
You ushered in a revolution
You were a guide when alive
You would be a guide even after death
If you had not ordered patience in hour of grief
I would have shed tears of blood from my eyes
The entire world is dark without you
Your passing away is a great loss
But we resign ourselves to the will of God
From God you came, and to God you have returned,
May your soul rest in peace in proximity to God."

Election of Hadrat Abu Bakr as the Caliph : After the death of the Holy Prophet when his body was still to be buried, the Ansars met at Saqifa Bani Saada to urge that the successor to the Holy Prophet should be chosen out of them. When the Muhajirin came to know of this gathering Hadrat. Abu Bakr, Hadrat Umar and some other Quraish leaders attended the meeting. The. Ansars demanded that the caliph should be elected out of them. When the Quraish made a counter claim, the Ansars suggested that one Amir be elected from among the Ansars and another Amir from among the Muhajirin. The Muhajirin contended that such dual caliphate would lead to disunity in the ranks of the Muslims which would be against the interests of Islam. After a good deal of discussion, the Ansars gave way and Hadrat Abu Bakr from among the Muhajirin was elected as the Caliph.

Hadrat Ali's Reaction : In Nahj-ul-Balagha we come across certain passages which indicate the reaction of Hadrat Ali to the election of Hadrat. Abu Bakr as the Caliph. When the meeting at Saqifa Bani Saada was brought to the notice of Hadrat Ali by someone, Hadrat Ali asked him as to what did the Ansar ask for. He was told that the Amir should be elected from them and if the Muhajirin also desired the office, one Amir might be elected from the Ansar and one from the Muhajirin. Thereupon Hadrat Ali said, "Was it not brought to their notice that the Holy Prophet had willed that after him the Ansar should be well-treated and if they made any lapse it should be overlooked Hadrat Ali was asked how did this will establish that the Caliph was not to be elected from among the Ansars. Hadrat Ali said that if the Ansars were to have the caliphate, there was no point in asking those in power to pay due regard to the Ansars. Hadrat Ali then enquired as to what argument the Muhajirin had advanced in support of their claim to the caliphate. He was told that the Muhajirin based their claim on the ground that they belonged to the tree to which the Holy Prophet belonged. Thereupon Hadrat Ali said, "What a pity that they look to the tree, but overlook its fruit". The implication was that the Muhajirin should have offered the caliphate to him and not to any one else.

In a passage in Nahj-ul-Balagha, Hadrat Ali is said to have expressed his reaction to the election of Hadrat. Abu Bakr in the following terms:

> "The son of Abu Quhafa has assumed the mantle of the caliphate forcibly although he knew that I was essential for the caliphate as the handle is for the grinding stone which moves it. In Islamic learning I excel every one else and the caliphate should have come to me as a matter of course. At this disregard of my right I became confused. I began to think whether I should assert my claim or whether I should practice forbearance and patience. After a good deal of thinking I decided to adopt the later course. "

Offer of Allegiance : After Hadrat. Abu Bakr had been elected as the caliph, Ibn. Abbas and Abu Sufyan approached Hadrat Ali and offered him allegiance as the caliph. Hadrat Ali did not accept the offer on the ground that this would create dissensions among the Muslims. From a passage in Nahj-ul-Balagha wherein Hadrat Ali is reported to have expressed his feelings at this stage in the following terms:

> "If I say something about the caliphate the people would say that I am ambitious for power. If I remain silent there are people who would say that I am afraid of death. I have suffered many wrongs. The people should have known that the son of Abu Talib is as much fond of death as the infant is fond of the milk of its mother. My silence is because of the secret which I alone know. If I reveal the secret you will tremble and shudder as the strings binding a vessel shake when the vessel is lowered in the well."

Property at Fidak : After the conquest of Khyber, the Jews of Fidak, a neighbouring settlement, had surrendered without any fight. They were offered the same terms as the Jews of Khyber. The Holy Prophet took over the property of the Jews at Fidak in his personal custody and the income from the property was earmarked by the Holy Prophet for meeting his household expenses and for looking after the needy and the wayfarer. After the demise of the Holy Prophet, Hadrat Ali lodged a claim before Hadrat Abu Bakr for the transfer of the property at Fidak to him. Hadrat Abu Bakr did not accept the claim on the ground that according to a tradition of the Holy Prophet, prophets leave no inheritance and whatever they leave belongs to the community as a whole. Hadrat Abu Bakr declared that the property in question would remain in his custody but he would utilise the income therefrom for the same purposes as was the practice of the Holy Prophet. As a part of the income would be earmarked for meeting the expenses of the household of the Holy Prophet, Hadrat Fatima and Hadrat Ali would have their due share This decision did not satisfy Hadrat Fatima and Hadrat Ali.

Activities of Hadrat Ali during the Caliphate of Hadrat Abu Bakr : From the source books that have come down to us, we do not have a proper account of the activities of Hadrat Ali during the caliphate of Hadrat Abu Bakr. Unfortunately most of the accounts available are coloured because of sectarian and partisan considerations. It appears that Hadrat Ali did not take the oath of allegiance to Hadrat Abu Bakr for some time and he remained aloof from the state politics. It appears that after the death of Hadrat Fatima, Hadrat Abu Bakr tried to console Hadrat Ali in his grief and win over his goodwill. It appears that Hadrat Ali took the oath of allegiance to Hadrat Abu Bakr some time after the death of Hadrat Fatima and got reconciled to him. When Hadrat Abu Bakr died Hadrat Ali in the funeral oration highly praised Hadrat Abu Bakr. This shows that in the later part of the caliphate of Hadrat Abu Bakr the relationship between Hadrat. Abu Bakr and Hadrat Ali was cordial. Hadrat Ali however did not take any part in the apostasy wars that were fought during the caliphate of Hadrat Abu Bakr. It appears that Hadrat Ali during the period confined his activities to domestic affairs and religious pursuits.

Death of Hadrat Fatima : Hadrat Fatima took the death of the Holy Prophet to heart and she passed away in early 633 C. E., barely six months after the passing away of the Holy Prophet. She was only twenty-nine years old at the time of her death. Her marriage lasted for short period of eight or nine years only. During this period she gave birth to five children, three sons and two daughters. Her three sons were Hassan, Hussain, and Mohsin. Mohsin died during infancy. Hassan was about seven years old while Hussain was about six years old at the time of her death

Hadrat Ali's Grief : Hadrat Ali was much grieved at the death of Hadrat Fatima. Her passing away soon after the death of the Holy Prophet was a great blow for Hadrat Ali. He felt disconsolate. He poured his grief in the following elegiac verses"

> "Afflicted as I feel
> With many a wordly disease.
> Verily, men in this world
> Would suffer as long as they live

In this vale of tears and sorrow
Verily, after the demise of the Holy Prophet
Fatima's loss has shown
That friends do not last forever."

In this hour of grief, Hadrat Ali addressed the soul of the Holy Prophet in the following terms:

"O Messenger of God please accept my greetings and the greetings from your daughter who has hastened to join you. O Prophet of God my patience has been exhausted at her death. I am most distressed and disconsolate. At your death I suppressed my grief with great difficulty. I laid you in the grave with my own hands. Verily, from God you came and to God you have returned. We all belong to God and to Him we have to return. Fatima was a trust with me which has now been taken away from me. My state of affairs will be told to you by your daughter. Please do enquire about me from her. Much time has not elapsed to your death and the memory of your passing away is very much alive with me. I pay my greetings and respects to you as I can expect relief in my distress only from you. If I move away from your grave, it will not be because of any indifferences on my part. And if I stay here, it will not be so because of having lost confidence in the promise that God has made to those who are patient. "

Hadrat Ali used to visit the grave of Hadrat Fatima frequently and used to write verses to express his grief. On one occasion he wrote:

"O thou grave, to thee I resort
For paying homage to thee.
O thou, the repository of my beloved
Thou answer me not
O thou beloved tomb, what ails thee
Thou respondeth not to my supplications.
Art thou, out of humour,
Because of the love that I bear thee. "

The Married Life : The married life of Hadrat Ali and Hadrat Fatima did not last beyond nine years. It was a happy union. Nevertheless there were differences between the pair occasionally. Once, after having quarrelled with Hadrat Fatima, Hadrat Ali went to the mosque and lay on bare earth. That made the Holy Prophet call Hadrat Ali by the appellation of "Abu Turab"— Father of the earth. At one time, Hadrat Ali entertained the idea of marrying a daughter of Abu Jahl. Hadrat Fatima complained to the Holy Prophet. The Holy Prophet felt annoyed and while addressing the people in the mosque he said that verily, Fatima was part and parcel of him and that if All wanted to marry the daughter of Abu Jahl, it was open to him to do so, but he should divorce Fatima in the first instance for the daughter of the Prophet and the daughter of Abu Jahl, could not live under the same roof. Thereupon Hadrat Ali dropped the idea of marrying the daughter of Abu Jahl. There were some temperamental differences between Hadrat Ali and Hadrat Fatima and the Holy Prophet always counselled Hadrat Fatima to fall in line with the wishes of her husband for after her father he was the best of men.

Hadrat Fatima Zahra—an Assessment : Hadrat Fatima Zahra is regarded as one of the four perfect women of all times, the other three women being Aishah, the wife of the Pharaoh of Egypt who mothered Moses, Mary, the mother of Jesus Christ, and Hadrat Khadija, the first wife of the Holy Prophet of Islam, and the mother of Hadrat Fatima Zahra. One day Hadrat Fatima enquired of the Holy Prophet why she was called Fatima. He said that it was so because fire would not touch her soul. She was also called "Batool" because she devoted herself all out to Allah and fervently followed the dictates of the Holy Prophet (PBUH). Hadrat Fatima resembled the Holy Prophet in countenance, in elegance of speech and in general deportment. Whenever Hadrat Fatima paid a visit to the Holy Prophet, he would kiss her on the forehead and would make her sit on his seat. He would say, "Fatima is part of me and whoever angers her, angers me, and whoever injures her, injures me ". It was customary for the Holy Prophet that when he went on a journey the last person of whom he took leave was Hadrat Fatima and when he returned from the journey the first person he would see was Hadrat Fatima. When the Holy Prophet was about to die, Hadrat Fatima visited him. The Holy Prophet whispered to her something that made her weep. Then he again whispered something and Hadrat Fatima laughed. She was asked what made her weep and laugh in succession. She did not disclose the secret, but later, after the passing away of the Holy Prophet, Hadrat. Aishah asked her about it and she said that she had wept on being informed of the impending end of the Holy Prophet but laughed on his assurance that she was to join him soon.

When the Holy Prophet died, the whole world became dark for her. She wept and mourned the death of the Holy Prophet in pathetic verses. She said:

> "It is not wondrous that whoever
> Smells the fragrance of Muhammad's tomb
> Will never smell another perfume.

Destiny hurt me with a bereavement
So sad and so dark,
That if it had fallen on the days
They would have been turned into eternal nights."

Oration on the Death of Hadrat Abu Bakr : When Hadrat Abu Bakr died in 634 C. E. Hadrat Ali delivered an oration which was not only a faithful summing up of the character and personality of Hadrat. Abu Bakr but was also a masterpiece of oratory. The speech has been preserved and quoted hereunder in full

"Mercy of God on you O Abu Bakr.'

You were an affectionate Companion and friend of the Prophet of Allah, a source of joy to him, and he who knew his secrets, and enjoyed the privilege of being consulted by him. You were the first person to embrace Islam, you had the purest faith, and your belief in Islam was unshakable. Of all, you feared Allah most, and you were the source of the greatest advantage to his faith. You had been with the Prophet more than any one else and your love for Islam was superior to others. A blessing to the Companions, you were the best of associates. Master of many virtues, excelling others in accomplishments, and superior to all in position, you resembles the Holy Prophet more than any other person in the uprightness of character and conduct and in kindness and excellence your rank was noble, and your position sublime, and you enjoyed the greatest confidence of the Prophet. May God reward you for your services to Islam and the Prophet.

For the Prophet you were like his very sight and hearing. You corroborated the truth of his message at a time when everybody belied him, and so you were called As-Sadiq" (the Veracious) by Allah in His revelations. He says, "The one who came with the Truth and the one who corroborated the Truth—the one who came with the truth was Muhammad, and the one who corroborated the truth was Abu Bakr. You supported him when others had deserted and you remained firm in helping him in misfortunes when other had withdrawn their support. In the days of hardship you were his best Companion, you were the second of the two, and his companion in the cave. You were the person on whom God conferred tranquillity of mind. You were the only Companion of the Prophet in his migration to Medina and you were his Caliph among his followers and in the religion of Allah. You discharged the functions of the Khilafat in a most excellent manner at a moment when the people had taken to apostasy and exhibited much firmness in enforcing the commands of Allah as had never been exhibited by the Khalifa of any other prophet.

You rose to the occasion when your colleagues showed lassitude and you became bold when they exhibited weakness. You were strong when they were weak. You retained your adherence to the ways of the Prophet when others had deviated from them You were his true Caliph with no dispute of difference although this gave offence to hypocrites and umbrage to the infidels You stuck to the commands of. Allah when others showed cowardice You remained firm when others went astray

You had the lowest voice and the highest distinction. Your conversation was most salutary and your reasoning was forceful. Your silence was longest in duration and your speech was most eloquent. You were bravest among men. You were well informed about matters. Your action was most dignified. You were the leader of the believers. You came towards the faith when others were away from it. Indeed you acted like a kind father to the believers and your filial affection made them your children. You bore the heavy burden which they could not and you preferred to do what they had omitted. You preserved that what they had lost. You taught them what they knew not. You took the risk when they were helpless. You did not lose patience when they were impatient.

You redressed the grievances of those who asked for justice. They turned to you for guidance and you guided them to success. They got through you what they had never dreamt of. For the infidels you were a source of terrible punishment and great fear. For the believers you were all kindness, affection and protection.

You fed in the atmosphere of piety, you attained its noble reward and won in superiority. Your argument was never weak and your judgement was never faulty. You were never guilty of cowardice and your heart was never crooked or misdirected. You were like a rock which stands firm in the face of hard blows of dashing winds and waves. You were, as the Prophet of Allah has said, the most generous of men in friendship and in giving money. Again, as he said, you were weak in body, but strong in enforcing the commands of Allah You were humble in your manners but dignified in the estimation of God. You were great in the eyes of men and you commanded respect with them. No one could even as much as wink at you, nor could any one taunt you. You were kind to all and partial to none. The weak and the humble were strong with you as you made secure their rights. The strong were weak and humble with you as you made them surrender the rights of others. No matter those who were near you and those who were far from you were all equal. Those who obeyed and feared. Allah were nearest to you. Your dignity lay in righteousness, truth and benevolence. Your word was imperative and definite. Your commad was mild and cautious. Your Judgement was fair and wise. You extirpated evil and made way for the truth clear. You solved difficulties. You extinguished the fires of evil and discord.

You brought moderation to the faith, strength to belief, firmness to Islam and the Muslims and triumph to the command of Allah You were a source of grief to the infidels because of your extraordinary qualities. You have created difficulties for your successors who would have to work hard to maintain the standard set by you.

Evidently, you attained a high position in doing good. You are far above mourning and lamentation. Mourning for you is great in the. Heaven. Your death has broken the backbone of the people, and we recite the verse 'From God you came, and to God you have returned '. We submit to what has been ordained by Allah and are ready to obey. His commands by Allah never shall the Muslims suffer after the death of the Prophet, a calamity greater than your death.

You were a source of honour, protection and support to the faith and for the believers you were a stronghold and a place of refuge. For the hypocrites you were all strictness and terror. May Allah take you near to your Prophet and may He not deprive us of the fruits of your efforts and may we not be misled after you. We recite once again 'From God you came and to God you have returned " May your soul rest in peace.'"

Chief Justice

Nomination of Hadrat Umar as the Caliph : Before his death bed, Hadrat Abu Bakr nominated Hadrat Umar as his successor.

Hadrat Ali not only took the oath of allegiance to Hadrat Umar but also married his daughter Umm Kulthum to Hadrat Umar and quite contrary to the biased allegations perfect cordiality prevailed between Hadrat Ali and Hadrat Umar. Hadrat Ali held the office of the chief justice. He acted as the principal counsellor of Hadrat Umar. He acted as chief secretary as well. The services of Hadrat Ali were highly appreciated by Hadrat Umar. In these circumstances the views expressed in some quarters that Hadrat Umar was the worst enemy of Hadrat Ali is far from truth and cannot be accepted.

Battle of Yermuk : During the time of Hadrat. Abu Bakr the Muslims captured a greater part of Syria including Damascus. When Hadrat Umar became the caliph the Byzantine made strong preparations and concentrated a very large army at Yermuk with a view to expelling the Muslims from Syria. The Muslims had to evacuate Damascus and the cities in northern Syria with a view to facing the Byzantines in battle at Yermuk in southern Syria. It was a critical state of affairs for the Muslims. At this juncture Hadrat Umar was of the view that he should himself go to Syria to command the Muslim forces. Hadrat Umar sought the advice of Hadrat Ali on the point Hadrat Ali advised in the following terms:

> "God is the protector of the Muslims. He guards their secrets God helped the Muslims when they were few in number and could not face the enemy. God

> defended them when they could not defend themselves. When God helped the Muslims in the early years we can depend on His help even now when we have gained in numbers. God is alive and would never die. We are fighting in His cause and we should have perfect faith that He would help us If you yourself go to fight against the Byzantines and God forbid are defeated that will cause a great confusion and would demoralise the Muslims. That would create a precarious situation for the Muslims in the areas bordering Syria. The proper course for you would be to remain in Medina and direct the operations from there You may place a seasoned General in command of the Muslim forces in Syria God willing, the Muslims would be victorious "

Hadrat Umar acted on the advice of Hadrat Ali and the Muslims won an astounding victory at the battle of Yermuk.

Conquest of Jerusalem : After the battle of Yermuk the Muslims won other battles in Syria and the Byzantines were forced to evacuate Syria. The Muslim forces attacked Jerusalem. The Lord Bishop of Jerusalem proposed to surrender Jerusalem in case Hadrat Umar, the Caliph of the Muslims, came to take over the city himself. Some of the companions of Hadrat Umar advised that the Caliph should not go to Jerusalem and the Christians after having been defeated could not dictate terms. When the advice of Hadrat Ali was sought he said:

> I had advised you not to go to Syria when the war was imminent for in the case of defeat that would have led to demoralisation on the part of the Muslims. Now that God has rewarded the Muslims with victory and the Christians desire that the Caliph should come himself to get the surrender of Jerusalem. I would advise that the Caliph should go to Jerusalem, for he will be going there as a victor. The presence of the Caliph of the Muslims in Syria would add to the prestige of the Muslims and would be instrumental in converting the Christians to Islam. Jerusalem is not merely sacred to the Christians, it is sacred to the Muslims as well. It was from Jerusalem that the Holy Prophet ascended the. Heavens and the sanctity of the place demands that its occupation should be taken by no one other then the Caliph of the Muslims"

Hadrat Umar accepted the advice of Hadrat Ali and personally went to Jerusalem to obtain the surrender of the city.

Ornaments of Kaaba : In the Holy Kaaba there were many ornaments which had been gifted by the devotees from time to time and embellished the walls of the House of God. Hadrat Umar was of the opinion that all such ornaments should be removed from the

Holy Kaaba and used for the purpose of the state. Hadrat Umar sought the advice of Hadrat Ali, who advised as follows:

> "When Mecca was conquered the Holy Prophet demolished the idols in the Holy Kaaba, but he did not touch the ornaments which embellished the walls of the Holy Kaaba. If there had been anything objectionable to the decoration of the walls of the Holy Kaaba, the Holy Prophet would have removed them. As he did not do so, it means that there is no objection to such ornamentation. Now if such ornaments are removed it would mean that you are depriving the House of God of something to which the Holy Prophet had not objected. I would not advise you to do anything of which the Holy Prophet was aware but chose to take no action"

Hadrat Umar accepted the advice of Hadrat Ali and let the ornaments remain in the Holy Kaaba.

The Hijri Era : In the time of Hadrat Umar it was felt that the Muslims should have a calendar of their own. The question that arose for consideration was as to form which event such era of the Muslims should begin. Many suggestions were made in this connection. When Hadrat Umar sought the advice of Hadrat Ali he advised as follows:

> "The migration is a turning point in the history of Islam Prior to migration, the Muslims were a persecuted people and they had to struggle for survival. It was only after the migration that the Muslims came into their own and were able to establish a polity which became a starting point for the consolidation of Islam. In the defence of Islam the Ansars have played an important role and as such the new era should be such wherein both the Muhajirs and the Ansars can share. As such the new Muslim calendar should begin with the 'Hijra, the day when the Holy Prophet first set his foot in Medina."

Hadrat Umar accepted the advice of Hadrat Ali and the Muslims calendar had its start with the migration of the Holy Prophet to Medina.

Counsels in Judicial Matters : Hadrat Umar frequently consulted Hadrat Ali in judicial matters and the advice given by Hadrat Ali was invariably followed. Once some persons while in the state of "Ihram" ate eight eggs of ostrichs. The point that arose for consideration was as to how these men should atone for the wrong they had done Hadrat Umar sought the advice of Hadrat Ali Hadrat Ali advised that these persons should mate eight camels with eight she camels and their offsprings should be sacrificed.

Once a mad woman was found guilty of adultery Hadrat Umar was inclined to punish the woman by being stoned to death. Hadrat Umar sought the advice of Hadrat Ali. He said that a mad person who had no control over the senses could not be declared guilty. The woman was accordingly let off.

A woman gave birth to a child six months after her marriage. She was accused of adultery. The case was referred to Hadrat Ali. Hadrat Ali advised that as there was no evidence of adultery and the woman could not be punished merely on the ground that she had given birth to a child six months after the marriage. Hadrat Ali observed that according to the Holy Quran the period from conception to the weaning of the child had been stated at thirty months and at another place the period of the weaning of the child after birth had been stated to be two years. This means that though the normal period for the birth of a child is nine months in some cases a child can be born after six months as well.

In the Shariah there were no specific orders for punishment in the case of drinking. The usual practice heretofore was that men found guilty of drinking were awarded forty lashes. It was found that this punishment was not deterrent. Hadrat Umar sought the counsel of Hadrat Ali. Hadrat Ali observed that in the case of calumny a punishment of eighty lashes was prescribed. When a man drank he lost his senses and could indulge in calumny. Hadrat Ali advised that for drinking the punishment should be the same as for the offence of calumny that is eighty lashes. This advice was accepted and it was laid down that henceforward the punishment for drinking would be eighty lashes.

In view of the soundness of his judicial opinions, Hadrat Ali was held by Hadrat Umar to be the best judge Hadrat Umar paid the highest tribute to Hadrat Ali when he said "But for All, Umar would have been lost."

Claim to Property : In the time of Hadrat Abu Bakr, Hadrat Ali and Hadrat Fatima had lodged a claim for the Holy Prophet's property at Fadak. Hadrat. Abu Bakr had not accepted the claim on the ground that according to a tradition of the Holy Prophet, prophets have no heirs. In the time of Hadrat Umar, Hadrat Ali lodged a claim again for the Holy Prophet's property at Fadak and Medina. Hadrat Umar upheld the decision of Hadrat. Abu Bakr with regard to the property at Fadak. He, however, transferred the Holy Prophet's property in Medina to Hadrat Ali. Hadrat Umar held that in Medina the Holy Prophet had fraternised with Hadrat Ali and as such Hadrat Ali had a share in such property. The property in Medina was transferred to Hadrat Ali on the condition that after keeping his share Hadrat Ali should spend the rest of the income from such property in the way the Holy Prophet used to do. Hadrat Umar held that the case of the property at Fadak was different. It belonged exclusively to the Prophet and was marked for public purposes in which Hadrat Ali had no fraternal share.

Hadrat Ali's Observation on the Death of Hadrat Umar : When Hadrat Umar passed away, Hadrat Ali mourned his death in the following terms:

> "May God bless the soul of Hadrat Umar'. He made things straight. He cured the malady. He enforced the Shan'ah. He established law and order. He was noble, virtuous and free from faults. He availed of what was good of the caliphate and avoided what was evil thereof. He obeyed God and served His cause well. After his passing away the people have taken to different paths where those who have strayed cannot find the way and those who have followed the straight way cannot long keep it."

Election of Hadrat Uthman as the Caliph : At his death bed, Hadrat Umar nominated a board of six members consisting of Zubayr b. Awwam, Saad b. Abi Waqqas,. Abdur Rahman b. Auf, Talha b Ubaidullah, Hadrat Ali b. Abu Talib and Hadrat Uthman b. Affan. During his lifetime, the Holy Prophet had given tidings of paradise to ten persons. The six persons nominated by Hadrat Umar were the survivors of the original ten persons who had been given the tidings of paradise during their lifetime. The three persons out of the blessed ten who had died by this time were Hadrat. Abu Bakr, Hadrat Umar, Hadrat Ubaidullah b Jarrah and Hadrat Saeed b Zaid, while the tenth one was Hadrat Umar himself. These six persons were required to elect one of themselves as the Caliph. When the board met, it ran into difficulties in electing the Caliph. Out of the six members, Zubayr withdrew his candidature in favour of Hadrat Uthman and Saad b. Abi Waqas withdrew his candidature in favour of Abdur Rahman b. Auf. This left three candidates in the field. Out of these three candidates Abdur Rahman b. Auf decided to withdraw, leaving two candidates namely Hadrat Uthman and Hadrat Ali. Abdur Rahman was appointed as the arbitrator to choose between the remaining two candidates, namely Hadrat Uthman and Hadrat Ali. Both Hadrat Uthman and Hadrat Ali undertook to abide by the decision of the arbitrator. Abdur Rahman b. Auf deliberated over the matter, considered the relative merits of the candidates and also consulted the Companions. After such consultation,. Abdur Rahman formed the impression that the majority of the people favoured the election of Hadrat Uthman. Contacting the two candidates separately he put to them the question whether they would follow in the footsteps of the previous Caliphs. Hadrat Ali said that he would do so as far as possible subject to his best judgement in the light of the Quran and Sunnah. Hadrat Uthman replied to the question in the affirmative without any reservation. Thereupon, Abdur Rahman gave his verdict in favour of Hadrat Uthman, who was acclaimed as the Caliph and the people offered the oath of allegiance to him. Hadrat Ali offered the oath of allegiance to Hadrat Uthman. In Nahj-ul-Balagha, there is a short statement of Hadrat Ali which shows his reaction to the election of Hadrat Uthman. Hadrat Ali is reported to have said:

"All know that in the matter of the Caliphate, I am more qualified and deserving than any other person Even though my claims have been ignored I will be motivated by considerations of selflessness in the interests of the solidarity of the Muslim Ummah. I acknowledge the new Caliph in the interest of the Muslim community, regardless of whatever hardship I may have to endure. "

Activities of Hadrat Ali during the caliphate of Hadrat Uthman : During the caliphate of Hadrat Umar, Hadrat Ali held the dual offices of chief justice as well as chief secretary. Hadrat Uthman conferred the office of the chief secretary on his cousin Marwan Hadrat Ali remained as the chief justice. He continued to be a member of the Majlisi-Shura. The accounts that have come down to us are mostly silent about the activities of Hadrat Ali. In the various history books we come across the judgements that Hadrat Ali delivered during the caliphate of Hadrat Umar and marvel at the highly developed sense of judgement of Hadrat Ali. But we have not come across any judgement delivered by Hadrat Ali during the caliphate of Hadrat Uthman though Hadrat Ali is said to have held the office of the chief Justice during this period. Although the Hashimites and the Umayyads belonged to the same stock there was rivalry between the two houses. After the death of Abdul Muttalib, power passed on to Umayyads who enjoyed great wealth. Then the Holy Prophet declared his mission, the Umayyads led the Quraish in hostility against the Holy Prophet and the Muslims. The Umayyads accepted Islam after the conquest of Mecca in 680 C. E. Thereafter the Umayyads acknowledged the superiority of the Hashimites. This position lasted for a short period of two years only as the Holy Prophet died in 632 C. E. Hadrat. Abu Bakr and Hadrat Umar who were elected as the Caliphs thereafter did not belong either to the Hashimites or Umayyads section of the Quraish. Hadrat Uthman was an Umayyad and during his caliphate the Umayyads gained in power at the cost of the Hashimites.

There is a passage in Nahj-ul-Balagha wherein Hadrat Ali complains that the Umayyads were withholding from him what was his due as the camelman withholds the like of the she-camel from her young one. It appears that during the caliphate of Hadrat Uthman, Hadrat Ali led a more or less retired life and did not take any active part in politics. By this time Hadrat Ali had four wives and a number of children. During this period Hadrat Ali devoted most of his time to religious exercise and domestic activities. After the death of the Persian emperor Yezdjurd his daughters were taken captive and brought to Medina. When put to open auction the oldest princess slapped the auctioner on the face. Hadrat Ali advised that it was not proper that such distinguished persons should be put to open auction. The proper line of action was that the standard price should be fixed and whosoever paid the amount should get the princess. Hadrat Ali purchased two princess. He married one of them to his son Hussain and the other to his step son

Muhammad bin. Abu Bakr. This shows that by this time the financial condition of Hadrat Ali had considerably improved.

Abu Dhar Ghifari : Hadrat Uthman known by the epithet of "Ghani" was a rich man. Hadrat Umar had placed restrictions on the purchase of lands by the. Arabs in conquered territories Hadrat Uthman removed these restrictions, with the result, the Arabs became big landlords. Islam stood for an egalitarian society wherein all people were equal politically as well as economically. On account of the liberal policies adopted by Hadrat Uthman, a moneyed class sprang up which took to a luxurious way of life. Men of this class built palatial buildings in Medina. In Syria the Governor Muawiyyah, a cousin of Hadrat Uthman, adopted a princely way of life. In Damishq Abu Dhar Ghifari, an eminent Companion vehemently criticised the luxurious way of life of Muawiyyah, and the men around him. Muawiyyah complained to Hadrat Uthman and Hadrat Uthman asked Muawiyyah to send Abu Dhar Ghifari to Medina. In Medina,. Abu Dhar Ghifari criticised Hadrat Uthman for his economic policies. Hadrat Uthman shifted Abu Dhar Ghifan to the interior of the desert at some distance from Medina. When. Abu Dhar Ghifan left Medina, Hadrat Ali addressed him in the following terms:

> "O Abu Dhar, you have suffered because of your goodwill for God. Therefore you should hope for His mercy. Those people are afraid of you because of their love for the world. You are afraid of these people because of your faith. Give the world to the people for which they are afraid of you. Escape from them with the thing of which you are afraid of them. Withhold your faith from them and do not covet what is dear to them as compared with faith in them. Hereafter, verily you will stand to profit while they will be at loss O. Abu Dhar bear in mind that the people may or may not like you but you should not abandon what you deem to be the truth. These people will befriend you only when you befriend their world. That will be a great price for you to pay. Therefore, there should be no regret when they turn you out of their world. A better Hereafter awaits you."

The Revolt : During the first six years of the caliphate of Hadrat Uthman the process of foreign conquests went apace and the people were satisfied. During the later part of the caliphate of Hadrat Uthman, the process of foreign conquests came to a grinding halt and discontentment began to mount among the people. The government of Hadrat Uthman was accused of nepotism, corruption and inefficiency. A crisis was reached in 656 C. E. when the mal-contents from Egypt, Kufa and Basra marched to Medina to demand the redress of their grievances. A body of the mal-contents approached Hadrat Ali and requested him to bring their grievances to the notice of the Caliph. Hadrat Ali visited Hadrat Uthman and said:

> "O Caliph, the people bid me expostulate with you, yet what can I say to you, son in-law as you were of the Holy Prophet and his bosom friend and you already know what I know. The way lies plain and wide before you but perhaps your eyes are closed and you cannot see it. If blood is once shed it will not cease to flow till Day of Judgements. The right will be blotted and treason would rage like the foaming waves of the sea."

Hadrat Ali observed that the complaint of that was the Caliph had appointed his close relatives to the highest offices under the State. Hadrat Uthman stated that if he had appointed some of his relatives they were competent people who had delivered goods. He added that Muawiyyah had been appointed as the Governor of Syria by Hadrat Umar and not by him. Hadrat Ali said that Hadrat Umar kept the Governors under strict control but under him the Governors had become independent and they were doing what pleased· them. Hadrat Uthman promised that he would make the necessary amends.

Inquiry into Complaints : Hadrat Uthman deputed special emissaries to the provinces and inquired into the complaints of the people. Muhammad b Muslim was deputed to Kufa, Usama b Zaid to Basra,. Abdul Rahman b Umar to Syria and Ammar b Yaser to Egypt. Muhammad b Mussailma, Usama b Zaid and Abdullah Rahman b Umar reported that the complaints of the people were frivolous and there was nothing wrong with the administration. Ammar b Yaser formed the view that the complaints of the people were genuine and instead of returning to Medina he chose to stay in Egypt. On the occasion of the Hajj in 655 C. E. Hadrat Uthman asked those who had any grievances to come to Mecca when their complaints would be looked in. He asked the Governors of the various provinces to come to Mecca well prepared to meet the charges levelled by the people against the provincial administration. No complaints were made on the occasion of the Hajj keeping in view the sanctity of the occasion. When Hadrat Uthman returned from the pilgrimage the mal-contents from various provinces gathered in large numbers in Medina. These people contacted Hadrat Ali to use his influence with the malcontents to disperse. Hadrat Ali approached the people and they complained that the previous instructions issued by the Caliph to the Governor of Egypt had no effect and they would not disperse unless the Governor was removed. Thereupon Hadrat Uthman agreed to pass orders for the removal of Abdullah b. Abi Sarh, the Governor of Egypt. This satisfied the malcontents and they dispersed

Assassination of Hadrat Uthman : After a few days the rebels returned to Medina again. They said that they had caught a slave of the Caliph who was carrying a letter to the Governor of Egypt asking him to execute the ring leaders of the rebels. The rebels brought this letter to Hadrat Ali, who took it to Hadrat Uthman Hadrat Uthman acknowledged about the contents of the letter. According to one account the letter was in the handwriting of Marwan, secretary to the Caliph. The letter remained a mystery, but the Caliph undertook to dismiss the officials at fault within three days No action was taken within the stipulated period and on the following Friday, Hadrat Uthman addressed the congregation. The Caliph criticised the rebels for having revolted against his authority and held that thereby they had invited the wrath of God and in the. Hereafter they would be doomed to hell. That led to a great uproar. The rebels threw stones at Hadrat Uthman who was wounded and was carried home in an unconscious state Hadrat Ali visited the Caliph and tried to avert the crisis. The crisis deepened and the rebels blockaded the house of the Caliph. The siege lasted for some days. A rumour was circulated that the Caliph has asked the provincial Governors to send some troops to Medina. When the rebels came to know that troops might soon arrive in Medina they broke into the house of the Caliph and assassinated him. That was a tragedy too deep for tears which cast a dismal shadow on the subsequent history of Islam.

FIVE

FOURTH CALIPH

ELECTED CALIPH

Period of Anarchy : After the assassination of Hadrat Uthman a state of anarchy came to prevail in the affairs of Medina. There was no government. The rebels let loose a reign of terror and the peaceful citizens of Medina chose to remain indoors. The rebels were divided into three groups, namely the Egyptian, the Kufans, and the Basntes. Although they had made common cause in the assassination of Hadrat Uthman, they differed among themselves on other points. After four days, the rebels decided to return to their homes but they felt that in their interest it was necessary that the new Caliph should be chosen before they left Medina. In the matter of the election of the Caliph, there were differences among the rebels. One group favoured the election of Hadrat Ali, another group favoured the election of Hadrat Talha and yet another group favoured the election of Hadrat Zubayr. It appears that at this stage the people of Medina themselves had lost the initiative and they were completely at the mercy of the rebels. Among the rebels themselves there was no outstanding leader whose opinion could prevail. Things were in a state of complete confusion.

No Candidate for Election : The Egyptians waited on Hadrat Ali and requested him to accept the office of the Caliph. He declined the offer and said that someone else should be elected as the Caliph. He assured them that whosoever was elected as the Caliph he would pay allegiance to him. Some prominent Companions of the Holy Prophet also waited on Hadrat Ali and tried to persuade him to accept the office. Hadrat Ali thanked them for their regard of him but did not agree to accept the office. On the refusal of Hadrat

Ali the rebels contacted Hadrat Zubayr and Hadrat Talha offered them the Caliphate. Like Hadrat Ali they also refused to accept the office. The rebels next approached the Ansars and requested them to choose a Caliph from among themselves. They too refused the offer. They were of the opinion that in the presence of Hadrat Ali no one else deserved to be elected as the Caliph. The rebels waited on Hadrat Ali again and tried to persuade him to reconsider his decision. He maintained his previous decision and persisted in declining the offer. The rebels next approached Saad b. Abi Waqas, Saeed b Zaid and Abdullah b Umar to accept the caliphate. All of them refused to accept the office. There was now a complete deadlock in the matter of the election of the Caliph. The rebels thereupon gave the ultimatum that in case the people of Medina chose the Caliph within the next twenty-four hours they would be forced to take some drastic action.

Election of Hadrat Ali : In order to resolve the deadlock, all the Muslims assembled in the Prophet's mosque. The people raised solgans in favour of Hadrat Ali. The leader of the Egyptian rebels took over the stage. He said they had risen against the caliphate of Hadrat Uthman because the administration had become loose and the grievances of the people had piled up. He added that it was necessary that the Muslims should choose a new Caliph in succession to Hadrat Uthman and the man they should choose for the office should be conspicuous for his learning, bravery, piety and nearness to the Holy Prophet. He observed that Hadrat Ali was the only person who fulfilled these qualities. Thereafter he went to Hadrat Ali, requested him to stretch his hand. When Hadrat Ali stretched his hand the people rushed to offer allegiance to him This process went on for several hours and the people vociferously welcomed the election of Hadrat Ali as the Caliph.

The Dissidents : Although Hadrat Ali was elected by an overwhelming majority there were some persons who abstained from offering him their allegiance. The Umayyads by and large abstained from participating in the process of election. After the assassination of Hadrat Uthman most of them had escaped to Syria. The few Umayyads who were still in Medina remained in their homes. Saad b. Abi Waqas did not offer any allegiance but he assured Hadrat Ali that he had no ill-will against him and his failure to take the oath of allegiance should not be construed as an act of any disloyalty to him. Abdullah b Umar abstained from offering allegiance, but he assured Hadrat Ali that no harm could be expected from him. The men of "Ahl-i-Safa" of the Sufi bent of mind abstained from offering allegiance as they were not interested in politics. Talha and Zubayr remained absent. There are some differences in the account pertaining to the allegiance of these two companions. According to one account they did not offer any allegiance to Hadrat Ali and slipped away from the city at the time when the other people had gathered in the mosque. According to another account the rebels fetched Hadrat Talha and Hadrat Zubayr to the mosque and made them offer allegiance to Hadrat Ali. According to one account the hand that Hadrat Talha offered in allegiance to Hadrat Ali was maimed and disfigured because of wounds received in various wars. This was regarded as a bad augury by some of the persons assembled in the mosque.

Address by Hadrat Ali : After his election, Hadrat Ali addressed the people. He said that he had no intention to accept the office of the Caliph but as the office had been forced on him he would do his best to discharge the duties of the office according to the commandments of God and the tradition of the Holy Prophet. He pointed out that a generation had passed since the demise of the Holy Prophet and during this period the Muslim polity had come to be plagued with dissensions and discord. He observed that the events that had culminated in the assassination of Hadrat Uthman were most deplorable and regrettable. He said that it would be his endeavour to purge Islam of all the evils from which it had come to suffer in the past. He made it clear that towards this end he would have to administer law and order with a stern hand. He warned all concerned that he would tolerate no sedition and all found guilty of subversive activities would be dealt with harshly. He advised the people to mend their ways and behave as true Muslims. Hadrat Ali was not the man to mince words. He felt disgusted with the state of political affairs and spoke in strong and bitter terms.

The Helplessness : The caliphate of Hadrat Ali had a shaky start. In spite of his determination to set things right, Hadrat Ali soon found that he was helpless and was the prisoner of forces which he could not control. When after his inaugural address Hadrat Ali was about to retire to his house the rebels approached him and said:

> "O, Caliph, beware that we are the people who would pursue things to their bitter end. We can turn things upside down and wreck regimes "

Hadrat Ali asked them not to indulge in such vainglorious boasts and should return to their camps. The rebels chose to remain quiet but Hadrat Ali could very well see a look of defiance in their eyes.

As Hadrat Ali came home, he felt very unhappy. The caliphate had taken long to come and when it came, it came in the wrong way. The caliphate had come to him as the gift of the rebels and he could not take any action against them. On the other hand, he was so helpless at the outset of his caliphate that he could not do anything against the wishes of the rebels.

At his house his son Imam Hassan and his cousin Abdullah b. Abbas advised him to leave Medina and retire to some place of safety in the desert. Their view was that he should let things settle down and in course of time the people would themselves come to him and assure him of their loyalty.

There was a good deal of weight in what Abdullah b. Abbas and Imam Hassan said but Hadrat Ali could not make up his mind to fall in line with the action proposed by them. Hadrat Ali, a man conspicuous for his valour, thought that it would be an act of cowardice on his part to run away from the office which he had once accepted. He said that he would face the situation, however grim, in complete trust in God.

The Controversy : Unfortunately, after the death of the Holy Prophet, the caliphate issue became a source of controversy among the Muslims and has led to sectarian differences thereby adversely affecting the solidarity of the Ummah. There is a school of thought which holds that Hadrat Ali alone had the right to succeed the Holy Prophet and that the three Caliphs—Hadrat. Abu Bakr, Hadrat Umarand Hadrat Uthman were usurpers. Another school of thought which commands majority does not subscribe to this view. We may examine some salient aspects of the issue.

Right to Succeed : The basic point for consideration is, whether any right in fact accrued to Hadrat Ali to succeed the Holy Prophet. It may be recalled that when Hadrat. Abu Bakr was deputed by the Holy Prophet as "Amir-ul-Hajj" (the Leader of the Pilgrimage), and the verses of the Holy Quran entitled "Declaration of Immunity" were revealed subsequently, Hadrat Ali was commissioned to proceed to Mecca to announce these verses to the people assembled on the occasion of the pilgrimage. Hadrat. Abu Bakr remained the "Amir-ul-Hajj" and he presided over all the ceremonies connected with the "Hajj" but the verses about the "Declaration of Immunity" were announced by Hadrat Ali. It was later clarified by the Holy Prophet that a divine message had to be communicated to the people either by himself personally or by a member of his family. That brings out the point that while a divine message could be communicated by a member of the household of the Holy Prophet alone, any other office could be held by any other person.

As the Holy Prophet was the last of the prophets and there was to be no prophet after him that was the end of the divine mission. As the divine mission came to an end with the death of the Holy Prophet, the grounds with reference to which Hadrat Ali could claim preferences in the matter of succession ceased to exist.

Will of the Holy Prophet : We have next to consider whether the Holy Prophet made any will about his succession. Everything about the activities of the Holy Prophet including the minutest details is fully documented. No will of the Holy Prophet is on record and as such it is a fact that the Holy Prophet made no will. It is alleged in some quarters that before his death the Holy Prophet had expressed the desire to record his will but Hadrat Umar frustrated the attempt by declaring that the Holy Quran was enough for them. Hadrat Aishah refuted this allegation and observed that the Holy Prophet did not express any desire to record his will.

It may be recalled that even during his illness the Holy Prophet attended the mosque on two occasions and addressed the people. On one occasion the reprimanded the people for their objection to the command of an expedition against Syria by Usama b Zaid. If the Holy Prophet, in spite of his illness, could advocate the cause of Usama's command, he could have advocate the cause of the succession of Hadrat Ali as well, if he had so desired.

Another point that arises for consideration in this respect is whether the failure to record the will was an omission or was it deliberate'? The Holy Prophet did not pass away suddenly. He had ample time to settle his affairs before his death. Even at the Farewell Pilgrimage three months before his death, he knew that his end was near. He had been sent by God to complete his mission. If the nomination of a successor was to be a part of the divine mission with which he had been entrusted, he would have nominated a successor to complete his mission. As he did not nominate a successor and as his mission had been completed, it means that the nomination of a successor was no part of his mission. After him whosoever was to succeed him was to be temporal ruler only, and the right to choose such ruler vested in the people. This means that the Holy Prophet did not nominate his successor deliberately. Obviously the intention was that the people should elect their leader themselves.

Allah Himself declared that He had chosen Islam as the religion for the people and the Muslims were the best community. It cannot, therefore, be said that what happened in the matter of succession was an omission on the part of the Holy Prophet or disinterestedness on the part of Allah (God forbid).

Will of Allah : It is our faith that all that happened had the sanction of Allah and was in accordance with His Will .This is evident from the fact that during the caliphates of Hadrat Abu Bakr and Hadrat Umar, extensive conquests were made which changed the course of history. It was nothing sort of a miracle that the Arabs of the desert overpowered the mighty kingdom of Persia in the east and the empire of the Byzantines in the west. This would not have been possible if the blessings of God were not with the regime which had come to be established after the death of the Holy Prophet. When God favoured these Caliphs, it hardly lies in the mouth of any one to say that they were usurpers.

Islamic Concept of Office : According to the traditions, the Holy Prophet said in definite terms that he who seeks an office does not deserve it. It is, therefore, difficult to believe that Hadrat Ali coveted the office of the caliphate at any stage. There are some passages in Nahj-ul-Balagha which show that Hadrat Ali did not covet the office but he held that the caliphate was his right. There is ample evidence in Nahj-ul-Balagha to the effect that Hadrat Ali felt embittered at the election of Hadrat Abu Bakr, Hadrat Umar or Hadrat Uthman. According to one passage, Hadrat Ali is reported to have said that the son of Abu Quhafa (Hadrat Abu Bakr) had worn the mantle of the caliphate forcibly, although he knew that he (Hadrat Ali) was as essential for the caliphate as the handle is necessary for moving the grinding stone. There is some confusion on the point whether Hadrat Ali considered that the caliphate was his right, or whether he considered himself to be the most deserving person to be the Caliph. If the Holy Prophet had nominated Hadrat Ali as his successor he would have automatically become the Caliph and question of election by the people would not have arisen. As the Holy Prophet had made no nomination, the Caliph had necessarily to be chosen by the people. Where the choice vested with the people, it was for the people to elect whosoever they deemed fit and no person can claim to have the right to be chosen. In the circumstances the position of Hadrat Ali vis a vis the caliphate is vague and it is not clear on what basis it can be held that Hadrat Ali had the right to be elected as the Caliph and that if any other person had been elected as the Caliph, his right had been usurped.

Relationship of Hadrat Ali with his Predecessors : It appears that Hadrat Ali did not take the oath of allegiance to Hadrat. Abu Bakr immediately. He, however, took the oath after sometime. In his oration at the funeral of Hadrat. Abu Bakr, Hadrat Ali spoke in glowing terms about Hadrat Abu Bakr both as a man and a Caliph. When Hadrat Abu Bakr nominated Hadrat Umar as his successor Hadrat Ali did not feel happy at the nomination. He, however, took the oath of allegiance to Hadrat Umar. Hadrat Ali even married his daughter to Hadrat Umar, and the relationship between Hadrat Ali and Hadrat Umar was throughout cordial. When Hadrat Uthman was elected as the caliph, Hadrat Ali took the oath of allegiance to him. When Hadrat Ali offered allegiance to his predecessors the implications is that he acknowledged their caliphate and waived his own right to the caliphate even if he had any claim. When Hadrat Ali himself acknowledged these Caliphs it is not clear how does it lie in the mouth of anyone to say that these Caliphs were usurpers.

Nature of the Issue : In our study of the issue of the caliphate, we have to consider the question of the nature of the issue. That question to be considered is whether the election of the Caliph is a religious or a political issue. The commandments of religion are contained in the Holy Quran and the Sunnah. There is no mention about the Caliph in the Holy Quran and the Sunnah. In the Holy Quran the word "Caliph" has been used with reference to men in general when he is said to be the Caliph of God. This means that the people in general are the Caliph of God. The Caliph to be the Head of the State is a political functionary only. Political issues must necessarily be limited to the milieu in which they arise and political issues cannot be kept alive for indefinite period. In Islam the State and the Church are not separate. This merely means that in an Islamic State the political affairs would be administered in accordance with the injunctions of Islam. It does not mean that every political issue would become a religious issue. A religious issue must be directly based on the Quran and the Sunnah and any political issue cannot become a part of religion. Election of a functionary is for a limited period and when that period is over all disputes about the election come to an end. Even if it is conceded that Hadrat Ali should have succeded the Holy Prophet in preference to any other person the controversy should have ceased with the close of the rule of the rightly-guided Caliphs. To keep this political issue alive for all times and make it a ground for sectarian differences does not appear to be in accordance with the spirit of Islam. Even if Hadrat Ali did not get the caliphate, he did get the caliphate after all and with his assumption of the caliphate the controversy about the validity or otherwise about the election of the previous Caliphs should have come to an end being time barred.

Vengeance for the Blood of Hadrat Uthman : After Hadrat Ali had assumed office the rebels left for their home towns. The departure of the rebels brought no peace to the city of Medina. The Umayyads who had consolidated their position in Syria raised the cry of vengeance for the blood of Hadrat Uthman. The blood-stained clothes of Hadrat Uthman and the fingers of his wife Naila which had been cut by the rioters while she defended her husband were exhibited in the mosque at Damascus. The Umayyads incited the emotions of the people to a high pitch and they declared with due solemnity that they would not rest content until the death of Hadrat Uthman had been avenged. The cry of the Umayyads raised in Damascus found its echo in Medina and Mecca as well and many persons in Medina and Mecca also joined the chorus for vengeance for the blood of Hadrat Uthman Talha and Zubayr, two prominent Companions who had taken the oath of allegiance of Hadrat Ali, supported the call for vengeance. Even Hadrat Aishah, the favourite wife of the Holy Prophet, joined the camp which raised the cry for vengeance.

Nature of the Crime : The assassination of Hadrat Uthman was a very tragic event in the annals of Islam. Particular sanctity is attached to the office of the Caliph and if the Caliphs were to be murdered in cold blood as in the case of Hadrat Uthman, that boded ill for the Muslim polity. According to the Islamic law the heirs of a dead person have the right to claim blood money (Qasas) for such murder. It is the obligation of the State to enforce such right. In view of this legal position the heirs of Hadrat Uthman had a prima facie case to claim vengeance for the murder of Hadrat Uthman. The law of Qasas applies in a normal case of murder when the person committing the murder can be apprehended. Where the case is complex and murder cannot be attributed to a particular person or persons, the law of Qasas would not apply in the conventional sense. The assassination of Hadrat Uthman was not a murder simpliciter; it was in fact a revolt and coup d'etat. The natural law is that where a revolt fails the rebels have to pay for such revolt with their lives. On the other hand where the revolt succeeds, the rebels capture power and their is no question of taking any action against them for they are the victors and the victors cannot be called to account for any bloodshed that they might have caused necessary for their victory. In this case the revolt against Hadrat Uthman had been successful, Hadrat Uthman had been killed and the power had been captured by the rebels. The rebels voluntarily transferred the power captured by them to the people and asked them to elect the Caliph. The people elected Hadrat Ali as the Caliph. The people in this case exercised the power delegated to them by the rebels and as such Hadrat Ali owed his election to the rebels. In the circumstances the cry for vengeance for the blood of Hadrat Uthman had become infructuous and it could not be raised before Hadrat Ali.

Purpose of the Cry for Vengeance : As in view of the circumstances referred to above, the cry for vengeance was infructuous, the purpose of the cry was really not to seek Qasas, but to cause confusion and create difficulties for Hadrat Ali. If those who raised the cry wanted Hadrat Ali to take action against the rebels, that was not possible as the revolt had succeeded and Hadrat Ali owed his election to the rebels. If the purpose of the cry was to accuse Hadrat Ali of the murder it was sheer perversity for Hadrat Ali was not even remotely connected with the murder. And if for the sake of argument he was involved in the murder in anyway, he could not be called to account as he was himself out of power. As a matter of fact those who raised the cry for vengeance were themselves responsible for the murder of Hadrat Uthman and they raised the cry merely to disguise their own guilt.

When Hadrat Uthman was the Caliph all authority vested in him and Hadrat Ali, had no authority. As such Hadrat Ali could not suppress the revolt, it was for Hadrat Uthman to take the necessary action. Hadrat Uthman, a noble soul, followed the policy of drift which culminated in his assassination. As such Hadrat Uthman was himself responsible for his own assassination. When the house of Hadrat Uthman had been besieged he had in fact called for aid from the provincial Governors. All the Governors including Muawiyyah delayed the despatch of relief. That provided an opportunity to the rebels to assassinate Hadrat Uthman. Thus Muawiyyah was himself guilty of the murder of Hadrat Uthman and it did not lie in his mouth to raise the cry for vengeance and demand such vengeance from Hadrat Ali Talha who later defected from the oath of allegiance to Hadrat Ali was indeed with the rebels when they besieged the house of Hadrat Uthman.

Ulterior Motive : The cry for vengeance was a mere subterfuge and the real purpose was to dethrone Hadrat Ali. The rivalry between Banu Hashim and Umayyah existed since long. The Banu Umayyah had led the Quraish of Mecca in the various battles against the Muslims. In the battles of early Islam, Hadrat Ali had killed the maternal grandfather maternal uncle and brother of Muawiyyah. Hadrat Ali had killed several other men of the Banu Umayyah. Hadrat Ali had killed the father of Umru. The Banu Umayyah thus bore a personal grudge against Hadrat Ali. After the conquest of Mecca by the Muslims the Banu Umayyah accepted Islam and acknowledged the supermacy of Banu Hashim. When Hadrat Uthman became the Caliph the tables were turned and Banu Umayyah took steps to establish their supremacy over the Banu Hashim. There is a passage in Nahj-ul-Balagha which shows that during the caliphate of Hadrat Uthman, the Banu Umayyah withheld from Hadrat Ali what was due to him just as the milkman withhold the milk of the she-camel from its young one. Hadrat Ali is reported to have said on the occasion that if he came into power he would deal with the Banu Umayyah as the butcher removed the skin from a dead animal. As such it was the endeavour of Muawiyyah to create difficulties for Hadrat Ali with a view to dethroning him from power. Hadrat Uthman was a capitalist and during his caliphate most of the Muslims took to the luxurious way of life in preference to the austere way of Islam. Hadrat Uthman had awarded jagirs to many persons. When Hadrat Ali was elected as the Caliph, a generation-term has elapsed since the death of the Holy Prophet and a well to-do class had sprung up among the Muslims. Hadrat Ali was known for his resolutionery views. The well-to-do class among the Muslims which included Talha, Zubayr, Muawiyyah and other men of Banu Umayyah were afraid that under Hadrat Ali their interests were likely to be adversely affected. They accordingly joined in the call for vengeance for the blood of Hadrat Uthman with a view to safeguarding their personal interests by creating troubles for Hadrat Ali. The real aim of those who raised the cry for vengeance for the blood of Hadrat Uthman was to capture power for themselves by means fair or foul.

Deposition of Governors : On assuming the caliphate, Hadrat Ali decided to depose the provincial Governors appointed by Hadrat Uthman and appoint new Governors in their stead. Some of the Governors like Muawiyyah in Syria had been in office for more or less twenty years and had grown too powerful. Such concentration of power in a single person was fraught with danger to the body politic and Hadrat Ali felt that in the interest of the State it was necessary that there should be a change in the provincial Governors. As a matter of fact one of the main allegations against Hadrat Uthman which had triggered off the revolt was nepotism in the appointment of Governors. Hadrat Ali felt that even if Hadrat Uthman had any justification for the appointment of his favourites as Governors, such justification was no longer there after his death. As such a change was necessary in general interest. Because of the unfortunate revolt against Hadrat Uthman, the administration stood shattered in some parts of the country. For the proper rehabilitation of administration a change in personnel was essential. Hadrat Ali had noticed that for some time past the Muslims had departed from the austere way of the life of Islam and had taken to the luxurious way of living borrowed from the non-Muslims. Hadrat Ali had a programme for the restoration of Islam to its pristine purity. For the implementation of such programme likely to have political, religious and social repercussions it was necessary that Hadrat Ali should have, as the provincial heads, persons in whom he had confidence and who could be depended upon to carry out his policies into action. Hadrat Ali did not wish to give the impression that he intended to victimise any particular individual, his proposal accordingly envisaged the deposition of all existing Governors and their replacement by new men of established integrity.

Mughira b. Shuba : Mughira b. Shuba was considered to be a wise man among the Arabs. He advised Hadrat Ali that he should not take the hasty steps of deposing all the Governors at the outset of his caliphate. He suggested that Hadrat Ali should bide his time and he should transfer or depose the Governors after he had consolidated his own position. Hadrat Ali advanced his argument in justification of the proposal to depose the Governors. The discussion lasted for a few hours but it proved to be indecisive. Hadrat Ali did not agree with the view of Mughira. The meeting on the first day came to close with the observation that they would meet the following day and reconsider the matter. When Mughira came to see Hadrat Ali the following day, he said that he had reconsidered the matter and he had come to the conclusion that provincial Governors should be deposed forthwith.

Abdullah b. Abbas : Abdullah b. Abbas, a cousin of Hadrat Ali, came to see him from Mecca Ibn. Abbas was very emphatic in his counsel that Hadrat Ali should not take the hasty steps of deposing the Governors. He said that with the assassination of Hadrat Uthman the prestige of the central government had fallen low and it was necessary that its prestige should be re-established before any attempt was made to remove the Governors Ibn. Abbas observed that in principle Hadrat Ali was right that he should have Governors who enjoyed his confidence, but in view of the unsettled condition when the people in the provinces, particularly Syria, had yet to take the oath of allegiance to him the proper course was that the orders for the deposition of the Governors should be held up till the people in all the provinces had taken the oath of allegiance to him. He said that Muawiyyah was strongly entrenched in power in Syria and if any orders for his deposition were passed he would defy them. Hadrat Ali said that he wanted him (Ibn. Abbas) to be appointed as the Governor of Syria Ibn. Abbas said that he could not accept the appointment, for Muawiyyah would not allow him to take charge. The difficulty in this respect was that while Muawiyyah had a force at his disposal the central government had no force at its disposal at that stage to take the field if any provincial governor chose to defy the order of the Caliph. Hadrat Ali observed that Mughira had originally offered advice against the deposition of the Governors but on reconsideration he had favoured the proposal for the deposition of the Governors Ibn. Abbas said that the advice that he had offered in the first instance was based on sincerity and he withdrew his advice because of some ulterior motives.

Orders for the Deposition : In spite of what Ibn. Abbas advised, Hadrat Ali issued orders for the deposition of the Governors. Hadrat Ali appointed Suhail b Hanifa as the Governor of Syria, Saad b. Ubaidullah as the Governor of Egypt, Ummarah b Shahab as the Governor of Kufa, Uthman b Hanif as the Governor of Basra, and. Abdullah b. Abbas as the Governor of Yemen. When the nominee of Hadrat Ali went to Basra, he was able to assume the charge and no resistance was offered to him. Similarly there was no resistance to the new Governor in Egypt, and he assumed the charge without any difficulty. Abdullah b. Abbas succeeded in assuming the charge in Yemen but the previous Governor escaped to Mecca and carried away the entire treasure with him. When the nominee of Hadrat Ali for the governorship of Syria reached Tabuk on the border of Syria, he was met by the Syrian force, who advised him to go back as they did not acknowledge Hadrat Ali as the Caliph. Similarly the nominee of Hadrat Ali to the governorship of Kufa had to return to Medina after having failed to assume the charge of his office.

Defection by Syria and Kufa : Thus at the outset of his rule as Caliph, Hadrat Ali had to face a crisis. The failure of the nominees of Hadrat Ali to assume charge implied a political schism in the body politic of Islam. The situation that emerged on the ground was that the Governors appointed by Hadrat Ali assumed office in Egypt, Basra and Yemen and the people in these provinces took the oath of allegiance to Hadrat Ali. The people of Kufa took the oath of allegiance to Hadrat Ali, but did not want any change in their Governor and they made the nominee of Hadrat Ali go back. Syria refused to acknowledge the authority of Hadrat Ali. In Mecca the position was confused. In Mecca some persons offered allegiance to Hadrat Ali, but the majority of the Quraish withheld their allegiance to Hadrat Ali. It appears that at that stage, Hadrat Ali did not appoint a Governor for Mecca and the Governor appointed by Hadrat Uthman continued in office. He did not offer allegiance to Hadrat Ali. Syria was definitely hostile to Hadrat Ali. Kufa was not hostile, but as the people of Kufa had played a leading role in the assassination of Hadrat Uthman and the election of Hadrat Ali, they wanted that Hadrat Ali should be subservient to them Mecca did not want to defy Hadrat Ali, but they did not want to support him either.

At the outset of his caliphate Hadrat Ali had to face an administrative crisis in the country. Among the historians there is some controversy on the point whether in the deposition of Governors, Hadrat Ali acted rashly or otherwise. Some of the writers have taken the view that as advised by Ibn. Abbas he should have bided his time and deferred the deposition of Governors. If we study the question in the light of what happened subsequently we arrived at the conclusion that their was nothing wrong in what Hadrat Ali did. Muawiyyah had no intention of owing allegiance to Hadrat Ali and if had been allowed to carry on as a Governor of Hadrat Ali, he would have been a source of greater trouble for Hadrat Ali. By such deposition, Hadrat Ali was able to establish his authority in a greater part of the country. If Hadrat Ali succeeded in consolidation of his rule in those provinces where his nominees held the office, he could have overpowered Syria without much difficulty. Unfortunately other complications took place and Hadrat Ali had to face trouble even in provinces where his Governor held office.

Emergence of Rivalry

The failure of the nominees of Hadrat Ali to assume office as the Governor of Syria and Kufa was a great challenge for Hadrat Ali. Musa, the Governor of Kufa, tried to temporise, though he acknowledged the authority of Hadrat Ali. In Syria the story was different. To start with the stand of Muawiyyah was that he would acknowledge the caliphate of Hadrat Ali after those who were responsible for the assassination of Hadrat Uthman had been brought to book. Hadrat Ali sent an emissary to Muawiyyah to explain to him the position. He assured him that every possible effort would be made tc trace the murderers of Hadrat Uthman. He observed that this would need time. He wanted the support of Muawiyyah in tracing the culprits. He advised that in the meantime, Muawiyyah should step aside from the office of the Governor and cooperate with the nominee of the central government in the interest of the solidarity of Islam. He pointed out that any dissensions among the Muslims at the stage would work to the advantage of the enemies of Islam.

Muawiyyah detained the emissary of Hadrat Ali for over three months. In the meantime he whipped up his propaganda campaign exploiting the murder of Hadrat Uthman. He sent his agents to Mecca and other parts of the country to relate the story of the assassination of Hadrat Uthman in pathetic terms and win the sympathy of the people. As the propaganda gathered momentum Hadrat Ali came to be accused of being an accomplice in the murder of Hadrat Uthman. The burden of the propaganda was that as the hands of Hadrat Ali were dyed with the blood of Hadrat Uthman he was not qualified to be the Caliph and those who had withheld their allegiance to him were justified in their refusal to acknowledge his authority.

After three months, Muawiyyah allowed the emissary of Hadrat Ali to return to Medina. He said that he would be sending his own emissary with a message for Hadrat Ali. The letter of Muawiyyah was brought to Medina by a Bedouin chief Kabisa. The cover bore the address "From Muawiyyah to All". When the cover opened, it contained a blank paper with no writing thereon. In a fit of anger, Hadrat Ali asked the bearer what did that mean? Kabisa pleaded for the safety of his life before he could answer the question. Hadrat Ali said that he was free to speak and he had his promise of safety. On this assurance the messenger said: "Know you then that there are no less than 60,000 Syrians whose beards are wet with tears and who are rallying around Hadrat Uthman's bloody shirt which they have made their war standard, have armed themselves and are bent on avenging the murder of Hadrat Uthman."

On hearing these words the anger of Hadrat Ali knew no bounds but he controlled his anger and said, "This is pure sedition. " Someone from among the congregation shouted "Kill the Syrian messenger for his impudence". At this Kabisa took to heels and retorted, "Four thousand chosen warriors are near at hand. Take care of your homes and hearths " Hadrat Ali said to the envoy, "Begone, for I have promised you the safety of your life"

Kabisa went away, but the defiant attitude of Muawiyyah was a great challenge for Hadrat Ali. To those of the Muslims who were present in the mosque, Hadrat Ali addressed in the following terms:

> "Beware! Satan has gathered his forces. His army is multiplying. By his wiles, Satan is attracting the people to him. Their propaganda is a tissue of lies. Their accusations against me are most unjust and unfair. They demand from me the right which they themselves had abandoned. They demand from me blood for blood which they themselves have shed. Their repeated demand for taking vengeance from the murderers of Hadrat Uthman is like demanding milk from a woman which has dried up. He who invites me to war should know that under all circumstances I will follow the teachings of the Holy Quran and the Prophet. If they refuse to abide by the injunctions of Islam, the sword which helps the upholders of truth and destroys the mischief makers would decide the issue. It is surprising that in spite of their stand on falsehood they give me the challenges of war. May God curse them' War can never frighten me to abandon the truth I am not afraid of death I will live for Islam and die for Islam."

Proclamation of Jihad : In order to meet the challenge of Muawiyyah, Hadrat Ali ordered the raising of levies with a view to undertaking an expedition against Syria. Despatches were sent to the various provincial Governors to send reinforcements and provide whatever succour they could. Hadrat Ali as Caliph issued the decree of Jihad and exhorted the people to join the campaign in large numbers for the vindication of the truth of Islam. When the Muslims of Medina gathered in the mosque, he addressed them in the following terms

Now or never if you fail to fight you will lose power and these accursed schismatics will destroy the solidarity of Islam. I have, however, high hopes in the mercy of God, Who will set right that which these people are bent on setting wrong "

The appeal did not have the desired result and the response to Hadrat Ali's call to arms in the defence of Islam was poor. Hadrat Ali felt grieved at the apathy of the people of Medina to Jihad. He called a special gathering of the people of Medina in the Prophet's mosque and addressed them on the importance of Jihad. His speech is preserved in the collection of his writings bearing the title Nahj-ul-Balagha. He addressed the people in the following terms;

> "Jihad' is one of the doors of heaven. God opens it for his friends. It is the dress of piety. It is useful and beneficial armour with which the faithful should be equipped. It is a strong shield for the believers If a man gives it up, God will make him wear the robes of disgrace and shame. He will be the victim of misfortune. He will be dishonoured

Beware! I urge you to take up arms against the upholders of falsehood I want you to attack them before they attack us. By God' know that those who shift their responsibilities to others court ruin and disaster. Know that Muawiyyah has attacked. Amber with his cavalry and has killed Hassan b Hassan Bakr the chief of that place I am told that one of his soldiers entered a house and took away ornaments and jewels of the lady of the house. It is both surprising and heartrending. Followers of Muawiyyah are misguided and mistaken, yet they are united and though you are the upholders of a true cause, you are disunited and divided. How sad that they kill you and you cannot destroy them. They fight against you and you evade fighting. The commandments of God are being defied and sins are being committed in open daylight and you see these things as passive onlookers. When I ask you to march in the summer season, you request me to delay the expedition till the hot season is over and when I ask you to march in the winter, you complain of excessive cold and want me to postpone the campaign till the cold season is over. These are lame excuses. If you are afraid of the excessive heat or cold, you are apt to run away at the sight of the sword. O men, you do not deserve to be called men. By God, I am ashamed at the sight of you. May God destroy you. You have broken my heart. You have made me lose my temper. You have upset all my plans, through your sins and disobedience. You have always made me drink the draught of sorrow. The Quraish now say that the son of Abu Talib is undoubtedly brave but he is ignorant of the art of war. Is there anyone from amongst their ranks who was more steadfast in war than me? I have been fighting in wars when I was barely twenty years old, and now I am sixty I do not know what should I do with you, for suggestions and plans are of little values to me who do not act upon them."

Strong and Bitter Words : From the historical accounts and the biography of Hadrat Ali that have come down to us, it is not very clear what exactly happened which made Hadrat Ali address the people of Medina in such strong and bitter words Reading between the lines of the speech of Hadrat Ali, it seems that he felt annoyed with the attitude of the people of Medina and he even reproached and cursed them. It appears that Hadrat Ali had a plan for an immediate attack on Syria but the plan did not materialise as adequate response from the people of Medina was not forthcoming. From the account of Taban it appears that Hadrat Ali had in fact given an order for the march to Syria. He had handed over the war standard to his son Muhammad b Hanifa. He had appointed. Abdullah b. Abbas, Umar b. Abi Salma and. Abu Laila b Umar b. Al Jarah as his Generals to command the various wings of the army. Hadrat Ali was to lead the army in person and he had appointed Qatam b. Abbas as the Governor of Medina during his absence. The people of Medina were loath that the Muslims should fight among themselves and before the army of Hadrat Ali could march to Syria many persons chose to withdraw. In the circumstances for one reason or the other, the expedition to Syria was delayed and this delay worked to the advantage of Muawiyyah and the disadvantage of Hadrat Ali. Things became further difficult when Hadrat Ali had to face another crisis, namely the defection of Talha and Zubayr who had sworn allegiance to him.

Defection of Talha and Zubayr : Talha and Zubayr were two eminent companions of the Holy Prophet. Talha belonged to the Tamim section of the Quraish. Talha became a Muslim at the young age of fifteen. He took part in the battles fought under the command of the Holy Prophet. He played a conspicuous part in the battle of Uhud and received many wounds in warding off the attacks on the Holy Prophet. He was married to a daughter of Hadrat. Abu Bakr. He was a magnate and was very rich. His daily income in reported to be over a thousand dirhams. He was critical of the administration of Hadrat Uthman and was popular with rebels from Basra. After the assassination of Hadrat Uthman the rebels offered him the caliphate, but he declined the offer on account of the uncertainty of the situation.

Zubayr b. Al. Awwam was nephew of Hadrat Khadija. His mother Safia was a paternal aunt of the Holy Prophet. He was thus a first cousin of the Holy Prophet. He fought in most of the battles of early Islam. He was a rich merchant. He was popular with the people of Kufa and when Hadrat Uthman was assassinated the rebels from Kufa approached him to accept the caliphate in succession to Hadrat Uthman. He declined the offer because of the uncertainty of the situation.

The Holy Prophet gave tidings of paradise to ten of his Companions during their lifetime and these ten included Talha and Zubayr.

Talha and Zubayr's Oath of Allegiance : When Hadrat Ali was elected as the Caliph both Talha and Zubayr took the oath of allegiance to him. Accounts differ as to the circumstances under which they took the oath of allegiance to Hadrat Ali. According to one account they took the oath of allegiance to Hadrat Ali voluntarily and were the first persons to take such oath. According to another account they took the oath of allegiance to Hadrat Ali subject to the condition that they were to share power with Hadrat Ali. According to yet another account when the oath of allegiance to Hadrat Ali was taken in the mosque, Talha and Zubayr shut themselves in their houses but the rebels took them from their houses to the mosque and forced them to take the oath of allegiance to Hadrat Ali. Talha had received many wounds in the wars and his hand was mangled. When Talha offered his allegiance with the mangled hand, some of the. Arabs prone to omens felt that such oath with a mangled hand did not augur will for the future.

Further Defection : When the oath of allegiance was taken to Hadrat Ali, the state of affairs in Medina was not normal. The majority of the Muslims in Medina took the oath of allegiance but a few persons abstained from taking the oath. These included Saad b. Abi Waqas. Abdullah b Umar, Usama b Zaid and Muhammad b Musailmah Ansan. They, however, assured Hadrat Ali that they would not create any trouble for him. On such assurance, Hadrat Ali did not press for their allegiance.

As the crisis in Medina deepened and Hadrat Ali gave the call for military action against Muawiyyah, even the people who had taken the oath of allegiance did not respond to the call. The people of Medina were generally loath that the Muslims should fight against Muslims. Talha and Zubayr met Hadrat Ali and suggested to him that if one of them was appointed as the Governor of Kufa and the other was appointed as the Governor of Basra they would help in the consolidation of his rule. Hadrat Ali did not accept the offer. He preferred to appoint his own men as the provincial Governors. He told Talha and Zubayr that he wanted them to remain at Medina by his side as his Counsellor. Frustrated in their attempt to get governorship Talha and Zubayr felt embittered. They requested Hadrat Ali to permit them to go to Mecca for performing the "Umra" Hadrat Ali refused the permission on the ground that he wanted their presence in Medina in public interest. Thereupon, Talha and Zubayr escaped from Medina secretly. At Mecca, Talha and Zubayr joined Hadrat Aishah. Both of them were related to Hadrat Aishah. One sister of Hadrat Aishah was married to Zubayr and another sister was married to Talha.

Hadrat Ali's Letter : Hadrat Ali felt much disturbed at the defection of Talha and Zubayr. He felt that Talha and Zubayr had defected under some misunderstanding. He decided that instead of taking any punitive action against them, an effort should be made to conciliate them. He accordingly addressed them a letter in the following terms and sent it to them at Mecca through a special messenger

> "Verily, both of your know very well that I did not approach the people to elect me as the Caliph. On the other hand it were the people who forced me to accept the office of the Caliph in the interest of Islam. Again I did not ask the people to swear allegiance to me, they did so of their own accord. Both

of you also stepped towards me and took the oath of fealty. The people did swear allegiance to me neither through any dread of fear nor from any hope of worldly gain or profit. So, if you took the oath voluntarily how can you retrace and recant. If you swore under compulsions even then you have proved the case against yourself because you outwardly rendered obedience to me and concealed your treachery from me. By God, such hypocrisy did not behove Muhajirs of your calibre. There was a good deal of scope left for you before you took the oath, but when you had taken the oath, no margin was left to you from recanting from that holy contract which you had entered of your own accord. You say that I am the murderer of Uthman. Come forward and let the people of Medina who did not take side with either of the party judge between you and me. Their judgement would reveal what I and you did on that occasion. You are experienced old men, and it behoves you to repent of what you have done. It is bad enough that you have incurred the odium of the people of the world, but beware that, in the life to come, for such deviation from the right you will have to face hell."

This letter had no effect on Talha and Zubayr. In Mecca they joined Hadrat. Aishah and raised the cry for vengeance for the blood of Hadrat Uthman.

Hadrat Ali's address about the defection of Talha and Zubayr

In an address to the people of Medina in the Prophet's mosque Hadrat Ali commented on the defection of Talha and Zubayr in the following terms:

"You know I had refused to accept the caliphate. It was only because of your insistence that I reluctantly agreed to accept the office. I was moved to do so, because the interest of Islam demanded that someone should head the State. You all took the oath of allegiance to me. In accepting the office I had laid down the condition that I expected your unstinted loyalty and support. The oath of allegiance is a sacred part between you and the person you have elected as the Caliph. Once the oath had been taken it is irrevocable. Like all of you Talha and Zubayr took the oath of allegiance to me. Now they have repudiated the oath and taken to the wrong way. They have given no reason for this change of face. They are eminent companions of the Holy Prophet and they fully know that the oath of allegiance once taken cannot be repudiated. I was no stranger to them. They are fully aware of my antecedents, my relationship with the Holy Prophet and my services to the cause of Islam. They are Quraish and I am also Quraish. Zubayr is in fact cousin. By rebelling against my authority they have created dissension among the Muslims which is a definite disservice to Islam. They have raised the cry for vengeance for the blood of Uthman. The implication of this cry is that they accuse me of the murder of Hadrat Uthman or my involvement. The assassination of Hadrat Uthman is deplorable, but the imputation of any blame on me in this respect is most unjust and unfair. All that took place happened before your eyes. I was neither concerned with the administration of law and order, nor did I command any influence with the rebels. Indeed I took all measures that I could, to protect the person of Hadrat Uthman. It is an undeniable fact that my sons were wounded while guarding the house of Hadrat Uthman. On the other hand it is well know that Talha was present among the rebels and he did not respond to the call of Hadrat Uthman when he called him. It is surprising and sheer perversion of truth that they should levy the charge of the murder of Hadrat Uthman against me when they themselves were the murderers. It is not merely uncharitable, it is criminal in character. As Talha and Zubayr have assumed the role of rebels, they will have to be treated as such. If they do not repent, I will have no option but to take punitive action against them. I cannot allow the rebels to gather force and create mischief. I am not like a bear which is lulled to sleep and the hunter hunts it while it is asleep I will lead a force against the rebels and destroy them howsoever painful the act might be."

Hadrat Aishah's Role : Hadrat Aishah was the favourite wife of the Holy Prophet. In 633 C. E. in one of the expeditions, Hadrat Aishah accompanied the Holy Prophet. On the way back she lost her necklace and when she went to search for the necklace in the desert where she had earlier gone for the call of nature, the caravan left in her absençe. Her camel-man was under the impression that she was in the litter on the camel. Later, she was picked by a camelman and brought to Medina. The mischief-mongers and the enemies of Islam made this incident the subject of calumny and Hadrat Aishah was accused of unseemly conduct. Because of the virulent propaganda campaign waged by the evil-doers the Holy Prophet became estranged to Hadrat Aishah and she left for the house of her father. During the period of estrangement, Hadrat Ali advised the Holy Prophet that there was no dearth of women and he could divorce Hadrat Aishah and marry some other beautiful woman. Later,. Allah revealed that Hadrat Aishah was innocent and no blame rested on her. As a consequence the Holy Prophet and Hadrat Aishah were reconciled. Hadrat Aishah bore grudge against Hadrat Ali for the advice that he had given to the Holy Prophet to divorce her. Hadrat Aishah was a stepmother of Hadrat Fatima, the wife of Hadrat Ali. Both of them were more or less of the same age. While Hadrat Aishah was the favourite wife of the Holy Prophet, Hadrat Fatima was his favourite daughter resulting in a natural jealousy. Once Hadrat Fatima complained to the Holy Prophet for favouring Hadrat Aishah. The Holy Prophet advised her, "Then my dear daughter, why should you not love the person whom your father loves". This relationship came to be further strained when after the death of the Holy Prophet, Hadrat Fatima and Hadrat Ali claimed the estate of Fidak as an inheritance but Hadrat. Abu Bakr did not accept the claim and declared the estate to be public property. After the death of Hadrat. Abu Bakr his wife. Asma, a stepmother of Hadrat Aishah, married Hadrat Ali. Hadrat Aishah felt unhappy at this marriage

Hadrat Aishah in Mecca : When Hadrat Uthman was assassinated, Hadrat Aishah was not in Medina. She had gone to Mecca a few weeks earlier for performing the pilgrimage. She came to know of the assassination of Hadrat Uthman and the election of Hadrat Ali as the Caliph when she was on the way back to Medina. She was much shocked at the murder of Hadrat Uthman. She felt unhappy at the election of Hadrat Ali with whom she had outstanding differences. On hearing of the news instead of proceeding to Medina she retraced her steps and returned to Mecca. Hadrat Uthman had been a popular figure among the Quraish of Mecca. When in Syria Muawiyyah raised the cry for the vengeance the blood for Hadrat Uthman. The cry was echoed in Mecca as well. The people of Mecca temporised in taking the oath of allegiance to Hadrat Ali. The tendency of the people of Mecca was to wait and watch further developments. The people of Mecca had at that stage no leader with them under whose direction they could take a specific course of action.

The return of Hadrat Aishah to Mecca changed the situation. In view of the great prestige and respect that she commanded as the "Mother of the Faithful" she soon assumed the role of a leader and the people assembled around her in large number. During the lifetime of Hadrat Uthman she had been critical of this policies, but after his death she decided to espouse his cause and join in the cry seeking vengeance for his blood. Her address to the people of Mecca is on record. She said:

> "O ye people'. The rebels from different provinces have murdered the innocent Uthman. These people levelled some allegation against the Caliph at the outset and when they could not establish the charges against him they rebelled against him. What had been ordained as unlawful by. Allah was made lawful by the regicides. They violated the sanctity of the city of the Holy Prophet in the sacred month of Hajj when the shedding of blood is prohibited. They plundered and looted the citizens of Medina. By God, a single finger of Uthman was more precious than the lives of all the regicides. The mischief has not been crushed and the murderers of Uthman have not been brought to book. It befits you now to seek satisfaction on these murderers. It is vengeance alone for the blood of Uthman that can vindicate the honour of Islam"

Call to War : The fiery address of Hadrat Aishah was virtually the call to war. It set a match to the smouldering fire of discontent among the people. The first man to respond to the call of Hadrat Aishah was Abdullah b. Aamar al-Hadhrami. He was the Governor of Mecca appointed by Hadrat Uthman. In view of the uncertain state of affairs in Mecca, Hadrat Ali had not replaced him so far by a nominee of his own. He knew that with Hadrat Ali as the Caliph he could not hold his office for long. He, therefore, placed all resources available to him as the Governor of Mecca at the disposal of Hadrat Aishah for any war that she might wage to seek vengeance for the blood of Hadrat Uthman Yala b Umayyah, the ex-Governor of Yemen who had been deposed by Hadrat Ali, responded enthusiastically to the call for war. On his deposition, he had brought all the treasure of the province of Yemen with him. He placed this treasure at the disposal of Hadrat Aishah for financing the war project. Abdullah b. Aamar of the Umayyad section, the ex-Governor of Basra who had been deposed by Hadrat Ali also joined the confederates. All the Umayyads of Mecca, and those who had escaped from Medina after the assassination of Hadrat Uthman offered themselves for war service. These included Saeed b. Al. Aas Mughira b Shuba and Walid b Uqba Talha and Zubayr who arrived from Medina in the meantime also joined the confederates. Both of them were related to Hadrat Aishah. One of the sisters of Hadrat Aishah was married to Zubayr and another was married to Talha. They became the right-hand men for Hadrat Aishah and the Commanders of the force of Hadrat Aishah.

Plan for War : Within a short time, Hadrat Aishah was able to set up a war organisation in opposition to Hadrat Ali. Though the confederates raised the cry for avenging the murder of Hadrat Uthman, their real aim was to dethrone Hadrat Ali. After building up a war organisation Hadrat Aishah and her party had to consider where the blow was to be struck Hadrat Aishah was personally of the view that an attack should be led on Medina as it was expedient that the malady should be uprooted root and branch. Apparently her idea was to overthrow Hadrat Ali and capture power. Most of her followers were of the view that it would not be advisable that the wife of the Holy Prophet should lead an expedition against the city of the Holy Prophet and violate its sanctity. The Umayyads proposed that they should proceed to Syria and join Muawiyyah. This view was not favoured by the non-Umayyad followers of Hadrat Aishah as such a step was likely to shift the balance of power in favour of Muawiyyah and strengthen his claim for the caliphate. Another proposal was that they should advance to Kufa This proposal was dropped on the ground that it was uncertain how far the people of Kufa would support the war against Hadrat Ali, particularly when most of the rebels responsible for the assassination of Hadrat Uthman belonged to Kufa. Talha suggested that he had considerable influence in Basra and if they advanced to Basra most of the people there would join them. This proposal was supported by. Abdullah b. Aamar who had been the Governor of Basra and had been deposed by Hadrat Ali. He said that he had many supporters in Basra and these people would join them in case they advanced to Basra. After a good deal of discussion and deliberation it was decided that they should in the first instance march to Basra and should undertake further campaigns against Hadrat Ali with Basra as the base. Addressing her followers Hadrat Aishah said:

> "A great tragedy has taken place and the innocent Caliph of the Muslims has been assassinated by the miscreants for ulterior ends. They have captured power and this is fraught with grave danger to the Muslim Ummah. As true Muslims, it is your bounden duty to rise to a man and take vengeance for the blood of Hadrat Uthman. To seek this end let us in the first instance march to our brethren in Basra and make that city our base for further operations. May God help us in our mission."

The Proclamation : Having taken the decision to open the campaign by a march on Basra, the confederates issued a proclamation in the following terms:

> "The Mother of the Faithful, Hadrat Talha and Hadrat Zubayr, two eminent Companions of the Holy Prophet, are leading an army to Basra and whosoever has any spark of faith in him should join the ranks to defend the faith and fight to seek vengeance for the blood of Uthman. Those who do not have the means of the journey will be provided with conveyance, arms and other necessities. It is an obligation on the part of the Muslims to rise to vindicate the truth. "

The Army : The proclamation had a good effect and many people joined the ranks. A majority of the people of Mecca favoured the confederates. A section of the population led by Abdullah b Umar decided to remain neutral and favour no party. A small section favoured Hadrat Ali. Al Fazal, the wife of Abbas, an uncle of Hadrat Ali, sent a letter to Hadrat Ali through a special messenger informing him of the plan of Hadrat Aishah.

The confederates were able to raise an army of three thousand strong people from Mecca. Envoys were sent to the tribes who inhabited the desert on the way to Basra to join the main army on the way.

Hadrat Aishah's Address : As the troops assembled at Mecca, Hadrat Aishah addressed them. She exhorted them to fight for upholding the truth and the suppression of falsehood. She said that the assassination of Hadrat Uthman, the Caliph of the Muslims was a great challenge for the faithful and they could not rest content till those guilty of the crime were brought to book and killed

Talha and Zubayr urged the troops to perform deeds of heroic gallantry which were the characteristics of" Ghazis". They told them that they had left Medina and its people in a state of quandary. In Medina right had been mixed up with wrong in such a way that the people knew not in which way to turn Talha and Zubayr made out the point that in the circumstances it was for the people of Mecca to give the lead and teach a lesson to the traitors who had assassinated the innocent Caliph, Hadrat Uthman.

The confederates justified their cause on the basis of the following verse of the Holy Quran:

> "And if two parties of the believers quarrel, make peace between them, but if one of them acts wrongly towards the other, fight that which acts wrongfully, until it return to Allah's command. Then, if it returns, make peace between them with justice and act equitably, for Allah loves those who act equitably."

Day of Tears : Hadrat Aishah mounting on a camel took command of the army and it set off on the march to Basra. The prominent women of Mecca travelled with Hadrat Aishah for some distance outside Mecca to see her off. These included Hadrat Hafsa, another wife of the Holy Prophet. Hadrat Hafsa intended to accompany Hadrat Aishah to Basra, but her brother Abdullah b Umar persuaded her to return to Mecca as in the war between the two parties of the Muslims it was expedient to remain neutral. As the women took leave of Hadrat Aishah they wept bitterly because of the uncertainty of fortune that lay in store for the army of Mecca. Here a dead camel was sighted from which blood flew profusely. This was taken to be a bad omen indicating that as a result of the campaign they were undertaking much blood was likely to flow. According to the Arab chronicles the day of the departure of the army of the confederates for Basra came to be known as the "Day of Tears", on account of the heavy tears shed at the time of the departure of the troops.

Desertions from the Army : The army of the confederates had hardly proceeded a few stages from Mecca when the followers of Talha and Zubayr began to quarrel among themselves on the point as to who out of Talha and Zubayr should become the Caliph in the event of victory. Hadrat Aishah tried to end the dispute by declaring that the issue was premature and that at the proper time it was for the people of Medina to choose the Caliph as they had elected the previous Caliphs. Hadrat Aishah appointed a neutral person to lead the prayers. The quarrel, however, did its damage. Some of the people who belonged neither to the party of Talha, nor to that of Zubayr came to feel that the war was being fought because of personal motives of Talha and Zubayr. Some persons suggested that as they had taken up arms to avenge the blood of Hadrat Uthman it was proper that a son of Hadrat Uthman should be chosen as the Caliph. This suggestion was turned down by the followers of Talha and Zubayr on the ground that only some veteran Companion could be chosen as the Commander of the Faithful. Because of these quarrels doubts began to assail some of the people who had joined the ranks under the impression that they were going to fight in the cause of Islam. They felt uncertain as to where the truth lay. Both the sides claimed to fight for the truth and it was obvious that both of them could not be in the right at the same time. One of them was bound to be in the wrong, but it could not be said who exactly was in the wrong. On one side was the "Mother of the Faithful", and on the other side was the "Commander of the Faithful" In the circumstances the proper course for the faithful was not to support either party until things appeared in their true colour. Saeed b. Al. Aas, an ex-Governor of Kufa who had joined the army of the confederates thought it advisable to desert and return to Mecca. Some other persons also returned with him. In response to the battle cry "On to Basra to kill the murderers of Hadrat Uthman", Saeed said, "Why go so far. The objects of your vengeance, Talha and Zubayr are riding on their camels before you, kill them and return home."

Hadrat Aishah at Hauab : In the way some desert tribes joined the forces of the confederates. When the cavalcade reached the watering place of Hauab, the dogs of the village came out and barked at Hadrat Aishah. She enquired about the name of the place and when she was told that it was Hauab, a shudder ran through her. She recalled a prediction of the Holy Prophet who while sitting among his wives one day had said that on one of his wives the gods of Hauab would bark. That unnerved Hadrat Aishah. She felt much concerned at the revelation that she was the wretched woman about whom the Holy Prophet had made the unsavoury prediction. The army camped at the watering place and Hadrat Aishah gave expression to her desire to abandon the expedition and return to Mecca. The following morning Talha and Zubayr played a ruse on Hadrat Aishah. They produced some witnesses who averred that the place was not Hauab. They also spread a false alarm that the forces of Hadrat Ali were advancing on the road from Mecca and there was no option with them but to hurry forward to Basra and occupy the city before an encounter with the forces of Hadrat Ali.

After forced marches the troops of Hadrat Aishah reached Basra and camped outside the city. The die was cast. Basra, heretofore a peaceful city, had to face a storm and become the theatre of an unfortunate civil war which was to lead to bloodshed and destroy unity among the Muslims.

Battle for Basra : When the army of Hadrat Aishah camped outside the city of Basra, Uthman b Hanif, the Waleed Governor of Basra sent a delegation from Basra to wait on Hadrat Aishah and ascertain from her the cause of her arrival there with an army. The delegation comprised two men, Imran b Hussain and Abul Aswad. Hadrat Aishah received the delegation with due courtesy and addressed them as follows:

"I swear by Almighty God that a woman of my rank and status cannot hide the truth and no mother can conceal anything from her sons. It is well known to you that rebels from various parts of the country including Basra invaded Medina, violated the sanctity of the Holy City and caused mischief. They shed the blood of the innocent Caliph. They stand guilty before God and His Apostle. The rebels perpetrated great atrocities on the people of Medina. I have come to Basra to apprise you of the great harm that these people have done to Islam. I have come to seek your help in wreaking vengeance for the blood of Hadrat Uthman. The purpose of our visit is to restore better relations between the believers in faith. We do not seek war. We want peace. Such peace must necessarily rest on the confidence of the people. At present there is a chaos in the affairs of the Muslims. We wish to set things right and your help in this behalf is solicited."

Preparation for War : On return from Hadrat Aishah, Imran b Hussain advised Uthman b Hanif that he should not involve himself in war with Hadrat Aishah for she had talked in the language of peace and not in that of war. Abul. Aswad, the other member of the delegation, who was a staunch supporter of Hadrat Ali, advised Uthman b Hanif that as the Governor of Hadrat Ali, he should fight against the enemies of Hadrat Ali. Talha and Zubayr had taken the oath of allegiance to Hadrat Ali and were now rebelling against Ali. Their purpose in coming over to Basra with an army could not be based on peaceful motives.

Uthman b Hanif required the people of Basra to assemble in the mosque to consider what action should be taken against the confederates.

The congregation was addressed in the first instance by Qais b. Al. Aqd. He was critical of the arrival of the confederates. He said that if these people had come to Basra to seek protection that was absurd for they themselves came from a place where even birds were assured of safety. He added that if they had come to seek vengeance for the blood of Hadrat Uthman, they should know that the people of Basra had not killed Hadrat Uthman. He exhorted the people of Basra to take up arms and drive away the confederates from their city.

Uthman b Hanif addressed the people in the following terms

"O ye people, you have sworn allegiance to Hadrat Ali in the name of God and his hand is over your hands. Whosoever recants his allegiance is guilty before men and God. I swear by God that had there been a worthier candidate than Hadrat Ali for the caliphate, he would not have accepted the burden of the office Had the people sworn allegiance to anyone else except Hadrat Ali, he would have also sworn allegiance to him. In that case Hadrat Ali would have obeyed the Caliph without any reservation. Remember that Hadrat Ali had no ill will against any of the Companions of the Holy Prophet. Both Talha and Zubayr took the oath of fealty to Hadrat Ali but their aim in taking such oath was not to obey God. Instead of seeing recompense from God they seek recompense from men. Now both of them assert that they had taken the oath under compulsion when the sword was placed on their necks. We have to see what is the opinion of the people. Where there is majority, their lies the truth of guidance. It is an open secret that the majority have elected Hadrat Ali as the Caliph and there can be no doubt that the truth is on the side of Hadrat Ali. It is therefore incumbent on you to fight against those who have rebelled against the authority of the Caliph and thereby espoused the cause of falsehood."

Hakim b Jabala, the Deputy Governor, took a more violent stand. He exhorted the people of Basra to take up arms against the people who had rebelled against the authority of the Caliph. He added that should all the people forsake him, he would fight against the rebels single handed until he met his martyrdom fighting in the cause of the truth.

Aswad b Harith al Saadi contradicted the stand of those who had advocated war. He said that Islam was the religion of peace and all disputes between the Muslims should be resolved through peaceful means. He held out that the confederates had not come to Basra to wage war. They had come to seek the aid of the citizens of Basra in their campaign against the murderers of Hadrat Uthman and in that behalf it behoved the citizens of Basra to treat them as honoured guests, particularly when they were led by the Mother of the Faithful. Some other speeches were made in favour of Hadrat Aishah. That led to an uproar among the people assembled in the mosque. Some people were loud in their support for Hadrat Ali and some were loud in their support for Hadrat Aishah. The meeting in the mosque ended in a stare of confusion. Those who favoured Hadrat Aishah joined the camp of Hadrat Aishah. Those who favoured Hadrat Ali responded to the call of Uthman b Hanif and took up arms to fight against the confederates.

The Battle : Some attempts were made to negotiate peace but such attempts failed and the armies on both the sides took themselves to the battlefield. Before the battle began, the representatives of each side in the usual Arab way declaimed the righteousness of their cause. After Talha and Zubayr had spoken, Hadrat Aishah addressed the people of Basra. She said that she had no intention of fighting against the people of Basra and shedding unnecessary blood. She added that her object was to seek vengeance for the blood of the innocent Uthman. He was the Caliph of the entire Muslim world including Basra and as such it was an obligation on their part to help in seeking such vengeance and bringing the murderers of Hadrat Uthman to task. She observed that the war was no solution of the matter and her very presence there was a positive proof to the effect that she wanted a peaceful resolution of the crisis that had overtaken the Muslims just as any mother would like any dispute between her sons to be settled peacefully and amicably. Her speech was impressive and effective. It started a good deal of argument and disagreement among the ranks of the army of Basra and some of the persons withdrew.

In spite of some defections from the ranks of the army of Basra there was no weakening of their will to give a fight to the confederates Janya b Qadama, a distinguished citizen of Basra, stepped forward from the ranks, and addressing Hadrat Aishah said that though the assassination of Hadrat Uthman was painful to the people of Basra, her discarding of the veil and leading an army was more painful to them. He wanted her to return to Mecca or Medina and not to meddle in politics which did not behove her as the Mother of the Faithful. Another citizen of Basra taunted Talha and Zubayr for leaving their wives and mothers at their homes and dragging the Mother of the Faithful to the battlefield. Talha and Zubayr were also criticised for taking the oath of allegiance to Hadrat Ali and then breaking it. Another Basnte addressed Hadrat Aishah in the following terms:

> "Mother if you have come here of your own free will, go back to your house
> If you have been brought here by force, we can conduct you to your house
> with honour and safety"

By this time excitement among the warriors on both the sides reached a high pitch and the war began with an attack on the forces of the confederates led by Hakim b Jabala, the deputy of Uthman b Hanif Hakim under a mistaken notion of his loyalty to Hadrat Ali hurled abuses on Hadrat Aishah. When his own men objected to such conduct on his part he shot dead those who objected. Hadrat Aishah instructed her men to remain on the defensive hoping that the fury of the attack of the Basntes would soon be over and it would be possible to stop the war. When Hakim and his men penetrated deep into the ranks of the confederates, she ordered a counter charge. The battle continued till nightfall. There was considerable loss of lives on both the sides but the loss in the ranks of the forces of Basra was much heavier.

After nightfall when the forces of Uthman b Hanif had retired those people of Basra who had joined the ranks of the confederates advised that at midnight the confederates should occupy that part of Basra which was largely populated by those who were opposed to the Walids. The operations was successfully carried into effect and the following day the fight had to take place in the city of Basra itself. That put the forces of Uthman b Hanif to disadvantage and many persons of these forces were killed. By the end of the day, Uthman b Hanif was faced with defeat and he sued for peace.

The Truce : Negotiations for peace led to an agreement for truce. It was decided that the parties in occupation of the two parts of Basra should continue to hold their parts. As emissary was to be sent from Basra to Medina to ascertain whether Talha and Zubayr had taken the oath of allegiance to Hadrat Ali voluntarily or under compulsion. If the enquiry revealed that the oath had been taken voluntarily the confederates would withdraw from Basra. If the enquiry revealed that the oath had been taken under compulsion the entire city of Basra would be handed over to the confederates. Till then the parties were to maintain cease fire.

Hadrat Aishah's Occupation of Basra : In pursuance of the truce agreement between Uthman b Hanif and the confederates, Kaab b Sur, the Qadi of Basra was commissioned to go to Medina to ascertain whether Talha and Zubayr had taken the oath of allegiance to Hadrat Ali voluntarily or under some compulsion Kaab b Sur was originally a Christian. He was attracted by Islam and became a Muslim. He was a man of great learning and piety and was very popular among the people of Basra. On arrival at Medina he proceeded to the Prophet's mosque and addressing the congregation said that he had come from Basra to ascertain whether Talha and Zubayr had taken the oath of allegiance to Hadrat Ali voluntarily or under compulsion. The men in the mosque maintained silence but Usama b Zaid stood up to say that Talha and Zubayr had taken the oath of allegiance under compulsion. At this Sahl b Hanif, the brother of Uthman b Hanif, the Governor of Basra rushed with his men to beat Usama. Usama's father Zaid was an adopted son of the Holy Prophet and the Holy Prophet loved Usama as a grandson. During the time of Hadrat. Abu Bakr, Usama had led a campaign to Syria. Some Companions came to the rescue of Usama and they too declared that Talha and Zubayr had taken the oath of allegiance under compulsion. Kaab b Sur came to the conclusion that Talha and Zubayr had in fact taken the oath of allegiance under compulsion.

War in Basra : On return to Basra, Kaab submitted his report that Talha and Zubayr had taken the oath of allegiance to Hadrat Ali under compulsion. According to the truce agreement, Uthman b Hanif had to surrender the complete control of the city of Basra to the confederates. By this time Uthman b Hanif had received instruction from Hadrat Ali that he was coming to Basra with a large force and that he should hold the city till his arrival. Uthman b Hanif accordingly refused to vacate the city on the ground that the report of Kaab was not correct. On the following Friday when the people of Basra had assembled in the main mosque, Talha and Zubayr addressed them apprising them of the terms of the truce, the report of Kaab b Sur, and the breach of faith on the part of Uthman b Hanif. The people assembled in the mosque came to be divided into two groups. One group supported Uthman b Hanif while the other group supported Talha and Zubayr. Hot words were exchanged between the two groups and that led to an armed conflict. Swords were freely used by both sides. The conflict lasted for several hours as a result of which many persons were killed and the mosque was dyed with the blood of the Muslims. In the conflict the party of Uthman b Hanif suffered heavy loos of life.

At nightfall the pro-Aishah group attacked the house of Uthman b Hanif. It was a dark and stormy night. The guards on duty were overpowered. The mob then broke into the house and Uthman b Hanif was taken captive. The mob wanted to kill him but under the orders of Hadrat Aishah he was imprisoned and lodged in jail. His beard was plucked and he was tortured by the mob.

Hakim b. Jabala : The following day the pro-Alid group took the field under the command of Hakim b Jabala. Hadrat Aishah made a proclamation to the effect that her quarrel was with the murderers of Hadrat Uthman only and as such those who were not involved in the murder of Hadrat Uthman should withdraw from fighting. It was also declared that those who fought would be deemed to be involved in the murder of Uthman. Kaab b Sur tried to bring about peace between the two sides, but all efforts to bring about reconciliation between the contending parties failed. The battle that followed proved to be a bloody one. The pre-Alid group was outnumbered but the men of the group fought desperately. Hakim b Jabala fought like a hero. He raised slogans in favour of Hadrat Ali and hurled abuses on Hadrat Aishah, Talha and Zubayr. A warrior of the army of the confederates struck Hakim b Jabala and severed one of his legs. In spite of this disability he continued fighting and sang:

"I do not mind if my leg has been severed.
My hands are still there.
It's no matter of shame for me to die.
Shame lies in flying from the battlefield.
Life lies in keeping honour alive.
I have lived with honour,
And I will die with honour. "

Hakim b. Jabala died in the battlefield. With his death his men lost heart and laid down arms. Many of them involved in the murder of Hadrat Uthman had fallen in the battle. Those who survived were executed. There were still some murderers of Hadrat Uthman who had not taken part in the battle. The tribes were asked to hand over such men. They were brought to Basra and executed. In this way all the people from Basra who were involved in the assassination of Hadrat Uthman were killed. Only one man escaped from such massacre. He was Harqus b Zubayr. He belonged to the Banu Saad tribe. The tribe refused to hand over Harqus. The tribe which was heretofore pro-confederates changed their loyalties and offered allegiance to Hadrat Ali. The tribe of Abul Qais whose many persons had been executed alienated from the confederates and transferred its loyalty to Hadrat Ali. Over six hundred persons belonging to Basra or the neighbouring tribes were executed or killed as the " Qasas" for the blood of Hadrat Uthman.

Administration of Basra : The confederates now became the master of the entire city of Basra. The pro-Ali group evacuated the city and those who remained in the city recognised the authority of the confederates. Supreme authority vested in Hadrat Aishah and Talha and Zubayr acted as her Ministers. The Baitul-Mal was seized and the men of the pro-confederate group who had suffered loss of life or property were duly compensated. Hadrat Aishah wrote a letter to Muawiyyah in Syria informing him how the confederates had taken vengeance for the blood of Hadrat Uthman. He was advised to undertake campaigns on similar lines to take vengeance for the blood of Hadrat Uthman.

Battle of the Camel

Hadrat Ali's Plan of Action : Hadrat Ali's original plan was to undertake an expedition against Syria. The implementation of the plan had to be deferred because the people of Medina had not favourably responded to his call for arms. The crisis deepened when Talha and Zubayr escaped from Medina and at Mecca Hadrat Aishah raised the cry for the vengeance for the blood of Hadrat Uthman. Hadrat Ali had thought that Hadrat. Aishah's call would be a mere storm in the tea cup and she would not or could not go to the extent of precipitating war. When Hadrat Ali came to know that Hadrat Aishah had assembled a force and was planning a march to Basra he felt that no further time could be lost and immediate action was called for to frustrate the efforts of Hadrat Aishah in gaining further strength. It was with some difficulty that Hadrat Ali was able to raise a small force at Medina. By and large the people of Medina shut themselves in their houses and remained indifferent to the call of Hadrat Ali. The force that Hadrat Ali was able to muster comprised mostly of the Sabites who had participated in the revolt against Hadrat Uthman. Some people of Medina who were devoted to Hadrat Ali, however, joined the ranks. Abu Qatada, a leader of the. Ansars, and a veteran warrior waited on Hadrat Ali and offered his services. Hadrat Umm Salma, a wife of the Holy Prophet came to see Hadrat Ali and said that if other women were to accompany him she would be glad to accompany. She had a son Umar by a former husband and he joined the army of Hadrat Ali. Hadrat Ali appointed Tamam b. Abbas as the Governor of Medina. He sent an emissary to Mecca to recruit whatever volunteers he could from the people of Mecca. The strength of the force that Hadrat Ali was able to muster in Medina did not exceed nine hundred. At the head of this force, Hadrat Ali marched out of Medina. When Hadrat Ali was about to depart. Abdullah b Salam, a veteran Companion of the Holy Prophet, held up the reins of the horse of Hadrat Ali and said:

> "O Commander of the Faithful, do not go out of Medina. If you once leave Medina you will not be able to return to Medina again. Medina would thereafter cease to be the capital of the Muslim world."

The Sabite followers of Hadrat Ali wanted to deal roughly with the old man, but Hadrat Ali warned them not to touch the person of Abdullah b Salam for he was an eminent Companion of the Holy Prophet. Hadrat Ali assured Abdullah b Salam that he would soon return to Medina. That was, however, not to be Hadrat Ali never came back to Medina and Medina ceased to be the capital of the Muslim commonwealth.

Hadrat Ali at Rabda : After some forced marches, Hadrat Ali reached Rabda. It was a junction from where one road led to Medina, one to Mecca, one to Kufa and another to Basra. Here he came to know that the army of Hadrat Aishah had already reached Basra and he had been late in intercepting the army of Hadrat Aishah half-way. Hadrat Ali now felt that a battle would have to be fought at Basra. The army at the disposal of Hadrat Ali was inadequate for the purpose. Imam Hassan, the son of Hadrat Ali, advised his father not to play with fire. He said:

> "I fear like Uthman you will be assassinated I have been advising you not to play with fire but you have not listened to me"

Hadrat Ali wanted him to indicate what was his advice to which he had not listened. Thereupon Imam Hassan said:

> "When the house of Hadrat Uthman was besieged by the rebels I had advised you to go out of Medina, for the assassination of Hadrat Uthman while you were present in Medina was not in you interest. When Hadrat Uthman had been assassinated I had advised you not to accept the caliphate unless deputations came to you from various parts of the country to request you to accept the caliphate. When Talha and Zubayr defected I advised you to shut yourself in your house and leave it to the people to decide the question of the vengeance for the blood of Hadrat Uthman themselves. I had advised you to keep aloof from the controversy but you did not accept my advice. "

Hadrat Ali said he did not leave Medina when the house of Hadrat Uthman was besieged for in that case the rebels would have chased and he would have met the same fate as had befallen to Hadrat Uthman. The caliphate was offered to me by the people of Medina. They alone were competent to do so and other towns had to conform to the decision taken by the people of Medina. He explained that when he had accepted the office of the Caliph he could not shut himself in his house and evade the responsibilities of the office.

Banu Tay : From Rabda, Hadrat Ali sent envoys to the neighbouring tribes to seek volunteers. The Banu Tay were the first to rally to the support of Hadrat Ali During the time of the Holy Prophet, Hadrat Ali had played an important role in espousing their cause and converting them to Islam. The tribe had particular attachments for Hadrat Ali and they enthusiastically responded to Hadrat Ali's call for volunteers. Saeed b Ubaid, the chief of the Banu Tay, waited on Hadrat Ali and said:

> "O Commander of the Faithful, there are many persons who do not speak openly what is in their hearts but such is not the case with me. I have always held you in the greatest esteem. I have looked upon you as the leader both openly and inwardly and have resolved to support you and fight against your enemies whosoever they be I consider you to be a person of the highest merit more worthy than anyone else of this or any other age to be called a superman"

With these words the chief swore allegiance to Hadrat Ali and thereafter the other men of the tribe also swore their allegiance. The men of the Banu Asad allied with Banu Tay also swore allegiance to Hadrat Ali. Most of the other tribes in the neighbourhood chose to remain neutral and not to side with any party at that stage.

Letters to Governor of Basra : From the camp at Rabda, Hadrat Ali addressed a letter to his Governor of Basra to the following effect:

> "Calling God to witness I say that Talha and Zubayr swore allegiance to me and then broke it. The devil has instigated them to follow a path which is not acceptable to God. These people are not afraid of God's wrath. When they come to you, persuade them to stick to the path of fidelity for which they swore at Medina. If they submit, behave kindly towards them. Should they persist in their treachery fight them until God decides between us"

Before this letter reached him Uthman b Hanif had made a truce with Hadrat Aishah and deputed an emissary to Medina to enquire whether Talha and Zubayr had taken the oath of allegiance to Hadrat Ali voluntarily and under some duress. When Hadrat Ali came to know of this development, he addressed another letter to Uthman b Hanif in the following terms.

> "Talha and Zubayr swore allegiance to me under no compulsion. Even if they did so under fear or compulsion such a constraint was used on them for preserving solidarity of Islam and not for creating discord among the believers If they recant from what they have sworn and aim at forcing my abdication they are without any cause. If they have any other grievance besides their aspiration to the caliphate I will be prepared to consider it."

It appears that before the second letter could reach Uthman b Hanif, Basra had already been occupied by the forces of the confederates and the Governor of Hadrat Ali had been overthrown.

Need for Reinforcements : In spite of the accession of the tribes of Banu Tay and Banu. Asad the forces at the disposal of Hadrat Ali were still too inadequate for any big showdown. The crisis had deepened after the occupation of Basra by Hadrat Aishah and the confederates. To dislodge the rebels from Basra, a large army was needed and such large force could come from Kufa alone. Hadrat Ali accordingly decided to win over Kufa to his cause before proceeding to Basra.

Mission to Kufa : Before Hadrat Ali could proceed to Basra, he had to tackle the problem of Kufa. The people of Kufa had played a leading role in the revolt against Hadrat Uthman. After the assassination of Hadrat Uthman they offered the caliphate to Zubayr, but on his refusal they supported the caliphate of Hadrat Ali. When Hadrat Ali was elected as the Caliph, the people of Kufa took the oath of allegiance to him. Abu Musa. Ashari was the Governor of Kufa appointed by Hadrat Uthman. When Hadrat Ali deposed the Governors of the previous regime and sent his nominee to assume the charge of the governorship of Kufa in place of Abu Musa. Ashari, the people of Kufa refused to accept the new Governor and wanted Abu Musa to continue in his office. Hadrat Ali accepted the demand of the people of Kufa and allowed Abu Musa. Ashari to continue as the Governor. Abu Musa. Ashari took the oath of allegiance to Hadrat Ali. The situation in Kufa was intriguing. Though the Kufans had taken the oath of allegiance to Hadrat Ali they believed themselves to be strong enough to act independently. In this context although Abu Musa owed his appointment to Hadrat Ali he did not deem it necessary to follow the orders of Hadrat Ali in all respects.

Muhammad b. Jafar and Muhammad b. Abu Bakr's Mission : When Muawiyyah had raised the standard of revolt in the west in Syria and Hadrat Aishah had led her forces to Basra in the east, Hadrat Ali could not afford to undertake a punitive expedition against Kufa to cut the Governor to proper size. Hadrat Ali accordingly decided to win over the people of Kufa and their Governor through conciliatory means From Rabda, Hadrat Ali sent a mission to Kufa comprising Muhammad b Jafar and Muhammad b. Abu Bakr. Both of them were the sons of Asma. Asma was originally the wife of Jafar. After the death of Jafar,. Asma married Hadrat Abu Bakr. After the death of Hadrat. Abu Bakr she married Hadrat Ali. The two Muhammads were thus the stepsons of Hadrat Ali. About their mission to Kufa, Hadrat Ali instructed his envoys as follows

> "Should the people of Kufa respond to my call, tell them how I prefer them to all other people of the commonwealth. Give them the tidings that I intend to make Kufa the capital of the empire. Treat the Kufans with kindness and ask them to come and arbitrate between us and those who have separated from us. Point out to them that I am putting up trust in them at this critical juncture. Let them come forward to help the religion of God and adopt such measures as may help to reunite the divided Muslims"

The envoys of Hadrat Ali were received by Abu Musa. Ashan coldly. He behaved as if he was not an appointee of Hadrat Ali but was the ruler of an independent country. He wanted the envoys of Hadrat Ali to carry the following message to their master

> "The assumption of the caliphate has placed Hadrat Ali in an awkward position. Therefore, we the people of Kufa have decided not to engage ourselves in the struggle. Let it be understood that we shall not take sides, until you have rid yourselves of the murderers of Hadrat Uthman"

Mission of Ibn Abbas : The stand taken by Abu Musa Ashan was preposterous. As the Governor owing allegiance to Hadrat Ali he was under an obligation to carry out the policies of Hadrat Ali. He could not sit in judgement over the command of Hadrat Ali. Hadrat Ali, however, took a lenient view of the matter and on the failure of the first mission he sent another mission to Kufa headed by Abdullah b. Abbas, an eminent companion and a cousin of Hadrat Ali as well as the Holy Prophet. This mission was also received coldly by Abu Musa Ashan. The mission did not succeed in making Abu Musa see reasons or realise his obligation to the Caliph. He asked the delegation to carry the following message from him to Hadrat Ali

> "The Companions of Muhammad (peace be on him) know more of God and His Apostle than those who have not had the opportunity of meeting him. Certainly the Companions have a right over us. My humble advice to all of you is that you should not assume the air of having God's authority with you and should not make war on God. Let you followers who have come from Medina go back to their homes till they all agree on a unanimous decision and they know who is to be relied upon. The present rebellion can best be epitomised in the famous saying of the Holy Prophet who predicted of the approaching time when he said, 'He that sleeps is better than he who sits. He

who sits is better than he who stands. He who stands is better than he who walks. He who walks is better than he who rides. 'Therefore, I will give you this advice: sheathe your swords, put off your lances, cut your bow strings and take the injured into your houses till a solution is found to the present crisis and disturbances cease."

Mission of Imam Hassan : The failure of two successive missions to Kufa set Hadrat Ali thinking. It transpired that the mission sent heretofore had merely met Abu Musa. Ashan and he had not allowed the members of the mission see the people. He had appropriated to himself the right to speak on behalf of the people of Kufa. Hadrat Ali was advised that if Kufa was to be won, a bolder line of action should be followed. After a good deal of discussion and deliberation it was decided that an effort should be made to contact the people of Kufa direct. Among the troops of Hadrat Ali there were some persons who belonged to Kufa or commanded influence with the people of Kufa. They were sent to Kufa to contact their friends and relatives and win them over to the side of Hadrat Ali. This time the mission to Kufa was led by Imam Hassan. It was felt that as long as Abu Musa. Ashan was the Governor of Kufa, the chances of the success of the mission were slender. Hadrat Ali accordingly authorised Imam Hassan that if the circumstances in Kufa were favourable, he could depose. Abu Musa. Ashan and appoint a new Governor.

The agents of Hadrat Ali succeeded in winning over many people to the side of Hadrat Ali. These agents brought home the point that as most of the people of Kufa had joined in the revolt against Hadrat Uthman, the cry for the vengeance for the blood of Hadrat Uthman was really aimed at the massacre of the people of Kufa. It was argued that in the circumstances it was in the interest of the people of Kufa that they should side with Hadrat Ali and fight against those who raise the cry for the vengeance for the blood of Hadrat Uthman merely as pretext for capturing power. The argument appealed to the people as they decided to opt for Hadrat Ali

Imam Hassan arrived at Kufa on Friday at the time of noon day prayers and he proceeded straight away to the main mosque. The agents of Hadrat Ali had brought the supporters of Hadrat Ali to the mosque in large numbers. As Imam Hassan entered the mosque, he was given a standing ovation by the people. Abu Musa. Ashan who was present in the mosque welcomed Imam Hassan to Kufa. Imam Hassan took the stage and after praising God and the Holy Prophet conveyed the message of goodwill of Hadrat Ali for the people of Kufa. He exhorted the people to strengthen the hands of Hadrat Ali in his fight against those who wanted to sow discord among the Muslims. Some of the people raised shouts in favour of Hadrat Aishah. To these people, Imam Hassan posed the question

> "Did God not enjoin upon Hadrat Aishah the duty of living quietly in her house and leaving it to the men to fight in the battlefield until the sedition was quelled? What an irony of fate that she should command us to do her part and has taken upon herself to do our part"

At this stage, Zaid b Sehwan, a prominent citizen of Kufa, rose up to say that he had received a letter from Hadrat Aishah wherein she had advised the people of Kufa to remain in their houses and not to take part in any fight. At this Imam Hassan put the following question to the assembly.

> "Is it not strange that she should advise the citizens of Kufa to abstain from fighting while she is herself leading a fight against the citizens of Basra"

Abu Musa. Ashan took the stage and said that in this crisis when two parties of the Muslims were at loggerheads the best course for the people of Kufa was to remain neutral.

Thereafter a long dialogue followed between Imam Hassan and Abu Musa. Ashan. Imam Hassan asked Abu Musa. Ashan the question

> "Did Talha and Zubayr not take oath of allegiance to Hadrat. Ali?"

Abu Musa said that they had taken the oath. Then Imam Hassan asked the question, 'What wrong had Hadrat Ali done to justify Talha and Zubayr revolt against him'?". Abu Musa said that he was not aware of any reason which could justify the revolt of Talha and Zubayr?" Imam Hassan next asked "If someone revolts against established authority, will such authority not be authorised to take action against those who have revolted?". Abu Musa answered the question in the affirmative "Then on what ground you do not justify the action that Hadrat Ali, the duly elected Caliph, has taken against those who have rebelled against his authority?". Abu Musa said that his ground was that it would lead to bloodshed among the Muslims. "But why should the Muslims help those who have rebelled against authority when God has enjoined the faithful to obey those in authority" asked Imam Hassan and to this question. Abu Musa had no reply. Imam Hassan next enquired of Abu Musa whether he had taken the oath of allegiance to Hadrat Ali and Abu Musa replied to this question in the affirmative. "You owe your office of the Governor to Hadrat Ali" was the next question and to this question again Abu Musa answered "Yes". "Are you not under an obligation to obey the command of the Caliph and not to do any act which helps his enemies directly or indirectly" Imam Hassan asked and this question was also answered in the affirmative. Imam Hassan thereafter posed the following question: "Your Caliph asks you to help him in his fight against his enemies. His enemies have asked the people of Kufa to remain confined to their houses and not to participate in the war. You also ask the people of Kufa to abstain from war. This means that by your acts you are helping the enemies of the Caliph although you have taken the oath of allegiance to him and owe your appointment to him. This is sedition." To this Abu Musa had no answer.

At this the supporters of Hadrat Ali raised the cry, "Down with the Governor. He is a traitor". Some voices were raised in support of Abu Musa and there was exchange of blows and hot words between the two sides. The fight between the parties spread outside the mosque. A party led by Ashtar took possession of the Governor's House and captured the Baitul Mal. That was the end of the governorship of Abu Musa. Ashan. He escaped to Mecca and under the authority delegated to him by Hadrat Ali, Imam Hassan appointed Qarda b Kaab as the new Governor of Kufa.

Pro-Ali Government in Kufa : With the departure of Abu Musa. Ashari from Kufa, a pro-Ali government was set up in Kufa. The new government proclaimed their full support to Hadrat Ali. The new Governor addressed the people of Kufa in the mosque and exhorted them to enrol themselves in the ranks of Hadrat Ali and strengthen his hands to enable him fight for the truth. Imam Hassan also addressed the people. He said:

> "Hadrat Ali had sent me to you with his message of goodwill for you. Of all the people in the commonwealth he has the greatest regard for you. He intends to make Kufa the capital of the Muslim empire. This is a great honour but Kufa deserves it. You are the people who can distinguish truth from falsehood. The way in which you have risen in the cause of Hadrat Ali is a positive proof of your love for the truth. Your Caliph needs your assistance. It is both in your interest and duly incumbent on you to help him. Can you give any reason for refusing his help? Is there anyone who can reasonably accuse him of having shown any covetous inclinations or withholding or perverting justice? Can anyone amongst you say that he thrust himself into the caliphate or that he proved himself unworthy of this dignity in anyway? Beware of those rebels who pretend to have taken up arms to avenge the murder of Hadrat Uthman. O ye people of Kufa, the avenging for the murder of Hadrat Uthman is merely a pretext to dethrone the Caliph Hadrat Ali. Hadrat Ali was elected as the Caliph unanimously by the people of Medina. Talha and Zubayr who now lead the rebels, took the oath of allegiance to him. Indeed they were the first to support him. Now they are the first to forswear him. Therefore O ye the people of Kufa it is incumbent on you to come and do what is good and forbid what is evil. Islam expects you to do your duty and your duty lies in supporting your Caliph."

The magnetic personality of Imam Hassan and his inspiring address won the hearts of the people of Kufa and they declared that they would stand by their Caliph through thick and thin. The people began to flock to the standard of Imam Hassan in large numbers and enrolled themselves as volunteers. Within a week a force ten thousand strong men was raised from Kufa to support Hadrat Ali.

March to Basra : When Hadrat Ali came to know that his mission in Kufa had succeeded and a force of ten thousand men from Kufa was coming to swell his ranks, he felt very happy. He proceeded one stage from ar-Rabda to welcome the man from Kufa. When he met the men from Kufa, he welcomed them enthusiastically. Addressing them he said:

> "Brave warriors of Kufa? You were always distinguished for your prowess and bravery. It was you who overran Persia. Your highly developed sense of love for religion and justice has always led you to help the weaker against the stronger and the right against the wrong. Unfortunately some of our brethren have chosen to follow the wrong way and sown discord among the community. I have sought your help in restoring unity among the Muslims. Those who have separated from us have no cause. They are misguided and I want them to see the light of reason. I have no intention of leading you to any sanguinary battie. You are to be the volunteers of peace and we have to proceed to Basra on mission of peace. I am sure your presence in such a large number will tilt the scale in favour of right. The services of the people in the cause of peace would not be forgotten and after the problem of Basra has been tackled, I will shift the capital from Medina to Kufa. That would greatly add to the importance of Kufa and to the prosperity of its people."

In reply to the address of Hadrat Ali some leaders of the people of Kufa paid tribute to the greatness of Hadrat Ali. They said that in view of his relationship with the Holy Prophet, his learning, his piety and his meritorious record of service in the cause of Islam he was the most suitable person among the Muslims to be their Caliph. They accordingly offered him their support without any reservation. They assured him that they would stand by him in thick and thin and in peace and war.

A Strong Army : The ten thousand strong army from Kufa added materially to the strength of Hadrat Ali. The force from Kufa included some veteran warriors who had distinguished themselves in the wars against Persia during the caliphate of Hadrat. Abu Bakr and Hadrat Umar.

When the Bedouin tribes who had heretofore followed the policy of sitting on the fence saw that the people of Kufa had joined Hadrat Ali in large numbers, they also decided to cast in their lot with Hadrat Ali and offered to serve in the ranks under him. When Hadrat Ali had left Medina he had hardly nine hundred men at his disposal. The strength of the army with him had now risen to twenty thousand. This considerably strengthened his position and he could confidently undertake the campaign to Basra. In the raising of the army there was, however, one point which could be a cause of embarrassment. Most of the Bedouins and the people of Kufa who had volunteered to join him were the men who had taken part in the rebellion against Hadrat Uthman. Indeed they were the people who were the most ardent supporters of Hadrat Ali. At this juncture when Hadrat Ali stood in great need of allies he could not afford to alienate the men who had volunteered to support his cause. As Hadrat Ali pondered over this aspect of the matter he felt that the people who had rebelled against him after taking the oath of allegiance to him were responsible for this awkward state of affairs. If such men had cooperated with him after consolidating his rule he could have taken some punitive action against the persons who had participated in the rebellion against Hadrat Uthman. If the rebels were sincere in their demand for the vengeance of the blood of Hadrat Uthman, it was incumbent on them to have strengthened his hands. By rebelling against him they had frustrated the object which they intended to achieve. The truth of the matter was that the cry for vengeance for the blood of Hadrat Uthman was a mere pretext; their real purpose was to capture power. Hadrat Ali was never keen to be elected as the Caliph, but now that he had been elected as the Caliph, he had to see that the sacred office of the Caliph should not become a plaything for adventurers.

Another point that worried Hadrat Ali was that as the Caliph it was incumbent on him that he should avoid any blood shedding among the Muslims. He accordingly resolved that though he would take a large army to Basra, he would avoid war and the sheer strength of his army would act as a brake against any rash action on the part of his opponents. After weighing such pros and cons of the case, Hadrat Ali broke the camp at ar-Rabda and took the road to Basra at the head of a large army of twenty thousand strong men.

Camp at Dhulkan : When Hadrat Ali and his troops halted at Dhulkan midway between ar-Rabda and Basra, they were joined by Uthman b Hanif, the Alid Governor of Basra. The Governor had been taken captive by the rebels and lodged in the prison. Later he was released under the orders of Hadrat Aishah Uthman b Hanif was in a sorry state when he confronted Hadrat Ali, half dead from the treatment that he had received at the hands of the rebels. He said, O Commander of the Faithful, you sent me to Basra with a beard but now I return to you disgraced having none. Hadrat Ali consoled him and said that his services in the cause of Islam would be recognised and he would be compensated for the privation that he had suffered. Hadrat Ali humorously remarked that he was old when he had sent him to Basra but he had returned to him looking younger Uthman b Hanif joined the retinue and accompanied Hadrat Ali to Basra.

On the Way to Basra : On the way to Basra at one of the halts, a "Kahin" met Hadrat Ali. The "Kahin" said that he saw blood flowing profusely on all sides. Hadrat Ali cursed him for his evil prognostication.

The tribes of Rabih and Abdul Qais had originally joined the troops of Hadrat. Aishah but later they withdrew their support from her and marched out of Basra to join the forces of Hadrat Ali. Hadrat Ali welcomed them and praised them for their ability to discern the truth.

As the troops of Hadrat Ali moved forward news were received that Basra had been occupied by the confederates and that all the people of Basra who were suspected of having participated in the murder of Hadrat Uthman had been executed. Thereupon Hadrat Ali is reported to have said:

> "Now that they have taken the "Qasas" and killed the people whom they considered guilty of the murder of Hadrat Uthman, what more do they want in Basra? O God, rid me of Talha and Zubayr."

Camp at Basra : On reaching Basra, the troops of Hadrat Ali camped outside the city. It was a large army and the camp was spread over several miles. The pro-Alid people of Basra who had evacuated the city on its cooperation by the confederates also joined the camp. Some other tribes in the neighbourhood of Basra also joined the camp. Hadrat Ali instructed his men to remain at peace. According to his instruction war was not to be resorted to until all possibilities of peace had been exhausted.

Peace Parleys : Although Hadrat Ali had led an army to Basra, he was averse to any armed conflict between the Muslims. He felt that those who had rebelled against his authority laboured under some misunderstanding. It was his endeavour that such misunderstanding should be removed and unity should be restored among the Muslims. When his army Generals asked his instruction about beginning the war operations, he commanded that war was not to be resorted to until all possibilities of an equitable settlement through peaceful means had been exhausted. He ordered that even on the failure of the peace parleys, the first shot was not to be fired from his side. "Let the other side take the initiative in the war, if they are not inclined to listen to the voice of reason" he said.

Mission to Hadrat Aishah : In his quest for peace, Hadrat Ali sent a peace mission to Hadrat Aishah. The peace mission was headed by Qaaqa, a prominent leader from Kufa. He was a renowned warrior and was well known for his heroic exploits in the wars against the Persians during the caliphates of Hadrat Abu Bakr and Hadrat Umar. The mission was instructed by Hadrat Ali not to adopt a threatening or a patronising attitude. No attempt was to be made to over awe the other side with the superior strength of the force at the disposal of the caliphate. Hadrat Ali desired that the negotiations between the parties should be a heart to heart dialogue and every possible effort should be made to remove the misunderstanding between the parties. Hadrat Ali instructed the members of the mission that due respect should be shown to Hadrat Aishah, the Mother of the Faithful. He sent a message of goodwill and great regards to Hadrat Aishah saying that in spite of the unfortunate misunderstanding that had cropped up between them he looked to her as a mother and expected a motherly treatment from her.

The Issues : The mission was received by Hadrat Aishah, Talha and Zubayr with due courtesy. The message of Hadrat Ali was duly delivered and Hadrat Aishah said that she would be glad if the misunderstandings were removed and unity among the Muslims was restored. Qaaqa enquired of Hadrat Aishah as to what were the objects before her which had prompted her to take the field. She said that the objects before her were to seek vengeance for the blood of Hadrat Uthman and to promote the cause of Islam.

Vengeance for the Blood : With regard to the issue about the vengeance for the blood of Hadrat Uthman, Qaaqa posed the question "Mother, tell me keeping God in view whether you accuse Hadrat Ali for the murder of Hadrat Uthman as a criminal or as an accomplice?" Hadrat Aishah said that she did not accuse Hadrat Ali for involvement in the assassination of Hadrat Uthman, her grievance was that as Caliph, Hadrat Ali had not taken any action to apprehend the murderers of Hadrat Uthman. Qaaqa then asked whether such murder was the act of one man, or was it the act of a mob. Hadrat Aishah said that obviously it was the act of a mob. Qaaqa next asked the question "Have things settled down after the murder of Hadrat Uthman" Hadrat Aishah said that the things were still very much in a state of disarray. Qaaqa thereupon said, "If things are still unsettled how could Hadrat Ali take against the people who were still in control of the situation and from whom another coup could be expected? To this question Hadrat Aishah, Talha or Zubayr had no satisfactory answer.

Qaaqa then posed another question, "Do you know that by rebelling against the authority of Hadrat Ali you have done great harm to the cause for the vengeance of the blood of Hadrat Uthman''''' "How was that", asked Hadrat Aishah. Qaaqa said, "By rebelling against the authority of Hadrat Ali, you have forced Hadrat Ali to deal with you instead of dealing with the murderers of Hadrat Uthman. In this crisis, Hadrat Ali had naturally to seek allies and when you have forsaken Hadrat Ali, those who had rebelled against Hadrat Uthman have come to the aid of Hadrat Ali in large numbers. Because they feel that the troubles of Hadrat Ali are because of them. Things have thus moved in a vicious circle and by rebelling against Hadrat Ali you have thrown him in the lap of the persons from whom you seek vengeance. By your action you have strengthened the murderers of Hadrat Uthman and weakened the Muslims "That set Hadrat Aishah thinking and she could not know how the argument advanced by Qaaqa could be met.

Promoting the Cause of Islam : Qaaqa then took up the question of promoting the cause of Islam. He pointed out that when the Muslims were united under Hadrat Abu Bakr and Hadrat Umar they made large conquests both in the east and the west. In the early years of the caliphate of Hadrat Uthman the process of conquests continued. When the Muslims rebelled against the authority of Hadrat Uthman and came to be divided among themselves the process of conquest came to a grinding halt. He observed that the enemies of Islam were on the borders of the Muslim State ready to take advantage of any division in the ranks of the Muslims. Qaaqa posed the question, "How can you promote the cause of Islam, if you seek to divide the Muslims for one cause or the other. Addressing the confederates he asked, "Did you promote the cause of Islam when you killed six hundred men of Basra and the mosque was dyed with blood? Did you thereby avenge the murder of Hadrat Uthman when such persons were not even remotely connected with the murder of Hadrat Uthman? If you killed them because rightly or wrongly you suspected them of being involved in the assassination of Hadrat Uthman, then is your demand for the "Qasas" for the blood of Hadrat Uthman not yet satisfied? He respectfully addressed Hadrat Aishah saying:

> "O Mother of the Faithful' Did God not enjoin you to sit quietly in your home? Did the Holy Prophet not warn you that the dogs of Hauab would bark on you?. Then how did you promote the cause of Islam by violating these instruction?". Addressing Talha and Zubayr he said "Did you not take the oath of allegiance to Hadrat Ali. If you took the oath of allegiance to Hadrat Ali under some compulsion, tell us the man for whom you would have voted if you were free. Is any man more qualified and more worthy to be the Caliph of the Muslims than Hadrat Ali? Verily Hadrat Ali is the best man to be the Caliph of the Muslims and by putting difficulties in his way you do not promote the cause of Islam you do great harm to Islam."

Reaction of Hadrat Aishah : The arguments advanced by Qaaqa had their way. They were most effective and impressive Hadrat Aishah asked Qaaqa, "Then, what do you suggest? ". He said, "I suggest that instead of fighting, make peace, strengthen the hands of Hadrat Ali and when law and order is fully established the Muslims acting in concert should determine how the vengeance for the blood of Hadrat Uthman could be taken". Thereupon Hadrat Aishah said, "If that be the view of Hadrat Ali as well, we agree to make peace on honourable terms" Qaaqa respectfully took leave of Hadrat Aishah and returned to Hadrat Ali to report the success of his mission.

Negotiations for Peace : When Hadrat Ali came to know of the success of the mission of his emissary Qaaqa to Hadrat Aishah, Talha and Zubayr he felt very happy. The two armies encamped in the "Wadi-us-Saba" (Valley of the Lion) near the village of Khuraiba outside Basra, facing each other. It was decided that the following day when the two armies assembled in the valley, the terms of peace would be negotiated and the proclamation of peace would be issued.

The following day as the two forces assembled, Hadrat Ali posted a man in the centre carrying a copy of the Holy Quran on his head. This was indicative of the desire on the part of Hadrat Ali to decide the dispute peacefully in the light of the teachings of the Holy Quran.

Hadrat Ali rode to the centre of the valley and called upon Talha and Zubayr to step forward to meet him. When Talha and Zubayr came forward he asked them why they had rebelled against his authority when they had taken the oath of allegiance to him. They said that they had taken the oath under duress and it was not binding. He asked them after all what did they want. They said that they wanted "Qasas" for the assassination of Hadrat Uthman. Hadrat Ali said that this matter could be considered under condition of peace.

Talha and Zubayr said that if Hadrat Ali was prepared to take "Qasas" from the murderers of Hadrat Uthman they were prepared to make peace and acknowledge Hadrat Ali as the Caliph. Hadrat Ali replied that he would consider their demand favourably.

Turning to Zubayr, Hadrat Ali said ' Have you forgotten that you are my cousin, being a son of my paternal aunt can you not recall that at one of our sittings with the Holy Prophet, he commended me to you? The Holy Prophet at that time predicted that I was to suffer harm at your hands and you undertook to safeguard my interests and not to forsake me". At these words, Zubayr shuddered and said "All you have spoken the truth I had forgotten the interview with the Holy Prophet. Now that you have reminded me of that I will not harm your interest and would be prepared to make peace with you."

The meeting ended in an atmosphere of goodwill from both the sides. Thereafter the two armies retired to their camps and the general impression was that peace would be made and war would be avoided. Emissaries were exchanged between the two sides and by the evening the general impression that the terms of peace had been mutually agreed upon and that the necessary peace treaty would be executed the following day.

The Regicides : The armies on the two sides heaved a sigh of relief on coming to know that peace was to be made the following day. At nightfall the men of the two armies retired to rest with easy hearts. The case with the regicides, the persons who had participated in the assassination of Hadrat Uthman was however different. In the army of Hadrat Ali there were two to three thousand men of Kufa who were involved in the revolt against Hadrat Uthman. When the confederates had occupied Basra they had executed all such men of Basra who were involved in the assassination of Hadrat Uthman as "Qasas" for the blood of Hadrat Uthman. The regicides of Kufa apprehended that in case peace was made between Hadrat Ali and the confederates the terms of the agreement of peace were likely to be that the confederates would acknowledge the caliphate of Hadrat Ali and Hadrat Ali would, in turn, order the execution of the regicides of Kufa like the execution of the regicides belonging to Basra. The leaders of the regicides of Kufa met in conference secretly to decide what course of action they should take to save their skins. It was proposed that Hadrat Ali, Talha and Zubayr should be killed. This proposal was turned down on the ground that such action on their part was likely to reunite the confederates and the followers of Hadrat Ali and they would together fight not only for the "Qasas" of Hadrat Uthman, but for the "Qasas" of Hadrat Ali, Talha and Zubayr as well. Many other proposals were considered. It was ultimately decided that they should take steps to ensure that the two sides were locked in battle before the peace agreement was executed. In pursuance of this plan before the day break the regicides attacked the army of the confederates. When this attack came to the notice of Talha and Zubayr they ordered their forces to meet the attack. They said that they knew before-hand that Hadrat Ali did not really mean to execute an agreement of peace. When the army of the confederates made a counter attack, the regicides made Hadrat Ali believe that the confederates had made a surprise attack. Hadrat Ali asked his forces to take up arms and beat back. Hadrat Ali said that he already knew that Talha and Zubayr were not serious in their peace proposals.

The Battle : Before it was day break the two armies had taken the field and engaged in a life and death struggle. The regicides fought most desperately and their attacks were resisted by the confederates. The battle accordingly took a sanguinary turn. It was a deplorably engagement when the Muslims cut the throats of Muslims. It appeared that the injunctions of Islam had been forgotten and the people reverted to the pre-Islamic practice of setting their disputes through the arbitration of the sword. According to chronicles when the opposing sides came together breast to breast with a furious shock the noise that was produced was like the sound of thunder. The forces of the two sides fought with the ferocity of lions and men fell on the battlefield from both the sides like the fall of autumn leaves. Talha fought bravely and he killed many warriors of the army of Hadrat Ali. He was, however, mortally wounded by the arrows that hit him. He was carried in an unconscious state to a house in Basra where he soon expired. By noon the tide of the battle began to turn against the confederates. At this stage Zubayr is also reported to have escaped from the battlefield and taken the road to Mecca. When Hadrat Aishah came to know of the state of the battle, she came to the battle seated in a litter on a camel. She exhorted the people to stop fighting. She posted Kaab b Sur, the Qadi of Basra, in the centre of the battlefield with a copy of the Holy Quran on his head. He exhorted the men of the army of Hadrat Ali to stop fighting in the name of God. Some men of the army of Hadrat Ali were inclined to listen to the call of Kaab b Sur, well known for his piety and learning. The regicides who were in the forefront of the fight cried. He is the man who reported that Talha and Zubayr had not taken the oath of allegiance to Hadrat Ali voluntarily Kill him "The regicides rained arrows on Kaab b Sur and he fell dead. The confederates shot arrows in return killing some of the regicides. The frenzy of the combatants appeared to know no bounds. The appalling carnage continued unabated and the dead and the dying lay pilled in heaps. Hadrat Aishah seated in a litter on a camel became the main target for attack by the forces of Hadrat Ali. The followers of Hadrat Aishah flocked round her camel to protect her. A devoted follower held the reins of the camel and as anyone from the army of Hadrat Ali advanced to attack the camels, the man holding the reins of the camel cut him with his sword. In such duels many persons fell on both the sides. Over two dozen persons of the army of the confederates lost their heads while holding the bridle of the camel of Hadrat Aishah. The casualties in the case of the warriors of the army of Hadrat Ali who dashed against the camel were much heavier. Hadrat Ali felt that as long as the camel of Hadrat Aishah stood, the battle would continue In order to end the battle, Hadrat Ali directed his men to slip behind the camel and cut off its legs. Some warriors of the forces of Hadrat Ali managed to slip behind the camel and cut off its legs. As the beast fell on the ground dead it gave such a shriek that made the men shiver in their shoes Hadrat Aishah escaped with her life although the litter in which she had been sitting was pierced with arrows Hadrat Aishah was lifted out of the litter and borne to a house in Basra.

End of the Battle : With the fall of Hadrat. Aishah's camel, the battle ended in the victory of Hadrat Ali and the defeat of the confederates. As in this battle the camel of Hadrat Aishah became the main target of attack the battle came to be known as the battle of the camel. The loss on both the sides was considerable. Over ten thousand persons were killed in the battle. Among the dead on both the sides there were many prominent Companions of the Holy Prophet who had fought in the wars under the Holy Prophet and the rightly guided Caliphs— Hadrat Abu Bakr, Hadrat Umar and Hadrat Uthman.

Talha, the confederate leader, died because of the wounds received in the battle. Zubayr escaped from the battlefield and he took the road to Mecca. He had proceeded for some distance from Basra when he came across a detachment led by the Banu Qais chief. Ahnaf b Qais. Here Zubayr halted to offer prayers. When Zubayr prostrated himself in prayers one of the men of. Ahnaf cut off the head of Zubayr with the blow of his sword. Ahnaf brought the head of Zubayr to Hadrat Ali hoping to be awarded for killing his enemy. At the sight of the gory head of his cousin, Hadrat Ali burst into sobs and turning to Ahnaf said, "You have done a ghastly deed and verily your lot is heel fire". Ahnaf was surprised at the remarks of Hadrat Ali. Addressing Hadrat Ali he said, "You are an evil judge of men. If someone delivers you from your enemies you pronounce the penalty of hell fire on him" Bitterly resenting what he felt to be a great injustice,. Ahnaf drew his sword and plunged it into his own breast.

Return of Basra : When after the battle, Hadrat Ali inspected the battlefield, he found it piled up with dead bodies and littered with severed limbs. The plain outside Basra was virtually soaked with blood. Among the dead on both sides there were many faces familiar to Hadrat Ali and he was much grieved over their death. These included some eminent Companions. Hadrat Ali felt that if as a result of the battle men of such eminence were to die, he would not have resorted to war. It was a deplorable sight that Muslims had cut the throats of Muslims and at this tragedy nobody could grieve more than Hadrat Ali. As long as the battle waged, there was enmity between the two sides. After the battle there was no enmity between the dead Hadrat Ali arranged for the funeral prayers, and the burial of the dead from the both the sides. Many vultures invaded the battlefield and carried away the limbs. A vulture carried a limb to Medina and it was found to be a severed hand containing a ring bearing the name of Abdur Rahman b. Atab, an eminent Companion. Hadrat Ali did not celebrate the victory as an occasion of joy. He ordered the observance of mourning for three days in the memory of the dead. These three days were spent in the burial of the dead.

Treatment of the People : Some of the followers of Hadrat Ali demanded that having been defeated the survivors should be distributed as slaves among the soldiers of the victorious army. Hadrat Ali turned down the demand saying that as the Caliph of the Muslims he could not allow the Muslims to be enslaved by Muslims in a country which was "Dar-ul-Islam". The soldiers of the army of Hadrat Ali desired that if they were not to be allowed to enslave the people of Basra, they should be allowed to plunder their property. Hadrat Ali turned down this demand as well with great force. He held that whatever arms and equipments had been brought to the battlefield on the occasion of the battle could be treated as "Ghanima" (war booty) and captured, but whatever lay in the homes of the people belonged to them and he could not permit his men to deprive the people of Basra of their rightful belongings. Whatever booty was collected from the battlefield was distributed among the soldiers, according to the Islamic law, and they were asked to abstain from seizing any property of the people of Basra by force.

Occupation of Basra : After the three days of mourning were over, Hadrat Ali entered the city of Basra and occupied it. He declared amnesty for the people of Basra and asked them to assemble in the principal mosque of the city. When all the people had assembled, Hadrat Ali addressed them. He said that his heart bled at the tragedy that had overtaken the people of Basra. For this they were themselves to blame. They had taken the oath of allegiance to him, but later they were misguided to repudiate such oath without cause. He observed that particular sanctity was attached to such oath and could not be repudiated. He narrated at length the circumstances under which Hadrat Uthman had been killed and how he had been elected as the Caliph. He added that Talha and Zubayr were the first to offer allegiance to him and they were the first to repudiate it. Thereafter, he explained at length how the demand for the vengeance for the blood of Hadrat Uthman was merely a pretext for gaining some ulterior end. As regards Hadrat Aishah he said he had the greatest respect and regard for her. There were some minor points of differences between him and her but there was hardly any justification for making such petty differences the ground for an armed conflict.

It was not worthy of a lady of her rank and status to take to arms when according to the injunctions of Islam, ladies were required to sit in their homes and the Holy Prophet himself had warned his wives in that respect. He added that those who had led the revolt laboured under some misunderstanding, and they were misguided in taking to arms. Because of such misguidance the Muslim Ummah had suffered and at this suffering and disaster none was more grieved than he. He said, "At this moment Basra lies bleeding, my heart bleeds at the tragedy that has befallen your city". He observed that he had granted annesty to the people of Basra and was prepared to forgive and forget the past, provided the people of Basra assured him of their loyalty. The speech of Hadrat Ali had its effect. The spokesmen of the people of Basra regretted all that had happened and assured Hadrat Ali of their loyalty. Thereafter all the people of Basra offered allegiance to Hadrat Ali. "Fatiha" was offered for the souls of the dead from both the sides. Someone asked him whether he regarded the people who had opposed him and had died as martyrs. He said that he regarded all the Muslims to whatever side they belonged and had died as martyrs, for rightly or wrongly they were of the conviction that they were fighting for cause. Hadrat Ali led the prayers and after the prayers mercy of Allah was craved for keeping the Muslims united. Hadrat Ali made the necessary arrangements for the administration of Basra. He took hold of the Baitul Mal and compensated the people who had lost their dear ones. He made arrangements for the treatment of the wounded. It was noticed that some people of Basra who were in the forefront in opposition to Hadrat Ali and had escaped to seek the protection of tribes in the desert. Hadrat Ali issued a proclamation that they were free to come to their homes in Basra and no action would be taken for their sins of omission or commission in the past.

Hadrat Aishah : The strain of the battle, the humiliation of her defeat, the failure of her mission and the death of her dear ones were too much for Hadrat Aishah to bear. Although a brave woman she took to weeping day and night and fell sick. Hadrat Ali visited her frequently and tried to calm her feelings. He made arrangements that she was properly looked after and was provided all facilities. Ashtar, the leader of the regicides, purchased the most valuable camel in Basra and sent it to Hadrat Aishah in lieu of the camel that had been killed in the battle. Hadrat Aishah refused to accept the gift and cursed Ashtar as the evil genius who was responsible for the troubles of the Muslims Ummah. When Hadrat Aishah recovered from her illness she expressed the desire to be sent to Medina. Hadrat Ali made elaborate arrangements for her journey. A group of women from Basra accompanied her to Medina. Muhammad b. Abu Bakr, a step brother of Hadrat Aishah, was commissioned by Hadrat Ali to escort her to Medina. Hadrat Ali himself travelled with her caravan for one stage beyond Basra and there saw her off requesting her to forgive and forget, for no one could say whether they were destined to meet again or not. Hadrat Aishah reciprocated that goodwill of Hadrat Ali and the two parted as friends. Back in Medina, Hadrat Aishah led a retired life and did not thereafter take part in politics. She contented herself with narrating the traditions of the Holy Prophet and in this field of scholarship she came to be recognised as an authority.

Consequences of the Victory : Hadrat Ali won the battle of the Camel. As a result of this victory, Hadrat Ali's caliphate came to be acknowledged by the entire Muslim world except Syria. From the victory of Basra the victory of Damascus could have been one step but that was not to be Basra could not become a stepping stone to further conquest. In the long run, Hadrat Ali's victory over Basra proved to be more elusive than real. The carnage in Basra had been heavy. Almost every family to whichever side they belonged lost one or more dear ones. Though the people took the oath of allegiance to Hadrat Ali but they did not feel happy General discontentment continues to smoulder in the hearts of the people.

In normal circumstances Hadrat Ali's victory of Basra should have strengthened his position and overawed those who were still opposed to him Things however did not turn that way If peace could have been made at Basra and Talha and Zubayr had acknowledged the caliphate of Hadrat Ali, the position of Hadrat Ali would have been strenghth ened. The death of Talha and Zubayr, as subsequent events showed worked to the advantage of Muawiyyah If they had been alive Muawiyyah was bound to contend against three rivals— Hadrat Ali, Talha and Zubayr. After the battle of Basra he had to contend against Hadrat Ali alone and this was something in his favour. Heretofore Muawiyyah had contented himself with cold war. He had abstained from taking to arms for he was afraid that such rebellion against established authority was likely to be looked by the Muslims with disfavour. The battle of Basra sanctioned the use of the sword as an arbiter in the matter of succession to the caliphate. It provided an arguments to Muawiyyah that if the people of Basra could fight against Hadrat Ali, so could the people of Syria

The victory of Basra instead of proving a source of strength for Hadrat Ali proved in the long run to be a source of weakness Most of the people had joined Hadrat Ali in the hope that as in other wars they would amass wealth by plundering the defeated people. When Hadrat Ali forbade such plunder that led to discontentment and those who had participated in the battle came to feel that nothing was to be gained by fighting for Hadrat Ali. That created difficulties for Hadrat Ali in recruiting men to fight against Muawiyyah

The battle of Basra was indeed precipitated by the regicides much against the wished of Hadrat Ali. The victory of Basra made the regicides more powerful. That led to very embarrassing results for Hadrat Ali In Basra, Hadrat Aishah had executed all the regicides of Basra. That provided an argument to Muawiyyah and other enemies of Hadrat Ali that he was involved in the murder of Hadrat Uthman for he had taken no action against the regicides and was instead protecting them

As the peace parleys at Basra before the outbreak of the battle showed, Hadrat Ali want to take action against the regicides of Kufa as Hadrat Aishah had taken action against the regicides of Basra Subsequent developments, however, made things difficult for Hadrat Ali. These people, rebellious by nature, became a source of great headache for Hadrat Ali. When Hadrat Ali appointed his cousin. Abdullah b. Abbas as the Governor of Basra these men viewed the appointment critically and said, "If every Caliph is to appoint his relatives as the Governors, why did we kill the old man Uthman?". As with the passage of time the crisis deepened these people progressively gained in power and importance and Hadrat Ali in spite of all his valour, integrity and other notable qualities became a virtual prisoner in the hands of those "rebels"

Fatal Shadow : The battle of Basra has cast a fatal shadow across the history of Islam. It was the first civil war between the Muslims and it set the unfortunate precedent for the Muslims to fight among themselves to seek some secular end. The battle of the Camel served as a prelude to the massacre of Karbala a generation later. The argument of Yazid was that if Hadrat Ali could take to the sword to assert his right to the caliphate, so could he when most of the people had in fact taken the oath of allegiance to him. If the people of Basra were rebels and Hadrat Ali was justified in military action against them thus he was justified in taking action against Imam Hussain who had rebelled against his authority.

Six

THE KUFA YEARS

Shift of Capital

Kufa, the New Capital : From Basra, Hadrat Ali did not proceed to Medina. He proceeded to Kufa instead. When Hadrat Ali had sent a mission to Kufa to get volunteers for the fight against Basra, he had promised the people of Kufa that he would make their city the capital of the caliphate. After his victory of Basra, Hadrat Ali declared Kufa to be the capital of the Muslim Commonwealth. When Hadrat Ali had left Medina for his campaign against Talha and Zubayr little did he imagine that he was not destined to visit Medina again.

After winning the victory at Basra, Hadrat Ali came to feel that as he had won a victory at Basra against Hadrat Aishah, Talha and Zubayr, so would he be able to win a victory against Muawiyyah For a campaign against Syria the response from the people of Medina had been poor. As the people of Medina were religiously more advanced, they were averse to side with any party for an armed conflict among the Muslims Some eminent companions in Medina had even abstained from taking the oath of allegiance to Hadrat Ali and had preferred to follow a policy of neutrality. As such Hadrat Ali felt that for any confrontation with Muawiyyah, Medina could not serve as a base

When Hadrat Uthman had been assassinated, the rebels had violated the sanctity of the holy city of the Holy Prophet. Hadrat Ali was accordingly of the view that in order to preserve the sanctity of the holy city of Medina, it was expedient that the political capital should be shifted elsewhere so that the sacred city should be spared the ordeals of facing political storms

In the campaign against Basra, Hadrat Ali had succeeded in raising a large force from Kufa Hadrat Ali hoped that after the victory of Basra, the prospects of raising a still larger force from Kufa for the campaign against Syria would be brighter Geographically Kufa was more centrally located and a war against Syria could be carried more advantageously with the base at Kufa instead of Medina. Those considerations promoted Hadrat Ali to establish his capital at Kufa.

The Characteristics : Kufa was a new colony town founded in the late thirties of the seventh century during the caliphate of Hadrat Umar. It was founded as a military cantonment consequent upon the Muslim conquest of Iraq. The town was populated by the Beduins of Northern Arabia. These tribes originally belonged to Yemen. In the ancient period Yemen was known for its highly developed culture. The Yemenites boasted that they were the people who had taken their culture to ancient Egypt. They claimed to be the fathers of Arabian culture. Their culture was tribal in character and though they had accepted Islam their culture at all retained many features of the pre-Islamic culture of the age of ignorance.

The city of Kufa was divided into a number of quarters and each quarter was populated by one tribe. These people were late-comers to Islam. Most of them apostatised after the death of the Holy Prophet. As a result of the apostasy wars during the caliphate of Hadrat Abu Bakr, they were reconverted to Islam. During the caliphate of Ḥadrat Umar they played an important part in the conquest of Persia, Iran and Syria. Ḣadrat Umar availed of the services of the men of Kufa in the ranks of his army but he did not confer on them higher posts of trust and responsibility. Under Hadrat Uthman they came to hold high army posts. As long as the process of foreign conquests continued, all things remained quiet within the country. When the process of foreign conquests came to a grinding halt, disturbances broke out within the country. In the revolt against Hadrat Uthman the people of Kufa had taken the main part. When after the death of Hadrat Uthman, Hadrat Ali became the Caliph, the cry for the vengeance for the blood of Hadrat Uthman was raised and things became difficult for Hadrat Ali, he had to seek the help of the people of Kufa. Indeed the victory of Basra was mainly due to the support of Hadrat Ali by the people of Kufa. The rebels of Kufa who had participated in the murder of Hadrat Uthman had favoured the election of Zubayr as the Caliph but later, they chose to support Hadrat Ali and fight against Zubayr at Basra. As the people of Kufa were late-comers to the fold of Islam they had not fully imbibed the Islamic values and they became notorious for their perfidy and treachery. The purer Arabs of Hijaz regarded the Kufans as the "Beduin element" the rabble of the Arabian stock.

Hadrat Ali at Kufa : Hadrat Ali recognised the administration. He appointed Governors and administrators for various provinces and districts. He appointed Qadis for the various cities. He issued instructions requiring his officers to administer justice with a stern hand. He asked the tax collectors to be prompt in the collection of taxes. They were, however, warned not to adopt oppressive measures. He exhorted his officials to be scrupulously honest. He asked all concerned to do their duties diligently and conscientiously. He wanted that law and order should be maintained strictly, that all miscreants should be rounded up and suitably punished. He brought home to all concerned that he would not tolerate any dereliction of duty on the part of any official high or low. He emphasised the need of promoting Islamic values.

The plan of Hadrat Ali was that soon after the victory of Basra when the morale of his forces was high, he should invade Syria and bring Muawiyyah to his knees. Hadrat Ali soon found that there were difficulties in the materialisation of such plan. The Beduins of Kufa were once again at their game of creating discontent against the established authority. In the battle of the Camel, in spite of the victory of Hadrat Ali many persons of Kufa had been killed. There was hardly any family which had not lost some one in the battle. The people of Kufa mourned the death of such persons and they were not inclined to risk another war. At Basra Hadrat Ali had prohibited his men from pillage of Basra, enslave the Basntes or plunder their property. The battle of Basra had not brought any material gain to the people of Kufa and they were reluctant to undertake another campaign unless they were assured of some material advantage

Hadrat Ali appointed his relatives and friends as the Governors of some provinces. Ashtar the Beduin leader of Kufa, stirred trouble by criticising Hadrat Ali for such appointments. To the people of Kufa he said, "What benefit has accrued to us in shedding the blood of Hadrat Uthman for his favouritism when his successor is to indulge in the same practice? 'Those who mourned for the deaths of their dear ones in the battle of Basra posed the question, "What have we gained in fighting against the Mother of the Faithful?" Thus hardly had Hadrat Ali begun his rule in Kufa when the embers of discontent began to smoulder in the capital city. The irony of the situation was that Hadrat Ali had hardly any military force at his disposal which he could put into the field by his order. He had to raise volunteers for any action and the people had their own moods. The initiative had thus came to rest with them and they dictated terms subject to which they would fight. By shifting the capital from Medina, Hadrat Ali could not expect much help from Medina or Mecca and he had to depend heavily on the people of Kufa. The difficulty with the people of Kufa was that they would not fight for a cause, they could be induced to fight only for some material advantage.

The difficulties of Hadrat Ali increased when trouble began in the province of System. The trouble was created by the followers of Abdullah b Saba, the man who had led the revolt against Hadrat Uthman. The extremist section among these rebels considered that there was no fun in killing one Caliph when he was to be succeeded by another Caliph. The aim of these rebels was that they should capture power for themselves and set up an independent state. When Hadrat Aishah had captured she executed all such Basntes who were involved in the assassination of Hadrat Uthman. Although Hadrat Ali defeated the confederates yet he had taken no action to avenge the death of those Basntes. The followers of Ibn Sabah raised the cry for the vengeance for the execution of these Basntes. They gained ascendancy in Seestan, which province broke into open revolt and refused to pay taxes. Hadrat Ali sent a force from Kufa to put down the revolt. The force of Hadrat Ali suffered defeat. Another force sent from Kufa met a similar fate. It appears that there was some treachery in the ranks of the force of Hadrat Ali. Hadrat Ali thereafter raised another force from Yemen and other parts of the empire and sent it to Seestan under the command to. Abdullah b. Abbas, the Governor of Basra This time the rebels were defeated and the revolt was suppressed. The campaigns in Seestan affected the prestige of the caliphate and proved to be a great strain on the already meager resources at the disposal of the caliphate. In the campaign against Seestan much time was lost and this loss of time worked to the advantage of Muawiyyah and the disadvantage of Hadrat Ali. According to one account the trouble in Seestan was created by the agents of Muawiyyah who had no scruples in making common cause with the murderers of Hadrat Uthman.

Importance of Egypt : Among the provinces of the Muslim Commonwealth, Egypt was the most important province. In the revolt against Hadrat Uthman the Egyptian rebels had played the leading role. Hadrat Ali was popular among the Egyptians and the proposal to elect Hadrat Ali as the Caliph was in the first instance sponsored by the Egyptians. When Muawiyyah who led the opposition against Hadrat Ali strongly entrenched in Syria, it was vital for Hadrat Ali that he should have a strong hold on Egypt. In this context the question of the appointment of a Governor for Egypt was a matter of utmost importance.

Qais bin Saad : During the caliphate of Hadrat Uthman,. Abdullah b. Abi Sarah was the Governor of Egypt. When the opposition to Hadrat Uthman gathered strength,. Abdullah b. Abi Sarah was overthrown by Muhammad b Hudaifa. Muhammad b Hudaifa was a cousin of Hadrat Uthman. When Hudaifa died, Hadrat Uthman took over the responsibility for the upbringing of Muhammad and treated him as a son. When Muhammad grew up he fell out with Hadrat Uthman and escaped to Egypt where he incited the people to rebel against the authority of Hadrat Uthman. In the confusion following the assassination of Hadrat Uthman, Muhammad b. Abi Hudaifa was enticed by Muawiyyah to come to Ansh on the borders of Palestine where he was murdered treacherously Muawiyyah's attempt to conquer Egypt, however, failed.

On becoming the Caliph, Hadrat Ali appointed Qais b Saad as the Governor of Egypt. He was a seasoned warrior and enjoyed great fame for his wisdom and diplomacy. He belonged to a distinguished. Ansar family of Medina. He was proud of his lineage and was much devoted to Hadrat Ali. Hadrat Ali asked him to take with him some troops from Medina. Qais said that the Caliph needed the troops at Medina and he would not like to weaken the defences of Medina in any way. Qais left for Medina with a retinue consisting of seven persons only.

Affairs of Egypt : The affairs of Egypt were at that time in a state of great disarray By great skill and bravery, Qais succeeded in assuming the charge of the governorship of Egypt. He addressed the people in the mosque and delivered to them Hadrat Ali's message of goodwill. He took the oath of allegiance to Hadrat Ali from the people. Saddled in power, Qais sent his agents to the various parts of Egypt to obtain the oath of allegiance of the people to Hadrat Ali. Such oath was subscribed to by all the people with two exceptions. In Karbala, the Banu. Adiaj led by Yazid Harith did not take the oath of allegiance to Hadrat Ali. The tribe led by the chief Musailmah b Mukhalled were pro-Uthman and their sympathies were with the Umayyads and Muawiyyah. With great tact and diplomatic skill, Qais b Saad succeeded in making a treaty of neutrality with them. They undertook that if they were not pressed to take an oath of allegiance to Hadrat Ali they would not create any trouble for the government of Egypt or the caliphate of Hadrat Ali. Qais considered that to neutralise these people, was in the best interests of the caliphate and it was not expedient to press them to take the oath of allegiance to Hadrat Ali.

Intrigues of Muawiyyah : The plan of Muawiyyah was that with Yazid b Harith and Musailmah b Mukhalled he would create trouble for the government of Egypt. By making a treaty of neutrality with these people, Qais denied Muawiyyah the possibility of having a foothold in Egypt. Thereupon he tried to cultivate Qais. Muawiyyah asked Qais to join him and in lieu thereof he promised him and his posterity the governorship of Egypt in perpetuity. Qais spurned this offer and declared that he was loyal to Hadrat Ali and could not betray him at any cost. Muawiyyah changed his tactics and tried to make Qais believe that in supporting Hadrat Ali he was supporting the murderers of Hadrat Uthman. Qais repudiated this view. He said that he was in Medina when Hadrat Uthman was assassinated and it was incorrect that Hadrat Ali had supported the rebels or was involved in any way with the murder of Hadrat Uthman.

Having failed to win over Qais to his side, Muawiyyah resorted to intrigue to create suspicion between Hadrat Ali and Qais. Muawiyyah whipped up propaganda to the effect that Qais was his ally and would betray Hadrat Ali at the proper time for such revolt. In proof of his claim for the friendship of Qais he asserted that Qais had not suppressed the party of the Egyptians who demanded vengeance for the blood of Hadrat Uthman and had not taken the oath of allegiance to Hadrat Ali.

The agents of Muawiyyah carried the propaganda to Kufa and when Hadrat Ali came to know of these persistent rumours, he began to harbour doubts about the loyalty of Qais. Muhammad b Jafar and Muhammad b. Abu Bakr, the step sons of Hadrat Ali, pressed on Hadrat Ali to put Qais to test. The two young men argued prima facie that there appeared to be truth in the rumours, for Qais had in fact not taken any action against the people who had not taken the oath of allegiance to Hadrat Ali, but had on the other hand tried to conciliate them. In order to test the loyalty of Qais, Hadrat Ali directed Qais to take into custody the chiefs of the tribes who had not taken the oath of allegiance to Hadrat Ali and who stood for vengeance for the blood of Hadrat Uthman.

Qais wrote back to say that it would be inexpedient to arrest the chiefs of the people. They had entered into a treaty of neutrality with him and they were abiding by the treaty. The treaty stipulated that as long as they were not pressed to take the oath of allegiance to Hadrat Ali, they would not raise the cry for the vengeance for the blood of Hadrat Uthman. He observed that he had established law and order in the province with some difficulty and if the chiefs were arrested that would create unrest and worsen the law and order situation. The government of Egypt would in that case be accused of breach of faith and that would provide an opportunity to Muawiyyah to interfere in the affairs of Egypt. He pointed out that being the man on the spot he knew what course of action was in the interests of the caliphate. He pointed out that he had framed his policies in the interest of the caliphate and any change therein at that stage would adversely affect the interests of the caliphate. He advised Hadrat Ali to review his order and not to press for any action against the people who had not taken the oath of allegiance to Hadrat Ali, but were otherwise not creating any trouble for the administration. Qais added that if Hadrat Ali did not agree with him it was open to him to depose him and appoint another Governor.

Deposition of Qais : The arguments advanced by Qais did not carry weight with Hadrat Ali. That made Hadrat Ali suspicious of the loyalty of Qais. The stand taken by Qais against the orders of Hadrat Ali was interpreted by Hadrat Ali to be an evidence of Qais's alignment with those who wanted to create trouble for Hadrat Ali by raising the cry for vengeance for the blood of Hadrat Uthman. Hadrat Ali deposed Qais. When Muawiyyah came to know of these developments he felt happy that his plan to sow dissensions between Hadrat Ali and Qais had succeeded. He invited Qais to come over to Syria after his deposition and offered him a high office. Qais refused the offer. He held that though Hadrat Ali had misunderstood him and treated him unjustly yet this could not affect his loyalty to Hadrat Ali. After deposition Qais returned to Medina. The deposition of Qais from the governorship of Egypt proved to be a great mistake. It set the stage for the occupation of Egypt by Muawiyyah.

Qais and Hadrat Ali : Muawiyyah and his agents scored a victory when their intrigues succeeded and Qais was deposed. The next line of action on the part of Muawiyyah was to win over Qais to his side. When Muawiyyah failed in this object because of the unswerving loyalty of Qais to Hadrat Ali, Muawiyan made further efforts to ensure that Qais and Hadrat Ali did not reconcile. The agents of Muawiyyah in Medina tried to persuade Qais to abandon the cause of Hadrat Ali but when he refused to fall in line with them they began to taunt him for his loyalty to the man who did not appreciate his services and the way Hadrat Ali had treated him. Exasperated by such taunts, Qais decided to visit Hadrat Ali at Kufa and demand a fair hearing from Hadrat Ali. All received Qais with due courtesy. The two men had a heart to heart dialogue. As a result of these talks, Hadrat Ali was convinced of the loyalty of Qais Hadrat Ali wanted Qais to remain by his side and he appointed him as his Chief Adviser. The reaction of Muawiyyah to the appointment of the Qais as the Chief Adviser of Hadrat Ali was expressed by him in a letter to his agent in Medina who had taunted Qais in the following words:

> "By taunting Qais and thereby forcing him to join. All you have acted as a fool. Had you given a hundred thousand men to Ali, it would have been a lesser evil to me than to give the counsel of such a man as Qais to my enemy."

Ameer Muawiyyah : Hadrat Muawiyyah belonged to the Umayyad section of the Quraish of Mecca. Muawiyyah and the Holy Prophet had Abd Manaf as their common ancestor. The Holy Prophet was the son of Abdullah who was the son of Abdul Muttalib, who was the son of Hashim who was the son of Abd Manaf. Muawiyyah was the son of Abu Sufyan, who was the son of Harb, who was the son of Umayyah, who was the son of Abd Shams, who was the son of Abd Manaf Hashim and Abd Shams were the two sons of Abd Manaf. The Holy Prophet was a descendant of Hashim while Muawiyyah was a descendant of Abd Shams Umayyah, the son of Abd Shams was an important man of the line and his descendants came to be known after him as the Umayyads.

Abu Sufyan, the father of Muawiyyah was a Quraish magnate. When the Holy Prophet declared his mission, Abu Sufyan was conspicuous for his hostility to the Holy Prophet and Islam. He led the Quraish army against the Muslims in the battles of Uhud and the Trench Muawiyyah's mother was the atrocious woman who made necklaces and bracelets of the ears and noses of the Muslims slain at Uhud. She ripped the dead body of Hamza, an uncle of the Holy Prophet, martyred at Uhud, took out the liver and rent it with her teeth.

It was only after the conquest of Mecca by the Muslims that Abu Sufyan and his family including Muawiyyah submitted to Islam. After conversion to Islam Muawiyyah acted for some time as a secretary to the Holy Prophet. During the caliphate of Hadrat

Abu Bakr and Hadrat Umar, Muawiyyah and his elder brother. Abu Yazid fought against the Byzantines in Syria.

Hadrat Umar appointed Abu Ubaida b Jarrah as the Governor of Syria. On the death of Abu Ubaida, Abu Yazid, the brother of Muawiyyah, was appointed as the Governor of Syria. On the death of Abu Yazid, Hadrat Umar appointed Muawiyyah as the Governor of Syria. When Hadrat Uthman who was a cousin of Muawiyyah became the Caliph, he confirmed Muawiyyah in his appointment as the Governor of Syria and added some other territories to his jurisdiction.

The Character : Muawiyyah was a typical Arab and he had all the virtues and vices which characterised the Arabs before their conversion to Islam. As Governor of Syria he won the hearts of the people by gifts and concessions. He was a man tall, fair and handsome and of dignified bearing Hadrat Umar often said about Muawiyyah that he was the Caesar of the Arabs. His great personal charm, his affability, his attractive and pleasant disposition, his good manners and his eloquence endeared him to the people. He was known to his people as 'the silver tongued Amir". His intelligence, his sagacity, his pursuit of poetry, his shrewdness and his sense of humour made him the "beau ideal" of the people. He was proverbial for his forbearance. He was a diplomat and politician par excellence. In winning battles the relied more on the effective use of the tongue than on the sword. He was a past master in propaganda. He was of the view that it was the end and not the means that mattered and in the achievement of the end any means, fair or foul could be adopted. Islam had enjoined austerity in living but Muawiyyah preferring the Byzantine way followed a luxurious way of life. He was fond of pomp, ceremony and lavish ostentation. He built costly palaces for himself. For the people of Syria who were used to the Byzantine way of life there was nothing objectionable in such display of power and pelf to the orthodox Muslims such wayward luxuriance was frivolous and profane.

Conflict between Hadrat Ali and Muawiyyah : After his election as the Caliph, Hadrat Ali deposed Muawiyyah from the governorship of Syrin a Muawiyyah did not accept the orders of Hadrat Ali and refused to vacate office While in all other provinces oath of allegiance was taken to Hadrat Ali under the influence of Muawiyyah. Nobody in Syria took the oath of allegiance of his authority that amounted to rebellion pure and simple. At the outset of his rule Hadrat Ali planned an action against Syria to suppress the revolt.

Things, however, got complicated and instead of being resolved got tangled with the lapse of time. Muawiyyah enjoyed the support of the people of Syria. Hadrat Ali was thus not able to take disciplinary action against Muawiyyah as the Head of a State could ordinarily take against a defiant subordinate. If Muawiyyah had to be deposed, military action was necessary against the people of Syria. That obviously meant the Muslims fighting against the Muslims This was something repugnant to Islam and as such when Hadrat Ali gave the call to arms for a military action against Syria the response from the people of Medina was very poor. Expedition against Syria had therefore to be deferred for some reason or the other. The delay worked to the advantage of Muawiyyah as thereby he consolidated his power.

Difficulties were created for Ḥadrat Ali. When Talha and Zubayr who had taken oath of allegiance to him defected and were joined by Hadrat Aishah. Hadrat Aishah, Talha and Zubayr occupied Basra and Hadrat Ali had to lead a force against Basra instead of against Syria Hadrat Ali won the victory over the confederates but this was achieved at a heavy cost. Over ten thousand persons died in this battle and their death was deeply mourned by the Muslim world. That also proved to be a drain of the limited resources at the disposal of Hadrat Ạli. When after the Basra campaign Hadrat Ali turned to Syria, Muawiyyah had become stronger and things for Hadrat Ali became all the more difficult.

Strategy of Muawiyyah : The conflict between Hadrat Ali and Muawiyyah had its roots in history. The Hashimites and the Umayyads were cousins and there was usual rivalry and enmity between them. During the time of Abdul Muttalib the leadership of the Quraish vested in the Hashimites. After the death of Abdul Muttalib the leadership passed on to the Umayyads. When the Holy Prophet declared his mission, the Umayyads were in the forefront in opposition to the Holy Prophet. Apart from religious scruples, one of the grounds for such opposition was the apprehension of the Umayyads that if Islam gained strength the leadership would pass on to the Hashimites. When the Muslims conquered Mecca the Umayyads had to accept the leadership of the Hashimites. After the death of the Holy Prophet the caliphates was held by Hadrat Abu Bakr and Hadrat Umar who were neither Hashimites nor Umayyads. The third Caliph Hadrat Uthman was an Umayyad and during his caliphate, the Umayyads came to be strongly entrenched in power. Indeed one of the main allegations of the rebels against Hadrat Uthman was that he had unduly favoured the Umayyads. When after the assassination of Hadrat Uthman, Hadrat Ali was elected as the Caliph, the Umayyads became uneasy to the transfer of power to the Hashimites. The real aim of Muawiyyah was to create difficulties in the way of Hadrat Ali in order to pave the way for the transfer of power to the Umayyads. The conflict between Hadrat Ali and Muawiyyah was really the recrudesce of the old rivalry between the Hashimites and the Umayyads.

Hadrat Ali, an outspoken and straightforward man wanted to exert authority over Muawiyyah for the simple reason that he had been elected as the Caliph and all authority vested in him. Pressing all his qualities as shrewd politician into service, Muawiyyah proceeded to undermine the authority of Hadrat Ali by resorting to propaganda against

Hadrat Ali and adopting other underhand means. He raised the cry for vengeance for the blood of Hadrat Uthman. He displayed the blood-stained garments of Hadrat Uthman and the amputated fingers of Hadrat Uthman's wife Naila in the main mosque at Damascus. This display was backed up by propaganda which raised the emotions of the people to a high pitch. With all the vehemence at his command, he addressed the congregations accusing Hadrat Ali of complicity in the murder of Hadrat Uthman. He maintained that the election of Hadrat Ali as Caliph was irregular as it was held under the pressure of the rebels who had assassinated Hadrat Uthman. When Talha and Zubayr defected from Hadrat Ali and advanced the plea that they had taken the oath of allegiance to Hadrat Ali under the coercion of the rebels, that furnished Muawiyyah another argument for criticising Hadrat Ali. When Talha and Zubayr were killed at Basra, Muawiyyah presented them as martyrs who had given up their lives in seeking vengeance for the blood of Hadrat Uthman. He maintained that Hadrat Ali was not merely involved in the murder of Hadrat Uthman he was guilty of the murder of thousands of Muslims including Talha and Zubayr as well. He criticised Hadrat Ali for the ill treatment of Hadrat Aishah.

Muawiyyah did not rest content with carrying on propaganda against Hadrat Ali, he undertook steps to weaken the hold of Hadrat Ali on the territories held by him. Muawiyyah was shrewd enough to see that if Egypt held fast Hadrat Ali, it could stab a dagger in the back of Syna Muawiyyah, therefore, directed his efforts towards undermining the influence of Hadrat Ali in Egypt. At that time Hadrat Ali had a Governor in Egypt who was very loyal to him and who held the province well under control. Muawiyyah tried to bribe the Governor and win him over to his side. When he did not succeed in this effort, he resorted to intrigues to make Hadrat Ali suspicious of the loyalty of his Governor. Under some misunderstanding Hadrat Ali deposed his Governor. That weakened the hold of Hadrat Ali on Egypt. In order to take advantage of this tactical mistake on the part of Hadrat Ali, Muawiyyah stood in need of an ally who could conquer Egypt for him. He soon found such an ally in the person of Amr b. AI-Aas known to history as the 'Conqueror of Egypt". He was the Governor of Egypt during the reign of Hadrat Umar. Hadrat Uthman had deposed him. That created bitterness between Hadrat Uthman and Amr b. AI-Aas. Amr b. AI-Aas had in fact incited the Egyptians to rebel against the authority of Hadrat Uthman. He had gone to the extent of challenging Hadrat Uthman that he would raise even all the shepherds of the land against him. Muawiyyah, in spite of his cry for vengeance for the blood of Hadrat Uthman found no harm in making an alliance with a man who had in fact incited the rebellion against Hadrat Uthman. Amr b. AI-Aas, in spite of his bitter opposition to Hadrat Uthman, during his lifetime saw nothing wrong in joining the chorus for vengeance for the blood of man in whose murder he was indirectly, if not directly, involved.

Muawiyyah realised that if he had to go to fight against Hadrat Ali, the Byzantines could take advantage of such rift among the Muslims and invade Syria. He, therefore, made peace with the Byzantines on terms favourable to them and even agreed to pay them an annual tribute.

Muawiyyah was also shrewd enough to realise that in case he had to strive for capturing power he must have a strong army at his disposal. He accordingly built a strong standing army. On the other hand, Hadrat Ali had no large-standing army at his disposal and for each campaign he had to raise volunteers.

Since the election of Hadrat Ali as the Caliph, Muawiyyah had been raising the cry for vengeance for the blood of Hadrat Uthman and all the time had been trying to build up his strength. A year after the election of Hadrat Ali, Muawiyyah was strong enough to take the offensive against Hadrat Ali.

Amr Bin Al-Aas : Amr b. Al-Aas was a prominent member of the Banu Sahm section of the Quraish. His father Al-Aas b Wail was the chief of the Banu Sahm and was a well-to-do merchant who commanded great influence among the Quraish of Mecca. When the Holy Prophet of Islam announced his mission. Al-Aas was one of the prominent members of the Quraish who pressed all their influence into service to oppose the Holy Prophet and torture the Muslims. Hisham, a brother of Amr, however, accepted Islam in the early years of the mission of the Holy Prophet and in spite of the pressure of his father, he did not recant from Islam. Hisham was one of the Muslims to migrate to Abysinnia Amr headed the delegation that the Quraish sent to Abysinnia to prevail upon the ruler of. Abyssinia to turn away the Muslims from his country. The mission failed and the ruler of Abyssinia refused to oblige the Quraish. After the migration of the Holy Prophet to Medina Amr took part in all the battles that the Quraish fought against the Muslims.

Conversions to Islam : After the pact of Hudaibiya, the truth dawned on Amr b. Al-Aas and he hastened to Medina along with Khalid b Walid where they accepted Islam. After conversion to Islam, Amr b. Al-Aas proved to be a great asset for Islam. The Holy Prophet entrusted him with some important missions which he fulfilled successfully. Later the Holy Prophet appointed him as the Governor of Oman. After the death of the Holy Prophet, when Hadrat. Abu Bakr became the Caliph he was recalled from Oman to lead campaigns against some of the apostate tribes. After the end of the apostasy wars he was commissioned to undertake campaigns in Palestine and Syria. During the caliphate of Hadrat Umar he invaded Egypt and conquered it. In the history of Islam he enjoys fame as the "Conqueror of Egypt." Hadrat Umar appointed him as the Governor of Egypt. When Hadrat Uthman became the Caliph, he allowed Amr to continue as the Governor of Egypt for some time. Later Amr was deposed and Hadrat Uthman appointed his foster brother as the Governor of Egypt.

Amr's Opposition to Hadrat Uthman : Amr b. AI-Aas felt much grieved at his deposition Back in Medina, Amr had an interview with Hadrat Uthman which ended in bitterness. He began to criticise the administration of Hadrat Uthman in harsh terms. He played an important part in fanning discontent against the caliphate of Hadrat Uthman. In the revolt against Hadrat Uthman, the Egyptians were in the forefront and one of the grievances of the Egyptians was the deposition of Amr b. AI-Aas from the governorship of Egypt Amr b. AI-Aas made no secret of his opposition to Hadrat Uthman. He openly challenged Hadrat Uthman that he would raise the entire Muslims world against him. When the revolt against Hadrat Uthman gained momentum and Medina came to be thronged with rebels from various parts of the Muslim world, Amr b. AI-Aas left Medina for his land in Palestine. He was in Palestine when Hadrat Uthman was assassinated.

During Caliphate of Hadrat Ali : After the assassination of Hadrat Uthman, Amr b. AI-Aas decided to follow a policy of neutrality and watch further developments. When Hadrat Ali was elected as the Caliph, Amr b. AI-Aas neither took the oath of allegiance to Hadrat Ali nor opposed him Amr b. AI-Aas had expected that Hadrat Ali would offer him the governorship of Egypt. If Hadrat Ali had offered him the Governorship of Egypt he would have offered him allegiance. In the absence of such offer Amr d. AI-Aas decided to remain in Palestine and watch further developments. Hadrat Ali appointed Qais b Saad as the Governor of Egypt. Qais proved to be a good Governor and he kept Egypt safe for Hadrat Ali. Muawiyyah succeeded in creating differences between Hadrat Ali and Qais which culminated in the deposition of Qais Amr b. AI-Aas expected that Hadrat Ali would in his own interests appoint him as the Governor of Egypt. When Hadrat Ali appointed Muhammad b. Abu Bakr as the Governor of Egypt,. Amr b. AI-Aas despaired of any recognition from Hadrat Ali. That threw him in the lap of Muawiyyah.

Muawiyyah and Amr b. AI-Aas : Muawiyyah was shrewd enough to see that for any confrontation with Hadrat Ali, it was necessary that Egypt should be wrested from the control of Hadrat Ali. It was plain enough that if Egypt was to be with Hadrat Ali, Egypt could very well thrust a dagger in the back of Syria. It was in this context that Muawiyyah tried to get Qais removed from the governorship. He succeeded in this effort when Hadrat Ali deposed Qais b Saad and appointed Muhammad b. Abu Bakr in his place as the Governor of Egypt. Muhammad b. Abu Bakr was a rash impetuous young man and Muawiyyah felt sure that he would not be able to effectively control the affairs of Egypt Muawiyyah's plan was to create disturbance in Egypt and take advantage of such disturbances to capture Egypt. For this purpose he needed a man who commanded influence in Egypt. When he looked around he realised that the most suitable person for the purpose was Amr b. Al-Aas. He accordingly invited Amr b. Al-Aas to Damascus. When Amr came to Damascus he was given an almost royal reception. The two men agreed to make common cause against Hadrat Ali, Muawiyyah decided to make Amr the Commander-in-Chief of his forces. He was also promised the governorship of Egypt on the conquest of that province. Such alliance between Muawiyyah and Amr b. Al-Aas was to prove a great setback for Hadrat Ali. It is strange that Muawiyyah fought against Hadrat Ali to claim vengeance for the blood of Hadrat Uthman and yet entrusted the command of his forces to a man who had actually incited the Egyptians to revolt and had openly defied and thrown a challenge to Hadrat Uthman.

In Quest of Peace : After Hadrat Ali had established his capital at Kufa, the task before him was to tackle the problem of Syria through peaceful means, if possible, and through the use of sword, if otherwise. Muawiyyah had defied the authority of Hadrat Ali and in the interests of the solidarity of Islam, it was necessary that Muawiyyah should be persuaded to submit to the authority of Hadrat Ali and if he was not inclined to listen to reason, action should be taken against him as any government would take an action against a rebel.

As a matter of fact, Hadrat Ali planned an action against Syria immediately after his election. The expedition against Syria had to be deferred as the response of the people of Medina for a war against Syria was poor. Later, complications arose when Talha and Zubayr defected and under the leadership of Hadrat. Aishah the confederates occupied Basra. In the circumstances, Hadrat Ali was forced to march to Basra instead of Syria. Hadrat Ali won the victory at Basra and the revolt of the confederates was successfully suppressed, though with considerable loss.

Hadrat Ali had a plan to march against Syria just after his victory of Basra. The expedition had, however, to be deferred. Hadrat Ali needed some time to consolidate his rule at Kufa. Adequate response from the people of Kufa to undertake an expedition against Syria was not forthcoming. Further complications arose when a revolt broke out in Seestan. This revolt was suppressed with some difficulty.

Envoy to Syria : After suppression of the revolt in Seestan, Hadrat Ali once more turned to the affairs of Syria. By this time, an year had elapsed since the election of Hadrat Ali. During this period, Muawiyyah had added to his strength. He had persisted in his propaganda in the name of vengeance for the blood of Hadrat Uthman. Hadrat Ali felt that the expedition against Syria had already been sufficiently delayed and such immediate action to tackle the problem effectively was called for.

Although Hadrat Ali had every justification to lead a military expedition to Syria forthwith, he nevertheless decided to explore the possibilities of arriving at a settlement through peaceful means in the first instance. He wanted to send an envoy to Muawiyyah and in this connection he looked for man who commanded some influence with Muawiyyah. The choice of Hadrat Ali in this connection fell on Janr b. Abdullah. He was the Governor of Hamdan under Hadrat Uthman. Hadrat Ali had retained him in his office and he had taken the oath of allegiance to Hadrat Ali. He was a personal friend of Muawiyyah. Hadrat Ali summoned Janr b. Abdullah to Kufa and commissioned him to proceed as his envoy to Syria and prevail upon Muawiyyah to submit to the authority of Hadrat Ali Malik. Ashlar, the leader of the regicides, advised Hadrat Ali that Janr should not be sent to Syria for he was a friend of Muawiyyah and he would promote the interest of Muawiyyah rather than those of Hadrat Ali. Ashtar opted to go himself. As Malik. Ashtar was involved in the assassination of Hadrat Uthman, Hadrat Ali did not consider it advisable to send him as an envoy to Syria.

Janr b. Abdullah went to Syria. He was warmly received by Muawiyyah Janr tried to persuade Muawiyyah to submit to the authority of Hadrat Ali. Hadrat Ali, so argued Janr, was the elected Caliph and in the interest of the solidarity of Islam it was necessary to maintain the unity of Ummah Muawiyyah detained Janr and asked him to see things for himself In the main mosque of Damascus the blood stained shirt and the amputated fingers of Naila were displayed and as the faithful entered the mosque and looked at these relics they wept and mourned at the death of Hadrat Uthman. They took the oath that they would not rest content until they had avenged the murder of Hadrat Uthman. Janr b. Abdullah visited other cities in Syria and everywhere he saw the people prepared for war to avenge the death of Hadrat Uthman.

Jarir b. Abdullah returned to Kufa to report that the people of Syria were bent upon making war to avenge the death of Hadrat Uthman. On the failure of the mission of Janr, Malik. Ashtar said that he already knew that nothing could come out of his mission as he was Muawiyyah's man. Malik. Ashtar said that if he had been sent as an envoy the results would have been different. Janr retorted that the people of Syria would have murdered him. Ashtar said that he would have first murdered Muawiyyah. Hot words were exchanged between Malik. Ashtar and Janr. Janr felt disgusted and shifted to Syria where he was well looked after by Muawiyyah.

Muawiyyah's Envoy : When Muawiyyah incited the people of Syria to wage war against Hadrat Ali, there were some people who were averse to the Muslims fighting among themselves. A group of such persons led by Abu Muslim waited on Muawiyyah and advised him to abstain from war. Muawiyyah said that all that he wanted was "Qasas" for the murder of Hadrat Uthman which was a religious obligation for him. He added that if Hadrat Ali took the "Qasas" from those who were involved in the murder of Hadrat Uthman or handed over such persons to him he would be prepared to offer allegiance to Hadrat Ali. Abu Muslim volunteered to go to Kufa as an envoy of Muawiyyah. Muawiyyah agreed and sent him to Hadrat Ali as his envoy. Hadrat Ali took the envoy to the mosque and there explained to the people the purpose of his mission. Thereupon all the people assembled in the mosque cried with one voice "We all are the murderers of Hadrat Uthman". Turning to the envoy Hadrat Ali said "You may tell Muawiyyah what you have seen and heard". Abu Muslim returned disappointed to Syria Things had come to be tied in such knots that there appeared to be no possibility of resolving that dispute through peaceful means. On one side the people of Syria clamoured for war to avenge the murder of Hadrat Uthman and on the other side the people of Iraq held that they all were the murderers of Hadrat Uthman. In the circumstances war appeared to be inevitable Muawiyyah maintained that just as the confederates under Hadrat. Aishah invaded Basra to take action against such Basntes who were involved in the murder of Hadrat Uthman thus he would have to invade Iraq to punish those who were guilty of the murder of Hadrat Uthman. The stand of Hadrat Ali was that the cry for the vengeance for the blood of Hadrat Uthman was merely a pretext for capturing power, for in case Muawiyyah was really interested in claiming "Qasas" the proper course for him was to take the oath of allegiance to him and then lodge a claim for Qasas" in the usual way enjoined by law Hadrat Ali maintained that if Muawiyyah persisted in his stand and refused to listen to reason there would be no option with him (Hadrat Ali) but to fight against Muawiyyah as he had fought against the confederates at Basra.

Various Letters : In Nahj-ul-Balagha, there are some letters which Hadrat Ali addressed to Hadrat Muawiyyah. These letters command historical importance and provide the background material for assessing and evaluating what happened at this critical period of Islamic history.

Finality of the Election of the Caliph : Hadrat Muawiyyah objected to the election of Hadiat. All as the Caliph Hadrat Ali refused the objection in the following terms;

> "I was elected by the same electorate which had elected my three predecessors, namely, Abu Bakr, Umar and Uthman. After the election had taken place and the people had declared allegiance to the newly-elected Caliph, neither those who were present, nor those who were absent have the right to object to the election. The electorate consists of the Muhajirin and the Ansars only and if this electorate has elected the Caliph, the election is final and is binding on the entire Ummah.' In view of this legal position if anybody objects to such election and repudiates the decision of the competent electorate, he is a rebel and has to be treated as such O Muawiyyah, I solemnly declare that if you take a fair view of the matter without any prejudice or bias you will realise that I am not even remotely connected with the murder of Uthman. It is quite

another matter that you are levying this accusation against me only to promote your ulterior purpose."

Criticism of Muawiyyah : In reply to the above letter, Hadrat Muawiyyah used insolent words and maintained the accusation against Hadrat Ali of murdering Hadrat Uthman. Hadrat Ali replied to this letter in the following terms:

"I have received your letter which is a tissue of lies and which show your evil nature. Your letter is a letter of a person who had neither the light to lighten the dark way, nor any guide to lead him. It is the letter of a person who is obsessed with his ulterior motive and is deliberately treading the way of perdition. Your letter is meaningless and baseless. Under the law there is only one "baiyat" which has been held. It has attained finality and is not susceptible of any review or revision. He who objects to the "baiyat" in fact denounces Islam."

Delivery of the Murderers : Hadrat Muawiyyah demanded that the murderers of Hadrat Uthman should be handed over to him. In reply, Hadrat Ali wrote as follows:

> "Our community resolved to assassinate the Holy Prophet. They decided to uproot the descendants of the Holy Prophet. They made many plans to destroy us. They withheld water supply from us. They subjected us to great trials and tribulations. God, however, came to our help and saved his religion. During this period the believers advocated the cause but the infidels were moved by considerations of loyalty to the tribe. The practice of the Holy Prophet was that when any war was at its height, he would make his relatives face the brunt of the battle. In the battle of Badr, Ubaida b Harith was martyred. Hadrat Hamza met his martyrdom in the battle of Uhud. Jafar, my elder brother, was martyred in the battle of Mutah. I did not lag behind in these wars but martyrdom was withheld from me. It is a vicissitude of times that I have to deal with a man who cannot take even two steps with me and who cannot claim priority over me. If anyone raises a false claim, may God take care of. As regards the demand that the murderers of Uthman should be delivered to you, I cannot accept the demand for you have rebelled against my authority and I have to deal with you as a rebel"

Challenge to Muawiyyah : Hadrat Muawiyyah gave the threat of war and in reply Hadrat Ali challenged him as follows:

> "O Muawiyyah what will you do when this mantle of the world which you are wearing is taken off from you. The world has attracted you. It spread its net and you have been trapped therein. The world called you and you welcomed its call. You have forgotten that you will be summoned to a place where no

shield would protect you. Thus you should desist from the course you have adopted. Prepare your account and take steps to protect you from the disaster that is going to overwhelm you. Do not listen to the advice of those who have strayed from the right path. If you do not desist from the wrong course that you have adopted, bear in mind that I would bring to you to senses. What are you? You are merely a wayward profligate man who has been enslaved by Satan. Satan has now become your sole guide, the end all and be all of your existence. O Muawiyyah tell me when were you the leader of the community and the ruler of the people. You had no priority in Islam. Even in the age of ignorance you held no office. Seek the protection of God. Misfortune makes you tread the wrong way. Fired with ambition and greed you are proceeding on the way that leads to perdition.

You have invited me to war very well. Keep all the men aside, and step forward to meet me in single combat. Why engage all the troops in armed conflict. Let us decide this issue by a duel so that it may become evident as to who has gone astray and has become blind.

Have you forgotten that I am the man who in the battle of Badr killed your maternal grandfather, maternal uncle and brother. You accepted Islam as a matter of expediency and Islam is as yet not a matter of faith with you.

You have declared that you have stepped into the field to seek vengeance for the blood of Uthman. You know very well who were responsible for the murder of Uthman. If you are in earnest in your declaration, seek vengeance from the right quarters. But I am seeing something else. I very well see that when war is brought about, you will shriek like a wounded camel. I foresee that in the war afraid of the carnage your men will call me to the Book of God, although they have falsified the Word of God and violated the oath of allegiance that they had taken to me."

Partition of the Muslim State : Hadrat Muawiyyah suggested that the Muslim state be partitioned and Syria be assigned to him. Hadrat Ali replied in the following terms:

"As regards your proposal that Syria be assigned to you I cannot accept that proposal today which I have rejected yesterday. Your observation that war has eaten into the vital of the. Arabs, You should bear in mind that those who fought in the cause of God have earned paradise and those who fought to secure a wordly end have already been sentenced to hell. Your statement that in the matter of military strength we both are at par is mere presumption and presumption cannot take the place of conviction. Also keep in mind that the people of Iraq are as much desirous of paradise as the people of Syria covet the world. Your statement that we both are the descendants of Abd Manaf is correct but it should be remembered that the Banu Umayyah are not equal to Banu Hashim, Harb cannot equal. Abdul Muttalib, Sufyan is not equal to Abu Talib nor can falsehood equal the truth.

You have forgotten that we have the honour of prophethood with us. It was because of this prophethood that the powerful were humbled and the lowly were elevated. When Islam triumphed and the people willingly or unwillingly were converted to Islam you were among such late converts who accepted the faith because of fear or agreed. In the circumstances the proper thing for you is that you should not allow Satan to overpower you"

Hadrat Ali and his Predecessors : In a letter, Hadrat Muawiyyah took the stand that Hadrat Ali did not offer his wholehearted support to the previous three Caliphs, namely Hadrat. Abu Bakr, Hadrat Umar and Hadrat Uthman. The game of Muawiyyah was that Hadrat Ali should say something against his predecessors which Muawiyyah could exploit for the purposes of propaganda Hadrat Ali replied to this letter in the following terms:

You have told me that God chose the Holy Prophet for delivering His message and the companions accepted the message. To tell this to me who belongs to the household of the Holy Prophet is like the carrying of dates to Hijr which is known for the abundance of its dates. You have claimed that in Islam such and such persons have precedence. This assertion is such that if it is correct you are not even remotely connected, therewith, if it is not correct that would not harm you in anyway. How are you concerned with the matter as to who is superior or otherwise in the matter of Islam. Your sponsoring this issue is like making the criminal the judge.

Muawiyyah you are fast speeding on the road to perdition. You have transgressed all limits. Desist from your ignominy. Remember that we are the persons who have the honour of belonging to the household of the Holy Prophet and whom God has already tested. Have you ever thought that our clan is superior to your clan but nevertheless the Holy Prophet contracted some material relations with your household to save you from any feeling of inferiority complex. We claim precedence in Islam because we belong to the household of the Holy Prophet and we were most devoted to him You have alleged that I was jealous of all the Caliphs preceding me and was hostile to them. If what you say is for the sake of argument correct, I have not committed any fault for which I owe an explanation to you. You have said that in making me take the oath of allegiance to the previous Caliphs I was dragged as a camel with the bridle in its nose. You have thus presented me as a person who is deprived of his right and is oppressed. By your misguided criticism you have in fact praised me. You have referred to my attitude to Hadrat Uthman I must reply to this part of your letter for you are related to him. Please peep into your heart and say who set the net for his murder, you or I Is it not a fact that you remained indifferent to his protection, while I tried my best to the last to avert the crisis I owe you no apology when I admit that I did differ from him in the matter of his policies and I always tried to offer him sound advice which he did not or could not accept You have written that for me you have nothing but sword. That has made me laugh. When did you find the descendants of Abdul Muttalib fear the sword or shrank from war when it was forced on them. Do not worry I will soon bring my troops to face you in battle."

Battle of Siffin

When war between Hadrat Ali and Hadrat Muawiyyah became inevitable, preparations for a showdown were made by both sides. Hadrat Ali managed to raise an army 90,000 strong men. It included men from Kufa, Iraq, Basra and Medina. Hadrat Ali made Malik. Ashtar the Commander-in-Chief of his forces. The army was divided into a number of commands and each command had its own commander.

In the correspondence that was exchanged between the two sides option was given to Hadrat Ali to lead the forces to Syria or let the Syrian forces come to Iraq. Hadrat Ali opted to lead his forces to Syria. In March 657, Hadrat Ali set out from Kufa at the head of his army. From Kufa the army proceeded to Medina. Here some troops joined the army of Hadrat Ali. From Medina Hadrat Ali set out for Syria. His plan was to march through Upper Mesopotamia and invade Syria from the north. The advance guard of the army advanced along the western bank of the Euphrates. The main army under Hadrat Ali advanced upto the Tigris and thereafter entered the Mesopotamian desert.

March through the Desert : The march of the army through the desert was a great ordeal. The long trek across the desert exhausted the water supplies at the disposal of the troops and the absence of water became an acute problem. Hadrat Ali sent his scouts to enquire of the tribesmen in the desert whether there were any wells or springs in the neighbourhood which could supply water to the troops. The tribesmen said that there were no wells or springs in the neighbourhood.

Hadrat Ali had heard that some centuries ago the Israeli patriarchs had dug wells in the desert and he hoped to be able to find out these ancient sites. The scouts who contacted the tribes in the desert were not able to get any clue of a spring or a well in the desert. One of the scouts, however, brought back with him an old Christian hermit who said that there was indeed a cistern in the neighbourhood in the past, but it had gone dry. The hermit added that according to old legends, a hidden well existed somewhere in the neighbourhood and its mouth was covered with an enormous stone but no one knew about the actual site of the legendary well. He observed that according to popular beliefs no one could locate the hidden well except a prophet or the representative of a prophet.

Miracle of the Well : Hadrat Ali himself proceeded on a survey of the desert. At one place Hadrat Ali saw a huge stone and he asked his men to dig at that site. Miraculously a well was discovered at the site the water supply whereof was more than enough for the needs of the troops. As the ancient well was discovered, the Christian hermit was thrilled at the miracle. Addressing Hadrat Ali he said that verily he was the representative of the prophet about whose advent the scriptures had predicted. He hastened to accept Islam at the hands of Hadrat Ali. He presented to Hadrat Ali an old parchment belonging to Simon, a companion of Jesus Christ on which was recorded a prophesy about the advent of the last prophet. The parchment also foretold of the lifting of the stone of the well by a representative of the last prophet.

The discovery of the source of water in the desert came as a matter of great relief to the troops of Hadrat Ali. It raised their morale and fortified them with the faith they were fighting for the vindication of the truth. The news of the recovery of the well in the desert impressed the tribes in the neighbourhood and they joined Hadrat Ali in the war against Hadrat Muawiyyah.

Onward to Siffin : After crossing the desert, Hadrat Ali and his troops pushed on Al-Raqqa on the left bank of the Euphrates. Here they had to cross the river. They asked the people of Al-Raqqa to provide them boats and build a bridge of boats for them. The people of Al-Raqqa said that in the war between the Muslim people they would remain neutral and as such they could not construct the bridge for them. Thereupon Malik Ashtar, the Commander-in-Chief of the forces of Hadrat Ali challenged the people of Al-Raqqa that unless they provided the necessary boats and constructed the bridge for them, he would declare war against them and order their massacre. The people of Al-Raqqa consulted among themselves and ultimately agreed to construct the bridge of boats for the army of Hadrat Ali to cross the river.

After crossing the river, the troops of Hadrat Ali advanced along the right bank of the river in the direction of Aleppo. Here they came across the Syrian vanguard.

The Syrians did not risk a skirmish with the forces of Hadrat Ali and withdrew precipitately

At Sur-Rum along the border of Syria, the Allied forces had a skirmish with the Syrian guards. The Syrians suffered defeat and retreated. Thereafter the forces of Hadrat Ali reached the plain of Siffin where they found the Syrian forces under Muawiyyah drawn up in strength and waiting for them.

Battle for Water : As the troops of Hadrat Ali arrived in the valley of Siffin it was found that the forces of Muawiyyah had already occupied the best part of the valley. There was only one source of water supply in the valley and Muawiyyah had so arrayed his forces that they controlled the water supply of the whole valley and the troops of Hadrat Ali had no access to water at any place. The strategy of Muawiyyah obviously was to force a defeat on Hadrat Ali by exposing his troops to the rigours of thirst.

Negotiation for Access to Water : The first task of Hadrat Ali was to gain an access to the source of water supply. Hadrat Ali sent a letter to Muawiyyah through a delegation. Hadrat Ali pointed out to Muawiyyah that according to the injunctions of Islam as well as according to the rules of warfare, access to water supply could not be denied to the combatants. Hadrat Ali observed that any armed conflict between the two sides would lead to great loss of life on both the sides. He was, therefore, keen that the disputes between the two sides should be decided through peaceful negotiations. He added that he was not going to lead an attack unless all possibilities of peace were exhausted. He brought home the point that in this context it was necessary that both the sides should have equal opportunities of access to water and the area around the source of water supply should be declared a neutral zone.

On receiving the letter of Hadrat Ali, Hadrat Muawiyyah called his council of war. Amr b. Al. Aas, the Commander-in-Chief of the forces of Muawiyyah, observed that according to the rules of warfare access to water had to be provided to the combatants from both the sides. He suggested that while maintaining overall control over the source of water supply they should allow the men of the forces of Hadrat Ali to obtain water for their needs at specified hours subjected to terms which might be mutually agreed upon.

Abdullah b. Abi Sirah, a former Governor of Egypt and a foster brother of Hadrat Uthman suggested that they should adopt the tactics of delay by neither providing access to the water supply to the other side, nor refusing to do so. He was of the view that because of such delay the forces of Hadrat Ali would have no option but to retreat from the valley and when they were on a retreat they could be attacked in the rear.

Some councillors of Muawiyyah held that they were seeking vengeance for the blood of Hadrat Uthman. The rebels had denied access to water to Hadrat Uthman. It was accordingly necessary that those who had subjected Hadrat Uthman to the rigours of thirst should likewise be subjected to the suffering.

Hadrat Muawiyyah gave an evasive reply to the delegation that he had received from Hadrat Ali. He did not refuse the demand outright but did not accept it either. His game was to play for time. In the meantime he sent reinforcements for his troops that guarded the sources of water supply.

The Battle : When the delegation of Hadrat Ali returned from Muawiyyah, Hadrat Ali called for his own council of war. After deliberations it was decided that an immediate attack should be made to gain control of the source of water supply. In the action that followed there was hard fighting with lances and swords. Some persons were killed from both sides but ultimately the forces of Hadrat Ali had the upper hand and they dislodged the Syrians from all the points commanding access to the source of water supply.

Now the position was reversed and Hadrat Muawiyyah had to approach Hadrat Ali to allow the Syrian access to the source of water supply. Some of the councillors of Hadrat Ali advised him to pay the Syrians in their own coins and to refuse them access to the source of water supply. Hadrat Ali overruled them saying that Islam did not permit them to stop the supply of water to their enemy. He said that he had to be guided by the Book of God and he could not act in the way the people acted during the Age of Ignorance. While the troops of Hadrat Ali maintained the overall control of the source of water supply, the troops of Hadrat Muawiyyah were allowed to have the water they needed at specified hours. During such hours men from both sides came in contact and the general feeling was that instead of resorting to an armed conflict the disputes between the two sides should be settled through peaceful means.

Months of Suspense : The armies that lay in camp at Siffin facing each other were the largest armies so far assembled in the history of Islam. The irony was that such large armies had not been assembled to fight against the non-Muslims in the name of God. The misfortune was that the Muslims were arrayed to fight against the Muslims and each side claimed that it had taken the field for cause. Nevertheless both sides wished to gain the end they had in view without an armed conflict.

Hadrat Ali instructed his men that they should not fire the first shot. Hadrat Muawiyyah likewise hesitated to take the initiative in beginning the war. With such large concentration of troops at one place, absolute peace was out of question. Isolated skirmishes took place every now and then leading to loss of life on both the sides. There was, however, no direct clash between the armies as a whole. For over two months the armies as whole remained quiet and in a state of suspense being officially neither at war nor at peace. Then came the months of Moharram and during this month the hostilities were officially suspended.

Overtures for Peace : During these months peace overtures were made and peace missions were exchanged between the two sides almost every day.

The missions that were sent by Hadrat Ali to Hadrat Muawiyyah tried to make out the point that Hadrat Muawiyyah should fear God and refrain from creating dissensions among the Muslims. He was told that as Hadrat Ali had been elected as the Caliph it was his bounden duty to owe allegiance to him. It was also pointed out that in view of his learning, piety, relationship with the Holy Prophet, services to Islam and other extraordinary qualities of head and heart, he was the most suitable person to be the Caliph of the Muslims.

The stand of Hadrat Muawiyyah was that the election of Hadrat Ali was irregular as it had been held under the pressure of the rebels. He accused Hadrat Ali of involvement in the murder of Hadrat Uthman. He observed that he was the cousin of Hadrat Uthman and according to the injunctions of Islam it was incumbent on him to seek "Qasas" for the murder of Hadrat Uthman.

To the charges of Hadrat Muawiyyah, the emissaries of Hadrat Ali maintained that Hadrat Ali had been elected by all the citizens of Medina. All previous regular elections of the Caliphs had been held by the people of Medina and in the case of the election of Hadrat Ali the electorate was the same. The rebels did not exercise pressure on the people of Medina to elect a particular person; their pressure was only to the extent that they should elect some person as the Caliph. The claims of all the eligible candidates were duly considered and by general consensus. Hadrat Ali was superior to all of them. In fact, all other candidates had withdrawn their claim, if any. Muawiyyah's contention was that Hadrat Ali's election was vitiated because of his involvement in the murder of Hadrat Uthman. The emissaries of Hadrat Ali observed that this accusation was false. Hadrat Ali was neither directly nor indirectly involved in the assassination of Hadrat Uthman. As a matter of fact, Hadrat Ali had tried his best to support Hadrat Uthman. They emphatically pointed out that to levy such a charge on a person of the calibre of Hadrat Ali was sheer sacrilege. Hadrat Muawiyyah maintained that if Hadrat Ali had supported Hadrat Uthman sincerely, the tragedy would have been avoided. The emissaries of Hadrat Ali posed the question: "You were entrenched in power in Syria and you had an army at your disposal. You were fully aware of the difficulties of the situation. Why did you not take proper steps to defend Hadrat Uthman? " Hadrat Muawiyyah had no satisfactory reply to this question. The emissaries of Hadrat Ali thereafter posed another question: "During the last days of the siege of his home, Hadrat Uthman had asked the provincial Governors including yourself to send him aid against the rebels. Why did you and the provincial Governors not send the aid? Are you then not indirectly responsible for the assassination of Hadrat Uthman?' Hadrat Muawiyyah had no answer to this question as well and that led to the exchange of hot and bitter words between Hadrat Muawiyyah and the emissaries of Hadrat Ali.

The emissaries of Hadrat Ali asked a further question "You say that if Hadrat Ali had supported Hadrat Uthman the tragedy would have been avoided? Did Ali have any force at his disposal? If you who had a large army at your disposal could not avert the tragedy? How could Hadrat Ali who had no force at his disposal avert the tragedy?" Hadrat Muawiyyah said that if Hadrat Ali was not involved in the murder of Hadrat Uthman he should hand over these murderers to him. The mission sent by Hadrat Ali pointed out that the proper way to ask for Qasas was that he should offer the oath of allegiance to Hadrat Ali and thereafter file a claim for Qasas before him. The delegates brought home to Hadrat Muawiyyah the fallacy in his stand. If his demand for Qasas was genuine he should have strengthened the hands of Hadrat Ali to enable him bring the murderers of Hadrat Uthman to book. By rebelling against the authority of Hadrat Ali he had enabled the murderers of Hadrat Uthman seek an alliance with Hadrat Ali. In such circumstances it was impossible for Hadrat Ali to take action against the persons who were his allies. It was pointed out with great force that the responsibility for complicating the state of affairs devolved on Hadrat Muawiyyah and not on Hadrat Ali, who would have himself avenged the murder of Hadrat Uthman if difficulties had not been created in his way.

Hadrat Muawiyyah suggested that a way out of the difficulty was that he should be recognised as the Caliph of Syria while Hadrat Ali could continue as the Caliph of the rest of the Muslim world. Hadrat Ali did not agree to this proposal as this was regarded to be repugnant to the spirit of Islam. Hadrat Ali also pointed out that this proposal on the part of Hadrat Muawiyyah had let the cat out of the bag and betrayed his real intention. That provided a conclusive proof to the effect that the cry for vengeance for the blood of Hadrat Uthman was merely a pretext to capture power.

Hadrat Ali sent a message to Hadrat Muawiyyah that if all this fuss was about the caliphate between himself and Muawiyyah why create dissenions among the Muslims and shed the blood of innocent persons? In the usual Arab way, Hadrat Ali proposed a duel with Muawiyyah. It was pointed out that in that way whosoever survived would be the Caliph Amr b. Al Aas advised Hadrat Muawiyyah that the proposal of Hadrat Ali should be accepted. Hadrat Muawiyyah hesitated to accept the proposal for he knew that Hadrat Ali had so far fought hundreds of duels, and in all such duels his adversaries had been killed Amr b. Al Aas pointed out that such was the case many years ago. With the lapse of time, Hadrat Ali had grown fat and unwieldly and in any personal combat he was apt to lose the balance and be overpowered. Hadrat Muawiyyah, however, could not make up his mind to take the risk of a personal combat with Hadrat Ali and he refused the offer.

Thereafter all negotiations for peace broke down and both the sides began to prepare for war.

Hostilities on a Limited Scale : When the sacred month of Moharram was over, and the possibilities of any settlement through peaceful means had receded, war between the two sides became imminent. Still hoping against hope, war on a full-fledged scale was avoided and hostilities began on a limited scale. A detachment from each side was led to fight each day. The battle waged for the whole day and the two detachments retired to thier respective camps at nightfall. The following day other detachments took the field and after a day-long combat retired to their camps when the night set. This process continued for a week. Losses of life occurred on both the sides but these contests were more like tournaments than battles. After a week the patience of both the sides was exhausted and the entire armies from both the sides took the field for a headlong clash.

The Main Battle : The main battle began on the 8th of Safar 37. A. H. The heralds from the army of Hadrat Ali stepped forward and shouted to the army of Hadrat Muawiyyah to accept the truth and acknowledge the caliphate of Hadrat Ali. The heralds from the army of Hadrat Muawiyyah shouted, "We seek vengeance for the blood of Hadrat Uthman. Hand us his murderers if you are in the truth". These calls proved ineffective and the two armies arrayed themselves for action. The army of Hadrat Ali was divided into three usual wings—the right wing, the left wing and the central wing. The central wing was commanded by Hadrat Ali himself and his wing comprised some veteran companions of Medina. One wing comprised contingents from Kufa and the other wing comprised contingents from Basra. The cavalry of the Kufa wing was led by Muslim. Ashtar while the infantry of this wing was led by Umar b Yasir. The cavalry of the Basra wing was led by Sahl b Hanif while its infantry was led by Qais b Sa'ad.

Before the war began Hadrat Ali addressed his army. He said that they were fighting in the cause of God and the vindication of the truth. He exhorted his men to prove their worth by performing prodigies of valour. If they survived they would be Ghazis, if they fell, paradise would await them. He asked his men not to fire the first shot. The enemy should take the initiative, but when the war began they should not rest content till they had defeated the enemy. The men were enjoined not to turn their backs. They were exhorted to play the role of heroes. They were instructed not to attack any wounded person, not to cut the limbs of a dead person, not to molest women, not to kill the aged and the children and not to plunder. They were asked to be steadfast, talk less and fear God.

Before the beginning of the battle proper, according to the usual Arab practice the challenge to personal duel was given. Hadrat Ali gave the challenge for personal combat with Hadrat Muawiyyah. Hadrat Muawiyyah did not accept the challenge. Then Malik. Ashtar the Commander-in-Chief of the forces of Hadrat Ali, stepped forward and gave a challenge for a personal duel with Amr b. Al Aas, the Commander-in-Chief of the forces of Muawiyyah Amr b. Al Aas, too did not accept the challenge.

In Battle Array : After the refusal of Hadrat Muawiyyah and Amr b. Al Aas to accept the challenge of personal combat the two armies drawn out in battle array fought for the whole day but neither side got the better of the other. The following day the combat was removed with greater vigour. Hadrat Ali was in the centre of his army with the flower of troops from Medina. Hadrat Muawiyyah had a pavilion pitched in the battlefield and there surrounded by his bodyguards he watched the course of the battle Amr b. Al-Aas with a great weight of horse charged the Kufa wing of the forces of Hadrat Ali which gave way and exposed Hadrat Ali to imminent peril. Hadrat Ali and the men of the central wing fought bravely and repulsed the charge. Malik Ashtar the Commander-in-Chief of the forces of Hadrat Ali, then led a charge against Hadrat Muawiyyah. The pavilion of Muawiyyah was surrounded by five columns of bodyguards ranged one after the other. Four of these five ranks were cut to pieces by Ashtar and his men. At this stage Hadrat Muawiyyah contemplated fight Amr b. Al-Aas rushed to his side and advised him not to lose heart. He said "Courage today, victory tomorrow" With great effort the forces of Muawiyyah beat back the attack and thereafter the two forces fought on equal terms. Feats of bravery were performed by men from both sides leading to heavy bloodshed.

On the third day the battle began again with unprecedented vigour. The Syrians pressed against the ranks of the forces of Hadrat Ali, but Ashtar drove them back with a good deal of slaughter. Then Ammaar b Yasir with his contingent dashed forward from the ranks of the forces of Hadrat Ali and attacked the forces of Hadrat Muawiyyah with the ferocity of a lion. He penetrated deep into the ranks of the enemy causing great havoc. Bent on seeking martyrdom Ammaar fell after he had broken the ranks of the enemy Ammaar was a distinguished Companion of the Holy Prophet. In the time of Hadrat Umar he was the Governor of Kufa. He developed some differences with Hadrat Uthman. When Hadrat Ali became the Caliph, Ammaar was his ardent supporter. He fought on the side of Hadrat Ali in the battle of the Camel. About him the Holy Prophet had prophesied that he would be killed by a group of godless and rebellious people Ammaar was ninety years old at the time of his martyrdom. When the people came to know of the martyrdom of Ammaar and recalled the prophesy of the Holy Prophet it demoralised the troops of Hadrat Muawiyyah. Hadrat Muawiyyah tried to keep up the morale of his people by saying that the responsibility for his death lay with Hadrat Ali who had brought him to fight irrespective of his old age. The death of Ammaar was a great personal loss for Hadrat Ali and he felt as if one of his hands had been cut off.

The following day the war was continued causing a good deal of slaughter. As the day wore on, the position of the army of Muawiyyah began worsening. Their supply of arrows was exhausted and they began pelting the forces of Hadrat Ali with stones. The Syrians next took to javelins and lances. Finally they fell on the troops of Hadrat Ali with swords. The battle continued during the night as well. In the nocturnal battle Hadrat Ali played the role of a hero. He stood firm as a rock and beat back the attacks of the Syrians killing, according to chronicles, as many as five hundred persons with his ponderous two-edged sword.

Ruse of Syrians : In the actions so far fought, the forces of Hadrat Ali had the upper hand and the final collapse of the Syrians was well in sight. In order to avert their defeat the Syrians now resorted to a ruse. The next day when the battle began again, the Syrians hung the leaves from the Holy Quran on their lances and raised the cry "O ye men of Iraq, should you kill us what would become of our families and should we slay you what would become of your wives and children. Let us stop this sad warfare and resort to the decision of the Book of God."

As soon as the men of Iraq heard the appeal of the Syrians, they threw down their arms and echoed the cry "Let the Book of God decide between us." Hadrat Ali expostulated with his men saying that this was nefarious device of Muawiyyah to cloak his defeat. Hadrat Ali warned his men not to fall into the trap but to fight to the finish This had no appeal for the men of Iraq. They argued that since they were fighting for the sake of God they could not refuse arbitration based on the Book of God. Hadrat Ali said that of all the people in the world he would be the first to accept the decision of the Book of God but he knew full well that neither Muawiyyah nor the people around him had any knowledge of the Quran or the injunctions of Islam. They were merely exploiting the Book of God for an ulterior purpose and it was necessary that they should be frustrated in their object. Hadrat Ali exhorted the people of Iraq to continue the fighting till they were victorious.

Revolt in Hadrat Ali's Army : The exhortations of Hadrat Ali had no effect. About 20,000 men of Iraq led by Zaid b Hassan and Musur bin Fidki openly revolted and laid down their arms. The rebels approached Hadrat Ali and calling him no longer their Caliph but simply. Ali, declared "Ali? You are appealing to the sword and they are appealing to the Quran. Let the issue of the caliphate be deferred to the judgement of God's Book". They adopted a hostile attitude and warned Hadrat Ali that if he did not submit to their demand he would meet the same fate as had befallen his predecessor, Hadrat Uthman.

Heart-broken at the treachery of his men, Hadrat Ali exclaimed with great grief Alas, you are deserting me at the critical time of need. Go and join the Syrian coalition against God and His Apostle." The rebels did not rest content with their revolt. A large section of the army under Ashtar was still fighting and they were having an upper hand. The rebels demanded that orders should be issued recalling. Ashtar from the battlefield. The rebels went to the extent of reproaching Hadrat Ali. He was accused of being an accomplice in the murder of Hadrat Uthman. He was accused of fighting against the Syrians to quench his thirst for self-aggrandisement. Hadrat Ali threatened them with grave consequences and they threatened him in turn. The pressure of the rebels increased and Hadrat Ali feeling helpless had to recall Ashtar from the front. Ashtar returned reluctantly and a fierce altercation ensued between him and the rebels. Ashtar upbraided them as traitors, hypocrites and villains. In return they reviled him. Because of this revolt in his army, Hadrat Ali had to suspend action against the Syrians and thus the victory which was in immediate sight evaded him. Henceforward misfortune was to stalk the steps of Hadrat Ali.

Arbitration Agreement : Hadrat Ali because of the treachery of his own men was no longer the master of his own will and he had to act in accordance with the dictates of the rebels. These rebels forced Hadrat Ali to depute the rebel General Ashas b Qais to enquire form Muawiyyah as to what was the significance of the display of the leaves of the Holy Quran on their lances. Muawiyyah said, "The significance of the display of the leaves of the Holy Quran on our lances is that we appeal from the decision of arms to the decision of the law of God. Let both sides retire from the battlefield and refer the case to the arbitration of two umpires, one umpire to be nominated by each side. The two umpires should decide according to the Holy Quran and the traditions of the Holy Prophet as to whom the sovereignty should go. The decision of the umpires should be binding on all" To this proposal Ashas gave his consent without consulting Hadrat Ali. Hadrat Ali was wroth at the acceptance of the proposal on his behalf. Hadrat Ali maintained that the issue of sovereignty was not in dispute. He was the duly elected Caliph and his right to the caliphate could not be adjudicated upon by the arbitrators. The rebels did not accept the contention of Hadrat Ali. Hadrat Ali in a state of utter helplessness said, "If you are not going to listen to me, then do whatever you like."

The Betrayer : Ashas b Qais who accepted the proposal of Hadrat Muawiyyah was the chief of the Banu Kindi. He was converted to Islam during the lifetime of the Holy Prophet. After the death of the Holy Prophet he apostatised. In the apostasy wars conducted during the caliphate of Hadrat Abu Bakr Ashas was defeated. He came to Medina, repented and was reconverted to Islam. Hadrat Abu Bakr married his sister Umm Fanda to him. During the time of Hadrat Umar he participated in the wars against the Persians. Hadrat Umar, however, did not trust him with any important office. Hadrat

Uthman made him the Governor of a province. Hadrat Ali deposed him. He came to Kufa and offered allegiance to Hadrat Ali Hadrat Ali made him a General of his army. He marched with Hadrat Ali to Siffin and played an important part in dislodging the Syrians from the source of water supply in the Siffin valley. To start with he showed a great deal of loyalty to Hadrat Ali but later he came to waver in his loyalty. Even before the Syrians displayed the leaves of the Holy Quran on their lances,. Ashas addressed the contingent of the Banu Kinda under his command in the following terms:

> "O ye Muslims, you have witnessed what has transpired during the course of this war and how many Muslims have been ruthlessly killed I have become old but I have never seen such dreadful carnage before. Whosoever hears me, it behoves him to pass on my message to others that we ought to resolve that we will not fight from henceforth and would refrain from killing the Muslims. By God I am not telling you these things because I am afraid of war or because cowardice has taken hold of me. I tell you these things because I pity the Muslim women and children who will suffer and mourn the loss of those who are killed in the battle."

This was outright treachery. It appears treachery was in the very blood of Ashas. His daughter was married to Imam Hassan. She poisoned Imam Hassan at the instigation of Yazid who promised to marry her in cases the poisoned Imam Hassan but refused to marry her when she had poisoned Imam Hassan on the ground that he could not trust a woman who could poison her husband.

Causes of Helplessness : The accounts of what happened at Siffin which have come down to us give no clue as to what was the cause of rebellion against Hadrat Ali when victory was almost in sight. It is not plausible that this sudden development took place at the display of the leaves of the Holy Quran on their lances by the Syrians. Obviously it was the culmination of some deep-set conspiracy. The exact extent of such conspiracy remains a mystery but it appears that the treachery of most of the army chiefs of Hadrat Ali was because of the bribery by Muawiyyah. The army that Hadrat Ali had brought to Siffin was mere a motley crowd than a disciplined force and this lack of discipline was its greatest weakness. It also appears that there was a good deal of jealousy among the Generals of the army of Hadrat Ali. When Hadrat Ali appointed Ashas as a General his appointment was opposed by Malik. Ashtar who was the Commander-in-Chief of the forces of Hadrat Ali and these differences between the two Generals persisted during the course of the war Hadrat Ali believed in the truth of his cause to such an extent that he did not sponsor any propaganda to support such cause. On the other hand Muawiyyah was a past master in making propaganda and in this respect he outwitted Hadrat Ali.

Arbitration Deed : When the arbitration deed came to be written up, altercation between the parties began over the first sentence of the preamble about the title of the parties. The supporters of Hadrat Ali insisted that he should be referred to as "All, the Commander of the Faithful". The other party objected to such title as they did not recognise him as the Caliph. The army chiefs of Hadrat Ali who had rebelled against the authority of Hadrat Ali overruled the view of the supporters of Hadrat Ali on the ground that in the case of the Hudaibiya pact when the Quraish objected to references to Muhammad (Peace be on him) as the prophet, the Holy Prophet agreed to the omission of such reference. The agreement that was drawn up provided for the truce between parties and the settlement of the dispute through arbitration of two umpires — one umpire to be appointed by each party. The umpires were required to give their decision in accordance with the injunctions of the Holy Quran. In the absence of any guidance from the Holy Quran, the traditions of the Holy Prophet were to be followed. The umpires were guaranteed the security of their life and property and of their families whatever the outcome of the arbitration might be. It was provided that the decision of the umpires was to be binding on all concerned. The umpires were required to give their decision within six months. They were required to meet at a neutral spot midway between Kufa and Damascus. The point to be determined by the umpires was as to whom out of Hadrat Ali and Muawiyyah the sovereignty was to belong. The supporters of Hadrat Ali pointed out that the issue of sovereignty was not the point in dispute, the dispute was about the "Qasas" for the assassination of Hadrat Uthman. The rebels against the authority of Hadrat Ali overruled this stand. They said that the real issue was that of the caliphate between Hadrat Ali and Muawiyyah and if this issue was decided the question of "Qasas" for the murder of Hadrat Uthman would be automatically decided. The arbitration deed as it was finally drawn up was nothing short of a death warrant for Hadrat Ali. He had, however, become so helpless that he had to agree to it.

The Umpires : After the arbitration deed had been drawn up, the arbiter to represent Hadrat Ali had to be appointed. Hadrat Ali wanted that his cousin Abdullah b. Abbas be appointed as the arbiter. The rebels said that they could not accept this nomination as Abdullah b. Abbas was related to him and he was apt to be partial. Hadrat Ali said that in that case let Malik Ashlar be appointed as the arbiter. The rebels vetoed this suggestion as well on the ground that Malik Ashtar had participated in the war and could not take an impartial view. The rebels said that they would nominate Abu Musa. Ashan, a former Governor of Kufa, in this behalf. Hadrat Ali pointed out that he had no confidence in Abu Musa. Ashan as he had deposed him from the governorship of Kufa. The rebels said that Abu Musa. Ashan was known for his neutrality and they could not agree to the nomination of any person other than. Abu Musa. Ashan as the arbiter. So helpless had Hadrat Ali become that he had to give way on this point as well and Abu

Musa. Ashan was appointed as the umpire to represent Hadrat Ali when Hadrat Ali had no confidence in him. On the side of Muawiyyah, Amr b. Al-Aas was appointed as the arbiter and no one objected that he had participated in the war and had developed certain prejudices.

The Return March

After the execution of the arbitration agreement the forces of both the sides had to withdraw from the battlefield. Although the arbitration agreement had been forced on him, Hadrat Ali as an honourable man found himself bound by the agreement. He accordingly ordered a return march for his forces. Hadrat Ali left the battlefield of Siffin with a heavy heart. Victory had eluded him because of the treachery of his own men. He had been betrayed. Heavy casualties had taken place from both the sides and he mourned at the death of so many Muslims. He had lost some of his best supporters like. Ammaar b Yasir and this vacuum could not be filled. He felt distressed that the Muslim Ummah had lost its unity. A generation after the death of the Holy Prophet the people were losing their Islamic character and were once again relapsing into the evils of the age of ignorance. It was heart-rending for him to see that truth was being suppressed and falsehood was getting the upper hand. It appeared to him that by subjecting him and the Muslims to such ordeals God intended the Muslims to be put to test. Hadrat Ali bowed his head to the will of God and prayed to the Almighty to grant him patience and courage to face the difficulties that beset his path. The return march was made by the shortest road on the right bank of the Euphrates. The troops that had marched to the battlefield fired with the urge to fight for the vindication of the truth were now a frustrated and disappointed people who were returning to their homes after losing much and gaining little. For such failure they reproached and accused one another. When the truce was called they had heaved a sigh of relief at the cessation of hostilities. On the way back when they reflected on the course of events which they had themselves precipitated they came to have second thoughts. It came to dawn on them that they were the victims of misfortune for which they themselves were to blame.

Back in Kufa, Hadrat Ali found the city plunged in gloom and grief. Almost from every house in the city rose the shrieks of women mourning the deaths of their dear ones who had fallen in the battle of Siffin. There was a sense of general discontentment with the people that the sacrifices that they had made had gone in vain and the campaign to Syria undertaken at a heavy cost had proved to be an exercise in futility. The general state of administration had fallen at a low ebb. Government was faced with acute financial difficulties. The law and order position became unsatisfactory. Hadrat Ali had to strive hard to restore some semblance of order. He sympathised with the families who had lost their men in the battle and assured them that such deaths would be avenged.

In his sermons to the congregation in the principal mosque of the city he exhorted the people to hold fast to the rope of God, cultivate the values of Islam, remain united among themselves and pray to God for their ultimate victory. He took the people into confidence and narrated at length how he had been betrayed at the battle of Siffin. He calmed the feelings of the people and sought their cooperation in another bid to avenge the truth.

The Kharijites : The battle of Siffin led to the birth of the first sect among the Muslims which came to be known as the Kharjites. The term literally means separatists, seceders or outgoers. The term is based on a verse of the Holy Quran (IV: 101) which refers to those who leave their homes among the unbelievers. They also called themselves as the Shurat, i. e., those who sell their lives and property in return for paradise. The movement had its origin among the tribes of Banu Tamim, Banu Bakr and Banu Hamdan. These people had participated in the revolt against Hadrat Uthman and were involved in his murder. When Hadrat Muawiyyah raised the cry for vengeance for the blood of Hadrat Uthman they allied themselves with Hadrat Ali. They fought on his side in the battle of the Camel. When Hadrat Ali led his forces to Syria these people formed an important component of the army of Hadrat Ali.

As the battle of Siffin dragged on without leading to any tangible results these people got wearied of the war. They felt that the war was in reality a struggle for power between Hadrat Ali and Muawiyyah. These people could boast of deep-rooted traditions of democracy and a struggle for power was repugnant to their way of life. They accordingly came to maintain that it was not advisable for them to be a pawn in the game of king making. When the troops of Muawiyyah displayed the leaves of the Holy Quran on their lances and appealed for decision to the Holy Quran instead of arms, these people responded to the call and forced Hadrat Ali to suspend hostilities, although victory for his forces was well in sight.

Thus these people though allied with Hadrat Ali indirectly promoted the cause of Hadrat Muawiyyah. Although he was after their blood because of their involvement in the murder of Hadrat Uthman Hadrat Muawiyyah was shrewd enough to appreciate their gesture and in the arbitration agreement that was subsequently drawn up, there was no reference to the murder of Hadrat Uthman. The point of dispute to be referred for arbitration was, as to out of Hadrat Ali and Hadrat Muawiyyah, to whom the sovereignty was to belong. On the return march these people had second thoughts on the matter. They felt that they had committed a sin in accepting the cease-fire. They became critical of the appointment of umpires. They were emphatically of the view that the decision of God alone should be sought for and it was a sin to vest the decision in the matter in human beings. They blamed Hadrat Ali for his acceptance of the proposal for the appointment of umpires.

In order to support their stand they worked out religious dogmas and their fundamental principle was "La Hukma ilia lillah" —no decision except the decision of God. They maintained that they stood for the establishment of the kingdom of God and not of men on the earth. As God was not to rule in person some Amir had to be appointed, but such Amir was bound to follow strictly the commands of God as revealed in the Holy Quran. The Amir could hold office as long as one observed the commands of God. When there was any dereliction on his part, he was liable to be killed. They acknowledged that they were involved in the assassination of Hadrat Uthman but they justified this act on the ground that Hadrat Uthman had acted against the commands of God. They held that when any person committed a sin he became a Kafir and it was necessary for him to offer repentance for re-entry in the fold of Islam. They had committed a sin in accepting the cease-fire. They repented publicly and sought the forgiveness of God. They held that they alone were true believers and all other persons who called themselves Muslims but did not subscribe to their views were unbelievers. They maintained that they had the right to kill unbelievers. It followed that they could not live in the midst of unbelievers. On return from Siffin they did not come back to Kufa. Instead they encamped at Harura, a few miles outside Kufa. In this way these people separated from the main body of the Muslims and came to be known as the Kharijites. Their strength was about twelve thousand. Their leaders were Shabath b Ribi al Riahl, Abdullah b Kauwa al Yeshkun Yazid b Qais al Harabi and. Abdullah b Wahab al Rasibi.

Hadrat Ali and Kharijites : As these people had formerly been the allies of Hadrat Ali and had defected under some misunderstanding, Hadrat Ali contacted them with a view to arriving at some conciliation with them. They criticised Hadrat Ali for his acceptance of arbitration. Hadrat Ali pointed out to them that he was against the acceptance of cease-fire when victory was almost in sight but he did so because of their pressure. They confessed that in putting pressure on him they had sinned and to atone for that sin they had offered repentance to God. They insisted that as Hadrat Ali had also sinned, he too should offer repentance. Hadrat Ali said that he had merely made a political mistake and not committed any sin and as such no particular act of repentance was called for. In his prayers he repented everyday and that cleared him before God. They said that it was wrong on his part to accept the verdict on human umpires instead of the decision of God. Hadrat Ali pointed out that according to the agreement the umpires were bound to give their verdict in accordance with the injunctions of Islam and if such decision was not in accord with the commands of God as revealed in the Holy Book, it could be repudiated. They demanded that Hadrat Ali should lead them to the battle again to fight against the Syrians Hadrat Ali said that he agreed with them and appreciated their offer but as he had entered into an agreement to keep peace it would not be advisable for them to take up arms for that would be against the injunction of Islam which enjoins the scrupulous observance of agreements. He assured them making God' his witness that if the decision of the umpires was not in accord with the injunction of Islam, he would lead them to war as desired by them. He observed that in the meantime they could make preparations for war so that they should be ready to march to the battlefield as soon as there was a violation of the agreement by the other side. That apparently satisfied the Kharijites and at the instance of Hadrat Ali they broke the camp at Harura and returned to their homes in Kufa.

Meeting of the Umpires : In pursuance of the arbitration agreement executed between Hadrat Ali and Hadrat Muawiyyah at Siffin the two umpires Abu Musa. Ashan and Amr b. Al Aas met a Dumatul Jandal midway between Kufa and Damascus in January 658 C. E.

Each side sent a retinue of four hundred persons to witness the proceedings. The retinue from Kufa was led by. Abdullah bin Abbas and Shuraih b Mani. The umpires invited some notable companions from Mecca and Medina who were known for their neutrality in the dispute between Hadrat Ali and Hadrat Muawiyyah to come to Dumatul Jandal. Those who responded to the invitation included. Abdullah b Umar,. Abdullah b Zubayr, Mughira b Shuba and Abdur Rahman b Harith. Sa'ad b. Abi Waqas was prevailed upon by his son to go to Dumatul Jandal but he declined to do so saying that he was not interested in the affair.

Arbitration Proceedings : According to the accounts that have come down to us, it appears that on the appointed day the two umpires met in camera. Amr b. Al. Aas asked Abu Musa. Ashan whether he held Hadrat Uthman to be innocent and his murder to be a crime. Abu Musa answered these questions in affirmative. Amr b. Al Aas next asked the question whether in the circumstances the claim of Hadrat Muawiyyah for "Qasas" for the blood of Hadrat Uthman was justified. Abu Musa said that according to the injunctions of the Holy Quran such claim could be made. Amr b. Al. Aas thereafter said that he objected to the caliphate of Hadrat Ali, because he was involved in the murder of Hadrat Uthman. Abu Musa said that this accusation was not correct and no proof could be given to establish his involvement in the murder of Hadrat Uthman. Amr b. Al-Aas said that Hadrat Ali had been asked to hand over the murderers of Hadrat Uthman to the heirs of Hadrat Uthman for taking "Qasas" but he had not done so. That implies his indirect if not direct involvement in the murder of Hadrat Uthman. Abu Musa said that the proper course for Hadrat Muawiyyah was to owe allegiance to Hadrat Ali and then lodge a claim for "Qasas" before him Amr b. Al-Aas said that as the murderers of Hadrat Uthman were allied with Hadrat Ali, the heirs of Hadrat Uthman could have no confidence in him in doing justice with regard to the claim for "Qasas". Amr b. Al. Aas suggested that in the circumstances proper course was that Hadrat Muawiyyah should be made the Caliph. Abu Musa said that in the matter of the caliphate, Hadrat Muawiyyah could not claim a precedence over Hadrat Ali. Hadrat Ali was one of the earliest converts to Islam. He was closely related to the Holy Prophet. He was the most learned man of the age. His services to Islam were well known. Amr b. Al. Aas said that though Hadrat Ali was superior to others in the matters of learning and piety, Hadrat Muawiyyah excelled others in matters of politics and statecraft Amr b. Al-Aas argued that the Caliph was to be the Head of the State and was primarily concerned with affairs of the world and in this respect Hadrat Muawiyyah would be a better choice. Abu Musa said that in an Islamic state the interest of the world could not be given preference over the interests of Islam and as such Hadrat Muawiyyah could not be preferred to Hadrat Ali in the matter of the caliphate.

Amr b. Al. Aas suggested that if with regard to the basic issue about the "Qasas" for the blood of Hadrat Uthman, Hadrat Ali could not be trusted because of his direct or indirect involvement in the murder of Hadrat Uthman and Hadrat Muawiyyah was not to be preferred to Hadrat Ali in the matter of the caliphate then the obvious course was that they should consider the names of some neutral persons for the office of the caliphate. To this course Abu Musa agreed. Abu Musa recalled the days of the glory of the Muslims during the caliphate of Hadrat Umar. He wished to have a caliph of the calibre of Hadrat Umar. That made the two umpires consider the name of Abdullah b Umar, who was present at Damatul Jandal, was contacted and he refused to be a candidate for the office of the Caliph, Sa'ad b. Abi Waqas was a suitable candidate, but he was not willing to be considered. The claims of Abdullah b Zubayr were considered but those were not accepted on the ground that as he had participated in the battle of the camel he could not be considered to be neutral in the matter. Some other names were considered but their claims were turned down on one ground or the other.

That led to a state of deadlock and the two umpires could not reach a decision. But some decision had necessarily to be taken. Thereupon Amr b. Al. Aas said, "If Hadrat Ali is not acceptable to us and Hadrat Muawiyyah is not acceptable to you and we have not been able to arrive at an agreement about any neutral person then what should be the way out in your considered opinion?"

Abu Musa said, "In my opinion the best course would be that we would depose both Hadrat Ali and Hadrat Muawiyyah and ask the community to decide the matter for themselves"

Amr b. Al. Aas said, "Alright, you make this announcement"

Announcement : Thereafter Abu Musa. Ashan took the stage to announce the decision. Abdullah b. Abbas asked. Abu Musa not to be the first in making the announcement. He advised him that he should let Amr b. Al. Aas speak first. Abu Musa did not pay any heed to the advice of Abdullah b. Abbas and announced the decision that both he and Amr b. Al Aas had agreed that Hadrat Ali as well as Hadrat Muawiyyah should be deposed and it should be for the community to elect whomsoever they liked as the Caliph. He observed that in accordance with this decision he deposed his candidate Hadrat Ali. Thereafter Amr b. Al. Aas took the stage. He said that according to the terms of the arbitration agreement, the umpires had to decide as to whom out of Hadrat Ali and Hadrat Muawiyyah the sovereignty was to belong. He observed that as the umpire representing Hadrat Ali had deposed him, Hadrat Muawiyyah was the only candidate left in the field and as such the sovereignty belonged to him.

There is some controversy as to what actually transpired between the umpires. According to the accounts that have come down to us it is said that both the umpires had agreed between themselves that both Hadrat Ali and Hadrat Muawiyyah should be deposed and that Amr b. Al. Aas went back on the agreement and betrayed Abu Musa. Ashan. This does not appear to be a correct account of what actually happened If both the umpires had originally agreed to the deposition of both Hadrat Ali and Hadrat Muawiyyah and. Amr b. Al. Aas went back on such agreement,. Abu Musa could have taken the stage and said that as Amr had violated his agreement with him his decision was of no effect. What appears to have happened is that when Abu Musa suggested that the matter should be referred to the community for the fresh election of the Caliph Amr merely asked him to make an announcement to that effect. Abu Musa was not shrewd enough to realise the implication of such announcement. It is well known that when Abu Musa was the Governor of Kufa he had advised the people of Kufa to remain neutral in the dispute between Hadrat Ali and Hadrat. Aishah in spite of the fact that he had taken the oath of allegiance to Hadrat Ali and was legally as well as morally bound to obey the command of Hadrat Ali. Hadrat Ali had to depose him Hadrat Ali had to accept his nomination as an umpire under pressure. Although Hadrat Ali did not have full confidence in Abu Musa, he still hoped that as Abu Musa was otherwise a pious Muslim he would act in a fair and impartial way according to the injunctions of Islam. Abu Musa was in fact so much obsessed with the idea of neutrality that he suggested the stepping aside of both Hadrat Ali and Hadrat Muawiyyah and the election of the Caliph by the community afresh. Such suggestion was not within the four corners of the agreement according to which the umpires had to decide as to whom out of Hadrat Ali and Hadrat Muawiyyah sovereignty was to belong. The accounts that come down to us provide that as soon as Abu Musa made this suggestion, "Amr b. Al. Aas jumped up and asked Abu Musa to announce that decision. Abu Musa considered that in asking him to make the announcement, Amr had agreed with him. Actually Amr had not made any agreement. He was shrewd enough to realise the implications of the suggestion. To be fair Amr did not violate any agreement with Abu Musa, he merely took advantage of the weakness in the stand of the umpire of Hadrat Ali. The life story of Hadrat Ali is a painful story of betrayals. To other betrayals one more betrayal was added as a consequence of the arbitration proceedings.

Hadrat Ali's Letter to Abu Musa : After the arbitration proceedings, Abu Musa did not have the courage to face Hadrat Ali. He slipped away to Mecca and from there wrote a letter to Hadrat Ali offering some sort of apology. Hadrat Ali replied to this letter, as follows:

> "Verily, many persons will be deprived of their rewards in the next world. They fall an easy prey to the temptations of the world, I am in a queer fix as regards the problem of the caliphate. A man, stiff necked in his conceit is at loggerheads with me. Surely, there is no one more anxious than me to keep the solidarity of the Muslims because I strongly hope that God would reward me for these selfless services of mine in the cause of the unity of the Muslims. Abu Musa, you turned against the right and deserted me. Surely there is none more unfortunate than you, because you were deprived of your wisdom and the faculty to act in the right way."

Battle of Nahrawan : The arbitration decision came as a great shock to Hadrat Ali. Hadrat Ali had hoped that as the umpires were to take the decision in accordance with the injunctions of the Holy Quran, they would act with a due sense of justice and fair play. The decision that was taken was neither just nor fair. It was taken in the spirit of the old. Arab traditions of the Age of Ignorance and was repugnant to Islamic values. The umpires were supposed to judge the relative merits of Hadrat Ali and Muawiyyah in the light of Islamic values and then choose one out of the two. The umpires did nothing of the sort. Abu Musa the umpire of Hadrat Ali, had some bias against Hadrat Ali because Hadrat Ali had deposed him from the governorship of Kufa and hence wittingly or unwittingly he acted against the interests of Hadrat Ali. Hadrat Ali had been duly elected as the Caliph by the authorised electorate and Abu Musa had no authority to depose Hadrat. Ali Amr b. Al Aas, the umpire of Hadrat Muawiyyah, was a clever man and taking advantage of the weakness in the stand of Abu Musa he manipulated victory for Hadrat Muawiyyah. The entire arbitration proceedings thus turned out to be a farce based on betrayal and trickery. It nevertheless created an embarrassing position for Hadrat Ali. The arbitration agreement had provided that the decision of the umpires was to be binding on both the parties. According to the terms of the agreement, Hadrat Ali was bound to accept the decision and step aside from the office of the Caliph. Hadrat Ali held the office as a trust from God and he could not betray such trust on the basis of a decision which was arbitrary, frivolous and capricious and therefore no decision. Hadrat Ali could not, therefore accept the decision and the only option left with him was to renew the war against Muawiyyah who had manipulated to win power through underhand means. Hadrat Ali accordingly gave call for arms and exhorted the people to join the war for the vindication of the truth and the suppression of falsehood. The people responded enthusiastically to the call and soon an army of 65,000 strong men was assembled.

Role of Kharijites : As started earlies, after the battle of Siffin the Kharijites had separated from the community and camped at Harura a few miles from Kufa. Their stand was that Hadrat Ali had made a mistake in accepting the arbitration of men. Hadrat Ali was asked by them to lead them to war against Muawiyyah. Hadrat Ali had tried to conciliate them and assured them that he would lead them to war in case the decision of the umpires was against the injunctions of Islam. Some sort of conciliation was brought about between Hadrat Ali and the Kharijites and most of the Kharijites returned to Kufa. The Kharijites were a restive and over-sensitive people of the extremist type. The Kharijites slipped from Kufa one by one, established a settlement at Nahrawan, a few miles to the east of the Tigris near Medina. The Kharijites from Basra and elsewhere in Iraq also migrated to Nahrawan. Here the Kharijites gathered in strength. They elected an Amir of their own. They were very meticulous in observing prayers and following other injunctions of Islam. They aspires to live sinless lives. They declared that they were not interested in the affairs of this world and that they had sold their lives to win paradise in the next world. Where a Kharijites picked up a date under a date tree and ate it he subsequently cut his right hand himself on the ground that the eating of the date without purchasing it from the owner amounted to a theft. On the other hand when any Muslim indulged in any controversy with them they invariably killed him. They held that no one except themselves was a Muslim and it devolved on them to get rid of such people who did not agree with them. They let loose a reign of terror in the countryside and created a problem of law and order for the administration. When the Kharijites of Basra migrated to Nahrawan they met in the way some Muslims including Abdullah, the son of an eminent companion Khabab. The Kharijites killed him as well as the woman who accompanied him.

When Hadrat Ali was ready for a march to Syria he sent a message to the Kharijites asking them to join him in the march to Syria. Hadrat Ali brought home to them the point that he had undertaken to lead them to war against Muawiyyah after decision of the arbitrators was known and now that he had repudiated the decision of the umpires and was leading a force to Syria they should join his ranks as originally agreed upon. The Kharijites gave an insolent reply to the invitation. They said that when they had asked Hadrat Ali to lead them to war he was the Caliph of the Muslims and it was incumbent on them to support him for thereby they were to serve the cause of God. After the decision of the umpires the position had been changed. According to this decision Hadrat Ali had been deposed and power had been vested in his rival Hadrat Muawiyyah.

In these circumstances Hadrat Ali was undertaking a campaign against Hadrat Muawiyyah for a personal end. They observed that as the warriors of God, they were committed to fight in the cause of God alone and not in the cause of any particular person to secure a worldly end.

Hadrat Ali felt that it was futile to argue with a fanatic people like the Kharijites. He was accordingly of the view that they should march to Syria without bothering for the assistance of the Kharijites. His armymen however, expressed the view that when they were to be away there was the danger that the fanatic Kharijites would terrorise and murder their families. Hadrat Ali accordingly prevailed upon to deal with the menace of the Kharijites before proceeding to Syria. Hadrat Ali agreed to this view and the force that was to proceed to Syria proceeded to Nahrawan instead.

The Battle : Hadrat Ali marched with his forces to Nahrawan. Reaching Nahrawan. Hadrat Ali planted a standard on the ground and declared that those who come under that standard would have amnesty and safe conduct. Some persons deserted the Kharijites camp and they were allowed amnesty and safe conduct to their houses. Thereafter Hadrat Ali sent a messenger to the Kharijites asking them that they should surrender the persons who were guilty of killing Abdullah b Khabab and other Muslims. The Kharijites refused to surrender any person and declared that they would consider it to be a virtue to fight against Hadrat Ali and his forces.

Hadrat Ali marshalled his force and launched an attack against the Kharijites. With the battle cry "On to Paradise", the Kharijites rushed on the troops of Hadrat Ali. The Kharijites hardly numbered four thousand while the troops of Hadrat Ali numbered about fifty thousand. The Kharijites fought desperately and frantically but they were outnumbered by the forces of Hadrat Ali. Out of four thousand Kharijites only two or three dozen Kharijites escaped, the rest were killed.

Hadrat Ali won a decisive victory at Nahrawan, but it proved to be a hollow and fatal victory which diverted Hadrat Ali from his main war against Hadrat Muawiyyah. After the victory of Nahrawan Hadrat Ali felt that the victory would raise the morale of his people. That was, however, not to be the case. Hadrat Ali wanted that from Nahrawan he should proceed direct to Syria. His army, however, desired that they should return to Kufa and thereafter proceed to Syria after taking some rest Hadrat Ali agreed with the wishes of his troops. The army returned to Kufa and camped at Nukhaila outside Kufa. The troops were given leave for two or three days and were commanded to return to the camp thereafter in order to proceed to Syria. The men left the camp but did not return to march to Syria. Hadrat Ali addressed the people in the mosques and exhorted them to join the camp. He reproached them for their disobedience and accused them of treachery. These exhortation, reproaches and accusations had no effect on the people and heart-broken Hadrat Ali had to abandon the campaign to Syria. When we reflect at the events that happened it appears that there was something wrong with the military organisation. The troops lacked discipline and instead of obeying orders from above, the troops indulged in giving orders. The troops betrayed Hadrat Ali at Siffin and forced him to stop the war when the victory was almost in sight. At Kufa Hadrat Ali was betrayed by his troops again when they refused to march to Syria. This naturally led to the advantage of Hadrat Muawiyyah. When he got the intelligence that Hadrat Ali was planning a march to Syria he led his forces to Siffin. When Hadrat Ali had to abandon the campaign to Syria, Muawiyyah withdrew his forces from Siffin and led them to Egypt with a view to wresting that prize province from the control of Hadrat Ali. Misfortune was now stalking the footsteps of Hadrat Ali. Henceforward, he was faced not with the loss of territories alone, he came to be exposed to the danger of losing his life as well. Though most of the Kharijites were killed at the battle of Nahrawan, some Kharijites escaped the massacre and these people conspicuous for their fanaticism vowed vengeance against Hadrat Ali. The victory of Nahrawan thus paved the way to the assassination of Hadrat Ali. A Kharijite assassinated Hadrat Ali two years later.

Loss of Egypt

On the deposition of Qais bin Saad, Hadrat Ali appointed Muhammad b. Abu Bakr as the Governor of Egypt. Muhammad b. Abu Bakr was the son of Hadrat. Abu Bakr Ṣiddiq, the first Caliph. On the death of Hadrat. Abu Bakr his wife Asma married Hadrat Ali and her son Muhammad was brought up by Hadrat Ali. Muhammad b. Abu Bakr was passionately devoted to Hadrat Ali. In the revolt against Hadrat Uthman he had sided with the rebels of Egypt. He had entered the room of Hadrat Uthman and held his bread. Hadrat Uthman upbraided him saying, "If your father had been alive, you would not have done like this. ". At this reproach Muhammad b. Abu Bakr withdrew. He was not present when Hadrat Uthman was assassinated.

Two Groups : Muhammad b. Abu Bakr was young and handsome. At the time of his appointment as Governor of Egypt he was twenty-two years of age. Muhammad b. Abu Bakr was popular with the young men of Egypt who had rebelled against the authority of Hadrat Uthman and were involved in his murder. All such persons called around Muhammad b. Abu Bakr and he conferred high favours on them. In Egypt there were two parties. One party was pro-Uthman. They held that Hadrat Uthman was innocent and those who had killed him were guilty of a crime. This party was led by Muawiyyah b Hudaij. As Sakuni and Musalamab Mukhalld. They had their concentration in Karbala in South Egypt. Qais b Sa'ad did not force these people to take the oath of allegiance to Hadrat Ali. He made a treaty of neutrality with them whereunder they undertook that if they were not pressed to take the oath of allegiance to Hadrat Ali they would remain at peace and would not create any difficulty for the state and would remain loyal to it. It was in pursuance of this treaty that when Hadrat Muawiyyah, the Amir of Syria, asked them to join him in raising the demand for vengeance for the blood of Hadrat Uthman, they refused to join him. In view of this treaty of neutrality, peace reigned in Egypt during the governorship of Qais b Sa'ad.

Muhammad b. Abu Bakr had the rashness of youth about him. He came to be surrounded by young men who had rebelled against Hadrat Uthman. Muhammad b. Abu Bakr and the people around him considered that they were strong enough to overawe the pro-Uthman party and force them to take the oath of allegiance to Hadrat Ali. Muhammad b. Abu Bakr as Governor commanded these men that they should take the oath of allegiance to Hadrat Ali within one month. The leaders of the pro-Uthman party waited on Muhammad b. Abu Bakr and said that his command was in violation of the treaty that they had executed with his predecessor. They advised him to maintain status quo otherwise the peace of the province would be disturbed. Muhammad b. Abu Bakr did not pay heed to their request and ordered the invasion of Karbala. In this action the forces of Muhammad b. Abu Bakr were defeated and the pro-Uthman party broke into open revolt which disturbed the peace of the province.

New Governor : When news about disturbances in Egypt reached Hadrat Ali he summoned Malik. Ashtar to Kufa for consultation. Malik Ashtar was the Commander-in-Chief of the forces of Hadrat Ali at the battle of Siffin. After the battle of Siffin he was appointed as the Governor of Mesopotamia and was stationed at Nisibin. Hadrat Ali had his consultation with Qais b Sa'ad about the affairs of Egypt. Hadrat Ali realised that he had made a mistake in deposing Qais b Sa'ad from the governorship of Egypt. He, however, could not spare Qais to be reposted as the Governor of Egypt for he wanted him to remain at Kufa by his side as his adviser. He, therefore, desired Ashtar to accept the office of the governorship of Egypt and restore order. Malik Ashtar was a good military general and he already commanded influence with the people of Egypt.

When Hadrat Muawiyyah came to know of the appointment of Malik. Ashtar as the Governor of Egypt he felt much concerned. Malik Ashtar was a strong man and Hadrat Muawiyyah feared that Malik Ashtar would be able to suppress the disturbances in Egypt with a strong hand and thus frustrate his (Muawiyyah's) efforts to wrest Egypt from the control of Hadrat Ali. Muawiyyah accordingly hatched a conspiracy to kill Malik. Ashtar before he could reach Egypt. He took into confidence the chief of Qalzauma, town on the border of Syria and Egypt and heavily bribed him to kill Malik Ashtar when he arrived there on the way to Egypt. When Malik Ashtar arrived at Qalzauma the chief of the town waited on him and provided for his stay in the city for the night. He was well looked after and served with sumptuous meals. Thereafter he was served with a cup of honey which was poisoned Malik. Ashtar died within a few hours.

When the news of the death of Malik. Ashtar reached Damascus, Muawiyyah was overjoyed. He announced the news to the people from the pulpit in the main mosque of Damascus. He said that Hadrat Ali had two arms. One of his arms was Amar b Yasir which had been cut in the battle of Siffin and with the death of Malik. Ashtar his second arm had also been cut off. When Hadrat Ali came to know of the death of Malik Ashtar he was overwhelmed with grief. The death of his right-hand man Malik Ashtar was a grievous blow for Hadrat Ali. Hadrat Ali now seemed to be fighting a losing battle. He was fast losing friends and the number of his enemies was fast multiplying.

When Hadrat Ali had appointed Malik Ashtar as the Governor of Egypt, Muhammad b. Abu Bakr felt dissatisfied at his deposition. Hadrat Ali wrote a letter to Muhammad b. Abu Bakr to say that he had passed the orders in his interest for he intended to appoint him as a Governor of some other peaceful province where things for him would be easier. With the death of Malik Ashtar Muhammad b. Abu Bakr had to continue in office and bear the brunt of the rebellion of the pro-Uthman group from within and the attack of Muawiyyah from outside.

The Propagenda : As long as the umpires had not given their decision at Dumatul Jandal and a truce obtained between Hadrat Ali and Muawiyyah did not interfere directly in the affairs of Egypt. He, however, indirectly helped the pro-Uthman group in Egypt led by Muawiyyah b Hudaij to maintain their stand against the government of Muhammad b. Abu Bakr. At Dumatul Jandal,. Abu Musa. Ashan declared the deposition of Hadrat Ali and Amr b. AI-Aas declared for the sovereignty of Muawiyyah. This decision, howsoever, reached and howsoever perverse turned the tables on Hadrat Ali. The implication of the decision was that henceforward Muawiyyah was the legitimate ruler of the Muslim state and Hadrat Ali was reduced to the status of a usurper or a rebel against the legitimate authority, in accordance with the propaganda of Muawiyyah. According to the pact between Muawiyyah and Amr b. AI-Aas Muawiyyah had promised the governorship of Egypt to Muawiyyah. After Amr b. AI-Aas had by a clever trick conferred the sovereignty on Muawiyyah, Muawiyyah commissioned Amr b. AI-Aas to conquer Egypt. When Amr departed at the head of an army on the expedition of Egypt Muawiyyah said to him," Amr you were the first conqueror of Egypt, go and reconquer Egypt "The plan of the pro-Uthman party was that while Muawiyyah b Hudaij would attack Muhammad b. Abu Bakr in Egypt itself, Amr should lead the attack from across the borders.

When Hadrat Ali had originally planned an expedition to Syria, Muhammad b. Abu Bakr had a sizable force at his disposal and he could deal with an internal rebellion. When after the battle of Nahrawan, Hadrat Ali had to abandon his expedition to Syria, Muawiyyah increased his pressure against Egypt. Under the changed circumstances many warriors of the forces of Muhammad b. Abu Bakr abandoned his cause and either joined the pro-Uthman party or preferred to be neutral and keep aloof from the struggle. Muhammad b. Abu Bakr was left with a small force of four thousand persons only when Muawiyyah b Hudaij and Amr b. AI-Aas launched their offensive Muhammad b. Abu Bakr requested Hadrat Ali to send him help. Accounts in this respect vary. According to one account Hadrat Ali because of the non-cooperation of the people of Kufa could not send any help. According to another account, Hadrat Ali sent some help but it was insignificant. According to yet another account whatever reinforcement was sent arrived in Egypt after all was over and Egypt had been captured in the name of Muawiyyah. The force with which Muhammad b. Abu Bakr fought consisted mostly of persons who were involved in the murder of Hadrat Uthman. These men were led by Bashr b Kinana Bashr b Kinana and they fought desperately and heroically but they were cut to pieces by the superior forces of the enemy. After Bashr b Kinana had been killed and further resistance became impossible, Muhammad b. Abu Bakr escaped from the battlefield and sought refuge in the ruins outside the city of Fustal. Muawiyyah b Hudaij secured the countryside and Muhammad b. Abu Bakr was taken captive and brought to Fustal. Abdul Rahman b. Abu Bakr waited on Amr b. AI-Aas and pleaded for the life of Muhammad b. Abu Bakr Amr b. AI-Aas sent words to Muawiyyah b Hudaij that the prisoner should be sent to him Muawiyyah b Hudaij said that he had taken to arms in vengeance for the blood of Hadrat Uthman and he could not show any mercy to the person who was guilty of the murder of Hadrat Uthman. Muhammad b. Abu Bakr asked for water from his captors. He was told that as he had refused water to Hadrat Uthman, thus no water could be allowed to him. Muhammad b. Abu Bakr was mercilessly slain. His corpse was wrapped in the skin of an ass and burnt.

Helplessness Again : When Hadrat Ali came to know of the end of Muhammad b. Abu Bakr and the fall of Egypt, his grief knew no bounds. In a letter addressed to his cousin Abdullah b. Abbas, Hadrat Ali mourned the death of Muhammad b. Abu Bakr in heartrending terms. The loss of Egypt was a grievous blow to the prestige of Hadrat Ali. Addressing the people from the pulpit in the main mosque of Kufa Hadrat Ali said:

> "O ye people' In the hour of need you have forsaken me Falsehood had overcome the truth and also no one is forthcoming to take up cudgels on behalf of the truth. I have lost Egypt I have lost a loyal son Who will avenge his death?Is no spark of faith left in you to fight for cause? What has happened to your oath of allegiance to me when you are not listening to me? Why have you become so deaf and dumb?"

Day after day, Hadrat Ali ascended the pulpit and poured out quotation from the Holy Quran and the traditions of the Holy Prophet, enjoining upon the Muslims their obligation to undertake Jihad. These harangues and exhortation had no effect on the people. Somehow they felt that the star of Hadrat Ali was waning and they were in no mood to worship the sun that was about to set. The state of the helplessness of Hadrat Ali is described by Dr. Ata Mohyuddin in the following words in his book. Ali, the Superman:

> "Hadrat Ali now lost heart completely, despair overwhelmed him, crippling his energies and paralysing all initiative. He completely lost faith in human nature and withdrew to a life of retirement. He no longer had any control over the army or over the people and presented the spectacle of a beaten man."

Trouble in Basra : After the conquest of Egypt the strategy of Muawiyyah was that discontent should be created in the territories under the control of Hadrat Ali. A vigorous propaganda campaign was whipped up accusing Hadrat Ali of breach of faith in not accepting the verdict of the umpires at Daumatul Jandal whereas according to the pact executed at Siffin such verdict was to be binding. In these territories there were already many tribes which were pro-Uthman. Those tribes were bribed to carry on propaganda against Hadrat Ali and sponsor activities likely to subvert the administration of Hadrat Ali in the various provinces.

The Game Plan : Muawiyyah tried to create trouble in Basra in the first instance. After Kufa the main concentration of the Kharijites was in Basra. After the battle of Nahrawan, the Kharijites had become the bitter enemies of Hadrat Ali. The game of Muawiyyah was to incite the Kharijites of Basra to create trouble for Hadrat Ali. There were many persons in Basra who were originally pro-Uthman but who had to take the oath of allegiance to Hadrat Ali after the battle of the Camel. The plan of Muawiyyah was to motivate such people to throw off their allegiance to Hadrat Ali.

The governorship of Basra was held by Abdullah b. Abbas, cousin of Hadrat Ali. Abdullah b. Abbas was present at Daumatul Jandal when the umpires gave their verdict. This verdict was a great shock for Hadrat Ali. Abdullah b. Abbas had comforted Hadrat Ali and had counselled him not to lose heart. He had advised Hadrat Ali to stick to his office for the decision of the umpires was a farce and therefore not binding.

Thereafter the troubles of Hadrat Ali continued to multiply. He had to fight against the Kharijites and though the battle of Naharwan was won, it brought further difficulties for Hadrat Ali. The army that he intended to lead to Syria to settle accounts with Muawiyyah refused to cooperate. A great blow fell on Hadrat Ali when the province of Egypt was lost. The death of Muhammad b. Abu Bakr, a ward of Hadrat Ali, greatly distressed and grieved Hadrat Ali. In order to condole the death of Muhammad b. Abu Bakr with Hadrat Ali,. Abdullah b. Abbas set out from Basra for Kufa. During his absence the charge of Basra was held by Ziyad b. Abihi. Ziyad was the son of a slave girl Samia and the name of his father was not known. Later Muawiyyah acknowledged Ziyad as a son of his father. Abu Sufyan from the slave girl Samia Ziyad was a capable person and at this stage he was very loyal to Hadrat Ali.

Force to Basra : After Abdullah b. Abbas had left Basra for Kufa, Muawiyyah sent a contingent of 2,000 horses under the command of Abdullah b Amr al Hadrami, a cousin of Hadrat Uthman. It was not an expedition of a regular invasion. The strategy adopted was that of peaceful penetration. The idea was to exploit the differences among the tribes in the area, flare up such dissensions and create problems for the administration of Hadrat Ali. On arrival in Basra, the Syrians became the guests of the Banu Tamim, a tribe known for its sympathy to Hadrat Uthman. Al Hadrami told the Banu Tamim that as a result of the decision of the umpires at Daumatul Jandal, sovereignty had passed on to Muawiyyah and as such they should owe allegiance to Muawiyyah. Banu Tamim accordingly took the oath of allegiance to Muawiyyah. There was a sizable section of the people of Basra proper who had originally sided with Hadrat. Aishah, but who were later forced to take the oath of allegiance to Hadrat Ali. These pro-Uthman persons joined the Banu Tamim and took the oath of allegiance to Muawiyyah. These defections weakend the position of the Alid government in Basra. In the circumstances Ziyad in charge of the government of Basra was forced to seek the protection of the Azd tribe, a tribe opposed to Banu Tamim.

At this stage the situation in Basra took the shape of conflict between the two tribes — Banu Tamim and Banu Azd. The government had ceased to function independently and was reduced to the status of a vassal of the. Azd tribe. Ziyad wrote to Hadrat Ali informing him of the situation in Basra. Hadrat Ali sent a small force from Kufa under the command of Abu Dhabiah Mujashi. He belonged to Banu Tamim and his mission was to prevail upon his tribe to repudiate their allegiance to Muawiyyah. Al Mujashi failed in his mission and he was killed by his own tribesmen.

At the death of Mujashi, Ziyad planned military action against Banu Tamim to seek vengeance for the blood of Mujashi. The two tribes of Azd and Banu Tamim, however, entered into a truce agreement to maintain the status quo and the military action contemplated by Ziyad could not be undertaken. Ziyad brought the state of affairs to the notice of Hadrat Ali. This time Hadrat Ali sent a force under Janah b Qadamah. He also belonged to the Banu Tamim tribe. The mission of Janah met with success and he was able to win many persons of the Banu Tamim to his side. Janah and his men besieged the house where Al Hadrami was lodged and set it on fire. Al Hadrami and his men were brunt alive. With the death of Al Hadrami, the government of Hadrat Ali regained the control of Basra.

A Sinister Hue : Abdullah b. Abbas returned from Kufa and assumed the office of the Governor of Basra. Although the government of Hadrat Ali had succeeded in regaining the control of Basra, that was not the end of the troubles in Basra. Most of the people who had repudiated the oath of allegiance of Hadrat Ali and had taken the oath of allegiance to Muawiyyah once again recanted and took the oath of allegiance to Hadrat Ali. Under the circumstances the process of oath taking lost its solemnity and became a farce. The people came to change their allegiance as they would change their clothes. That bred discontentment and a sense of insecurity among the people.

Things on the Basra front acquired a sinister hue when Abdullah b. Abbas, the Governor of Basra, defalcated the state funds. Abdul. Aswad, incharge of the Baitul Mal at Basra, brought to the notice of Hadrat Ali that heavy amounts had been received in the state treasury as "Kharaj", but these amounts had been defalcated by the Governor. Without disclosing the source of his information, Hadrat Ali wrote to Abdullah b. Abbas that it had come to his notice that he had defalcated heavy amounts from the state treasury. Hadrat Ali pointed out that the Government was merely a trustee of the state fund and according to the injunctions of Islam, such funds could not be diverted to serve personal ends. Abdullah b. Abbas wrote in reply that the report that had been made to Hadrat Ali was false. He added that he was fully conscious of his duties and obligations as the Governor and the Caliph should have no anxiety or misgiving on that score. This reply did not satisfy Hadrat Ali and he asked Abdullah b. Abbas to furnish detailed accounts as to the receipts and expenditure out of the state funds. Abdullah b. Abbas took offence at the order of Hadrat Ali requiring him to furnish accounts. He did not furnish any accounts, but instead resigned from his office and proceeded to Mecca taking away all the state treasury with him. Abdullah had been the righthand man of Hadrat Ali. He was closely related to him and was his chief counsellor. Such defalcation and desertion by his close relation and best friend came as a great blow to Hadrat Ali. With the ill-gotten money. Abdullah b. Abbas purchased some beautiful slave girls. When Hadrat Ali came to know of these purchases he wrote a letter to Abdullah b. Abbas bringing home to him the gravity of his crime. Abdullah b. Abbas wrote back to say that if what he had done was a crime, it was not as heinous as the crime committed by Hadrat Ali himself in causing the bloodshed of thousands of Muslims for the sake of personal power. That broke the heart of Hadrat Ali. Such shafts of ingratitude from a close associate and dear friend made Hadrat Ali feel bitter. That was a betrayal which made Hadrat Ali lose faith in human character.

In most of the source books that have come down to us an account of the defalcation and betrayal of Abdullah b. Abbas is given in terms what has been narrated above. There is, however, some controversy on the point. According to some accounts when. Abdullah b. Abbas saw that the days of the rule of Hadrat Ali were numbered and Muawiyyah was likely to capture power he took away all that was in the state treasurey to prevent it from falling into the hands of Muawiyyah. What he did was precedented. When Hadrat Ali deposed the Uthmanite Governor of Yemen and appointed. Abdullah b. Abbas as the Governor the previous Governor had taken away all the state treasury with him to Mecca.

According to one account the entire story of the defalcation and desertion of Ibn. Abbas is fictitious. According to this account it is held that Abdullah b. Abbas was the Governor of Basra when Hadrat Ali was assassinated. He held the office during the caliphate of Imam Hassan and relinquished the office only when Imam Hassan abdicated the caliphate in favour of Muawiyyah. It is alleged that when the Abbasids came to power and differences developed between the Abbasids and the Alids, some Shia writers invented the story of the defalcation of Abdullah b. Abbas to cast aspersions on the character of the Abbasids.

Revolt of Khurrit bin Raashid : Khurrit b Raashid was the chief of the Banu Najia tribe. He belonged to Bahrain. In the battle of Camel at Basra he was an ally of Hadrat Ali. He and his men fought on the side of Hadrat Ali against the Syrians. He developed differences with Hadrat Ali on the occasion of the battle of Nahrawan. According to some accounts he sympathised with the Kharijites and got alienated from Hadrat Ali because of the massacre of the Kharijites at the battle of Nahrawan. One day after the battle of Nahrawan he appeared before Hadrat Ali and accused him of breach of trust by first agreeing to abide by the verdict of the umpires and thereafter going back on this undertaking and refusing to be bound by the decision of the umpires. Hadrat Ali told him that he had not committed any breach of trust. The decision of the umpire was a force and had not been taken according to the injunctions of Islam as provided for in the agreement executed at Siffin. Hadrat Ali told him that if he wanted to be enlightened in the matter he could advance arguments in support of the righteousness of the course adopted by him in repudiating the decision of the umpires. Khurrit said that he would come to Hadrat Ali the next day to hear his arguments.

Flight of Khurrit : Khurrit b Raashid, however, did not keep up his words and before the next day dawned Khurrit b Raashid and his three hundred followers escaped from Kufa. In the way they came across two men, and asked them who they were. One of them said that he was a Jew. He was let off being a Dhimmi. The other man said that he was a Muslim. He was asked what he thought of Hadrat Ali. He said that he had high opinion about Hadrat Ali and regarded him as the Commander of the Faithful. Thereupon the Muslim was hacked to pieces by the men of Khurrit b Raashid.

When Hadrat Ali came to know of the flight of Khurrit b Raashid he sent a detachment of about three hundred persons under the command of Ziyad b Khasfa in pursuit of the fugitives. Ziyad overtook Khurrit at Mazar Ziyad asked Khurrit to surrender. Khurrit said that he would first like to have a talk with Ziyad. Ziyad allowed him to have his say. Khurrit accused Hadrat Ali of the breach of trust. He said that after the decision of the umpires, Hadrat Ali should have stepped aside from the caliphate and allowed the community to elect the Caliph. Ziyad pointed out that the umpires' decision about the reference of the issue to the community had not been accepted by the umpire of Muawiyyah. Sovereignty was declared to belong to Muawiyyah as farce and by no criteria Muawiyyah could claim preference over Hadrat Ali in the matter of the caliphate. Khurrit said that whatever the case he refused to acknowledge Hadrat Ali as the Caliph. Ziyad said that in that case he would be forced to take punitive action against him as a rebel. Khurrit said that he was not prepared to submit and the use of any force would be met with force. The two sides thereafter took to the sword. The battle waged for the whole of the day. Two men were killed from the troops of Ziyad, while five men were killed from the side of Khurrit. The battle proved indecisive and the troops retired to their respective camps at nightfall. Although the casualties were not large, the number of persons who were wounded from either side was sufficiently large. When the next day dawned, it was found that Khurrit and his men had escaped during the night. Ziyad and his men thereafter proceeded to Basra. Here the accounts brought the intelligence that Khurrit and his men had proceeded to Ahwaz. Ziyad and his men halted at Basra and sought for further instruction from Hadrat Ali.

Battle of Ahwaz : Hadrat Ali appreciated the services of Ziyad and his men. He asked them to return to Kufa. From Kufa Hadrat Ali sent a larger force comprising about 2,000 men under the command of Muaqil b Qais. This force proceeded direct to Ahwaz. The Governor of Basra was also asked to send a force from Basra in aid of the main force under Muaqil b Qais. In the neighbourhood of Ahwaz Khurrit was able to muster a considerable following. He incited the people not to pay taxes to the Government brigands and other disorderly persons also joined his ranks. A pitched battle was fought outside. Ahwaz, Khurrit and his men suffered defeat and fled to Ramhurmuz. The action that took place at Ramhurmus also ended in the reverse of Khurrit. Thereafter Khurrit escaped to Bahrain. The Alid forces purchased Khurrit to Bahrain. Here Muaqil issued a warning to the people that those who deserted Khurrit would be granted amnesty, but those who chose to fight would be allowed no mercy. Many persons availed of this amnesty and defected from Khurrit. Nevertheless many persons remained steadfast to his cause and fought desperately. In the bloody encounter that ensued Khurrit fell along with many comrades. Those who survived were taken captives and all was over with the revolt.

Reconversion : It transpired that during these disturbances many persons who were originally Christians but had converted to Islam were reconverted to Christianity. They felt the Christianity was a religion of peace, but Islam was a strange religion, the followers of which cut at one another's throat mercilessly. Muaqil gave an option to these persons to be reconverted to Islam, but those who refused were executed on the charge of apostasy. The number of captives exceeded five hundred. As these persons parted from their families their womenfolk raised heart-rending shrieks. The Alid Administrator of the city of Ardshir who belonged to the same tribe as the captives was touched at the plight of these unfortunate men. This officer, Masakala by name, offered to ransom all the captives. The amount of ransom was worked out at two lakh dirhams. He paid one lakh dirhams forthwith and promised to pay the balance after he had collected the amounts from the persons concerned. Muaqil accordingly handed over all the captives to Masakala. Hadrat Ali was happy at the suppression of the revolt of Khurrit. He appreciated the services of Muaqil and his men for the successful termination of the campaign. He was also well impressed at the action taken by Masakala on humane and compassionate grounds. Masakala realised the amounts from the persons concerned but he defalcated in depositing the amount in the state treasury. When pressed to pay the amount, he escaped to Syria where Muawiyyah welcomed him and gave him an office. Hadrat Ali was much grieved at this betrayal. It appeared the people had lost the Islamic values which the Holy Prophet had tried to inculcate in them.

Raids on Iraq and Hijaz : After the failure of Muawiyyah's mission in Basra, he decided to undertake raids on Iraq with a view to create a sense of insecurity among the people of Iraq in general and the people living in the border areas in particular. Muawiyyah organised raiding parties under different commanders and these parties were commanded to undertake raids in the territory of Iraq all along the border. A party under the command of Noman b Bashir was asked to ravage Ayn Tamr. A party under Sufyan b. Auf was required to operate against Hit and. Anbar. The third party under Abdullah b Masaada al Fazan was commanded to operate in the Taima section. Another party under Zohaq b Qais raided Upper Mesopotamia. The purpose of these raids was to ravage and plunder. As a result of these raids, the Syrians gathered considerable booty. These parties appeared as a whirlwind and after striking blows and ravaging the countryside they withdrew to their territory. Hadrat Ali strengthened the border security guard force. As a result of these raids, the Syrians were not able to occupy any area in Iraq, but such inroads had a considerable nuisance value and proved to be a great drain on the meagre financial resources at the disposal of Hadrat Ali. Even when there were disturbances along the border, the people of Kufa remained indifferent and they did not respond to Hadrat Ali's call to rise en masse in defence of their territories. It was with great difficulty that Hadrat Ali managed to raise some force to defend the border, but its strength was very small as compared with the extent of the danger that faced the State.

Expedition to Hijaz : In the beginning of 660 C. E. prior to the annual pilgrimage Muawiyyah, sent an expedition of 3,000 horses under the command of Basr b. Artat to ravage. Hijaz Basr was a hard-hearted savage brute, cruel by nature. His mission was to win over the people of Hijaz to the side of Muawiyyah. Basr began his campaign with Medina. Hadrat Ali had shifted the capital from Medina to Kufa in order to keep the war away from Medina and thereby respect the sanctity of the city of the Holy Prophet. Hadrat Ali had accordingly made no arrangements for the defence of Medina. When the force of Muawiyyah appeared before Medina, the Alid Governor fled the city and Basr occupied it without any resistance. Basr asked the people of Medina to assemble in the Prophet's mosque. Basr ascended the pulpit and accused the people of Medina in not coming to the help of their, Caliph, Uthman and let him be murdered in cold blood before their very eyes. He made a passionate plea for vengeance for the blood of Hadrat Uthman. He said that he would show no mercy to the murderers of Hadrat Uthman. The people assembled in the mosque shed tears of repentance and mourned the assassination of Hadrat Uthman. Thereafter all the people of Medina took the oath of allegiance to Muawiyyah. Basr deposed the Alid Governor of Medina and appointed a new Governor on behalf of Muawiyyah. Medina was thus lost to Hadrat Ali.

From Medina, the Syrians proceeded to Mecca. Qatam b. Abbas, the. Alid Governor of Mecca, fled the city and the people of Mecca did not offer any resistance. Like the people of Medina, the people of Mecca offered their allegiance to Muawiyyah. Those who did not take the oath of allegiance escaped from the city. Among them was Abu Musa. Ashan, one of the umpires at Daumatul Jandal. Abu Musa. Ashan had given his decision against Hadrat Ali, but he had not favoured Muawiyyah either. He was pursued and brought to Mecca where he was produced before Basr. Basr asked him why he had escaped from Mecca. He said that he had fled for his life. Basr said that if he valued his life, he should take the oath of allegiance to Muawiyyah. Like the other people of Mecca, Abu Musa. Ashan took the oath of allegiance to Muawiyyah. Thus Hijaz was lost to Hadrat Ali and that was obviously a great blow to his cause.

Expedition to Yemen : Basr deposed the Alid Governor of Mecca and appointed a new Governor on behalf of Muawiyyah. Thereafter Basr and his troops proceeded to Yemen. The Governor of Yemen was Ubaidullah b. Abbas, a cousin of Hadrat Ali. He made a feeble attempt to resist the invader but then fled from the battlefield leaving the command to his deputy Abdullah Harithi. In the action that followed, Abdullah was defeated and killed. Thereafter Basr entered the capital city of Yemen. He resorted to atrocities as a savage, brute and is referred to by some historians as a second Nero. He killed the young children of Ubaidullah. Most of the men of Yemen who had fought against the Syrians were taken captive and killed. Like the people of Medina and Mecca, the people of Yemen were made to take the oath of allegiance to Muawiyyah.

Hadrat Ali's Counter-attack : Hadrat Ali mustered a force 4,000 strong and sent it to Yemen under the command of Jariah b Qodamah and Wahaib b Masood al Thaqfi.

On the way to Yemen the forces of Hadrat Ali passed through the territory of Najran, the inhabitants whereof supported Muawiyyah. They resisted the advance of the Alid force. In the action that followed the Najranites were defeated and killed in large numbers. When Basr came to know that the. Alid force was advancing on Yemen, he could not make up his mind to risk an encounter with the Alid force. Before the Alid force reached Yemen, Basr and his Syrian troops made good their escape from Yemen and took the road to Syria. The Alid forces occupied Yemen and restored the rule of Hadrat Ali. The Governor appointed by Basr was deposed and the Governor of Hadrat Ali resumed his office. The people who had taken the oath of allegiance to Muawiyyah recanted and took the oath of allegiance to Hadrat Ali again.

After restoring the law an order in Yemen, the forces of Hadrat Ali marched to Mecca and then to Medina. At both the places the story of Yemen was repeated. The Governors of Muawiyyah deposed and the Governors of Hadrat Ali were reinstated. The people who had taken the oath of allegiance to Muawiyyah recanted and took the oath of allegiance to Hadrat Ali again.

Consequences of the Raids : As consequence of his raids of Muawiyyah was not able to acquire any territory. Because of these raids a greater part of the country was ravaged and many persons had been killed. Basr, the Commander of the forces of Muawiyyah, acted as a savage brute and let loose a reign of terror. When Basr killed the young children of Ubaidullah, the Alid Governor of Yemen and Hadrat Ali came to know of this atrocity he invoked the curse of God on Basr. Back in Syria, Basr was struck with insanity. In the fits of madness that came to seize him he would shriek for his sword whereby he could kill the people. He was provided a wooden sword and a stuffed animal skin on which to practise his skill. He wielded his sword with such mad fury that he died of exertion and the world was rid of him.

Apart from the ravaging of the countryside and the massacre of the people these raids led to the grave consequence of the demoralisation of the people. The people lost the sense of values and judgement. One day they took the oath of allegiance to one person and the other day they recanted and took the oath of allegiance to another person. Islam came to sit lightly on the people and instead of fighting in the cause of God, as enjoined by Islam, the people fought to seek worldly ends, a course repugnant to Islam.

Claim to Caliphate : That set both the sides thinking. According to the accounts that have come down to us, it is not clear what happened exactly after the failure of the raids undertaken by the forces of Muawiyyah in the territory held by Hadrat Ali. According to some authorities it was Hadrat Ali who made overtures for peace. According to other authorities, it was Muawiyyah who took the initiative in starting negotiations for peace. According to Taban the caliphate was partitioned and it was agreed that Muawiyyah was to be the Caliph for Egypt and Syria while Hadrat Ali was to be the Caliph for the rest of the territories under the control of the Muslims. The details of such agreement are not available. It may be recalled that prior to the battle of Siffin, Muawiyyah had proposed such partition but Hadrat Ali had not agreed thereto because he held such partition to be repugnant to Islam. Since then things had turned out to go in favour of Muawiyyah and according to the decision of the umpires, however obtained Muawiyyah had manipulated to secure the sovereignty of the whole of the Muslim world. Muawiyyah was not the man to lose the advantage that he had once secured. It appears to me that there was no regular agreement about a truce of the caliphate. The agreement was merely about a truce on the status quo basis whereunder Muawiyyah held Syria and Egypt and the rest of the Muslim territories were under the control of Hadrat Ali. This view gets support from the fact that a few months after this agreement, Muawiyyah declared himself to be the Caliph for the entire Muslim world. If there had been a previous agreement for the partition of the caliphate. Muawiyyah could not so soon go back upon such an agreement and declare himself to be the Caliph for all the Muslim lands. According to the political thought that obtained at the time, the caliphate was indivisible and there could not be more than one Caliph. That is why in spite of the decision of the umpires in his favour Muawiyyah had refrained from declaring himself as the Caliph so far. After the failure of his raids he made a truce to gain time and gather more strength. With the lapse of time the position of Hadrat Ali grew weaker and that of Muawiyyah grew stronger. By mid-660 C. E. Muawiyyah saw that the position of Hadrat Ali had become sufficiently weak and his best supporters like Abdullah b. Abbas had forsaken him. At that stage he felt himself to be strong enough to declare himself as the Caliph. This declaration stunned Hadrat Ali. He could not remain quiet at such declaration and yet he was not strong enough to undertake military action against the pretender. At this stage Hadrat Ali was the most distressed man who did not know what to do. He felt that God was putting him to test and as a true Muslim he decided to resign himself to the will of God.

The Martyrdom

Hadrat Ali defeated the Kharijites at the battle of Nahrawan, but that was not the end of the Kharijites because of the reverse met at Nahrawan they became all the more fanatic. Those who survived the disaster of Nahrawan burnt with the desire to seek vengeance for the blood of their comrades who had fallen in the battle of Nahrawan.

The Conspiracy : After the battle of Nahrawan, many Kharijites went to Mecca and sought sanctuary in the Kaaba. At Mecca they saw that the occupation of the city by Syrians, the people repudiated their oath of allegiance to Hadrat Ali and transferred their allegiance to Muawiyyah. Later they saw that when the Syrians were driven away from

Hijaz, the people of Mecca recanted from their oath of allegiance to Muawiyyah and took the oath of allegiance to Hadrat Ali again. The Kharijites felt sore that in this way the sanctity of the process of oath taking was violated and instead of establishing the kingdom of God on earth, the parties were trying to establish their own kingdoms. That was revolting to the way of thinking of the Kharijites. According to their view all those who were fighting for power had committed sin and had ceased to be Muslims. Fanatics as they were, they had the conviction that they would be serving the cause of God, if they murdered all such persons who were the principal characters in the struggle for power. They singled out three men for such murder, namely Hadrat Ali, Muawiyyah and Amr b. AI-Aas.

The Kharijites in Mecca met at the Kaaba and commissioned three young men to carry the plot of murder into effect. Abdur Rahman b Maljan al Salmi was chosen to assassinate Hadrat Ali at Kufa. Barq b. Abdullah was entrusted with the task of murdering Muawiyyah. Amr b Bakr was assigned the task of putting an end to Amr b. Al-Aas at Fustat. These young men whitened their swords with deadly poison. Thereafter they were required to proceed to the places assigned to them and there wait till the seventh of the month of the Ramadan when all the three assassins were to fall on their victims and kill them.

On the appointed date, Barq b. Abdullah attacked Muawiyyah at Damascus while he was leading the Fajr prayers. The murderer was caught red handed. His feet and tongue were cut off in the first instance. He was thereafter subjected to other tortures and ultimately put to death

The wound that Muawiyyah received was not fatal. His physicians offered him two alternative cures, one being cautery and other was the drinking of a draught which would neutralise the poison but would render him impotent. Muawiyyah adopted the second alternative and he was duly cured after a few days. The Kharijite plot to murder Muawiyyah thus came to nought.

At Fustat, the Kharijite assassin. Amr b Bakr went to the main mosque on the appointed day to assassinate Amr b. AI-Aas Amr b. AI-Aas was a child of fortune and during his life luck favoured him miraculously at critical moments. That day because of his illness due to colic pain, he did not attend the Fajr prayers in the mosque. Instead the prayers were led by his deputy Kharja b Hudhafa. The assassin had not seen Amr previously and he took Kharja for Amr Dashing Kharja, the assassin slew him with the stroke of the poisoned sword. Assassin was caught red handed and produced before Amr asked the assassin about his motive for killing Kharja. Amr said that he had really intended to kill him (Amr) and Kharja had been killed because he took him for Amr. Under the orders of Amr, the Kharijite assassin was tortured and put to death. The Kharijite plot of murdering Amr b. Al. Aas thus came to nought.

The Assassination : Abdur Rahman b Mulzim al Salmi, the assassin-designate of Hadrat Ali, reached Kufa well before the appointed date. Here he fell in love with a Kharijite girl Qataum by name. According to chronicles she was an outstanding beauty. She had a face as beautiful as the moon and her flowing jet black tresses were most captivating. Her father and brother had been killed in the battle of Nahrawan and she was fired with the desire to avenge their death. She agreed to marry. Abdur Rahman if he could present to her the head of Hadrat Ali as her dower. As he was already committed to the assassination of Hadrat Ali he readily accepted the condition laid down by his beloved. At the instance of Qataum two more Kharijites joined with Abdur Rahman in the conspiracy to assassinate Hadrat Ali. One of them was Werdan who was related to Qataum. The other was Shaubib b Bijrah who belonged to the tribe of Anjah.

On the fearful Friday morning of the seventeenth day of the month of Ramadan, the three conspirators went to the main mosque of Kufa just before the break of dawn. Here they took up their position in the narrow passage leading to the prayer hall. A little later Hadrat Ali came to the mosque when it was still dark and there was no one else in the mosque. When Hadrat Ali stood to pray. Werdan struck at Hadrat Ali but missed his mark. Then Abdur Rahman struck Hadrat Ali on the forehead with his poisoned sword which penetrated on the brain through the scar of an old wound. Thereafter the assassins fled from the mosque.

When the faithful assembled in the mosque for prayers they found Hadrat Ali lying wounded on the prayer mat. A hunt for the assassins was made. Werdan resisted being taken captive and was killed. Abdur Rahman was apprehended and taken into custody,. The third conspirator escaped from Kufa. Abdur Rahman confessed his guilt. He said that he had struck his blow at Hadrat Ali in the name of God for he considered that in seeking power Hadrat Ali had sinned and was guilty of killing thousands of innocent people. Hadrat Ali cursed Abdur Rahman for his misguided views. He however, instructed his men that the assassin should be kept in custody and should not be subjected to any hardship. He observed that if he recovered from the wound, he would himself decide what punishment should be awarded to him. If he died the assassin was to lose his life. He was, however, to be killed in one stroke and was neither to be mutilated nor made to suffer languishing death.

The wounds of Hadrat Ali proved to be fatal. No antidote could be found to the poison that had penetrated into the body of Hadrat Ali. The condition of Hadrat Ali steadily deteriorated and he breathed his last on the 24th of January 661 C. E. From God he came and to God he returned.

Will of Hadrat Ali : Before his death, Hadrat Ali made his will in the following terms:

"I declare in my will that except for God there is none who deserves to be worshipped. He is unique. He has no partner. Muhammad (peace be on him) is His Prophet and Messenger, whom He commissioned to give the people guidance through the religion Islam. Islam is the most perfect religion and it is destined to prevail over all other faiths. All our prayers, our sacrifices, our life, our death, our everything is for God. I require all my children and family members to fear God. I wish that all of you should die in Islam. Hold fast to the faith of Islam. Remain united, for according to the Holy Prophet unity in ranks is better than prayers. Be kind to your relatives so that Allah may be kind to you. Remain steadfast in piety and resign yourself to the will of God. Never aspire to anything which is beyond your reach. Be truthful always. Be kind to the orphans and in their affairs fear God. Do not wait for their seeing your help. See that in your presence they should not be overcome by any care or anxiety. Be afraid of God in respect of the rights of your neighbours over you. The Holy Prophet always willed for the right of the neighbours indeed to such an extent that we were afraid lest the neighbours be declared as heirs. Follow the Quran in letter and spirit and see that nobody takes precedence over you in the matter of the observance of the injunctions of the Holy Quran. In the matter of prayers be very particular for it is the basic pillar of Islam. As long as you are alive do not miss your prayers. Undertake Jihad with your life and property. Fear Allah in the matter of Zakat for it extinguishes the wrath of God. Fear God in respect of your regard for the companions of the Holy Prophet, for the Holy Prophet made particular mention of them in his will. Be afraid of God in the matter of the poor and the needy. Make them share your wealth. Your slaves have rights on you. Fulfil your obligations. Those who disparage your religion, do not be afraid of them. If they wish to harm you. Allah will be enough to protect you. Try to live in the world in a way which may help it become better. Stop the tyrant from his oppression. Act upon the commandments of God. Face the realities of life with courage and fortitude. Do not be ruffled by the obstacles that stand in your way. Help each other in the doing of good. Do not help those who rebel or do mischief May God be merciful to all who belong to the house of the Holy Prophet' I entrust you to the protection of God."

Hadrat Hassan's Oration : Hadrat Hassan delivered the following oration on the death of Hadrat Ali

"O misguided men of the Banu Murad, you have killed a man who was so dear to the Holy Prophet and Allah. Your crime is most heinous. You have orphaned the Muslim community. You have deprived the faithful of their commander. You have killed a man who was an ideal man, who stood heads and shoulders above the people around him. He was the man who was the bravest man of the age. He was the most learned man of the times. His services to Islam cannot be forgotten. In the Holy Quran there are references to his greatness. There are numerous traditions of the Holy Prophet which speak of his outstanding qualities as a great Muslim. Also you killed a great man on the day when the Holy Quran was revealed. It was on this date that Jesus Christ was lifted to the heavens. Verily I swear by God in Whose Hand is my life that for the Holy Prophet no person who has gone by, and no person who is to follow can excel Hadrat Ali in the matter of virtue and faith. May his soul rest in peace.

The Burial : Hadrat Ali instructed that his burial place should remain a secret. He had many enemies and he feared lest his body might be subjected to some indignity. According to legend the dead body of Hadrat Ali was placed on a camel which was driven from Kufa. The camel stopped a few miles west of Kufa, and here the dead body of Hadrat Ali was buried secretly. No tomb was raised and nobody knew of the burial place except a few trusted persons. It is narrated that more than a hundred years later, the. Abbasid Caliph Harun-ur-Rashid went deer hunting outside Kufa and the deer sought sanctuary at a place where the hounds would not pursue it. On enquiry as to why the place was a sanctuary, Harun-ur-Rashid was told that it was the burial place of Hadrat Ali. Harun-ur-Rashid ordered a mausoleum to be built on the spot. In due course the town of Najaf grew round the mausoleum.

Fate of the Assassin : Hadrat Ali had willed that his assassin should not be subjected to any torture but should be killed with one stroke of the sword. The assassin was a fanatic and instead of being remorseful at his ghastly deed and heinous crime he continued to boast of his services to Islam in assassinating Hadrat Ali. That annoyed the Muslims and contrary to the will of Hadrat Ali his assassin was subjected to torture. His eyes were seared and his limbs were cut off. Thereafter his dead body was put in a sack and burnt.

Elegy on the Demise : Abdul, Aswad, Al Dusli wrote the following elegy on the demise of Hadrat Ali:

"And now O eye, alas for thee, come to my aid
Now weep for the Prince of the Faithful
And let Umm Kulthum weep for him
With her flowing tears, for verily she has beheld death
Now say to the schismatics wheresoever they may be
May the eyes of the envious never be refreshed

In the month of fasting you have made us grieve
For the best of all men universally
You have slain the best of those that have mounted steeds
And tamed them or put foot upon a vessel
Of those who wear and adjust sandals
And of those who read the Quran and its perspicuous verses
And in him were the noblest virtues
And the love of the Apostle of God of the created things
Verily the Quraish know wheresoever they were
That you were the best of them in ancestry and faith
When I stood before the face of the father of Husain
I saw the radiance that shone above his eyes
And before his death were happy
Beholding the son-in-low of the Apostle of God among us
Establishing the truth in which there was no thought of evil
And acting equitably between enemies and kinsmen
Knowledge with him was not hidden
Nor was he created among the proud of heart
The people because when they lost Ali
Like unto the ostrich bewildered in a country bare of herbage
Rejoice not, Muawiyyah, son of Sufyan
For verily the continuance of the caliphate is with us."

Historic Testament : After the battle of Siffin, Hadrat Ali had written a detailed testament in favour of his son Imam Hassan. It is a brilliant code of counsel which provides guidance for every Muslim. The testament is found in Nahj-ul-Balagha and its running translation is given hereunder:

> "Son, I enjoin on you that you should fear God. Follow His commandments. Enliven your heart with His remembrance. Hold fast to His rope. No relationship is stronger than the relation that exists between you and God.

The Hereafter: O son, enlighten the heart with prayers. Suppress all lust with piety. Strengthen your heart with faith. Brighten it with wisdom. Overpower it with the remembrance of death. Let it beware of its mortality. Frighten it with the vicissitudes of the times. Make it take lesson from the fate of the dead. Wander through the ruins of the settlements of the past. Ask these ruins what did these people do, where have they gone, where they have settled now. This will make you realise that they have departed from their friends and relatives and that they now rest in the wilderness of the graveyard where you will also have to go sooner or later. Rectify your lapses. Hereafter for the world. Do not speak in the state of ignorance. Refrain from unnecessary talk do not tread on the path from which you can apprehend the danger of running astray. Withhold your step from evil for that is the way to safety.

Virtue and faith: If you will preach virtue, you will be among the virtuous. Counteract the evil with your tongue. Keep aloof from the wicked. Undertake Jihad in the way of God. In the affairs of God do not be afraid of the accusations of the evil mongers. For the vindication of the truth do not hesitate to face the storm of difficulties. Seek protection in faith.

Protection of God: In all that you do, seek the protection of God, for thereby you will be in citadel which is strongly fortified and invincible. In seeking anything do not make any partner with God, for all bounty is in the hands of God in all matters. Pursue the right. Do not covet what is undesirable.

The elders: Son, show no lapse in the fulfilment of your obligations. Follow in the footsteps of your elders. As you see yourself today they saw themselves likewise yesterday. As you think, they also thought. Experience taught them that they should tread the right path.

Your own way: If you are inclined to follow your own way as a result of your own experience you may do so but it should be done with due care and wisdom. Do not get yourself involved in doubts and debates. Before embarking on such adventure seek the support and help of God. Step into this valley only when you are convinced that your heart is receptive, your intelligence has mature and your intellect is sufficiently developed to distinguish the right from the wrong. Without such pre-requisites the way will be dark and you will liable to stray. It is necessary for the seeker of truth that he should neither stray from the right path nor be assailed by any doubts.

Tests of God: Son, understand that. He in Whose Hand is death has control over life as well. He who brings about birth brings about death as well. He tests you by putting you to troubles. He is our final refuge. See that you do not fail in. His test Believe that the world is subject to the well established law of God that in the world man is awarded bounty as well as subjected to trials and tribulations. The final award is made in the Hereafter of which we have no knowledge.

Resignation to the will of Allah: Son, if there is anything which you cannot comprehend, do not repudiate it, but you should mediate over it and attribute your failure to understand it to the limitations of your intellect. It may be appreciated that when you are born you are devoid of understanding and knowledge comes to you steadily as you grow up. Even when grown up, it cannot be said how many things there are still of which you are ignorant. There are things which excite your wonder, but knowledge about them dawns on you gradually. Therefore your attachment should be to that Being Who has created you, and Who had given you sustenance. Your prayers should be for Him and you should resign yourself to His Will. Son, no one had taught about God as the Holy Prophet. Make him your guide and seek your salvation through him.

Allah is One: Son, if there had been any god other than Allah, their prophets would have also come and they would have also established their dominions. There is, however, no sign of any such dominion. Verily Allah is One. He had no partner. He exists since eternity and will live forever. He is the first and the last. He has no beginning and no end. He is almighty, omnipotent and omniscient. Thus you should act in such way as a humble servant would act with reference to his mighty master. Remember that God has enjoined you to do good things and refrain from bad things.

Picture of the World: Son, I have presented to you a picture of the world. I have given you an account of its insignificance. So it is for you to keep this in mind and act accordingly. The people who have tested the world do not feel distressed on leaving it. They are in fact like persons who migrate from a famine-struck land to land of plenty. These people bear the ordeal of the journey and separation from friends and relatives so that they may arrive at a land where they can enjoy plenty. Their every step is a step forward bringing them closer to their destination. The people who are attached to the world cannot bear separation from it. They are like those people who leave a land of plenty for a famine-struck land. Their journey would be most troublesome and their end would be most tragic.

Balance between yourself and the People: Son, make yourself a balance between yourself and the people. Whatever you like for yourself, like it for others. Whatever is undesirable to you, consider it undesirable for others as well. If you do not want to be oppressed by any one, do not oppress anybody. Treat others as you wish to be treated by them. If the people behave with you as you behave with them, consider this to be a proper state of affairs. Do not say anything without proper knowledge. Do not say anything which you do not like to be heard against yourself.

Self Adulation: Self adulation is a folly and a cause of destruction for self. Do not become a treasurer for others. Seek enlightenment from God and fear God alone. Son, you have before you a long and hazardous journey. During this journey, good conduct should be your greatest asset During this journey you should not carry with you a burden a larger than what is necessary If you carry a burden which is heavier than what you can bear that will be a source of great embarrassment for you Do as much good as you can. If while you are rich someone asks for a loan from you, give it so that it is returned to you when you are in straitened circumstances.

The Journey to the Hereafter: Son, you have a steep rock to ascend. For climbing such height, a man without burden is at an advantage as compared with a person carrying a heavy burden. Thereafter there will be hell or paradise. Before reaching your destination send your goods in advance to ensure a comfortable accommodation when you arrive at your destination.

Access to God: After death, no apology will avail, nor any return to the world would be possible. Have faith that. He Who holds the treasures of the earth and the heavens has permitted you to ask for anything you want. Whatever you ask for, you will get. If you seek mercy you will have it. You can have free access to Him. No functionary stands in the way between you and Him. Worldly goods are of little value. They are for you; you are not for them.

Preparations for Death: Son, you are born for the Hereafter. Deaths lies in wait for you. Howsoever you may run from it, it will overreach you. You have to fall a victim to death sooner or later. Therefore be careful lest death comes to you before you have had the opportunity to repent. In that case you will be deemed to destruction. Son, you should be well prepared so that when death comes you will have no regret.

Temptations of the World: Son, do not be tempted by the world for God has revealed its worthlessness. Even the world itself is aware of its transitory nature. Those who are devoted to the world are like barking dogs and ferocious animals who fall at one another, the strong devouring the weak. Some of such beasts are tied down and are devoid of the power to harm. Some of them run amok like camels which roam about causing mischief. They are devoid of intelligence. They tread the path of destruction and are enveloped in darkness. They cannot see light. They have got themselves lost in the labyrinths of the world. They are enamoured of the world and have made it their God. The world is playing with them and they are playing with the world. They have completely forgotten the Hereafter.

Counsels to follow: Son, all your hopes cannot be realised. You cannot live for a period longer than what has been ordained for you. You have to tread the way which was trodden by the people before you. Be moderate in your desires. Do not transgress the limits. Do not become a slave of your desires. That good is no good which leads to evil. That wealth is no wealth which brings dishonour. Take care that ambition and greed do not lead you to destruction. Do not seek the favour of any one for whatever is ordained for you, you will get it at all cost.

Speech and Silence: Whatever harm accrues because of silence can be remedied, but whatever harm is done by speech cannot be remedied. Have you not seen that water is kept in the water skin by tying the mouth of the water skin. It is better to restrain your desires than to stretch your hand before others. A little that is earned because of honest labour is better than larger amount gained through dishonest means. Guard well your secret. Sometimes one is apt to harm himself by his own act. He who speaks more than what is necessary indulges in error.

Man and God: God is most merciful, when you violate your repentance. He does not take any vengeance. When you turn to Him again, He does not taunt you, nor does He take cognisance of your faults. He does not hesitate in accepting repentance. He does not make you despair of His mercy. He regards repentance as a virtue. Any dereliction minor or grave is counted as one, but every good deed is treated as ten virtues. He had kept the door of repentance open. He listens to your plaint. When you praise Him, He listens to you. It is He to Whom you tell your difficulties and afflictions and seek health, longevity and the fulfilment of desires. No one other than Him can fulfil your desires. If there is any delay in the acceptance of your prayer, do not give way to despair. The acceptance of the prayer depends on your bona fides. Sometimes there is delay in the acceptance of the prayer so that you may have a greater reward. Sometimes your prayer is not accepted for what you ask for is not in your interests. Therefore you should ask for such things which are really to your advantage.

Company: Keep the company of the virtuous. Refrain from the company of the wicked. To oppress the weak is the worst tyranny. When softness becomes hardness, hardness becomes softness. Sometimes cure becomes malady and malady becomes cure. Sometimes an evil wisher does what is good for you and a well-wisher does what is harmful to you. Do not bank on false hopes for that is the capital of the dead. Intelligence is the application of experience. The best experience is that which bears a lesson. Avail of the opportunity before it turns against you.

The Fate: Everyone who goes on a journey may not return. Do not waste things. Do not spoil your prospects of the Hereafter. The fate of man is previously ordained. Whatever is the decree of your destiny will come to pass. A trader is a gambler in some way. Sometimes scarcity may be more beneficent than plenty.

The Times: As long as the times favour you, march with the times. Beware that ambition does not blind you and enmity does not deprive you of your intelligence. If a friend loosens the bond of friendship, you should strengthen such bond. If he keeps distance from you, you should try to come closer to him. If he adopts a stiff attitude against you, you should adopt a gentler attitude towards him. If he makes a mistake you should find an excuse for him. Behave with a friend as if he is your master and you are his slave. Do not befriend the enemy of your friend. Do not refrain from tendering advice to your friend even though it might be bitter. Do not give way to anger. He who is harsh with you, be kind to him. He who has a good opinion about you, see that such opinion is not falsified. Do not ignore that rights of a friend under the false notion that he is a friend, for where rights are ignored, friendship suffers. Do not despair because of the oppression of a tyrant, for by such oppression he digs his own grave.

Sustenance: Son, sustenance is of two types, one that you seek and the other that seeks you. Thus if you do not seek sustenance it will seek you. In the world your share is to that extent which can stand you in good stead in the Hereafter. If you grieve even what you have lost, then you should grieve over everything which you have not got. Do not be like those people who are not impressed by any advice, but are moved by accusations. A wise man takes a lesson from even an ordinary lapse.

Patience and Faith: Overpower desires and suspicions by patience and faith. He who does not take the middle course strays. A friend is like a relative. A true friend is he who looks after your interest in your absence. A stranger is he who has no friend.

Words of Counsel: He who leaves the path of the truth treads the dark way. He who lives within his means keeps his honour safe. The strongest bond is that which binds man to the God. He who does not care for you is your enemy. When hopes are frustrated, despair becomes the way of life. Every lapse may not be noticed, nor can every opportunity be availed of. Sometimes he who has eyes may stumble, while the blind may tread without any mishap. He who trusts the world, the world betrays him. When there is a change in the ruler, the times also change. Before undertaking a journey look at the persons who are to be your companions. Before occupying a house look to the persons who are to be your neighbours. Take care that in your talk you do not indulge in ridiculing anyone. Do not consult women. Their intelligence is limited and their resolves lack strength. Keep them in seclusion. Let no stranger come in contact with them. Do not encourage them to make recommendations. Treat your servants well. Allot them distinct jobs so that each servant well allot them distinct jobs, so that each servant knows his duty. Respect your clan. It is the source of strength for you.

Conclusion: "Son, I entrust your world and your Hereafter to God and pray for your welfare both in this world and the Hereafter."

Seven

THE ACHIEVEMENTS

Great Administrator

Administrative Instructions : When Hadrat Ali appointed a person to a high office, with the letter of appointment he also issued a Memorandum of instructions setting out the guidelines to be followed for the purpose of administration. Some of these instructions which are on record are very much modern in character and show the insight of Hadrat Ali as an administrator.

Instructions to Malika Ashtar: When Malik. Ashtar was appointed as the Governor of Egypt, Hadrat Ali instructed him as follows

> "O Malik let it be known to you that you have been appointed to the governorship of Egypt"
>
> All of your actions as the Governor will be open to the criticism of the people. You should do good deeds. Keep your passions under control. Your dealings with your subjects should be just and fair. Treat them affectionately and love them.
>
> There are two kinds of subjects to be governed, firstly your brethren in Islam, and secondly the minorities whose protection has been guaranteed. Intentionally or unintentionally the people are apt to make mistakes. It will behove you to excuse them, as you expect that God will forgive your sins. Do not be ashamed if you pardon them. Never find pleasure in punishing them.

Do not be short tempered. Never say that you are Governor above them, for it breeds a feeling of inferiority in them. Should you ever take pride in your exalted office then think of the power and grandeur of God, for that is the only means to check your arrogance. Remember that God hates the cruel and the arrogant.

Be fair and just, for if you fail in it, you are a tyrant and tyrant is the enemy of God. God hearkens to the weak and the afflicted. Follow the path of moderation in your doings and try to please your subjects.

It is the common masses who are a power in the eyes of Islam. Freely mix with the masses and refrain from the company of the backbiters and the wicked. Be broad-minded, overlook the faults of others and forgive them. Do not bear malice against anyone and do not do anything which is below your dignity. The backbiters and the wicked are very cunning, never lend an ear to what they say. Do not seek the advice of a coward who will make you faint-hearted. Do not take the greedy persons as your advisers, for they will make you cruel. Above all bear in mind that miserliness, cowardice, and greed ruin a person.

In the selection of Ministers see that you appoint those persons who speak the truth, howsoever unpalatable it may be. Do not seek the advice of those who may flatter you, your face, for flattery breeds arrogance. Do not give an equal status to a bad and a good person. Treat a good person kindly and a bad person cruelly. Remember that it is better to rule over the people by love than by fear. Always try to satisfy and please your subjects.

Try to maintain the traditions of those early Muslims who brought amity and love amongst the believers in faith and tried to reform. In no way should you depart from these traditions. Should you try to introduce innovations you will come to grief. Always seek advice from the learned and wise concerning the reformation of the people. Your subjects are divided into different classes, some of them are soldiers who fight for God, some are Qadis, some are non-Muslims who pay Jizya, some of them are businessmen, some are craftsmen and artisans, while a few beggars. Remember that God has fixed a share for each of them.

The soldiers serve as a fort for the subjects. They are the ornament of the rulers, protecting religion and maintaining peace. Take good care of them as you take care of your children. Love them and treat them kindly.

When appointing Qadis, select holy and pious persons for the post. They should neither be greedy nor make errors in their judgements. In no way should they deviate from the truth deliberately. They should not become arrogant when flattered. But alas, such persons are few. Supervise your officials who should be appointed on merit and merit alone. Appoint the officials from those families who accepted Islam the earliest for those are the people who attach more importance to the next world than to this. Give them handsome pay so that they may not beguiled into monetary temptations. Have a good system of spies to observe their activities. And should any of these officials be found guilty of a bribery, misappropriation of government funds, or any similar offence, punish him immediately. Such officials should be suspended, disgraced and dismissed.

In the imposition of taxes you should see to it that the people are taxed according to their capacity. Try to populate those towns and places which are thinly populated. In the case of famine, failure of crops or the incidence of any other such calamity, you should remit taxes. Remission of taxes at such junctures mitigates the sufferings of the people. Such philanthropic measures will endear you to the people who will stand by you through thick and thin. Should the condition of farmers be poor, the cultivation of the land is bound to deteriorate. Should the ruler be greedy, the farmers are bound to be reduced to poverty.

Strictly supervise the work of your record keepers, who should be appointed form amongst those who are scrupulously honest and are humble. In no case should they be negligent on the discharge of their duty and they should carry out your orders implicitly.

Enjoin the businessmen and the industrialists to be honest and kind. They are the men who increase the wealth of a nation. Of peaceful nature, they are great benefactors of the people. Extend your protection to them and encourage them to develop trade and commerce. The prices must be reasonable and they should not be allowed to make exorbitant profits. Their weight must be correct and the accounts kept by them should not be false. Defaulters who set such orders at naught should be punished.

Be kind towards the poor and the destitute. Fear God and help them. They need your attention and you should not neglect them because of your other official duties and activities. Show mercy to the aged and the orphans who have no means of subsistence. Show them your generosity. Above all be humble and benevolent. When you give anything to them give it cheerfully with a smiling face. Address them kindly and do not put off till tomorrow what you can do toady. Fear God and observe prayers which should be perfect and not defective in any way.

Do not be isolated from your subjects and do not stay away from them for a long time, for if you do so, your officials will oppress the subjects.

Sometimes an offer may adopt unscrupulous and crooked means for self-aggrandisement. Avoid such men and do not show any favours to them. Do not show any nepotism to your relatives and do not bestow any land on them.

Be just in your dealings with everyone. If any relation of yours commits an offence, you should punish him according to the laws of God. Under no circumstances you should spare him and show him any mercy.

Should your subjects rebel against you because of your strict disciplinary measures you should explain to them fully the critical situation which has necessitated your adopting such measures and try to win them over. You should always try to make peace with your enemies for peace brings happiness and prosperity. Even after the conclusion of peace, be watchful of your enemies for they are sometimes apt to deceive you. You keep your promise to your enemy at any cost. Never violate the terms of a treaty.

Neither break your promise with your enemy nor try to deceive him. Avoid bloodshed. Never kill anyone without sufficient cause. Verily on the Day of Judgement God will punish those who have shed the blood of others unnecessarily. Never consolidate your position by putting men to the sword unnecessarily and unlawfully, for it is bound to weaken the kingdom.

Never take pride in your high rank. Treat the subjects kindly and you must act according to whatever promises you have made. Do the right thing at the right time in the right way. Should the people be unanimous about a particular course of action, never thrust your opinion on them.

Never lose your temper and try to keep your passions under control. Always remember God and try to follow in the footsteps of the Holy Prophet Muhammad (peace be on him). Follow these instructions faithfully and sincerely."

Instructions to Abdullah b. Abbas: Hadrat Ali issued the following instructions to Abdullah b. Abbas, the Governor of Basra.

> "You should know that Basra is the place where Satan descends. It is the home of dissensions. You should treat the people of Basra with kindness and remove fear from their hearts. I have come to know that you are oppressing the people of Bani Tamim. Bani Tamim are the people whose one star rises if another star sets. That was the case both in the time of ignorance and Islam. We are also closely related to them. It behoves us to strengthen those bonds. In your speech and your actions be careful and discern the right from the wrong. You are my nominee and I am responsible for your action I repose confidence in you, see that this confidence is not betrayed."

Letter to Ziyad b. Abiya: Hadrat Ali issued the following instructions to Ziyad b. Abiya, the Governor of Fars.

> "Beware that it is the matter of administration, any lapse on your part is brought to my notice, I will deal with you harshly and will not spare you. Tread the path of moderation and do not waste public funds. Today remember your tomorrow. Spend only so much which is absolutely necessary. Whatever is surplus save it for the rainy day. Do not be arrogant. Do you think God would reward you for humility when you are arrogant?. When you roll in luxury you cannot be expected to be rewarded for poverty. A man is rewarded only for his accomplishment. One reaps as he sows."

Instructions to the Collectors of Zakat: Hadrat Ali issued the following instructions to the Collectors of Zakat:

> "Proceed to your duty with pious intentions and faith in God. Do not threaten any Muslim. See that you do not indulge in any act which is not liked by the people. Do not collect anything beyond what is enjoined by the commandments of God. When you reach any settlement alight at the well outside the settlement. Do not alight at the house of anyone. Thereafter enter the residential area with due decorum and dignity. Greet the people. If they do not respond to your greeting, do not mind it. Thereafter tell them that the Caliph has sent you to there to seek compliance with the commandments of God. Ask them whether anything is due from them in accordance with the commandments of God. If anybody says that nothing is due from him, do not enter into argument with him. If he accepts the liability then proceed to collect the dues with due sympathy without harassing him in anyway. If Zakat is due in the shape of animals or camels do not enter the animal fold without the permission of the

> owner. When you enter such fold do not do anything which would annoy the owner. Do not try to create the impression that you are an officer. In assessing divide the property in two parts and give the owner the option to retain one part. Then divide the other part into two parts and give the owner the option to retain one part. Repeat the process of division till that part which is payable in Zakat is arrived at. If the owner objects to the process of division repeat the process to the satisfaction of the owner. Whatever is collected as Zakat, place it in the custody of a man in whose piety and integrity you have confidence. If any animal is taken in Zakat see that it is not lame, unhealthy or disabled in any way. When a she animal is taken see that its young one is not deprived of milk. While taking the animals to the headquarters see that they are well fed and are not subjected to any hardship.
>
> In doing your duty be afraid of God in your hearts of hearts. Do not comply with the commandment of God in such a way that outwardly it may appear to be in conformity with the commandment of God. But it may inwardly be repugnant to such commandment. See that what you do is in complete accord with what you say. Do not make your subordinates feel that you are an officer over them. You should not harass them in any way and should not make them feel inferior for under Islam all persons are equal. You can take your share out of the Zakat, but bear in mind that the poor, and the destitute should first have their due share. See that no one is deprived of what is due to him. See that what is in trust with you is not misappropriated in any way. The worst crime is the betrayal of trust and disloyalty to the Imam."

A Great Commander

Instructions for the Conduct of War: Hadrat Ali was a successful and skilled military General. Some of the instructions that he issued to his Generals and the army about the conduct of wars are on record and show his great military insight.

Instructions to his son Muhammad Hanifa: At the battle of Siffin, Hadrat Ali entrusted the flag of command to his son Muhammad Hanifa. Hadrat Ali issued him the following instructions:

> "O son, let mountains move from their places, but you should not move from the place that has been assigned to you in the battlefield. Install your feet firmly on the ground as though a nail has been driven into it. Let your one jaw of teeth rest firmly on the other jaw. Keep an eye on the rear of your enemy. Enter the battle with firm determination that you have sold your head to God. With all this, always think that success lies in the hands of God. Above

all never raise your hand against the sick, women, the aged and the children. Even if they abuse you, it behoves you to give them refuge. Never mutilate the limbs of the enemy or any other person. Give decent burial to the dead bodies of your enemies."

Instructions to the Generals of the Border Forces: Hadrat Ali issued the following instructions to the Generals of the forces operating in the border areas:

"It is the duty of the Officer Commanding that if he has attained a high office, he should not thereby change his attitude to his subordinates. On the other hand the greater the bounties that God has conferred on him, the greater should be his kindness to the people under his charge. It is your right on me that accept for war, I should not keep any secret from you. It is incumbent on me but for that the matters enjoined by the Shanah. I should consult you in all affairs of the state, and should not deprive you of any of your right. If I protect your rights, it is obligatory on you that you should obey me and should not hesitate to respond to my call for action. Do not be overawed by the difficulties that stand in the way of the vindication of truth. If you do not act accordingly, you will lower yourself in my estimation and you will be liable to be called to account for your lapse. You will have to face punishment on that score. Take note that I will not spare you and will not allow you any concession. As I deal with you should in turn deal with your subordinates on similar lines. Such mutual understanding will keep the affairs in order."

Treatment for the Rebels: Hadrat Ali issued the following instructions to a General in the matter of the treatment to be accorded to rebels.

"If the rebels repent and return to obedience, then accept their repentance and do not be harsh with them. If they persist in their revolt and are not prone to listen to reason, then suppress them with the aid of the people who are loyal to you. See that you depend only on those people who are sincere to you. Do not care for those who are indifferent. It is better not to own a person who is not with you wholeheartedly. It is better that such men should remain sitting and should not stand up."

Instruction to the Army: Hadrat Ali issued the following instructions to the army:

"When you camp in the battlefield, your camp should be at the base of a mountain, a hillock, or on the bank of a river or canal, so that this may ensure your safety. Post guards at the top of the mountain, hillock or any other

> strategic place, so that the enemy may not attack you unawares. Keep in mind that the vanguard of the force and its scouts are like the eyes and ears of a person. Make suitable arrangement for securing intelligence. See that there is no disunity in your ranks, when you are in camp or on the march, behave as one body. Make proper arrangements for watch and ward during nights. Your guardsmen should remain alert. You should be watchful even in your sleep and you should wake up and take up arms at the slightest indication of danger."

Strategy for Crisis: In the case of a crisis, Hadrat Ali laid down the following strategy to be adopted:

> "If in a battle there is a critical time and you have to fall back, do not forget to make such retreat a step for attacking the enemy again with redoubted force. Do not lose heart. Be stout hearted. Be prepared, keep swords ready. Suppress voices. Maintain silence for that is the way to overcome a crisis."

Prayers of Hadrat Ali: When starting operations in a battle, Hadrat Ali would pray to God in the following terms:

> "O God, our hearts are inclined to You. Our heads bow before You. We look to You for help. We are fighting in Your way, against the people who are fighting for selfish ends. We seek aid. All victory belongs to You."

An Ideal Judge : Hadrat Ali was the most learned man of the age in Islamic law. He acted as a Judge during the time of the Holy Prophet and the Caliphs Hadrat. Abu Bakr and Hadrat Umar. Some of the judgements delivered by Hadrat Ali are on record and show his highly developed sense of discerning the truth and doing justice.

The Story of Loaves: Once two companions went on a journey. One of them had five loaves with him and the other one had three loaves. In the way they were joined by a stranger who shared the loaves with them. On departure the stranger gave them an amount of eight dirhams. A dispute arose between the two companions about the division of the amount. The man who had five loaves wanted to keep five dirhams for himself and give three dirhams to his companion. His companion did not accept this decision and insisted that the amount should be divided equally between them and that each one of them should get four dirhams. The men wanted Hadrat Ali to decide their dispute. While entertaining the suit, Hadrat Ali asked the man who had three loaves that he should accept what his friend offered him namely three dirhams. He did not accept the offer and wanted that the matter should be adjudicated so that due justice was done. Hadrat Ali asked whether at the time of the sharing of loaves all the three persons concerned had equal shares. He was told that it was so Hadrat Ali thereupon gave the judgement that the man with three loaves was entitled to one dirham while the other man who had five loaves was entitled to seven dirhams. This bewildered the man with three loaves who would not accept even three dirhams. He wanted Hadrat Ali to enlighten him as to the basis of his judgement Hadrat Ali explained the position thus "You had three loaves and your companion had five loaves. There were thus eight loaves in all. As all the loaves were shared equally between three persons, divide each loaf into three pieces. That would make 24 pieces. Your companions owned five loaves or fifteen pieces while you owned three loaves or nine pieces. As these 24 pieces were shared equally, this means that each one of you ate eight pieces. You had nine pieces, and out of these you ate eight pieces yourself. Thus the stranger ate only one piece from your loaves. Your companions had fifteen pieces. Out of these he ate eight pieces himself leaving seven pieces which were eaten by the stranger. Thus the stranger ate one piece from you and seven pieces from your companion. It is, therefore, plain arithmetic that for one piece you are entitled to one dirham and your companion is entitled to seven dirhams for seven pieces."

Dispute about a Child: Once, a dispute arose between two women about the possession of a child. Each woman claimed to be the mother of the child. No proof could be adduced from either side, but each woman insisted emphatically that the child belonged to her. In the absence of any satisfactory evidence, Hadrat Ali was unable to decide to whom the child actually belonged. Exasperated addressing the women Hadrat Ali said that as no satisfactory evidence had been produced and as both the women insisted on the motherhood of the child, he had no option but decide that the child be cut in two parts, and thus the child be divided among them. Hearing this decision, one of the women burst into tears and said, "My Lord, do not kill the child. You may very well award it to the other woman". Thereupon Hadrat Ali declared that she was indeed the mother of the child and delivered the child to her.

Dispute about the Custody of Money: Once two friends proceeded on a journey. Before departing on the journey they kept some money in custody with a woman. She was enjoined not to return the money unless both of them came together to claim it. After some time, one of them came to the woman and said that as his other partner had died, the amount kept in custody be returned to him. He produced some sureties and the woman returned the amount to him. After sometime the other man who was reported to be dead appeared and claimed the money from the lady. She said that his other friend had taken away the money on the ground that he had died. The men insisted on payment on the ground that she was committed not to return the amount unless both of them were present. The dispute dragged on and the man brought the suit in the court of Hadrat

Ali. Addressing the plaintiff Hadrat Ali said, "Your stand is that the money was not to be returned unless both of you were present "The plaintiff said, "Yes my lord that is so" Hadrat Ali said, "Then go and bring your partner, so that the amount may be delivered to you." The man actually wanted to play a ruse and at this wise decision of Hadrat Ali, the attempt to fleece the poor woman was frustrated.

Detection of Murder: Once seven persons went on a journey. After sometime six of them returned and they could give no news about the seventh man. They gave confiscating accounts about him. Sometimes they said that he had died, sometimes they said that he had quarrelled with them and left their company. The wife of the man suspected that they had killed her husband. She accordingly lodged a complaint with the court of Hadrat Ali. Hadrat Ali summoned the six men. Each one of them was kept in separate rooms, where a security guard was posted. Thereafter one of them was called to the presence of Hadrat Ali. The man was charged with murder, but he insisted that he was innocent and knew nothing about the man. Thereupon Hadrat Ali ordered the court crier that he should give the "Adaan". As the "Adaan" sounded, the other persons segregated in the various rooms shuddered and thought that their companion had confessed the murder. Accordingly when they were summoned and presented before Hadrat Ali, they confessed their guilt Hadrat Ali accordingly ordered them to pay "Qasas" to the widow of the murdered person.

The Cow and the Ass: Once a complaint was lodged in the court of Hadrat Ali by a man that his ass had been killed by the cow of another person. Hadrat Ali summoned the owner of the cow and asked him to offer his defence if any. He said that as a matter of fact the ass had attacked the cow first and the cow had killed the ass in retaliation. Hadrat Ali asked the owner of the cow, "Where were you when the ass attacked the cow". He said that he was driving the cow. Then he asked the owner of the ass, "Where was the ass at the time". He said that it was tied. Addressing the owner of the cow Hadrat Ali said that as the ass was tied and the cow was untied his plea that the ass had first attacked the cow was untenable. He accordingly decreed that the owner of the cow should compensate the owner of the ass.

Mad Woman accused of Adultery: Once a mad woman was brought to the court of Hadrat Umar. The charge of adultery was established against her. Hadrat Umar was inclined to sentence her to the penalty of being stoned to death, but he deemed it necessary to consult Hadrat Ali before delivering the judgement. Hadrat Ali advised that the penal law of Islam was applicable only in such cases where the person concerned was in proper senses and could be held responsible for his action. Where a person was not in proper senses he could not be held accountable for his actions. The view of Hadrat Ali was accepted and the mad woman was let off.

Child born Six Months after Marriage: In the time of Hadrat Umar, a child was born to a woman six months after her marriage. When the case came to the notice of Hadrat Umar he was of the view that it was a prima facie case of adultery and as such the woman should be sentenced to punishment meant for adultery. Hadrat Umar referred the case to Hadrat Ali. No evidence was forthcoming to the effect that the woman had any illicit liaison before marriage. Hadrat Ali held that the mere fact that the child had been born six months after the marriage would not be a sufficient ground for convicting the woman. Hadrat Ali pointed out that in the Holy Quran the period from conception to the weaning of the child is laid down at thirty months and the period of the weaning of the child after birth is given as two years. This means that though under normal circumstances a child is born after nine months, a child may be born after six months under abnormal conditions. The woman was accordingly let off and absolved of the charge of adultery.

Share in the Property of a deceased Husband for a Divorced Wife: A companion had two wives. He divorced one of them. A little later he died. The divorced woman claimed a share in the property of her late husband. The suit was contested by the other wife on the ground that the plaintiff could not claim a share as she had been divorced. It transpired that the husband had died within three months of giving the divorce and the divorced wife did not have more than two monthly courses. Hadrat Ali accordingly awarded her a share in the property of her husband.

The man who Stole his Coat of Mail: An interesting story is on record in a case in which Hadrat Ali was himself the plaintiff. After the battle of Siffin, Hadrat Ali lost his valuable coat of mail. After some time, Hadrat Ali saw his coat of mail in the possession of Christian. When asked to return the coat of mail the man insisted that the coat belonged to him. Hadrat Ali filed a suit in the court of the Qadi of Kufa. The Qadi asked Hadrat Ali to produce witness in support of his claim Hadrat Ali could produce his son and his slave as witnesses. The Qadi held that he could not accept such evidence as it was interested. Under the circumstances the Qadi rejected these suit of Hadrat Ali. Instead of being aggrieved against the decision, Hadrat Ali appreciated the integrity of the Qadi. After the judgement the Christian came to Hadrat Ali and offered him the coat of mail saying that it in fact belonged to him. The man was so much impressed with the administration of justice under Islam that he hastened to accept Islam at the hands of Hadrat Ali. Hadrat Ali presented him the coat of mail as well as a horse. The man fought on the side of Hadrat Ali against the Kharijites in the battle of Nahrawan and was martyred.

A Great Man

A biographer is in some way an alter ego of the hero, whose biography he writes. There is some communion between the biographer and his hero transcending considerations of time and space. In writing 'his biography of Hadrat Ali, I have had some communion with the soul of Hadrat Ali and in some mysterious way I had the necessary guidance in appreciating such events in the life of Hadrat Ali which were otherwise obscure. Just as a lover lacks the image of his beloved in his heart, thus a biographer locks the image of his hero in his heart and he can enter into a dialogue with such image.

Biography and History : There is some difference in the approach of a biographer and a historian. A biography is usually an exercise in hero worship. A biographer is prone to paint the picture of his hero in bright colours. The approach of a historian is basically objective and constructively critical. Every hero of a biographer may not necessarily be a great man from the point of view of history. Where the hero is a great man in history, his biography has to be projected in the context of history. Hadrat Ali is verily a great man of the history of mankind in general and history of Islam in particular In undertaking this study in the life of Hadrat Ali, I have to act not merely as a biographer but as a historian as well. This means that besides narrating the main events in the life of Hadrat Ali, I have to examine the impact of such events on history. As such I have to subject the main events in the life story of Hadrat Ali to critical examination to ascertain their causes and effects. Of course such criticism has to be constructive.

Greatness of Hadrat Ali : Greatness is a phenomenon whereunder specially gifted person endowed with extraordinary qualities appear on the world stage from time to time. History is the science which studies the phenomenon of greatness. Usually every person who scales the heights of greatness and acquires a place in history is a success from the worldly point of view. There is some peculiarity in the greatness of Hadrat Ali. He is great indeed very great but he was not a success from the worldly point of view in the conventional sense in which the word "success" is understood. We have thus to undertake a study to probe into the cause that militated against the success of Hadrat Ali from the worldly point of view, in spite of his greatness. We will also have to consider how he is great, when he did not succeed from the worldly point of view.

Periods in the Life : The life of Hadrat Ali can be divided into three distinct periods. The first period comprises the first thirty two years of the life of Hadrat Ali and extends from 600 to 632 C. E. I call this period the period of education and action. It was during this period that Hadrat Ali received his education under the loving care of the Holy Prophet, imbibed the values of Islam and acquired all the attributes that contribute to greatness. In the post-Hijn years he emerged as the greatest warrior of the age. He distinguished himself as a great warrior in the battles of Badr, Uhud and the Ditch. His crowning success was his conquest of the Khyber. In the battles he killed more men than any other single man in history. All those who fought in the duels against him were invariably killed. He came to be known as the "Lion of God". He acted as a Justice and acquired fame for his wise and well-reasoned judgements. He acted as the Governor of Yemen and acquired good deal of experience as an administrator. He had the honour of announcing the verses of the Holy Quran about the "Declaration of Immunity" to the people on behalf of the Holy Prophet on the occasion of Hajj. When the Holy Prophet died, Hadrat Ali was in the prime of his youth, enlightened, experienced, wise valiant and an embodiment of virtues. He had expected that because of his outstanding qualities and his relationship to Holy Prophet he would be chosen as the Caliph. He was, however passed over and this state of affairs continued for 24 years when the office of the caliphate was held by Hadrat. Abu Bakr, Hadrat Umar and Hadrat Uthman. This period constitutes the second period of the life of Hadrat Ali. During this period although Hadrat Ali acted as a counsellor to the Caliphs he generally kept aloof from active politics I call this period as the period of inaction and contemplation. It was a period of inaction from the political point of view because he kept aloof from politics. It was the period of contemplation from the spiritual point of view, for this period was spent by Hadrat Ali mostly in prayers, religious exercise and dialogues with God. The further he went from the world, the nearer he got to God. The third period began when Hadrat Ali was elected as the Caliph. This period lasted for five years only. I call this period as the period of frustration.

Hadrat Ali found the caliphate to be a bed of thorns. During five years he had to fight three battles — the battle of the Camel, the battle of Siffin, and the battle of Nahrawan. All these battles were fought against the Muslims and led to considerable bloodshed. It was a matter of the greatest shock for Hadrat Ali that instead of fighting against the non-Muslims he had to fight against the Muslims. During this period, Hadrat Ali had to suffer from frustration because of repeated and continuous betrayals, even by men close to him. At the outset of his caliphate, he was betrayed by the Banu Umayyah, when Muawiyyah defied him and accused him of involvement in the murder of Hadrat Uthman. He was betrayed by the people of Medina who did not respond to his call to undertake "Jihad" against Muawiyyah. He was betrayed by Talha and Zubayr who took the oath of allegiance to him and later defected. He was betrayed by Hadrat. Aishah, his mother-in-law, who took up arms against him. He was betrayed by the people of Basra who had taken the oath of allegiance to him but later defected. At Siffin he was betrayed by his own army who would not fight when the victory was in sight. In the matter of arbitration he was betrayed by his umpire,. Abu Musa. Ashan, who instead of defending his cause deposed him. He had to face the secession of the Kharijites who had originally fought on his side at the battle of Siffin. He was betrayed by Khurnt b Raashid who had been his ally, but later revolted against him and created trouble in Basra. He was betrayed by his own brother Aquil who was not satisfied with the allowance that Hadrat Ali gave him and joined Muawiyyah who rewarded him handsomely. He was betrayed by his cousin. Abdullah b. Abbas when he had appointed him as the Governor of Basra and who left his post after misappropriating heavy funds from the Baitul-Mal. The final act of betrayal came when Hadrat Ali was martyred by a fanatic Kharijite.

Causes of Non-success of Hadrat Ali from the Worldly Point of View : The usual phenomenon of greatness is that men succeed in life and because of such success they acquire greatness. The usual law is that greatness is a consequence of success. Nothing succeeds like success and nothing fails like failure. This means that if you succeed you become great but if you fail you are pushed aside and are forgotten. In case of Hadrat Ali we come across extraordinary exception to the law of success and greatness. Hadrat Ali's greatness is of a different species. His greatness did not flow from any success in life. Such greatness was inherent in him; it preceded his encounter with the world and it outlived his death, although he did not succeed in his worldly life as the word "success" is understood in the conventional sense. As a matter of fact, Hadrat Ali became more famous after death than when he was alive.

We may next proceed to consider the cause which militated against the success of Hadrat Ali in spite of his greatness. As a matter of fact the greatness of Hadrat Ali was of such dimensions that he towered very high above the people around him. It was a case of Gulliver in the land of dwarfs. He was so high that he could not bend to meet the people and the people were so low that they could not rise to meet him. As such a proper equation could not be established between Hadrat Ali and the people around him and that was the main cause why he was frequently betrayed and why he did not succeed in the affairs of the world as the ordinary men succeed. Hadrat Ali was very much in advance of his age and the people of the age could not keep peace with him.

By the time Hadrat Ali came to office, a generation had passed since the death of the Holy Prophet. During this period the Muslims had made large conquests. That had brought great wealth and wealth had changed the life of the people. A capitalist class sprang up among the Muslims. Hadrat Ali, a great Muslim of the old type, wanted to enforce the austere discipline of original Islam. He himself led a very simple life and aimed to follow in the steps of Hadrat Umar. Hadrat Ali, however, lacked the harshness of Hadrat Umar and could not enforce the reform he had in view. There was a gulf between Hadrat Ali and the capitalist class who wielded considerable influence. Hadrat Ali was very parsimonious in the spending of public funds while Muawiyyah who himself led a luxurious life was very liberal in spending public funds. The capitalist class among the Muslims given to the worldly way of life preferred Muawiyyah to Hadrat Ali because of personal considerations. While Hadrat Ali was more concerned with the Hereafter than this world, the people around him were more concerned with the world than the Hereafter. This difference in outlook could not be bridged and that is why there are many betrayals in the camp of Hadrat Ali. These betrayals weekend the position of Hȧdrat Ali considerably. Hadrat Ali was a man of strong principles and he would not compromise with principles. The people opposed to him were masters of propaganda and they did not hesitate to adopt any means fair or foul to gain their end. Hadrat Ali lost the game because he would not abandon his principles at any cost.

Opposition of the Quraish : In the extension of the Muslim dominions the Quraish had played the leading role. Hadrat Ali was a Quraish but he could not win the support of the Quraish in his book. Ali, the Superman, Dr Mohyuddin has observed as follows about the opposition of the Quraish to Hadrat Ali:

> "Hadrat Ali hoped to establish a world of Islamic empire, a kingdom of God on earth where peace was to reign supreme and mankind could move steadily towards perfection. That he failed so completely in one of the enigmas of Islamic history. The student is perplexed and indeed despondent when he discovers that the entire tribe of the Quraish gave whole-hearted support to the first two Caliphs,. Abu Bakr who belonged to the tribe of the Banu. Adi, but not to their two successors, who also belonged to the Quraish tribe. It is baffling indeed that they obeyed. Abu Bakr and Umar blindly, but deserted Uthman and Ali, whom they bitterly opposed and finally murdered. From the moment that Ali came to power, he was resisted and obstructed by Quraishite, in spite of the fact that the aristocratic Quraish knew that Ali had noble blood in his veins, blood which had flowed in the veins of the Holy Prophet and that in addition he had those personal traits of character which made him unique amongst all the persons of his age. Ali's knowledge, piety, bravery, generalship, services for the propagation of Islam and his achievements on the battlefield for the defence of Islam, made him superior to the first two Caliphs, he was superbly equipped to fill the office of the Caliph, yet the entire race seems to have taken up arms against him. In spite of his qualities of mind and spirit he seems to have been sacrificed to the prevailing tribal spirit of his countrymen. Perhaps it was his superiority, more than anything else, which led to his downfall. He knew himself to be superior to his contemporaries and he hated the petty tribal chiefs of the Quraish who were interested only in their self-aggrandisement. What is more, he let them know his contempt for them, seldom bothering with the formalities of consulting them and frequently acting independently of them, in defiance of established custom."

The Personality : Hadrat Ali was of medium height. He had a superb head with a face as noble as the man himself. His nose was straight and his mouth was beautifully formed. His eyes were most commanding, being full of light and lustre. There was a tone of music in his voice. There was an aura of spirituality and a strong personal magnetism about him. In his youth, he was handsome and full of fiery vigour. In his latter age, he became corpulent and bulky. His grey hair of the head gave way to baldness. His beard, however, remained thick and luxuriant and he often dyed it red. He was stout, genial, charitable, meditative, reserved a man who towered high above the people around him because of his intellectual and spiritual attainments.

Hadrat Ali was endowed with all qualities that make a man great. He is not only great, he is regarded as a superman and ideal man. He was a paragon of virtue. He enjoyed fame for his piety and religious devotions. He was an embodiment of Islamic values. In his love of God and, His Messenger, he was second to none. While praying to God, his absorption was so intense that he often lost consciousness. His mind was so pure that he could hold communion with God. He had learnt the Holy Quran by heart and he could quote appropriate verses to suit every occasion. He was most truthful and honest. He was most humble. He was simple in his habits. He avoided display and luxury. He lived the life of an ascetic. Even when Caliph, he lived in an ordinary house. The doors of his house remained open for all at all times. He was most generous. He was most liberal in giving charity. He always came to the help of those who were distressed and involved in any difficulty. He looked after widows and orphans as if they were the members of his own household. He was a warrior, a General and a man conspicuous for his bravery and valour. Indeed he was braver than any other man in history. He fought hundreds of duels in his lifetime and in all such encounters his rivals were worsted. In the various battles he killed a record number of enemies. He was a skilful swordsman. His sword would never miss its mark. In the various battles that he fought he never turned his back. He was an embodiment of patience. In the battle of Uhud he received so many wounds that the nurses were unable to dress such wounds. He bore the pain with great patience.

The people around him misunderstood him, but he did not lose patience. He was most chivalrous and forgiving. He would forgive even his worst enemies. He was a great scholar. His book Nahj-ul-Balagha is a living proof of his scholarship and erudition. There was a sense of humour about him and sometimes he said things in a lighter vein to bring home the point he had in view. He was a master of similes and metaphors and when bringing home a point he always illustrated it with appropriate metaphors and similes. He was a great philosopher and there is great depth in his thoughts expressed in his writings. He was known for his wisdom. He was indeed wiser than Solomon. Most of his wise sayings have attained the dimensions of proverbs. He was a great orator. His sermons were most impressive. He was the master of rhetoric. He is regarded as the father of Islamic learning. He has left a deep mark on Islamic theology. He was the founder of Arabic grammar. He was a great poet. He was the Father to Sufism. He was the Father of Islamic jurisprudence. He was an impartial judge. His famous judgements are the most valuable assets of Islamic jurisprudence. He was a skilful administrator. He introduced numerous reforms. He was an eminent political thinker and his political thought has an air of modernity about it. The greatness of Hadrat Ali as a man is multidimensional in character and after the Holy Prophet he is the greatest Muslim whose memory is honoured by the Muslims all over the world.

Wives and Children : The principal wife of Hadrat Ali was Hadrat Fatima, the favourite daughter of the Holy Prophet. During the lifetime of Hadrat Fatima Hadrat Ali at one stage proposed to marry a daughter of Abu Jahl. When the Holy Prophet came to know of his proposal, he felt annoyed and declared that if Hadrat Ali wanted to marry another wife, he should divorce Hadrat Fatima in the first instance. Thereupon, Hadrat Ali abandoned the idea of marrying another wife. Hadrat Fatima was the mother of three sons and two daughters. The sons were Hassan, Hussain, and Mohsin. Mohsin died during childhood. The daughters were Zainab and Umm Kulthum.

After the death of Hadrat Fatima, Hadrat Ali married a number of wives. These were:

(1) Umm-ul-Bunian who was the daughter of Hazam b Khalid. Hadrat Ali had five sons from her, namely: Abdullah, Jafar,. Abbas, Uthman and Umar. All of them except Abbas were martyred in the battle of Karbala along with Hadrat Hussain.

(2) Khaula who was the daughter of Jafar Hanfiyah. She was the mother of a son known as Muhammad b Hanfiyah.

(3) Umm Habib who was a daughter of Rabia. She gave birth to a son Umar and a daughter Ruqiya.

(4) Asma who was the daughter of Umais. She was in the first instance married to Hadrat Jafar, an elder brother of Hadrat Ali. On the death of Hadrat Jafar, Hadrat. Abu Bakr married her. After the death of Hadrat. Abu Bakr she married Hadrat Ali. She had two sons from Hadrat Ali, namely: Yahya and Muhammad. Asghar.

(5) Laila who was the daughter of Masud. She was the mother of two sons, namely Ubaidullah and Abu Bakr.

(6) Umama who was a daughter of Abi. Al. Aas and Hadrat Zainab, an elder sister of Hadrat Fatima. Her son from Hadrat Ali bore the name of Muhammad Awsat.

(7) Umm Saeed who was a daughter of Urwa. She bore Hadrat Ali two daughters, namely: Umm-ul-Hassan and Ramla.

(8) Muhyat was a daughter of the famous Arab poet Imra-ul-Qais. She gave birth to a daughter who expired in infancy.

Hadrat Ali married nine wives in all including Hadrat Fatima. The number of wives at a time, however, did not exceed four. He had a few slave girls of whom Humla and Umm Sohaib bore him 12 daughters—Nafisa, Zainab, Ruqiya, Umm-ul-Karaam, Humaira, Umm Salma, Sughra, Khadija, Umm Hani, Umm Kulthum, Jamana and Maimuna Hadrat Ali was, in all, the father of fifteen sons and eighteen daughters.

Hadrat Ali's Generosity : Generosity was one of the main attributes of Hadrat Ali. According to Hadrat Ali when someone in need asks for your help and you help him that is liberality or munificence. When you help a man in need before he asks of hour help that is generosity. In Arab annals Hatim a Bedouin, is known for his generosity. According to the accounts that have come down to us, Hadrat Ali out-classed him in the matter of generosity. Hadrat Ali used to say "Woe to that man who spends his wealth in buying male and female slaves, but spends not his money on the free-born who, with a little alms, would become enslaved in gratitude to him forever."

Preference for the Supplicant to one's own Needs: Once a supplicant went to the house of the Holy Prophet to beg for food but there was none in the house. On being told of this by his wives the Holy Prophet asked whether there was anyone who could give relief to the supplicant. Hadrat Ali offered to take the beggar to his house. There Hadrat Fatima said that there was nothing in the house except a few loaves that she had cooked for the children. She however, gave the loaves to the supplicant saying that she would give them to the beggar and would rather see her children go hungry. It was on this occasion that the following verse of that Holy Quran was revealed:

> "They prefer the supplicant to themselves even though they may be hungry themselves. And who so is rid of the covetousness of his own soul will be triumphant"
>
> (59 9)

God accepted Hadrat Ali's Charity : It is related that once somebody presented 300 gold coins to the Holy Prophet, who made a present of them to Hadrat Ali. On the way home, Hadrat Ali saw a harlot to whom he gave one hundred coins. The next day the whole town was gossiping about Hadrat Ali's misplaced charity for giving the money to a woman of ill repute. Hadrat Ali felt offended and decided that he would give another hundred coins to a worthier person. This time he met a thief and he gave him one hundred coins. The people were critical of Hadrat Ali squandering the money by giving it to a brigand. Hadrat Ali decided that whatever money was left with him he would give it to a deserving person. This time he gave the money to a person who happened to be rich man. The people became loud in the criticism of Hadrat Ali in his charity to undeserving persons. It was, however, revealed to the Holy Prophet that God had accepted the charity of Hadrat Ali. The harlot after getting the money gave up her profession and decided to lead a chaste life. The thief after getting the money gave up robbery, the rich man on getting the alms felt so repentant that he distributed all his wealth among the poor.

Manifold Return for Charity : Once Hadrat Fatima gave some yarn that she had spun to Hadrat Ali to sell it in the market and buy therewith some provisions for cooking meals. Hadrat Ali sold the yarn for a gold coin. He came across some beggars and he distributed all the amount among the beggars. He had gone a few steps when he came across a man with a camel who said, "Ali, would you buy the camel" Hadrat Ali said that he had no money. The man said that he could sell the camel on credit. Thereupon the man gave the bridle of the camel to Hadrat Ali and disappeared. Hadrat Ali had gone a few steps when another person met him and purchased the camel for a hundred gold coins. Hadrat Ali thus got a hundred fold return for his charity.

A Legend of the Generosity : It is related that on one occasion a supplicant approached Hadrat Ali and asked him to give him some bread. Hadrat Ali asked his slave Qanbar to attend to the supplicant. Qanbar came to Hadrat Ali and said that the bread was in saddle bag Hadrat Ali said, "Give him the saddle bag". At this Qanbar said that the saddle bag was on the camel Hadrat Ali said, "Give him the camel" Qanbar said that the camel was in the row of camels Hadrat Ali said, "Give him all the camels."

The Golden Ring : It is related that at one time while the Holy Prophet and Hadrat Ali were offering prayers in a mosque, a supplicant came and said, "O God, bear witness that I have asked every one of the congregation to give me something in alms, but none has offered anything Hadrat Ali who was prostrating on the prayer mat at that time held out his finger which bore a gold ring, and pointed it out towards the beggar, who took it off.

Paying the Debt of a Dead Muslim : Once a Muslim died in Medina. The Holy Prophet along with Hadrat Ali attended the funeral. Before leading the funeral prayer the Holy Prophet enquired whether the deceased had to pay any debt. He was told that the deceased had to pay a debt of a few dinars. The Holy Prophet desired that someone should undertake responsibility for clearing the debt of the deceased. It was Hadrat Ali who undertook the responsibility for meeting the debt and it was only then that the Holy Prophet led the funeral prayer.

Paying for Dates : One day as Hadrat Ali passed through the market of Kufa he found a slave girl weeping while sitting on the roadside. Hadrat Ali enquired from the girl as to the cause of her distress. She said that she had purchased some dates from a date seller, but her master had not approved of the dates and when she wanted to return the dates to the date seller he refused to accept them. Hadrat Ali paid her the amount involved and asked her to eat the dates herself.

Highly Acclaimed

References of Hadrat Ali in the Holy Quran : According to the commentators of the Holy Quran there are numerous verses in the Holy Quran which have implied references to Hadrat Ali. According to the Shia commentators there are as many as three hundred verses of Holy Quran which have implied reference to Hadrat Ali. According to the Sunni commentators the number is much smaller. Some of the verses which according to the consensus of the commentators refer to Hadrat Ali are given hereunder:

Verse 33, Sura 33

Verse 33 of Sura 33 of the Holy Quran reads

> Allah's wish is to remove uncleanliness far from you O folk of the Prophet's household and cleanse you with enough cleaning" Hadrat Ali is obviously included in the expression "Folk of the Prophet's household."

Verse 361, Sura 3

Verse 361 of Sura 3 provides

> "And whose disputes with you concerning God after the knowledge which has come to you say to him 'Come, we will summon our sons, your sons, our women and your women and ourselves and yourselves. Then we will pray humbly to our Lord, and solemnly invoke the curse of Allah upon those who lie."

This verse alludes to the deputation of the Christians of Najran who came to Medina to hold discussion with the Holy Prophet about the truth of Islam. In this verse, the reference to "Our sons and our women," includes reference to Hadrat Ali, Hadrat Fatima, Hassan and Hussain.

Verse 3, Sura 9

Verse 3 of Sura 9 provides:

> "And a proclamation from God and His Apostle to the people on the day of 'Greater Pilgrimage' that Allah is free from obligation to the idolaters and so is His Messenger. So, if you repent it will be better for you, but if you are averse, then know that you cannot escape. Allah Give tidings O Muhammad of a painful doom to those who disbelieve."

In pursuance of this verse, the Holy Prophet commissioned Hadrat Ali to go to the Greater Pilgrimage' to announce the verses of the Sura of "Immunity" wherein God absolved the Muslims from all obligations under the treaties previously concluded with the idolaters.

Verse 23, Sura 42

Verse 23 of Sura 42 reads:

> "Say O Muhammad to mankind: I do not ask of you any reward for it, but love for relatives, and whosoever earns good."

According to traditions when the Holy Prophet was asked as to who were the relatives alluded to in the verse, the Holy Prophet said, "Verily, the reference is to Ali, Fatima, Hassan and Hussain."

Verse 21, Sura 45

Verse 21 of Sura 45 reads

> "Do those who commit evil deeds suppose that we shall treat them like those who believe and do good deeds—that their lives and their deaths shall be equal. No bad is their judgement."

According to Ibn. Abbas "the doers of good" referred to in this verse refer to Hadrat Ali, Hadrat Hamza and Hadrat Ubaydah b Harith

Verse 17, Sura 11

Verse 17 of Sura 11 reads

> "Is he to be counted equal with those who rely on a clear proof from his Lord and a witness from Him recites it, and before it was the Book of Moses, an example and a mercy? Such believe therein Who so disbelieves therein, the Fire is his appointed place. So be not you in doubt concerning it Lo, it is the truth from your Lord, but most of mankind believe it not."

One day in one of his sermons Hadrat Ali said that there was hardly a man from amongst the Quraish who had not been referred to in the Holy Quran. Hadrat Ali was asked to recite some verses which alluded to him. Thereupon he recited the above verse.

Verse 4, Sura 66

Verse 4 of Sura 66 reads

> "Now if both of you turn to Allah repentant it will be better for you, as your hearts are already so inclined. But if you back up each other against him, surely Allah is his helper, and Gabriel and the righteous among the believers, and furthermore all other angels too are his helpers."

According to Ibn. Abbas, the Holy Prophet said that the "righteous" men alluded to as "helper" in this verse refers to Hadrat Ali.

Verse 18, Sura 32

Verse 18 of Sura 32 reads

> "Is he who is a believer like him who is an evil doer? Verily they are not equal."

According to Ibn. Abbas "believer" in this verse refers to Hadrat Ali, and "evil doer" refers to Walid b Utba.

Verse 54, Sura 25

Verse 54 of Sura 25 reads:

And He it is who created man from water, and has appointed for him kindred by blood, and kindred by marriage and your Lord is all powerful."

According to traditions "kindred by blood and kindred by marriage "refers to Hadrat Ali.

Verse 36, Sura 24

Verse 36 of Sura 24 reads

> "The lamp of light is lit in houses which Allah has allowed to be exalted so that His name be remembered in them. Therein he is glorified in the mornings and evenings."

According to traditions, the Holy Prophet said that the "houses" referred to in this verse include the house of Hadrat Ali and Hadrat Fatima.

Verse 55, Sura 5

Verse 55 of Sura 5 reads

> "Your friend is only Allah and His Messenger, and the believers who observe prayer and pay the poor rate."

According to traditions "believers referred to in this verse includes a reference to Hadrat Ali.

Verse 12, Sura 58

Verse 12 of Sura 58 provides

> "O ye who believe'. When you consult the Messenger in private, give alms before your consultation. That is better and purer for you. But when you do not find the wherewithal, lo? Allah is Forgiving and Merciful."

According to traditions when this verse was revealed the Holy Prophet wanted to fix an amount which every person who consulted the Holy Prophet should pay. Hadrat Ali represented that as the people were generally poor no amount should be fixed and the option should rest with the person concerned to pay whatever alms he could.

Verse 181, Sura 7

Verse 181 of Sura 7 reads

> "And of those. We have created there are people that guide men with truth, and do justice therewith."

According to traditions, the reference to "people that guide men with truth" in this verse included a reference to Hadrat Ali.

Verse 57, Sura 43

Verse 57 of Sura 43 reads

> "And when the son of Mary is cited as an example, lo, the people jeer thereat"

According to traditions, the Holy Prophet is said to have told Hadrat Ali one day that his example would be like that of Jesus Christ. A section of the people would love him so much that they would willingly die for him while there would be some people who would fight against him.

Verse 29, Sura 48

Verse 29 of Sura 48 reads

> "Muhammad is the Apostle of God. And those with him are firm against the disbelievers, and merciful amongst themselves Thus see them bowing down, and prostrating themselves in prayer seeking grace from Allah and His pleasure. Their mark is upon their faces, being the traces of prostrations. Such is their description in the Torah. And their description in the Gospel is like a seed that sends forth its sprout, then makes it strong, it then becomes thick and stands on its stem, delighting the sowers, and causing the disbelievers to burn with rage at the sight of them. Allah has promised to those of them who believe and do good works, forgiveness and a great reward."

According to the commentary of Imam. Abu Musa this verse was revealed in favour of Hadrat Ali

Verse 43, Sura 13

Verse 43 of Sura 13 reads

> "And those who disbelieve say 'You are not a Messenger. ' Say to them 'Sufficient is Allah as a witness between me and you, and so is he who possess knowledge of the Book."

According to commentators, the phrase "Whosoever has the knowledge of the Book" alludes to Hadrat Ali.

Verse 64, Sura 8

Verse 64 of Sura 8 reads:

> "O Prophet! Allah is sufficient for you and for such of the followers as follow you."

According to commentators the phrase "such of the followers as follow you" alludes to Hadrat Ali.

Father of Sufism : Hadrat Ali is claimed as the "Father of Sufism" Most of the Sufi orders claim their descent from Hadrat Ali. According to Hadrat Ali Hajwen, the rank of Hadrat Ali is very high in the line up of Sufism. According to Hadrat Junayd of Baghdad, Hadrat Ali is the Sheikh as regards the principles and practices of Sufism.

Holy Prophet and Sufism : The roots of Sufism lie embedded in Islam itself. There are numerous passages in the Holy Quran which are of a mystical character. The Holy Prophet of Islam (peace be on him) himself displayed mystical inclination and he very often retired to the cave of Hirah for the purpose of devotion, meditation and contemplation. The Holy Prophet was recipient of two types of revelations—one embodied in the Holy Quran and the other that illuminated his heart. The former was meant for all, the latter for a selected few whose hearts could be illuminated with the Divine Light. The knowledge of the Holy Prophet was thus book knowledge (Ilm-i-Safina) and heart knowledge (Ilm-i-Sina) Hadrat Ali got this heart knowledge from the Holy Prophet. It is related that after the. Ascension, the Holy Prophet awarded a mantle to Hadrat Ali which led to the illumination of his heart.

Gnosis of God : According to Hadrat Ali, the base of religion is the gnosis of God. He held:

> "The height of gnosis is His confirmation. The height of confirmation is Tauhid. The height of Tauhid is the acknowledgement of the supremacy of God in all matters. He is beyond all attributes No particular of attribute can give an idea of His exact nature. He is not bound by anything, all things are bound by Him. He is infinite, limitless, boundless, beyond time, beyond space, beyond imagination. Time does not affect him. He existed when there was

nothing. He will exist forever. His existence is not subject of the law of birth or death. He is manifest in everything, but He is distinct from everything. He is not the cause of anything, everything is because of Him. He is unique, He has no partner. He is creator. He creates as well as destroys. All things are subject to His command He orders a thing to be and its is."

Hadrat Ali enjoined the severance of the heart from all things save God. Hadrat Ali was asked what was the purest things that could be acquired, and he said, "It is that which belongs to a heart made rich by God". When Hadrat Ali was asked about gnosis, he said, "1 know God by God, and I know that which is not God by the Light of God". When asked whether he had seen God he said that verily he had seen God for he could not warship Him unless he knew Him.

Prayers to God : When Hadrat Ali used to pray, his hair would stand on end. He would tremble and say, "The hour has come to fulfil a trust which the heavens and the earth were unable to bear". Abu Darda, an eminent companion of the Holy Prophet said," None in this world has excelled. All in prayer" While praying, so great was the intensity of the emotions of Hadrat Ali that he would fall into a swoon. It is related that on one occasion,. Abu Darda found Hadrat Ali lying rigid on the prayer mat and touching his cold body thought that All had breathed his last. When he broke this news to Hadrat Fatima she said that Hadrat Ali often became unconscious while praying. Abu Darda weeping profusely sprinkled some water on face of Hadrat Ali and he regained consciousness. Seeing the tears in the eyes of Abu Darda, Hadrat Ali said "Why are you crying? You shed tears when you see me in this state. Imagine what will happen to me when the angels drag me into the presence of God and I am forced to render an account of my deeds. They will bind me with fetters of iron and present me before God and those of my friends who will happen to be witnesses will be powerless to help me. They will lament my unhappy plight, but none save God will be able to help me on that day."

Communion with God : Very often Hadrat Ali would sob the whole night in prayers to God and God would reward him with a glimpse of the Inner Vision. According to Hadrat Ali, the highest purpose of knowledge is the awakening of latent spiritual faculties whereby one is enabled to discover his true and inner self. It is to this inner self that God reveals Himself when the self disappears in the vision of the "All. Absorbing Reality" Hadrat Ali often observed that man could have the joy and wonder of communion with God if one abandoned pride, disciplined the flesh, overcame the lust and submitted to the Will of God. He exhorted the people in his various sermons not to indulge in the gross licentiousness which had characterised. Arab society in the Days of Ignorance" But should instead live in piety and simplicity as enjoined by Islam. Hadrat Ali said, "Man is a wave in the boundless Sea of God. As long as man's vision is clouded by ignorance and sensuality he will consider himself a separate entity, different from God. But when the evil between him and God is lifted he will then know what he really is. The wave will then merge with the ocean" Hadrat Ali held that enlightenment is needed so that one can first get to know himself. Only then he get to know God Hadrat Ali held that to this end religious exercise must be practised. Sufism for which Hadrat Ali stood derived its strength from the Shanah. Hadrat Ali preached that any form of knowledge which failed to show the Infinite Reality in man was useless, because it could not fill that vacuum of which the aching soul of every individual was so pathetically conscious. Hadrat Ali wanted men to be virtuous as virtues purify the soul and it is only the purified soul that can be the recipient of spiritual enlightenment This is the doctrine of Inner Light which was enunciated by Hadrat Ali as the core of Sufi thought Hadrat Ali accordingly acknowledged as the "Father of Sufism" and the prince of saints.

Doctrine of Preference : Hadrat Ali also enunciated the doctrine of preference. He stood for preferring the claims of others to one's own claims. He gave an outstanding demonstration of this doctrine when he slept on the bed of the Holy Prophet on the night of the Holy Prophet's migration from Mecca, when the infidels were seeking to slay him Hadrat Ali risked his life for the sake of the Holy Prophet, because of the preference that Hadrat Ali gave to the life of the Holy Prophet as compared with his own life. After the death of the Holy Prophet, Hadrat Ali considered that he was the most deserving person to be elected as the Caliph. When his claims were overlooked and other persons were elected as the Caliph, he offered them allegiance in pursuance of the doctrine of preference. It was this spirit of preference that motivated Hadrat Ali to plunge on the thick of the battle to meet the challenge of the enemy regardless of his own personal safety. It is related that when after the Ascension, the Holy Prophet gave Hadrat Ali a mantle, he asked him as to the use that he would make of the mantle. Hadrat Ali said that he would use it to cover the faults of others. The true Sufi way lies in covering the faults of others.

Fasting : According to Hadrat Ali fasting was not a mere formality or a ritual, it was an exercise for the purification of the soul. Because of his constant fasting, Hadrat Ali earned the epithets if "Qaim-ul-Lail" (praying most of the night without sleep), and "Saim-ul-Nahar" (Fasting mostly during the day) Hadrat Ali held that hunger sharpens the intelligence and improves the mind and health. Hunger involves some affliction for the body, but it illumines the heart, purifies the soul and leads the spirit into the presence of God. One who cultivates his spiritual nature by means of hunger in order to devote himself entirely to God and detach himself from worldly ties is at a much higher level than the person who cultivates his body by means of glutony and lust. Hadrat Ali acted on the advice of the Holy Prophet, "Fast so that perchance your hearts may see God in this world". And verily, because of his fasting and other spiritual exercise, Hadrat Ali did see God in this world. The Holy Prophet had enjoined, "When you fast, let your ear, your eye, your tongue, your hand, and your every limb fast" Hadrat Ali followed this advice in letter as well as in spirit. By the discipline of fasting Hadrat Ali was able to subordinate the physical senses to spiritual requirements in such a way that they could respond only to what was pure and became dead to what was impure. Hadrat Ali thus led a purified life:

Zakat : Hadrat Ali held

> "Of the most meritorious acts of a believer and one of the most acceptable things to God is Zakat. It behoves every one to give charity, because from amongst the acts of worship this is the most pleasing to God."

In his sermons, Hadrat Ali exhorted the people in the following terms

> "O ye people send a part of your wealth to God so that it may stand you in good stead in the next world. Do not leave your entire wealth here so as to be a source to annoyance to you in the world to come"

In the annals of the Arabs, Hatim Tay enjoys fame for his munificence and generosity. Hadrat Ali outclassed Hatim in the matter of generosity. Some of the stories of his generosity which have attained the dimensions of legends are narrated in another Chapter of this book.

Pilgrimage : Hadrat Ali was born in the Kaaba. He had, therefore, a strong emotional attachment for the Kaaba. Hadrat Ali observed that the Holy Kaaba was sited in a territory known for its stony wastes and wilderness where no water was available. God had ordained the Muslims to bear the hardships involved in a journey through such inhospitable land cheerfully so that these very privations might ultimately become a source of salvation. The pilgrimage is symbolic of the fact that whatever hardship one bears in the trials of life and endeavours to fulfil the will of God, he acquires goodness and righteousness by them. The darkest things in the world is the beloved's house without the beloved. What is really important for a lover is the beloved and not the house of the beloved. According to Hadrat Ali the spirit of pilgrimage did not lie in a bare visit to the Kaaba, it lay in developing the inner vision whereby one could see God, the Lord of the Kaaba.

Jihad : Hadrat Ali held that Jihad is the gateway to Paradise.

He said:

> "God has opened this gate for His friends. It is the mantle of piety. It is the shield of faith. He who avoids it, God subjects him to disgrace."

Hadrat Ali held that Jihad did not lie in merely taking up arms in the cause of God, it comprehends incessant struggle against falsehood in all spheres of life. Jihad is the main piller on which Islam rests.

Repentance : The first stage in the path of Sufism is repentance. Repentance is described as the awakening of the soul from the slumber of heedlessness, so that the sinner becomes aware of his evil ways and feels contribution for past disobedience. Hadrat Ali repeatedly prayed for the forgiveness of God. His typical prayer was:

> "O God, forgive me my sins of which you are more aware than me. And if I commit these sins again even then forgive me. Whatever promises I had made with myself to follow your commands have not been fulfilled. I seek Your forbearance. If I have sought Your proximity with my tongue, but my heart did not keep pace with my tongue, overlook my lapse. O God, forgive me for my futile talk, vain desires and lapses of the tongue."

Detachment : Hadrat Ali exhorted that while living in the world, one should not renounce the world, yet he should not have an undue attachment for the world. Detachment from the world Zuhd is the means of attaining God. It is related that someone begged Hadrat Ali to give him a precept Hadrat Ali said:

> "Do not let your wives and children be a cause of concern for you, for if they be the friends of God,. He will look after. His friends, and if they are the enemies of God, why should you take care of God's enemies."

Patience : On the mystic way the traveller has to meet many trials and tribulations. God subjects His lovers to severe testing and he alone can pass such tests who is patient. Hadrat Ali was the personification of patience and for his patience he won the epithet of "Job, the Second" In the battle of Uhud Hadrat Ali received as many as sixty-one wounds on his person so that his whole body looked like one big wound which the nurses could not dress. Hadrat Ali though in mortal agony said:

> "May God grant me patience to bear this suffering. Is it not a favour of God that He gave me the courage to stand and fight, and not to leave the field?"

About the patience of Hadrat Ali, Dr. Ata Mohyuddin writes as follows in his. All, the Superman:

> "All used to say that at no time in his life had he ever known peace and tranquillity. From the time he went in infancy, to the home of the Holy Prophet it was a ferment of turbulence and turmoil. The Holy Prophet was constantly persecuted by the Meccan pagans. Then, from adolescence onwards,. Ali was

constantly fighting in Jihad and after the death of the Holy Prophet, he was embroiled, against his wish, in the political intrigues of others. Even, when elected Caliph the implacable enemies of Islam arose and rebelled against him yet he bore all these afflictions with patience, thanking God that he had acquitted himself well in the tests and trials to which the Almighty had thought fit to subject him."

Gate of Knowledge

Hadrat Ali was the most learned man of the age. He was a living encyclopaedia of knowledge. The Holy Prophet said, "I am the City of Knowledge, verily. All is the Gate of it. " He was the first person to have learnt the Holy Quran by heart. He possessed a prodigious memory; he was a keen observer, he was a deep thinker, he had an enlightened mind and he carried in his brain a vast store house of knowledge. He was a versatile genius and he exhibited extraordinary talents in all disciplines of knowledge. He was a master of philosophy and rhetoric. He was a distinguished poet. He was a great preacher and teacher. His knowledge extended to such disciplines as logic, mathematics, physics, astronomy, medicine and history.

His Concept of Knowledge : Hadrat Ali held that the principal aim of knowledge is the inculcation of virtue, promotion of faith and understanding of God. He held that knowledge enlivens the soul, it is health and life; it kills ignorance. He defined knowledge as the sum total of excellence. He held that the pursuit of knowledge is better than the pursuit of riches, that knowledge is the ornament of the rich and the riches of the poor and that knowledge is better than riches. He held that the learned live even after their death. He maintained that the learned are the living ones in the dead mass of ignorance. He observed that to respect the learned is to respect God. About the respect of the teacher he held that one who teaches you a letter binds you with the fetter of gratitude. He maintained that the talk of a learned man carried with it the fragrance of the garden of Paradise.

Superiority of Knowledge over Wealth : It is related that once ten learned men approached Hadrat Ali and wanted to know how knowledge was better than wealth. They requested that each one of them be given a separate answer. Hadrat Ali answered them as follows:

(1) Knowledge is the legacy of the Prophets, wealth is the inheritance of the Pharaohs. As the Prophets are superior to the Pharaohs, so knowledge is better than wealth.

(2) You have to guard your wealth, but knowledge guards you. Therefore, knowledge is better than wealth.

(3) When knowledge is distributed it increases. When wealth is distributed it decreases. As such knowledge is better than wealth.

(4) A man of wealth has many enemies, while a man of knowledge has many friends. Therefore knowledge is better than wealth.

(5) A learned man because of his wider outlook is apt to be generous while a rich man because of his love for money is apt to be miser. As such knowledge is better than wealth.

(6) Knowledge cannot be stolen, while wealth is constantly exposed to the danger of being stolen. Accordingly knowledge is better than wealth.

(7) With the lapse of time knowledge gains in depth and dimensions. Hoarded coins get rusty, or cease to be legal tender. Therefore knowledge is better than wealth.

(8) You can keep account of wealth because it is limited, but you cannot keep account of knowledge because it is boundless. That is why knowledge is better than wealth.

(9) Knowledge illuminates the mind, while wealth is apt to blacken it. Therefore, knowledge is better than wealth.

(10) Knowledge is better than wealth because knowledge induced the humanity in the Holy Prophet to say to God "We worship. Thee as we are Thine servants", while wealth engendered in Pharaoh and Nimrod, the vanity which made them claim Godhead.

As a Poet : Hadrat Ali was a distinguished poet In his book. Ali, the Superman Dr. Ata Mohyuddin has assessed the poetry of Hadrat Ali in the following terms:

> "All in his poems is shown as a moralist, freely expressing the righteousness of his cause. In them, as in his sermons, he exhorts the pious to be sincere and steadfast, to refrain from wrongdoing and to stick to the faith. The poetry is neither romantic nor lyrical, but reformative. It contains no sensuous feelings or imagery and has nothing about it of the themes on which the old school of Arab poets delighted to dwell. There is no praise of women, wine, music, amusement and even of the sword. Ali's eloquence is reserved for the praise of patriotism, humility, modesty, chastity, piety and resignation to God's will. Some of his verses are addressed to his followers and are complaints about their infidelity, others extol the virtue of loyalty to the community. Indeed he may be said to have laid the foundation of a national poetry. The style of the verses, which like. Ali's prose, is racy, lively and unstilted, makes the ethical truths expounded in them much more palatable than they might otherwise have been. The literary form adopted by Ali in his verses exerted a great

influence on the trend of Arabic poetry in general. These verses still retrain an importance second to none in Arabic literature".

The Deewan : There is some controversy about Deewan or the collection of the poems of Hadrat Ali. According to one school, his "Deewan", a collection of 1500 verses and bearing the title "Anwar Oqueil" is extant. According to another account this collection includes poems written by the followers of Hadrat Ali.

Samples of the poetry of Hadrat Ali

In his book History of the Caliphs, Suyuti has given some samples of the poetry of Hadrat Ali. These are:

(1) Where hearts contain despair

And the spacious breast is stifled by what is within it,
And cares make their abode and repose,
And sorrows anchor in their habitations,
And no way is seen for the dispelling of distress,
And the stratagem of the cunning availeth not
There shall come to thee in thy despair a helper
When the answerer of prayer who is nigh shall bring
For all sorrows when they have reached their term
There is linked to them an approaching joy"

(2) "Consort not with a foolish brother, beware of him. For how many a fool hath corrupted the gentle. When he hath fraternised with them'. A man is judged by the man with whom he consorteth. For their are comparisons and similitudes for one thing with another.

The measure of a sandal is made when it is matched with it,. And the evidence of the feeling of one heart toward another is when they meet".

(3) "Men lust for the world and plot for it,

Yet its clearness is mingled for them with impurities
They do not give thou of it thy portion
According to thy wisdom when it is distributed
But men have their allotted shares according to their destinies
How many there are of the wise and sagacious unprospered

While a fool has gained his wealth by errors,
If it could be acquired by force and rapine
Falcons would sweep off with subsistence of sparrows."

(4) "Disclose not thy secret but to thyself
For every confidant hath a confidant
For verily I have seen erring men
Who do not aspire to a high sense of honour."

The Distinctions : Hadrat Ali was a man of many distinctions. He owed his distinctions to his relationship with Holy Prophet, his valour, his knowledge and his spiritual attainments.

His Birth: He had the distinctions of being a Hashimite both on the side of his father as well as his mother.

He had the distinction of having a name which was a derivative of the name of Allah. No other person before him bore the name of Ali.

His relationship with the Holy Prophet

On opening his eyes after his birth the first person whom he saw was the Holy Prophet.

He was named by the Holy Prophet.

As an infant he had the honour of sucking the tongue of the Holy Prophet.

He was the first cousin of the Holy Prophet. He became a ward of the Holy Prophet and was brought up as a family member of the household of the Holy Prophet.

He received his training under the loving care and guidance of the Holy Prophet.

When the Holy Prophet declared his mission he was the first teenager to be converted to Islam.

Hadrat Khadija and Hadrat Ali were the first two persons to pray after the Holy Prophet.

When the Holy Prophet invited the Hashimites to a dinner and asked them to aid him in his mission, Hadrat Ali was the only person to respond to the call of the Holy Prophet.

He risked his life for the sake of the Holy Prophet and slept on his bed when the Holy Prophet left for Medina and the Quraish youth besieged the house with a view to killing the Holy Prophet.

When the Holy Prophet left for Medina he entrusted to Hadrat Ali the task to return the belongings of the people to them which they had placed in the custody of the Holy Prophet.

When the Holy Prophet joined the Muhajirs and the Ansars in fraternity in Medina, he allied himself in fraternity with Hadrat Ali.

The Holy Prophet married his beloved daughter Fatima Zahra to Hadrat Ali.

He was commissioned by the Holy Prophet to write the agreement which came to be known as the Hudaibiya Pact.

After the conquest of Mecca he had the unique distinction of standing on the shoulders of the Holy Prophet and destroying the idols in the Kaaba.

He was entrusted by the Holy Prophet with the special mission of announcing the Quranic Surah "Al Baraat" (Immunity) to the people on the occasion of the pilgrimage.

He was the only person to whom the Holy Prophet referred to as the "Maula" of the Ummah.

When the Holy Prophet proposed "Mubahala" with the Christians of Najran, he chose Hadrat Ali as his "second man."

The progeny of the Holy Prophet descends through Hadrat Ali

He was the only person to whom the Holy Prophet imparted 'inward knowledge."

The Holy Prophet conferred many appellations on Hadrat Ali such as Haidar-i-Karrar, Abu Turab, Asad Allah, Syedul, Arab, etc.

The Holy Prophet declared his relationship to Hadrat Ali as those of Moses and Aaron.

When the Holy Prophet died, Hadrat Ali washed him and prepared his dead body for burial.

His Valour : He participated in all the wars of early Islam fought under the command of the Holy Prophet.

In all the battles, Hadrat Ali was the flag bearer of the forces of the Muslims.

He was the bravest man among the Muslims. For his unusual bravery he won such titles as "Asad. Allah," the lion of God or "Haidar-i-Karrar" the warrior whom nobody could match.

During his lifetime he killed over a thousand persons of the enemies. In the battle of Badr alone he killed two dozen persons.

He fought over a hundred duels and in all the duels his adversaries however strong were killed.

He was the Conqueror of the Khyber.

His Knowledge : He was the most learned man of his age. He was a living encyclopaedia of knowledge and learning.

After the Holy Prophet he was the most eloquent person of the age.

Because of his knowledge and wisdom he is known as the "second Solomon".

His wise sayings and aphorisms have attained the status of classical proverbs.

He was the first person to write a grammar of the Arabic language.

Among the early Muslims he is the only person whose collections of writings have come down to us under the title of Nahj-ul-Balagha.

He was a distinguished poet.

He enjoys fame as the "Father of Rhetoric".

He was an authority on mathematics.

He was a master of the science of physics.

He had deep medical knowledge.

After the Holy Prophet he is regarded as the greatest philosopher of Islam.

He was a calligrapher and wrote a beautiful hand His spiritual attainments.

He was the first person to lean the Quran by heart.

According to commentators there are at least three hundred verses in the Holy Quran which have an implied reference to Hadrat Ali.

After the Holy Prophet he was the Chief Judge among the early Muslims. He is regarded as the "Father of Fiqh".

He is the first revivalist among the Muslims. He interpreted the doctrine of Islam and systematised them.

He is regarded as the "Father of Sufism". All schools of Tasawwuff trace their origin to him.

His Appellations : Because of his multi-dimensional greatness and outstanding qualities, Hadrat Ali is known by many appellations and each appellation projects some particular aspect of his greatness. Some of these appellations are as follows:

(1) Murtada-he with whom God is pleased.

(2) Maula—the master.

(3) Haidar-i-Karrar—the brave warrior against whom no one could stand.

(4) Asad Allah—the lion of God.

(5) Al-Ghahb—the victorious.

(6) Sher-i-Yazdan—the bravest man of the age.

(7) Mushkil-Kusha—one who resolved the difficulties of the people.

(8) Shah-i-Awlia—the king of saints.

(9) Shah-i-Momin— the king of the pious.

(10) Abu Turab-Father of the Earth.

(11) Amir-ul-Momineen—the leader of the faithful.

(12) Amin-ul-Momineen—the trustee of the faithful.

(13) Imam-ul-Muttaqeen—the leader of the god-fearing.

(14) Sayedul-Arab—the chief of the Arabs.

(15) Al Wasi—the testamenter.

(16) Al Hadir—the guide.

(17) Al Zahid-the chaste.

(18) Al Abid-the pious.

(19) Al Salah-the reformer.

Scholars' Views

Abdullah b. Masud : Abdullah b Masud used to say that throughout, Arabia there was no more impartial judge than Ali. He also said that Hadrat Ali was the founder of Arabic grammar.

Abu Saeed Khudri : Abu Saeed Khudri held that he could easily detect a hypocrite by his enmity towards Ali.

Imam Hanbal : Imam Hanbal said:

> "Ali had numerous enemies and all of them tried to find fault with him, but they searched in vain and could not find any flaw in him. At long last they Joined hands with Muawiyyah and declared war on Ali. When they failed to defeat him by fair means they took to treacherous and deceitful courses to defeat him. "

Ibn Athir : Ibn Athir, the great biographist, held:

> "Ali was the first Caliph both of whose parents were pure Hashimites. He was so judicial minded that he could not put up with the dishonesty of his relations or friends and was so much engrossed in piety that at the time of his marriage with Fatima he did not possess anything save a camel skin on which he fed his camels in the day and which he converted into a bedsheet at night. The Prophet in his table talk has not extolled anyone of his companions as much as he has Ali surely, Ali never spoke a lie during his lifetime."

Darema : Darema was a sharp tongued Arab lady who was very loud in the praise of Hadrat Ali and the denunciation of Muawiyyah. After the death of Hadrat Ali, Muawiyyah summoned her to his court and enquired of her why she had supported Ali. She said that she had done so because Hadrat Ali was a lover of justice who honoured the pious and sympathised with the poor.

Ibn Nadim : In his work. Al Fihinst writing about Hadrat Ali, Ibn Nadim has held that Hadrat Ali arranged the Chapters of the Holy Quran in the order of revelation. He exercised utmost circumspection in editing traditions.

Umar b. Abdul Aziz : Umar b. Abdul Aziz, the Umayyad Caliph, was asked as to whom he considered to be the most pious man in the world. He said:

> "Ali excelled mankind in piety. Not only did he practise its virtues, but he tried zealously to reform his friends, associates, acquaintances and all those who came in contact with him.

Masudi : Masudi, the great historian, writes:

> "If the glorious name of being among the first Muslims, a comrade of the Prophet in exile, his faithful companion in the struggle for the faith, his intimate friend in life and his kinsman, if a true knowledge of his teachings and of the book, if self abnegation and practice of justice, if honesty, purity and love of truth, if a knowledge of law and science constitutes a claim to pre-eminence then all must regard. All as one of the foremost Muslims"

Shah wali Ullah : Shah wali Ullah has observed:

> "Chivalry and strength of character, humanity and sincerity which are attributes of great men were represented in abundance by Hadrat Ali. He is the father of Islamic learning and his intellectual attainments were due to the ideal training of the Holy Prophet. He was Hafiz and a great authority on the Quran. He was the greatest Mujtahid and jurist of his time and one of the greatest of all times. He was one of the greatest orators of early Islam."

Syed Amir Ali : Syed Amir Ali has assessed the achievements of Hadrat Ali in the following terms:

> "His bravery won him the title of the "Lion of God", and his learning that of the "Gate of Knowledge. " Chivalrous, humane and forbearing to the verge of weakness as a ruler, he came before his time. Most of the grand undertakings initiated by Umar for the welfare of the people were due to his counsel. Ever ready to succour the weak and to redress the wrongs of the injured, the accounts of his valorous deeds are recited with enthusiasm from the bazars in Cano to those of Delhi. With his dying breath he inculcated lessons of charity, love, humility and self abnegation to his sons. He expressly ordered them that no harshness should be shown towards his murderer who should be executed with one blow."

Dr. Ata Mohyuddin : In his book Ali, the Superman, Dr. Ata Mohyuddin has assessed Hadrat Ali in the following terms:

> "Ali has meant many different things to many generations, each of whom has found something to inspire it out of all the diverse wealth of his mind. During his lifetime he was thought of primarily as a warrior fighting at first in the battles of God and later for a decade against schismatics. He was also respected for his knowledge and learning and in later years many thought of him as a saint but it was until after his death that the effect which he had exercised over the ethical life of his time began to be appreciated. He was the founder of a movement which aimed to rejuvenate the ethical life of the Muslims. The. Arabs had begun to forsake the unity of Islam in favour of the tribal laws of the 'Days of Ignorance". All had of fight against the disintegrating social forces that were everywhere around him and attempted almost single handed to restore the religious policy of Islam. That he succeeded as well as he did was due to moral earnestness of his own character and to the colossal store of spiritual knowledge from which he drew his strength. In subsequent ages his ethical pronouncements which fell largely on deaf ears during his lifetime were to have an invigorating effect on the Islam he served so well. The influence of Ali was to continue to make itself felt long after his death and to recreate earnestness among the believers. It still makes itself felt today"

Allama Iqbal : In his poem "Asrar-i-Khudi",. Allama Iqbal has paid tribute to Hadrat Ali in the following terms:

> "Ali, the son-in-law of the Prophet, was a man of many qualities.
>
> He gave fresh vigour to faith.

And brought honours to the community of the faithful.

He developed self-disciplines and killed avarice.

A person who knows and controls himself rules the world."

Philip Hitti : In his book. History of the Arabs, Professor Hitti assesses the character of Hadrat Ali as follows'

> "Valiant in battle, wise in counsel, eloquent in speech, true to his friends, magnanimous to his foes, All became both the paragon of Muslim nobility and chivalry and the Solomon of Arabic tradition around his name, poems, proverbs, sermonettes and anecdotes innumerable have clustered. He had a swarthy complexion, large black eyes, bald head, thick and long white beard and was opulent and of medium stature. His sabre Dhul Fiqar, wielded by the Prophet on the memorable battlefield of Badr, has been immortalised in the words of the verse found engraved on many medieval Arab records 'No sword can match Dhul Fiqar, and no young warrior can compare with Hadrat Ali". The later Fidayan movement which developed ceremonies and insignia savouring of medieval European chivalry and the modern scouts movement, took Ali for its Father and model. Regarded as wise and brave by all the Islamic world, as idealistic and exemplary by many Fidayan and Derwish fraternities, as sinless and infallible by his partisans and even held to be the incarnation of the deity by the Ghulah (extremists) among them, he whose worldly career was practically a failure, has continued to exert a posthumous influence second only to that of the Holy Prophet himself. The throngs of pilgrims that still stream to his Mashhad at Najaf and to that of his son Hussain, the Shia arch-saint and martyr at nearby Karbala and the passion-play enacted annually on the tenth of Moharram throughout the Shia world testify to the possibility that death may avail a Messiah more than life."

Sir William Muir : In his book. The Caliphate, its rise, decline and fall, Sir William Muir has paid his tribute to Hadrat Ali in the following words:

> "In the character of Ali there are many things to commend mild and beneficent, he treated Basra when prostrate at his feet with a generous forbearance. Towards theocratic fanatics, who wearied his patience by incessant intrigues and insensate rebellion, he showed no vindictiveness. Excepting Muawiyyah, the man of all others whom he ought not to have estranged, he carried the policy of conciliating his enemies to a dangerous extreme. In compromise indeed and in procrastination lay the failure of his caliphate. With greater vigour, spirit and determination, he might have averted the schism which for

a time threatened the existence of Islam and which has never ceased to weaken it. Ali was wise in counsel and many an adage and sapient proverbs have been attributed to him. But like Solomon, his wisdom was for others than for himself.

Charles Mills : In his book. A. History of Muhammadanism, Charles Mills assesses Hadrat Ali as follows:

> "As the chief of the family of Ḥashim and as the cousin and son-in-law of him whom the Arabians respected almost to idolatry, it is apparently incredible that Ali was not raised to the caliphate immediately after the death of Muhammad (peace be on him). In the advantage of his birth and marriage was added the friendship of the Prophet. The son of Abu Talib was one of the first converts to Islam and Muhammad's favourite appellation of him was the Aaron of a second Moses. His talents as an orator and his intrepedity as a warrior commended him to a nation in whose judgement courage was virtue and eloquence was wisdom. But the pride and loftiness of his spirit endured not the caution inseparable from schemes of policy and continually precipitated him into rashness. His opposition to Abu Bakr would not have ceased if Fatima had lived; but on he death, six months after that of her father, the Companions of Muhammad relaxed in their friendship to his family. In the reign of Abu Bakr, Umar and Uthman, a dignified independence was preserved by Ali. On the invitation of the Caliphs, he assisted in the councils of Medina, but he was principally occupied in the tranquil pursuits of domestic life and the various duties of his religion. On the murder of Uthman, the Egyptians who were at Medina offered him the caliphate. Indignant that the power of nomination should be usurped by the strangers. Ali declared that the suffrages of the inhabitants of Mecca and Medina alone could be available. The public voice soon echoed the opinion of the murderers and the scruples of Ali were soon removed. In apprehension of the enmity of Aishah, his relentless foe and of the whole family of Muawiyyah, he declined to receive in private the preferred allegiance of the chiefs. With his accustomed simplicity, he proceeded to the mosque clad in a cotton gown, a coarse turban on his head, his slippers were in one hand and a bow instead of a staff, occupied the other".

Professor Nicholson : In his book. A Literary History of the Arabs, Nicholson remarks as follows:

> "Ali was a gallant warrior, a wise counsellor, a true friend and a generous foe. He excelled in poetry and in eloquence, his verses and sayings are famous

> throughout the Muhammadan east, though few of them can be considered authentic. He can be compared with Montrose and Bayard in the fineness of spirit. He had no talent for the stern realities of statecraft and was overmatched by unscrupulous rivals who knew that war is a game of deceit. Thus, his career was in one sense a failure, his authority as a Caliph was never admitted while he lived by the whole community. On the other hand he has exerted down to the present day a posthumous influence only second to that of Muhammad himself. Within a century of his death he came to be regarded as the Prophet's successor jure divine as a blessed martyr, sinless and infallible, and by some even as incarnation of God. The All of Shiites legend is not a historical figure glorified, rather does he symbolise in purely ethical fashion the religious aspirations and political aims of a large section of the Muslim world."

John J. Pool : In his book Studies in Muhammadanism, John J Pool observes as follows:

> "The fact is that Ali was too mild a man for the stirring times in which he lived. He was too slow to resolve and too undecided in action. At any time he preferred compromise and delay to energy and promptness and with fatal results. The death of Ali was an epoch-making event. We come now to the parting of ways. Henceforward the Commanders of the Faithful ceased to be elected by the votes of the people of Medina or Mecca. Arabia was no longer to be the seat of temporal power. For the future, in Islam, might was to take the place of right."

Edward Gibbon : In his book Rise and Fall of the Roman Empire, Edward Gibbon observes as follows about the assassination of Hadrat Uthman and the succession of Hadrat Ali:

> "A tumultuous anarchy of five days after the martyrdom of Uthman was appeased by the inauguration of. Ali, his refusal would have provoked a general massacre. In this painful situation he supported the becoming pride of the chief of the Hashimites, declared that he would rather serve than reign, rebuked the presumption of the strangers and required the formal, if not the voluntary, assent of the chiefs of the nation. He has never been accused of promoting the assassination of Uthman, through Persia indirectly and secretly celebrates the festivals of that holy martyr. The quarrel between Uthman and his subjects was assuaged by the early mediation of Ali and Hassan, the eldest of his sons, was insulted and wounded in the defence of the Caliph."

While commenting on the failure of Hadrat Ali in matters pertaining to statecraft, Gibbon observes as follows:

> "A life of prayer and contemplation had not chilled the martial activity of Ali but in a mature age, after a long experience of mankind, he still betrayed in his conduct the rashness and indiscretion of youth."

Thomas Carlyle : In his book on "Heroes and Hero Worship", Thomas Carlyle observes as follows:

> "As for this young Ali, one cannot but like him a noble-minded creature, as he shows himself, now and always afterwards, full of affection, of fiery daring something chivalrous in him, brave as a lion, yet with a grace a truth and affection worthy of Christian Kinghood. He died by assassination in the mosque at Kufa, death occasioned by his own generous fairness, confidence on the fairness of others, he said if the wound proved not unto death, they must pardon the assassin, but if it did, they must slay him straightway, so that they two in the same hour might appear before God and see which side of that quarrel was the just one."

Dr. Henry Stubbe : In his book "An Account of the Rise and Progress of Muhammadanism" Dr. Henry Stubbe observes as follows:

> "Ali was of a brown complexion, a little man with a belly somewhat large, he had a contempt of the world, its glory and pomp. He feared God much, gave many alms, was just in all his actions, humble and affable, of an exceeding quick wit and of an ingenuity that was not common. He was exceedingly learned not only in those science that terminate in speculation, but those which extend to practice"

Major Price : In his book Memories of the Principal Events of Muhammadan. History Major Price observes as follows

> "His virtues and extraordinary qualities have been the subject of voluminous panegyrics and his war-like exploits from his youth upwards have been particularly celebrated in the "Khawer Nama", a poem well known in the east and which may perhaps contend in extravagance with the wildest effusions of European romance. With his acknowledged talents and magnanimity, it is however difficult to account for the train of civil mischief and perpetual discontent which continued to disturb him through the whole of his reign. His gallant spirit was probably incapable of bonding to the ordinary shifts of

political craft and it is perhaps true that the Arabian chiefs were not yet sufficiently disciplined to see the sovereign authority quietly monopolised by any particular family."

J. J. Saunders : In his book. A. History of Medieval Islam, J J Saunders observes as follows:

"His moral qualities were respectfully recognised. He was a brave fighter and eloquent orator and a loyal friend Many sayings of his are quoted to prove his mastery of proverbial wisdom, a gift highly honoured among the Semites. He displayed towards his foes a patience and magnanimity expressive of a humane and generous disposition. His religion was founded on a genuine piety. He was shocked by the growing luxury and corruption of the age and to his many doubts whether Uthman was an upholder or a violator of the law may be attributed the hesitating and ambiguous attitude he adopted towards the regicides, which proved so fatal to his rule and reputation. As his temper was indolent he drifted rather than led. He was easily outmatched by the astute and the forceful and he lacked the commanding personality to impose his will on a turbulent society. His authority was challenged by the politic shrewdness of Muawiyyah and the furious zealotry of the Kharijrtes, his inability to overcome either delivered Islam to schism and grave believers were driven to see in a reunion of the empire under the Umayyads the only escape from tribal and sectarian anarchy. Yet he has been raised by a powerful sect little below that of Muhammad himself, the Shia or a party of Ali laid it down as an article of faith that he was designated by God and the Prophet to be the lawful Caliph and Imam of Islam, his three predecessors being treated as usurpers and that divine revelation continued to be interpreted by his descendants and his supposed grave at Najaf, a sandhill on the edge of the desert six miles west of Kufa, is annually visited by thousands of devout pilgrims who curse his supplanters and fever him as the friend of God and the first of Imams."

Life at a Glance

599/600 C.E.	Birth of Hadrat Ali.
605 C.E.	Hadrat Ali becomes the ward of the Holy Prophet.
610/611 C.E.	Hadrat Ali is converted to Islam.
615 C.E.	A batch of Muslims migrate to Abyssinia under the leadership of Jafar, the elder brother of Hadrat Ali.

617/619 C.E.	The Hashimites are excommunicated by the Quraish.
619 C.E.	Year of Sorrow, Death of Abu Talib and Hadrat Khadija.
620 C.E.	The Ascension of the Holy Prophet.
622 C.E.	Hadrat Ali risks his life for the sake of the Holy Prophet and lies on his bed while the Holy Prophet leaves for Medina. Migration to Medina.
623 C.E.	Hadrat Ali settles in Medina Works in the construction of the Prophet's mosque.
624 C.E.	Battle of Badr. Operation against the Jews of Bani Qainuqa. Marriage of Hadrat Ali with Hadrat Fatima.
625 C.E.	Battle of Uhud. Operations against the Jews of the Banu Nadir. Birth of Hadrat Hassan.
627 C.E.	Battle of the Trench. Operation against Banu Quraiza. Operation against Banu Mustaliq. Operation against Banu Saad.
628 C.E.	Pilgrimage to Mecca. The Hudaibiyah pact. The Conquest of Khyber.
630 C.E.	The Conquest of Mecca. Battle of Hunain. Battle of Taif. Operations against Banu Tay.
631 C.E.	Mubahila with the Christians of Najran. Hadrat Ali is commissioned to announce the verses about the Declaration of "Discharge" on the occasion of Hajj at Mecca. Expedition against Banu Rumla. Operation against Banu Zubuda. Hadrat Ali's mission to Yemen.

632 C.E.	The Farewell Pilgrimage. The Holy Prophet's Khutba and Khum Ghadir. Demise of the Holy Prophet. Election of Hadrat. Abu Bakr as the Caliph.
633 C.E.	Death of Hadrat Fatima Zahra.
634 C.E.	Death of Hadrat. Abu Bakr. Election of Hadrat Umar as the Caliph.
644 C.E.	Death of Hadrat Umar. Election of Hadrat Uthman as the Caliph.
656 C.E.	Martyrdom of Hadrat Uthman. Election of Hadrat Ali as the Caliph. Rebellion of Talha, Zubayr and Hadrat Aishah. Battle of the Camel.
657 C.E.	Hadrat Ali shifts the capital to Kufa. Battle of Siffin.
658 C.E.	The Arbitration. The battle of Nahrawan.
659 C.E.	Muawiyyah's occupation of Egypt. Trouble in Basra. Revolt of Khurrit b Raashid. Raids of Muawiyyah.
660 C.E.	The Syrians are driven from Hijaz and Yemen. Muawiyyah declares himself as the caliph at Damascus.
661 C.E.	Martyrdom of Hadrat Ali.

EIGHT

ILLUSTRIOUS WIFE

HADRAT FATIMA ZOHRA (R.A.A.)

Hadrat Fatima was born 5 years before the Holy Prophet (PBUH) declared his mission. These were the auspicious days when the Quraishites were busy in the reconstruction of Kaaba. (Tabaqat).

Hadrat Abbas reports that she was born when the Holy Prophet (PBUH) was 35 years of age and Kaaba was under construction (Isaba). According to Isaba she was 5 years senior to Hadrat Aishah in age.

Name and Title : Her name is Fatima and her adopted name (Kunniyat) is Umm Muhammad. She is the youngest daughter of the Holy Prophet (PBUH). She is one of the four most celebrated and perfect women born so far. The Prophet of Allah (PBUH) has said:

> "Among men there have been many perfect; but among women only four: Aasia the wife of Pharroha, Mary the daughter of Imran, Khadijah the daughter of Khuwaylid, and Fatima, daughter of Muhammad (PBUH)".
>
> She is the chief of the women of the world and head of the women in the Paradise. Her titles are Tahira, Mutahira, Zakia, Razia, Marzia and Batul. (Isabah).

Explaining the significance of her names, Fatima, Batul and Zahra, Hafiz Ibn-e-Hajar says that she is named Fatima, because Allah will protect her and her friends from the fire of Hell and she is called Batul because she was distinguished among the ladies of her age as regards learning, piety and ancestry; and she got the honorific of Zahra, because according to Maulana Shaikh Abdul Haq, she excelled in feminine charms and human excellence, and therefore, she was called as such. Other authorities agree that this is correct explanation.

From her childhood Hadrat Fatima was very sober, suave and serious. Her other sisters used to take part in games and pastimes, but she would not join them. She did not like going out and visiting people unnecessarily and used to keep herself aloof, always sitting with her mother. The Holy Prophet (PBUH) used to appreciate her simplicity and her disregard of the worldly attachments, and therefore, she was called Batul. Because she resembled very much with her father, the Holy Prophet (PBUH) in features and habits, she was known as Zaika and Razia.

> ***Her Marriage :*** When the Holy Prophet (PBUH) migrated to Medina, Hadrat Fatima was unmarried. There were a number of proposals for her. First Hadrat Abu Bakr requested for her hand. The Prophet of Allah (PBUH) asked him to wait for a heavenly direction. (Tabaqat). Hadrat Abu Bakr discussed this matter with Hadrat Umar and asked him to also propose for his marriage with Hadrat Fatima, which he did and got the same reply from the Holy Prophet (PBUH). Then people persuaded Hadrat Ali to try his luck. But considering his straitened circumstances he was reluctant to propose. Moreover, keeping in view the turning down of the proposals of seniors like Abu Bakr and Umar he thought that he stood no chance. But people around him encouraged him to try on the score of his relationship with the Holy Prophet (PBUH). However, he put up his proposal before the bride's father, who accepted it. The Holy Prophet (PBUH) also talked over this point with Hadrat Fatima, saying that Hadrat Ali wanted to marry her. She kept quiet. This silence is considered as approval. Hadrat Fatima was married to Hadrat Ali during the month of Moharram of 2 A.H. some 4 months after the marriage of Hadrat Aishah with the Holy Prophet (PBUH)
>
> (Isba)

According to some other biographers her marriage with Hadrat Ali took place after the battle of Uhud. After 71/2 months she was sent to live with Hadrat Ali (Usud-ul-Ghaba). On the other hand some people say that Hadrat Fatima's marriage with Hadrat Ali took place after 5 1/2 months of Hadrat Aishah's wida (her coming to the house of the Holy Prophet (PBUH) and the former went to live with Hadrat Ali after 91/2 months of her marriage with him, when she was 15 years 5 months and 15 days of age and Hadrat Ali was 21 years 5 months and 15 days old. (Istiab). Thus Hadrat Ali was 6 years older than Hadrat Fatima.

> Hadrat Ali collected 480 dirhams by selling some goods to Hadrat Uthman in order to meet the expenses of his marriage. He placed this amount before the Holy Prophet (PBUH) who asked him to spend two-third on bridal dresses, etc., and one-third on other items of marriage.
>
> (Tabaqat).

Hadrat Ali himself relates the story of his marriage with Hadrat Fatima in these words:

> "I had a maid servant, whom I had freed sometime ago. She once suggested that I should propose for my marriage with Hadrat Fatima to the Holy Prophet (PBUH). I replied that I had nothing to meet the expenses of the marriage. Inspite of this, she insisted that I should approach the Holy Prophet (PBUH) and request him for the hand of his daughter. Therefore, thus encouraged by her insistence, I went to the Holy Prophet (PBUH) with this end in view. But when I met him, I was overawed by his personality and could not say anything, and kept quiet. The Holy Prophet (PBUH) himself enquired if I had gone to him with a proposal for the hand of Hadrat Fatima. I replied in the affirmative. He then asked me if I had anything for the payment of *Mehr* (Dower Money). I said nothing. He then suggested that I should sell the armour which the Holy Prophet (PBUH) had given to me after the battle of Badr, and pay for the dower money out of its sale proceeds. The Nikah was performed and the armour was given in lieu of dower money.
>
> (Usud-ul Ghaba)

According to another story, some Ansars suggested to Hadrat Ali to propose himself for his marriage with Hadrat Fatima. As such when he approached the Holy Prophet (PBUH) with this request, the latter replied with (Ahlan was marhaban" (welcome). When Hadrat Ali came back to this waiting Ansars, they enquired from him the outcome of his mission. Hadrat Ali repeated the words of the Holy Prophet (PBUH). The Ansars asserted that this was enough to convey his assent.

> After the Nikah (Marriage ceremony) the Holy Prophet (PBUH) said that to complete the ceremony a Walima feast (The wedding feast, which is generally given on the day after marriage) was also necessary. One of his companions, Hadrat Saad offered his goat and an Ansar tribe contributed towards the Walima expenses.
>
> (Tabaqat).

During these days Hadrat Ali was living in a small rented house, a little ahead of the house of the Holy Prophet (PBUH). The Holy Prophet (PBUH) sent off his venerable daughter along with his maid servant Umm Aiman to live with her husband. Soon after the departure of Hadrat Fatima, the Holy Prophet (PBUH) went to the house of Hadrat Ali, asked for some water, performed ablution and then sprinkled the remaining water on Hadrat Ali and read this prayer:

> "O Allah, bless both of them, shower Thy blessings upon both of them and bless their progeny".
>
> (Tabaqat).

According to another story, when Hadrat Fatima was leaving for the house of her husband, the Holy Prophet (PBUH) asked Hadrat Ali to wait for him at his house. As such when the Holy Prophet (PBUH) knocked at the door of their house, his maid servant Umm Aiman opened the door and the following dialogue took place between her and the Holy Prophet (PBUH).

> ***Holy Prophet:*** Is my brother inside this house?
>
> ***Maid Servant:*** How he can be now your brother when you have married your daughter to him?
>
> ***Holy Prophet:*** Yes, it is so. Is here Asma bint Amees as well, and have you come here to honour the daughter of the Prophet?
>
> ***Maid Servant:*** Yes, my Lord. Asma bint Amees is in, and I have come here to venerate the daughter of the Holy Prophet (PBUH).

The Holy Prophet (PBUH) then blessed Umm Aiman and after entering the house asked for some water. He drank a little (and according to yet another version of Tabaqat, it is said that he washed his hand) and sprinkled a little on the shoulders, arms and chest of Hadrat Ali, and then sprinkled some water on Hadrat Fatima and then told her that he has married her to the best man in his family.

Dower Money : As stated since Hadrat Ali had no money to pay for the dower of Hadrat Fatima, he had given his old armour to her as dowry. The price of this armour was then estimated to be about 400 dirhams. There are different stories about the valuation of this armour and the amount of Hadrat Fatima's dowry. But this is agreed that amount of her dower money was not less than 400 dirhams.

The articles which the Holy Prophet (PBUH) gave to his distinguished daughter on her marriage included:

1. A wooden bed with carved designs;
2. A leather pillow stuffed with the bark of the date trees;
3. One cup;
4. One leather skin to carry water;
5. Two grinding stones, and
6. Two earthen pots.

And these articles remained her only household goods throughout her life.

The Children : Hadrat Fatima had two sons and two daughters, namely Hadrat Hassan, Hadrat Hussain, Umm Kulthum and Zainab born to her from Hadrat Ali. These are well known in the future annals of Islamic history and have left deep and everlasting landmarks.

> The Holy Prophet (PBUH) loved these children very much. Among his daughters, only Hadrat Fatima had the honour to maintain the future generation of her august father.
>
> (Usud-ul Ghaba)

According to Zurqani, a third son, Mohsin and a third daughter Ruqayya also were born to her, but they died in childhood.

Excellence and Nobility : Hadrat Fatima excels the women of the world as regards her qualities of heart and head. The Muslims are unanimous that she is the chief of the womankind of the world. According to Istiab, the Holy Prophet (PBUH) has said that Hadrat Fatima is the leader of the women in the Heaven. Hadrat Ibn-e-Abbas quotes from the Holy Prophet (PBUH) that Hadrat Fatima alongwith the virgin Mary, Hadrat Khadijah and Aasia the wife of Pharaoh, will lead the women folk in Paradise. She is the only one woman in the world who on account of her unparalleled piety and divinity has been venerated and sanctified by the Muslim world and she is named and glorified in congregational sermons in prayers.

There are a number of persons who are included among the Ahl-e-Bait (family) of the Holy Prophet (PBUH) but Hadrat Fatima is the distinguished, unmatched and the most perfect person among them.

> Hadrat Fatima was a model of righteousness, courage and piety. Hadrat Aishah says: "I have not seen a person more truthful than (Hadrat) Fatima except her father the Holy Prophet (PBUH)."
>
> (Istiab)

Whenever the Holy Prophet (PBUH) returned from a journey, he used to visit his daughter, Hadrat Fatima first. Although she had other sisters also, some of whom were more intelligent and charming, but the Holy Prophet (PBUH) loved her the most. (Usud-ul Ghaba). Inspite of her being the most beloved child of her father, Hadrat Fatima did not take any worldly gain or benefit due to this relation.

Hadrat Fatima not only greatly resembled her august father in features, she meticulously followed his practices, habits and manners. Whenever she used to visit him, he would stand up to welcome her, kiss her forehead and make her sit in his place.

According to Bukhari, the Holy Prophet (PBUH) had declared that: "Fatima is a part of my body: one who annoys her, will annoy me".

> When a daughter is married and leaves her parental house to live with her husband, the situation is painfully sharp and pungent. The girl has to leave the house where she was born and brought up; where she spent her childhood and attained adolescence and where she spent the happiest and best days of her life. She goes to a new house in new environment with new people and to start a new life. She is naturally apprehensive of an uncertain future. In her modesty she tries to hide her discomfiture and anguish. She weeps but not loudly to attract attention. Hadrat Fatima was also a girl leaving the house of her affectionate father. The Holy Prophet (PBUH) seeing her weeping, said to her, "Darling! Why these tears! I have married you with a person who is supreme in learning and suavity and is the first (among the boys) in accepting Islam".
>
> (Usud-ul Ghaba)

> Once Hadrat Fatima fell ill and the Holy Prophet (PBUH) went to see her and enquired about the health of his dear daughter. She replied that she was not well and over and above that she had nothing to eat. The Holy Prophet (PBUH) asked if she did not like to be the leader of the womenfolk of the world. She asked him as to what was the position of Mariam bint Imran (Mother of Christ). He replied that she was the chief of the women of her time and you are the leader of the females of your time. He concluded, "By Allah, I have married you to a man who is a leader of this world and religion both".
>
> (Istiab).

Hadrat Ali had his house at some distance from that of the Holy Prophet (PBUH) who once desired that it would have been better and more convenient if he took a house closer to him. One of his companions, Hadrat Harith bin Noman had some houses closer to the residence of the Holy Prophet (PBUH). When this companion learnt about the desire of his Prophet he himself went to him and said:

"O Prophet of Allah, I understand you want a house for your daughter closer to your residence. All of my houses are at your disposal. Please send for Hadrat Fatima to live in any of them. My life and property may be sacrificed for the sake of Allah's Messenger. By Allah, if you take a thing from me, it will be far better if it is with you than it may be with me". The Holy Prophet (PBUH) blessed Harith and prayed for him. Hadrat Fatima then shifted to this house.

(Tabaqat).

Hard and Simple Life : Hadrat Fatima was an extremely pious, religious minded and contended lady. She had spent her entire life in want and penury. Both she and her august husband, lived in straitened circumstances. Inspite of these difficulties, Hadrat Fatima was an example of resignation and submission to the Will of Allah and always remained contended. She had no parallel in divinity, bashfulness, modesty and in all the virtues that nature demanded and desired of a member of fair sex. She used to do all the chores of her household herself. Due to working of the handmills, rashes had appeared on her soft and tender palms and due to constant carrying of water in the leather skin, her shoulders and waist had developed hard spots.

These were the days when the Muslims were conquering new lands and Medina was full of booty and the wealth of the conquered cities. But the Holy daughter of the holiest of the world, had no share in these riches. Whenever Hadrat Fatima requested her distinguished father for a maid servant from the Baitul Mal (Public Treasury) to help her in the household work, the burden of work or he would stress upon the short life in this world and that soon one would be freed from the strain and stress in this life; at times he would flatly refuse, saying that the public treasury was meant for the help and relief of poor persons and orphans. Once a number of war prisoners were brought to Medina. Both Hadrat Ali and his august wife, approached the Holy Prophet (PBUH) and requested for the allotment of a prisoner to help them in their domestic work, but the Holy Prophet (PBUH) refused to oblige them stating that these prisoners would be sold (released on ransom) and their sale proceeds would be utilised for the relief and succour of the poor and destitute. Instead, he taught them a prayer to be recited after each *salat* (Prayer) and also before retiring to bed for their relief and mental peace.

Hadrat Ali was very kind to Hadrat Fatima, and always tried his level best for her comfort and convenience. The Holy Prophet (PBUH) used to advise Hadrat Ali to treat Hadrat Fatima well and would call upon his daughter to obey her husband and serve him well. The Holy Prophet (PBUH) was always trying to make their home life happy by all possible means.

> The Holy Prophet (PBUH) ever took a keen and lively interest in the domestic affairs of his daughters and son-in-law and extended all help to make their life easy and peaceful. Whenever there was any difference of opinion or discord between the couple, the Holy Prophet (PBUH) would intervene, offer sound advice and reconcile them. On such an occasion he advised Hadrat Fatima to put up with trifles and not take small things too seriously by asserting that: "there is no couple, who does not have differences or squabbles". It is not absolutely necessary that the man should at all times work in accordance with the wishes of his wife.
>
> (Tabaqat).

The Holy Prophet (PBUH) did not life showing off or pomposity. As such he did not approve his children to be ostentatious or make a show. Once Hadrat Ali presented a golden necklace to Hadrat Fatima, when the Holy Prophet (PBUH) learnt about this he reprimanded her in these words: "O Fatima, would you like the people say that the daughter of the Messenger of Allah, wears a necklace of fire?" She at once sold out the golden necklace and purchased a slave.

> Once the Holy Prophet (PBUH) returned triumphantly from a battle. To welcome her father in a befitting manner, Hadrat Fatima decorated her house by hanging curtains on the doors and put on silver bracelets on the hands of her sons, Hadrat Hassan and Husain. The Holy Prophet (PBUH) who adhered pomp and show, returned from the door. Hadrat Fatima understood the reason for the return of her father, at once tore down the curtains and removed bracelets from the hands of her sons. The two sons, being still very young, did not appreciate the action of their mother and resented the taking away of bracelets from their hands. They approached their grandfather weeping. The Holy Prophet (PBUH) said that although they were his own kith and kin, yet he did not like them to be involved with the worldly wealth and empty pride. He, however, ordered the purchase of an ordinary necklace for his daughter and ivory bracelets for his grand sons.
>
> (Abu Daud, Nasai).

A brother of Abu Jahl, an implacable opponent of the Holy Prophet (PBUH), suggested to Hadrat Ali that he should marry Ghora bint Abu Jahal. Hadrat Ali appeared to be inclined to marry her. But when the Holy Prophet (PBUH) came to know about his intention, he was much annoyed, and in the course of his sermon from the pulpit in the mosque, he openly expressed his disapproval in these words:

> "The house of Hisham (Abu Jahl's family) seeks my permission to marry their daughter to Ali, son of Abu Talib. But I will not permit this; I will never allow

this. However, the son of Abu Talib (Ali) may divorce my daughter and marry their daughter (if he likes). Fatima is a part of my body, on who torments her, will hurt me. Anybody harming her will harm me" He further added: "I do not want to convert lawful into unlawful and unlawful into lawful. But by Allah, the daughter of the Messenger of Allah and the daughter of the enemy of Allah, cannot be put together.

(Bukhari and Usud-ul Ghaba).

As a result of this forthright assertion of the Holy Prophet (PBUH), Hadrat Ali did not have a second wife so long as Hadrat Fatima was alive. (Istiab).

According to Isaba, the Holy Prophet (PBUH) had told his daughter Hadrat Fatima, her husband Hadrat Ali, and her sons Hadrat Hassan and Husain, that "anybody who is antagonistic to you is antagonistic to me and one who is friendly to you is friendly to me".

(Istiab)

Once Hadrat Ali asked the Holy Prophet (PBUH) as to which of them (Ali and Fatima) is dearer to him. He replied "Fatima more than you and you are more than Fatima".

(Usud-ul-Ghaba).

By the Death Bed of Her Father : When the Holy Prophet (PBUH) passed away from this world, Hadrat Fatima was aged only 29 years. Hadrat Aishah says that just before his passing away, she was sitting near him, when Hadrat Fatima came to see him. Her mode of walking resembled her father. The Holy Prophet (PBUH) at once said: "Welcome, my daughter" and then made her seated by his side. He then whispered in her ears which made her weep; he again whispered in her ears, which made her smile. Hadrat Ayeshah says that she was wonder struck and could not resist asking Hadrat Fatima, the reason for her weeping and smiling. First Hadrat Fatima, refused to divulge the secret, but when after the demise of her august father, she was again asked, she replied that "the Holy Prophet (PBUH) first whispered in my ears that the Angel Jibbrail used to recite the Quran once a year, but this year contrary to his practice, he had recited the Quran twice. From this he (the Holy Prophet S.A.W.) inferred that his end was near and that of all the members of his family. (Ahl-e-Bait) I will be the first to meet him. This made me weep. He then asked me if I do not like to be the leader of the womenfolk of the world. This made me beam".

When the Holy Prophet (PBUH) was in the grip of death agony, Hadrat Fatima could not stand the anguish of her father and exclaimed: "I pity for my father's pain"

The Holy Prophet (PBUH) replied: "Your father shall not have to be in pain after this day".

After the demise of the Holy Prophet (PBUH) only Hadrat Fatima of all his daughters, was alive. His death had caused her the greatest grief. She used to weep almost constantly on the death of her exalted father. She lived only for 6 months after her father's death but during these months she never laughed or smiled and remained mournful throughout.

> After the last rites of the Holy Prophet (PBUH), his companions waited upon Hadrat Fatima and tried to console her. She then asked one of them - Hadrat Anas: "Have you buried the Messenger of Allah?" He replied "Yes Madam". She remarked: "How could you tolerate to bury him under tons of earth?"
> (Usud-ul-Ghaba).

She went to the grave of the Holy Prophet (PBUH) wept and applied the dust of his grave to her eyes and read the following couplet:

> "After having smelt the dust of the grave of the Holy Prophet (PBUH) one need not smell any other perfume. If the misfortunes that have fallen upon me, had fallen on the days, they would have turned into nights". These couplets have been composed by Hadrat Ali. The following elegy is said to have been composed by Hadrat Fatima on the death of her father:
>
> "The sky is covered with dust. The sun is wrapped up and the world is darkened. The earth is not only grief-striken after the passing away of the Holy Prophet (PBUH) but due to extreme sorrow has cracked down.
>
> The people living in the East and West and the tribe of Muzer and the people of Yaman are in tears for him. There is mourning for him on high mountains and in palaces. Oh! last of the prophets, may the blessings and mercies of Allah be upon you".
> (Durrul Mansur).

After the passing away of the Holy Prophet (PBUH) the question of distribution of his legacy cropped up. The history is witness to the fact that the distribution of Holy Prophet's (PBUH) patrimony is one of the causes which have divided the Muslims.

> The only things which the Holy Prophet (PBUH) left after his demise comprised of a white mule, some weapons and some landed property which included gardens in Medina, Khyber and Fidak. The Holy Prophet (PBUH) had declared

> that: "The Prophets have no inheritors. What we leave is the right of the Muslims as a whole".
>
> (Bukhari).

As regards the nature of properties in Khyber and Fidak, there was some difference of opinion among the companions of the Holy Prophet (PBUH) from the very beginning. Some said that these were as a trust with the Holy Prophet (PBUH), and some held that they were his personal properties and distributable. Among the latter were Hadrat Fatima, some wives of the Holy Prophet (PBUH) and his uncles Hadrat Abbas. As against these, Hadrat Abu Bakr, Hadrat Umar and some other senior companions held that these properties were trust for the benefit of all the Muslims. The Holy Prophet (PBUH) had already earmarked their income for the use of poor persons and destitutes.

Soon after the passing away of the Holy Prophet (S.A.W,) Hadrat Fatima requested Hadrat Abu Bakr to distribute her father's legacy (among the heirs).

> Hadrat Abu Bakr replied that to him the relatives of the Holy Prophet (PBUH) were dearer than his own, but the difficulty was that the Holy Prophet (PBUH) himself had stated that the prophets leave no legacy; as such he was unable to act contrary to the dictates and wishes of the Holy Prophet (PBUH). But this statement failed to satisfy Hadrat Fatima (Tabaqat) and she remained dissatisfied with Hadrat Abu Bakr so long as she was alive.
>
> (Bukhari).

> But a story in Tabaqat says that just before her death, Hadrat Abu Bakr, came to see Hadrat Fatima in her sickness and sought her permission to come in. When permitted, he came in and made enquiries about her health. This made her pleased.
>
> (Tabaqat).

The Demise : Like her other three sisters, Hadrat Fatima also died in her youth, only 6 months after the passing away of the Holy Prophet (PBUH). Some people say she died only 70 days after her august father's death: (Istiab); some other state that she outlived her father by 2 months and some record this period as 4 months. But according to authentic reports she died 6 months after her father's demise when she was 29 years of age on 3rd Ramadan of 11 A.H. (Istiab). Thus the prophecy of the Holy Prophet (PBUH) that of all the members of his family; she would be first to meet him after his death, proved true.

> Hadrat Abbas, the uncle of the Holy Prophet (PBUH) led her funeral prayers, and he along with Hadrat Ali and Hadrat Fazal lowered her body into the grave. (Tabaqat).

Nothing is known about the nature of her illness. It appears she died as a result of some ordinary disease and was not much confined to bed.

Hadrat Umm Salma says that at the time of the death of Hadrat Fatima, Hadrat Ali was not present in the house. She asked for some water for a bath and some neat and good clothes. She had a good bath and put on the clothes. She then asked for her bed to be made and went to bed facing the Kaaba. Thereafter she told Umm Salma that the time for her departure was near. Since she had already bathed, she did not need one after her death, nor there was any necessity for uncovering her body. Soon after this, she expired. When Hadrat Ali came to his house, Umm Salma related the whole story. Therefore, she was buried as desired by her. (Tabaqat). The same story is told by Umm Rafae in Isaba.

According to the wishes of Hadrat Fatima, her body was laid in the grave that very night without delay and very few persons had the chance to join the funeral.

Hadrat Fatima was extremely sober, suave, modest and bashful. Before her death she had instructed that her dead body be taken to the graveyard fully covered, unlike the practice among the Arabs. Accordingly, her coffin was fully increased. She is the first Muslim lady whose dead body was so thoroughly covered.

Hadrat Ali returned from the graveyard with a very heavy heart and in extreme sorrow recited the following verse:

> "I see that I am surrounded by many calamities of this world. And the people of the world will remain sick so long as they are in this world".
>
> "Two friends are bound to separate. The period other than separation, is short. After the Messenger of Allah, the separation of Fatima, proves that the friend does not live long". (Durrul Mansur).

Hadrat Ali used to visit the grave of his wife daily and used to shed tears for her.

Place of Burial : Some people say that she is buried in the grave-yard of Baqi, but Waqidi reports on the authority of Abdur Rahman bin Abul Maula, that she is buried in a corner of Dar Aqeel, by the side of a thoroughfare.

NINE

PRINCIPLES OF ADMINISTRATION

Hadrat Ali (R.A.) followed the administrative pattern set by Hadrat Umar (R.A.) and did not make any noticeable changes. He tried to improve the administration of those places where it was not proper during the time of Hadrat Uthman (R.A.). He usually gave useful advice to his governors at the time of their appointment. When he appointed Hadrat Kaab ibn Malik for supervision of various officers in various provinces he gave him the following instructions: "Check officers of each and every district of Iraq thoroughly so that they may not act wrongly"

General Morals

Like Hadrat Umar (R.A.), he was very particular for the standard of morals of his officers. He never allowed his"' officers to neglect their duties or to behave immorally. Once he found that Mundhar ibn Jarud, governor of Istakhr, spent most of his time hunting instead of giving attention to administration. He wrote to him: "I have been informed that you are spending much of your time in hunting and recreation and neglect your duties. If that is true you would be punished for that." When his negligence was proved, Hadrat Ali dismissed him. He wrote to another governor for his negligence: "It has come to my notice that you are leading a luxurious life. Your table is provided with different varieties of meals which common people cannot get. You behave un-Islamically while you are alone, but deliver sermons like most pious people (Siddiqin) on pulpits (Mimbars)..........If these complaints are true then remember that you are in loss and I would punish you............You can not hope for the reward given to righteous people in a position when you have spoiled the wealth of orphans and widows for your pleasure.......

Repent for your sins and give the right of Allah due upon you." Besides warning them in writing he also sent various commissions to watch the officers of various provinces.

Treasury and Revenue

He took care of "Baitul Mal" in the same way as was done by Hadrat Umar (R.A.). Once his cousin Hadrat Abdullah ibn Abbas (R.A.) took ten thousand Dirhams from Baitul Mal. When he knew about it he immediately wrote to Hadrat Abdullah ibn Abbas to return it and warned him for future.

He never allowed his family members to take from the "Baitul Mal" more than what they deserved. Once Hadrat Amr ibn Salamah brought some fat and honey from Isphahan in "Kharaj" (Land Tax). Hadrat Umm-i-Kulthum, daughter of Hadrat Ali took some honey and fat from that. When Hadrat Ali counted the barrels of honey and fat the next day he found that one barrel of each was missing. Then he was told that his daughter took them. He immediately paid the price of the honey and fat used by his daughter.

Hadrat Abu Rafi, the slave of the Holy Prophet, once took a pearl from the Baitul Mal for his daughter. When Hadrat Ali knew about it he not only took it back but also warned him not to do that ever again in future.

Hadrat Ali (R.A.) was very strict in the matter of public revenues and its administration. When-ever there was delay in receiving the tax he immediately wrote to the officers. Once Yazid ibn Qais was very late in sending the revenue tax, Hadrat Ali wrote him: "Explain the delay in sending the Kharaj. I advise you to fear Allah and warn you not to repeat it in future, otherwise your virtues would be lost and your Jihad (Holy War) for the sake of Allah would be spoiled. Fear Allah, and keep away from unlawful wealth. Don't give me a chance again to warn you for your mistakes.........."

Once Numan ibn Ujlan, a revenue officer, did not deposit the revenue in time and went to some other place. Hadrat Ali wrote to him: "One who embezzles the trust cannot be saved from the punishment of Allah. He destroys his world interests and the interests of the hereafter both ....You belong to a righteous family, repent before Allah for your misbehaviour, pay all the revenue you have charged from the public and do not compel me to punish you."

Hadrat Ali (R.A.) improved the taxation system. He imposed land tax on forests the produce of which was not been contributed fixed military expenditure or was being marketed.

Stipends from the "Baitul Mal" to the Poor : Hadrat Ali (R.A.) gave stipends to the needy persons and helped the poor from the "Baitul Mal." He was very generous in this respect. Even though Persians had revolted against him one time he treated them so generously that they were highly pleased with him and remembered him for a long time, and named him "Arabi Noshairwan" (the Just Arab).

Kindness to non-Muslims : He was very kind to his non-Muslim population (Dhimmis). He instructed his officers to treat them well and to take special care of their needs. Once he wrote to one of his officers, Amr ibn Muslimah: "It has come to my notice that the non-Muslims (Dhimmis) of your area are complaining about your strict behaviour. Treat them well and don't be so strict with them. Your strictness may cross limits and can turn into cruelty." Once a canal for irrigation belonging to non-Muslims was littered with rubbish. When Hadrat Ali was informed about it, he immediately wrote to the Officer-in-charge, Karzah ibn Kaab Ansari, "The non-Muslims (Dhimmis) of your area have complained that one of the irrigation canals belonging to them has been covered with rubbish. It is your duty to get it cleaned. I swear by Allah that it is better for you that the non-Muslims of your place continue living happily than migrating to other place because of difficulties."

The Justice

His justice was equal to both the Muslims and the non-Muslims, the poor and the rich and officer and subordinate. He had himself once appeared before the Judge (Qadi) and the decision was given against him because of lack of evidence. Once his Armour was lost. After sometime he saw it with a Christian. He filed a suit against him in the court of the famous Judge, Qadi Shuraih. Qadi Shuraih asked him to produce a witness but he could not do so. The Armour was returned to the Christian. The Christian was so impressed that he accepted Islam immediately saying: "This is the example set by Prophets. The Caliph's case has been rejected because he had no evidence for his lawful claim."

Armed Forces

Hadrat Ali (R.A.) was an experienced army general of Islam. He had fought a number of battles in the company of the Holy Prophet (Sallallahu 'alaihi wa Sallam). During his caliphate he gave a crushing defeat to his opponents in the battle of "Jamal" (Camel). He also defeated "Khawarij". As has been said before, he had the upper hand in the battle of "Siffin" but accepted arbitration only for the sake of Muslim Unity.

Hadrat Ali (R.A.) established a number of new cantonments in the state, and built a number of forts. He built a number of forts in Persia when there was a revolt. Hadrat Ali took special care of his border with Syria, which was under the control of Hadrat Muawiyyah (R.A.). He established a number of army posts all along the Syrian border.

He built a bridge over the river Euphrates which was very important from the defence point of view. The fort of Askhar, built in Persia was considered to be one of the strongest forts of his time.

Preaching of Islam

To preach true way of life i.e. Islam, is one of the foremost duties of a Khalifah. He paid special attention to it during his caliphate. Although he was not able to conquer many regions during his caliphate because of the civil war, yet a number of people accepted Islam because of the good treatment meted out to them. In Iran many people accepted Islam due to his kindness with the public. Those who forsook Islam re-joined the Faith because of Ali's teachings.

Thus we see that Hadrat Ali was a great administrator. He was one of the closest Companions of the Holy Prophet (Sallallahu 'alaihi wa Sallam) and possessed unparalleled courage, vigour and Faith.

Various Problems

The insurgents' shameful act of assassination of the Khalifah could never have been imagined by Hadrat Ali or any other eminent Companion at Medina. It came as a total surprise to Hadrat Ali (R.A.) whose two sons, Hasan and Hussain (R.A.) were guarding the gate of Uthman's residence. The insurgents after climbing the back wall of the residence had assassinated the Khalifah. The assassination of Hadrat Uthman was really due to creation of faction among the Muslim Community which was the goal of Abdullah Bin Saba and his followers (the insurgents), and they achieved it.

After the assassination of Hadrat Uthman, the insurgents virtually controlled the Capital, Medina for several days. The Muslims were frightened and sat behind closed doors. After the assassination of Hadrat Uthman (R.A.) an unprecedented calamity had fallen on the Muslims and for three days, Medina was without any government.

Afterwards the insurgents approached Hadrat Ali (R.A.) to be the Khalifah. Egyptians led by Ibn Saba and Ghafqi were the main group of insurgents behind the proposal for the Khilafat of Hadrat Ali (R.A.). Hadrat Ali first declined to bear the responsibility of this great office. But the insurgents pressed him to accept it. As a matter of fact Hadrat Ali wanted to approach Hadrat Talha and Hadrat Zubayr (R.A.) who were included in the panel of the six persons appointed by Hadrat Umar (R.A.) to select a Khalifah. He wanted to take pledge of loyalty (Baiat) at the hands of any of these two gentlemen. But at the end, pressed by the threats of the regicides he decided to put the matter before Muslim public in the Mosque of the Holy Prophet (Sallallahu 'alaihi wa Sallam). Most of the Companions in Medina considered him, to be the fittest person for "Khilafat" after Hadrat Uthman (R.A.). He then agreed to take the responsibility and gave his consent.

On 21st Dhul-Hijjah 35 A.H. pledge of loyalty took place at the hands of Hadrat Ali (R.A.). First of all the leading insurgents took the pledge of loyalty on his hands, followed by the general public, at Medina. Hadrat Talha and Zubayr (R.A.) did not want to take a pledge (Baiat) until the case of Hadrat Uthman assassination was decided. Before that Hadrat Ali had offered the office of Khilafat to both of them but they had declined. However under the threats of insurgents they took the pledge of loyalty at Hadrat Ali's hands, on the condition: "You (i.e. Ali) have to decide matters according to the Holy Quran and Sunnah (ways of the Holy Prophet) and would punish the guilty according to Islamic Law." Hadrat Ali (R.A.) agreed to their conditions. Hadrat Sad bin Waqqas said that he would take pledge when all the Muslims had done so. Following Companions did not take pledge at the hands of Hadrat Ali (R.A.): Muhammad bin Muslimah, Usamah bin Zaid, Hassan bin Thabit. Kaab bin Malik, Abu Said Khudri, Numan bin Bashir, Zaid bin Thabit, Mughirah bin Shubah and Abdullah bin Salam. Most of the members of Banu Umayyah (Uthman's family) also did not take pledge of loyalty at Hadrat Ali's hands. Some of such persons who did not take Baiat went to Syria.

However the majority of the Muslims in Medina took pledge at the hands of Hadrat Ali. According to "Ahli Sunnah wal Jamaah", Hadrat Ali was the most suitable and the fittest person for Khilafat after Hadrat Uthman (R.A). If some of the Companions did not take pledge on his hands, because of the political situation of that time, it did not mean that his Khilafat was not accepted by the Muslim majority. Besides Hadrat Ali (R.A.), nobody including Hadrat Muawiyyah (R.A.) claimed to be the Khalifah at that time. The difference between them was the question of punishment to the assassins, which took the shape of various battles.

As it would be seen afterwards Hadrat Amir Muawiyyah (R.A.) declared his Khilafat only after the death of Hadrat Ali (R.A.). Hadrat Ali was declared to be the Khalifah not only by the insurgents but by the Muslim public as well including the leading Ansar (Helpers) and Muhajirin (Emigrants). This could also be noticed with the fact that in the first battle which took place between Hadrat Ali and Hadrat Aishah (and her group) about 800 of those Companions who had participated in the Treaty of Hudaibiyah were with Hadrat Ali besides other Companions. As a matter of fact Hadrat Ali was the most popular figure at that time and was the most appropriate person to be the fourth caliph.

The Disobedience

On his third day as the Khalifah, Hadrat Ali asked all the Sabaites (insurgents) to return to their places. Some of them started to go back but a party headed by Abdullah bin Saba did not obey the Khalifah pretending all the while to be his friends. In the history of Islam this was the first incident of disobedience of a Khalifah. Their aim was to be with him in order to create mischief as it would be observed later.

Hadrat Ali (Radiallahu Anhu), faced a very difficult situation. His three main problems were:

(i) To establish peace in the State and to set right the deteriorating political situation.

(ii) To take action against the assassins of Hadrat Uthman (R.A.) who had gone underground after he took the office. Actually some of them were among the persons who requested Hadrat Ali (R.A.) to take office of the Khilafat, but neither he nor any other Muslim at that time knew the real assassins. It was the hardest job at that time to find out the real assassins because the persons who recognised them had already left Medina, and those among the Sabaites, who were present there did not tell Hadrat Ali the truth. All of the Sabaites told Ali (R.A.) that they did not want to assassinate Hadrat Uthman, that was done only by some of the wicked persons whom they did not recognise. Some time, therefore, was required to investigate the matter and that was possible only after peaceful atmosphere was restored in the state which, unfortunately, never occurred during the caliphate of Hadrat Ali as the situation continued to worsen.

(iii) The third problem was the attitude to be adopted towards those Companions (R.A.) who would not pledge loyalty at the hands of Hadrat Ali unless he either handed over the assassins to them or punish them according to Islamic Law. Though we cannot criticise the sincerity of their intention but in fairness to Ali. It has to be said that it was rather an impossible job for Ali (R.A.) to fulfil their demands immediately in that situation.

Hadrat Ali (R.A.) was a very straight-forward man who considered the "Khilafat" (Caliphate) as a great trust. His aim was to establish peace in the State which should be the first aim of every good ruler in such a place where certain elements try to destroy the order. According to leading Islamic Jurists it is quite right fora Muslim ruler to delay the cases of murder etc. in order to establish peace in an Islamic State (as mentioned by Qadi Abu Bakr Ibn al-Arabi in his book "Ahkam-ul-Quran"). Hadrat Ali (R.A.) was quite right in his decision to tackle the assassins on restoration of normally. The Majority of the Muslims, specially Ahli Sunnah wal-Jamaah had agreed with him on this point. The events which took place during the caliphate of Hadrat Ali in the form of various battles will be discussed in the light of the above facts.

Probe into Assassination

After assuming office, Hadrat Ali (R.A.) tried to find out the assassins of Hadrat Uthman (R.A.). He called Marwan bin al-Hakm, the chief secretary of Hadrat Uthman, who was present, in the house at the time of assassination, but he had already left for Damascus along with a number of Banu Umayyads.

The only other witness was Hadrat Nailah, wife of Hadrat Uthman (R.A.). But she was a housewife who used to live under "Hijab" (Purdah) in accordance with Islamic custom and as such she could not tell the names of the persons present at that time except the features of some of them. She could only name Muhammad bin Abu Bakr who had entered the house but as stated before he had left the house before Hadrat Uthman assassination. Moreover Muhammad bin Abu Bakr took an oath (in accordance to Islamic Law) that he was not an assassin and he had left the house as soon as Hadrat Uthman (R.A.) recognised him and said, "O my dear nephew,! if your father (Abu Bakr) were alive you would have not committed this." Hadrat Nailah gave her evidence in favour of Muhammad bin Abu Bakr and had confirmed that he was not one of the assassins. In spite of his efforts Hadrat Ali could not locate the assassins.

Dismissal of the Governors

In the opinion of Hadrat Ali (R.A.) the governors appointed by Hadrat Uthman (R.A.) were basically responsible for all the events. They did not pay much attention to check the subversive activities of the insurgents. So he dismissed all the governors appointed by Hadrat Uthman (R.A.). Some of the Companions did not agree with Hadrat Ali (R.A.) on this. Among such persons were Hadrat Mughirah bin Shubah and Hadrat Ibn Abbas (R.A.). They advised Hadrat Ali not to take such a hasty action. According to them it was not wise to dismiss them unless they pledged loyalty to Hadrat Ali, because Uthman's assassination could be an easy excuse for them to refuse the pledge of loyalty to Hadrat Ali's. Hadrat Ali did not listen to their advice because he believed that expediency should not be the guiding factor. Hadrat Mughirah bin Shubah (R.A.) was totally against Ali's action. He left Medina and went to Mecca.

He appointed Hadrat Abdullah bin Abbas as the governor of Yemen; Uthman bin Hanif as the governor of Basrah; Ammarah bin Hissan of Kufa, and Qais as the governor of Egypt. Hadrat Sahl Bin Hanif was asked to take charge of governorship of Syria from Hadrat Amir Muawiyyah (R.A.).

When the governors went to take charge they were faced with difficulties. Egypt was one of the provinces in favour of Ali (R.A.) but when the new governor, Qais reached there the public was divided in three groups. Some of them accepted him but others demanded that the assassins must be punished first. There was a third group, belonging to Sabaites and the insurgents, who demanded that the assassins must not be punished in any case. Same difficulty was faced by the newly appointed governor of Basrah. A group of people was in favour of the insurgents while the other was against them. While the governor of Kufa was on his way a spokesman of Kufis came and asked him to return to Medina because they did not want to change their governor Hadrat Musa Ashari (R.A.) in any case. So Hadrat Ammarah bin Hissan (R.A.), the governor designate, returned to Medina. The new governor of Yemen, Hadrat Abdullah bin Abbas did not face any difficulty because Yala, the old governor had already left Kufa for Mecca before Hadrat Ibn Abbas reached there. When Hadrat Sahl bin Hanif, the governor designate of Syria, reached Tabuk (the out-post of Syria), Amir Muawiyyah's cavalry men stopped him from proceeding any further and asked him to go back to Medina. Thus Kufa and Syria were the two provinces which had openly flouted Hadrat Ali's authority.

Hadrat Ali sent his special messengers to Kufa and Syria. The governor of Kufa, Hadrat Abu Musa Ashari (R.A.) sent a satisfactory reply and assured Hadrat Ali of his loyalty to him. Not only this he also wrote to him that he had already taken pledge of loyalty for him from the people of Kufa.

The case of Hadrat Muawiyyah (R.A.) was entirely different.

Hadrat Muawiyyah's Demand

After the assassination of Hadrat Uthman (R.A.) his family except his wife Nailah, reached Damascus and told Amir Muawiyyah (R.A.) the details. They also carried with them the blood stained shirt of Hadrat Uthman (R.A.) and the chopped off fingers of his wife Hadrat Nailah. Amir Muawiyyah, a kinsman of Hadrat Uthman (R.A.) was shocked on hearing the news, and when it was made public, all the Muslims of Syria were greatly perturbed. Hadrat Amir Muawiyyah (R.A.) was a great statesman and was in Syria for about 20 years. He hung the blood stained shirt and the chopped off fingers of Hadrat Uthman's wife on the "Mimber" (pulpit) of the Jami' Mosque of Damascus because of which the Syrian Muslims got inflamed. This was the situation of Syria when Sahl bin Hanif, the governor designate of Syria was forced to return to Medina from Tabuk.

On receiving the special messenger from Hadrat Ali, Amir Muawiyyah (R.A.) did not reply for about three months and detained the messenger. Then he sent his own messenger to Hadrat Ali (R.A.) in Rabiul Awwal, 36 A.H. The messenger handed over the letter to Hadrat Ali addressed as "From Muawiyyah to Ali". When the letter was opened it was a blank paper on which only "Bismilla-Hir-rahmanir Rahim "(In the name of Allah, most Gracious, most Merciful) was written. Hadrat Ali (R.A.) was amazed to see the letter, which was in fact, an insult to the office of the "Khalifah". The messenger also told Ali

(R.A.) that 50,000 sheikhs of Syria were bemoaning the death of Hadrat Uthman and were determined to fight until the assassins were handed over to them. Hadrat Ali replied, "O Allah! You know it well that I am free from any charge of Uthman's assassination. I swear by Allah that the assassins have escaped."

The Sabaites pretending to be friends of Hadrat Ali, tried to create another disturbance by trying to kill the messenger, but Hadrat Ali (R.A.) did not allow it. However exchange of hot words took place between them and the messenger.

Amir Muawiyyah's reply was a clear indication of his intention. The matter was not going to be settled without force. Therefore Hadrat Ali decided to use force against Muawiyyah (R.A.) and started preparations for it. Hadrat Ali's elder son, Imam Hasan (R.A.) was a man of rather mild temper. He requested his father to give up the Khilafa and not to think of fighting against Muslims (i.e., to start; civil war). But there was no other way and Hadrat Ali (Rad A.) had to handle the situation with an iron hand in order tot keep the provinces under the centre as they were since the time of Hadrat Abu Bakr (R.A.).

This was the first time in the history of Islam when the Muslims were preparing to fight against each other. As a Khalifah Hadrat Ali was quite right in his decision. Not to pledge loyalty was an open revolt against his authority and he had to deal boldly with any type of internal rebellion. Hadrat Amir Muawiyyah (R.A.), as a matter of fact, was over-excited on the tragic assassination. The family of Uthman (R.A.) which had reached there after the assassination was also a cause of this attitude. Moreover some of the Sabaites, whose only aim was to divide the Muslim community had reached Syria and incited the Muslims against Hadrat Ali. They were playing double role. On the one side a group of them was with Hadrat Ali (R.A.) to stir him up against Muawiyyah'.; (R.A.), while on the other side some of them went to Syria only to inflame the feelings of Muslims over there. Under such conditions Muawiyyah (R.A.) had no alternative but to insist upon his demand for punishment of the assassins before pledging loyalty to Hadrat Ali (R.A.).

Hadrat Aishah's Demand

While Hadrat Ali (R.A.) was preparing for war against Amir Muawiyyah another difficulty arose. After the assassination of Hadrat Uthman (R.A.) some members of his family went to Hadrat Aishah (R.A.) who was in Mecca to perform the Hajj. They and a number of Medinites informed her about the tragedy while she was on her way from Mecca to Medina after the Hajj. Hearing the news of assassination of Hadrat Uthman she returned to Mecca and appealed to the people over there to avenge the death of Hadrat Uthman (R.A.). Hundreds of people including the governor of Mecca came out at Hadrat Aishah's call. The governor of Yemen, Yala bin Munabbah also joined her in

Mecca. Among Banu Ummayyads who joined Hadrat Aishah in Mecca were Said bin As, Walid bin Uqbah and Marwan bin Hakam.

In the meantime Hadrat Talha and Zubayr (R.A.) demanded Hadrat Ali to punish the assassins. He told them, "Please wait. I will do my duty as soon as conditions allow me." Hadrat Talha and Zubayr were not satisfied with Hadrat Ali's reply and left Medina for Mecca to join Hadrat Aishah (R.A.). They had not correctly assessed the delicate situation in Medina. The city was not free from the grip of Sabaites and there was a general feeling against Umayyads in the public. Hadrat Ali (R.A.) was anxious to restore peace first so that the assassins could be punished.

In Mecca Hadrat Aishah (R.A.) started to march to Medina at the head of about two thousand men with the object of dealing with the assassins. Hadrat Abdullah bin Zubayr was also there. They also asked him to join but he declined to do so and remained neutral.

When Hadrat Aishah was about to march to Medina, proposals came to visit Basrah first to collect more supporters. She decided to go to Basrah.

Hadrat Aishah to Basrah

While Hadrat Aishah was on her way to Basrah more people joined her in the way. By the time she reached Basrah, there were three thousand men under her flag.

The governor of Basrah, Uthman bin Hanif (appointed by Hadrat Ali), sent some men to find out the object of her visit. She and other Muslims told them that they wanted to tell people of their duty towards the late Khalifah so that proper action would be taken to punish the assassins. The messenger of the governor asked Hadrat Talha and Zubayr for what reason they were breaking the Baiat on the hands of Hadrat Ali. They told them that the pledge (Baiat) was taken from them at the point of sword, and that they would have kept the pledge if Hadrat Ali had avenged Uthman's assassination. The governor of Basra decided not to allow them to enter the city till he got help from Hadrat Ali. He called a public meeting and asked people to fight against them. In the meeting some people favoured the governor while some of them supported Hadrat Aishah, Talha and Zubayr. The supporters of Hadrat Ali (R.A.) and the governor came out to fight.

Takeover of Basra

Hadrat Aishah gave a stirring speech before the Muslims. It was so impressive that half of the supporters of the governor left him and joined Hadrat Aishah. Seeing this she tried to settle the matter peacefully instead of fighting. But there were some agents of Abdullah bin Saba (Sabaites) specially his famous disciple, Hakim bin Hublah, who did not allow any settlement. He attacked Hadrat Aishah's army before the governor gave him permission to do so.

The fight took place but no result came out till the evening. In the meantime the governor got instructions from Hadrat Ali to resist Hadrat Aishah's army if they did not agree to pledge loyalty to him. Then a furious battle took place in which Uthman bin Hanif, the governor, was defeated and captured Hakim bin Hublah and some of his followers were killed, and Basra was occupied by Hadrat Aishah and her supporters.

Civil War

March to Basrah : The capture of Basrah by Hadrat Aishah (R.A.) made the situation very grave. The Islamic state was really on the verge of serious civil war. Hadrat Ali (R.A.) never wanted to start war against the Muslims but the internal situation at that time compelled him to do so. War was unavoidable.

The Khalifah, therefore, postponed his march to Syria for the time being in order to set things right in Iraq. He decided to march on to Basrah. A number of Ansar and other Companions were not in favour of Hadrat Ali (R.A.) 'leaving Medina, instead they asked him to send his army. When Hadrat Ali (R.A.) was leaving Medina, Abdullah bin Salam (R.A.) took hold of his camel and said, "O Amir-ul-Muminin (Leader of the believers) don't leave Medina. If you leave it at this moment, you would never come back and the Capital would be changed." But he decided to go ahead with his mission because of the seriousness of the situation.

Some of the Companions remained neutral and did not join Hadrat Ali (R.A.) even though he asked them to do so. Among such persons were: Abdullah bin Umar, Muhammad bin Muslimah, Sad bin Waqqas and Usamah bin Zaid (R.A.)

Hadrat Ali started for Basrah towards the end of Rabiul-Awwal, 36 (A. U.) *i.e.* Nov. 656 A. D.' Abdullah bin Saba and his followers were accompanying Hadrat Ali.

Help from Basrah : Hadrat Ali (R.A.) asked Abu Musa Ashari to send help but he got no response because Hadrat Abu Musa (R.A.) dreaded a civil war. Therefore Hadrat Ali (R.A.) sent his eldest son, Hasan (R.A.) to Kufa who addressed the people and pleaded for Ali (R.A.). The people were stirred on the appeal and about nine thousand men marched on to join Ali (R.A.).

Peace Sought

Hadrat Ali (R.A.) assured all the people accompanying him that he would try his best to avoid blood-shed and to set the things right peacefully. On reaching Dhi Qara place near Basrah, Hadrat Ali, with his characteristic aversion to blood-shed sent his cousin

Abdullah bin Abbas and Qaqa bin Amr (R.A.) to negotiate peacefully with Hadrat Aishah, Talha, and Zubayr (Rid. A.) who were preparing to face Hadrat Ali (R.A.) with a big army.

The messengers of Hadrat Ali (R.A.) assured Hadrat Aishah, Talha, and Zubayr (Rid. A.) that Hadrat Ali would avenge the assassins of Hadrat Uthman (R.A.) as soon as peace was established in the state. Hearing this they were satisfied and there were hopes for a peaceful settlement.

But in the army of Ali (R.A.) there were Abdullah bin Saba and his henchmen to whom peace was fatal. At the possibility of peaceful settlement they were much disturbed. They met in a secret council and whispered to each other that Ali (R.A.) was prepared to avenge the death of Hadrat Uthman (R.A.). They were determined to make the peaceful settlement a total failure. They sent their agents to Basrah to incite the Muslims population by saying that if Ali (R.A.) entered Basrah he would enslave all the inhabitants and would kill all the youths. The Basrites, therefore, must check and fight him back.

Hadrat Ali (R.A.) hoping for a peaceful settlement, marched towards Basrah to talk personally with Hadrat Talha and Zubayr (R.A.). The two armies were facing each other. Hadrat Ali gave an address to Basrites in which he said, "I am but your brother........I will avenge Uthman's assassins,"

Hadrat Talha, Zubayr and Basrites were fully satisfied with what Hadrat Ali (R.A.) told them. Ali (R.A.) also returned to his camp very satisfied. He gave strict orders to his men not to fight in any case, and prayed all the night to Allah.

But Ibn Saba and his henchmen had planned otherwise. In the darkness of night they made a sudden attack on Hadrat Aishah's army. Hadrat Talha and Zubayr were startled by the sudden attack and said that Ali (R.A.) could not desist from shedding Muslim blood and he has ordered a night attack. On the other hand Hadrat Ali (R.A.) was shocked when he was told by Sabaites that Talha and Zubayr had taken them by surprise. He also remarked in the same way that they did not stop from taking the blood of Muslims. According to Tabari the following Sabaites were the leaders behind this plan: Ashtar Nakhi Ibn Sauda, Khalid bin Muljam, Alba bin Haitham and Shuraib bin Aufa. Ibn Saba was the ring leader.

Battle of Camel

Soon a full scale war started. Hundreds of Muslims fell on each side. Hadrat Ali (R.A.) was greatly pained at the situation. He tried to stop the battle but the battle had already flared up.

In the dawn the troops of Hadrat Aishah (R.A.) apprised her of the situation and suggested that she should mount on a camel in Hijab (Purdah) so that the situation might ease. But it worked the other way and Basrites thought that Hadrat Aishah came in the field to fight with them. During the fight Hadrat Ali reminded Talha and Zubayr (R.A.) the words of the Holy Prophet: "One day you (Talha and Zubayr) will fight Ali wrongly." They remembered the saying and left the battlefield but when Talha was leaving the field somebody rained arrows on him and he was killed.

When the fight did not come to an end Hadrat Ali (R.A.) ordered one of his men to cut the hind legs of the camel on which Hadrat Aishah was mounting in a "howdah". The order of Hadrat Ali was carried out and the camel fell on its forelegs. Hadrat Aishah was taken out of the "howdah" with due respect. The battle came to an end in favour of Hadrat Ali (R.A.). Hadrat Aishah (R.A.) was sent with due respect to Medina escorted by her own brother, Muhammad bin Abu Bakr. In this battle about ten thousand Muslims on both sides lost their lives. Hadrat Ali (R.A.) felt deeply moved because of the loss of Muslim blood. Hadrat Zubayr who had already left the field after remembering the Holy Prophet's saying was going to Mecca. He stopped in a valley to perform his Salat, but was slain by a man, named Amr bin Jarmoz while he was busy in his Salat. When Hadrat Ali came to know, he rebuked the murderer by saying: "I have seen him fight for the Prophet of Allah several times. I give the murderer the news of hell-fire."

After the battle he took pledge of loyalty from the people of Basrah and appointed Hadrat Abdullah bin Abbas as the governor of Basrah. He gave general amnesty to all those who fought against him including Marwan bin Hakam and other persons of Banu Umayyah family. The address which Hadrat Ali (R.A.) gave at Jami Mosque of Basrah before the Baiat (pledge of loyalty) moved the Muslims, and they were convinced that Ali (R.A.) was a just Khalifah.

Change of Capital

Hadrat Ali (R.A.) was very much grieved on seeing the disrespect of the "Haram" (Forbidden Place) of Medina when the insurgents laid siege to the late Khalifah's house and then assassinated him. He wanted to change the Capital to save Medina from future political disturbance. After staying for a few days at Basrah, Hadrat Ali (R.A.) went to Kufa. There he was given a warm welcome. He got more supporters at Kufa and thought it to be a more suitable place as the Capital of his Khilafat. Therefore in Rajab 36 A.H., he decided to transfer the capital from Medina to Kufa.

Hadrat Ali's Final Invitation to Hadrat Muawiyyah : Hadrat Ali (R.A.) now turned his attention towards Hadrat Muawiyyah (R.A.). He was then ruling over the whole Islamic State with the exception of Syria. The peace-minded Hadrat Ali (R.A.) wanted a peaceful settlement. He, therefore, wrote a letter to Hadrat Muawiyyah (R.A.) asking him to take pledge of loyalty at his hand in the interest of Islam and the unity of the Muslims. But Hadrat Muawiyyah again demanded of him to avenge Hadrat Uthman's assassins first.

The show of Hadrat Uthman's blood-stained shirt and the chopped-off fingers of his wife, Hadrat Nailah, was still going on in the Jami' Masjid of Damascus. The powerful Syrians had rallied round Hadrat Muawiyyah. On the other hand Hadrat Ali (R.A.) was still unable to overcome the insurgents. When Hadrat Amir Muawiyyah's messenger came to Hadrat Ali to put the demand to hand over the assassins, 10,000 men of Hadrat Ali's army said with one voice: "All of us are the assassins of Uthman (R.A.)." Hadrat Ali (R.A.) then said to the messengers, Hadrat Muslimah, "You can see for yourself the situation. I am still unable to find out the real assassins." But Hadrat Muawiyyah was determined not to give up his demand. Hadrat Ali (R.A.) finding no other way, was compelled to declare war against Hadrat Muawiyyah (R.A.).

Battle of Siffin : The above situation forced Hadrat Ali (R.A.) to march out against Syria. In the beginning there was not much response for Hadrat Ali's call. But when Hadrat Ali explained the position to the Muslims, a large army gathered around Hadrat Ali and 50,000 Muslims came out under his banner to fight the Syrians. When Muawiyyah (R.A.) came to know about Hadrat Ali's advance, he too proceeded with a vast army and occupied a better position in the field. Hadrat Ali (R.A.) encamped at Siffin, and Amir Muawiyyah on the other side of Siffin.

Hadrat Ali's intention was not to shed Muslim blood in vain. He therefore again tried and sent a deputation of three men on peace mission to Amir Muawiyyah (R.A.). Amir Muawiyyah (R.A.) again demanded that the assassins of Hadrat Uthman must be slain before any compromise can be reached and that he was demanding this as a "Wali" (next of kin of a murdered person) of Hadrat Uthman. The demand was again refused by Hadrat Ali (R.A.) on the ground that he was not able to locate the real assassins and it would need some time, and that the Pledge of Loyalty must be taken without any condition.

In the month of Dhul Hijjah 36 A.H., Hadrat Ali (R.A.) ordered his troops to take positions. But there seemed unwillingness to fight on both the sides. Muslims were facing Muslims. However in the beginning fighting began with single combats followed by light encounters of single battalions. Thus the whole month of Dhul Hijjah ended without any big fight. When the moon of Muharram appeared Hadrat Ali and Muawiyyah made a truce for one month. During this time he again got an opportunity for renewed peace talks. Hadrat Ali (R.A.) sent another mission led by Adi bin Hatim Tai to Amir Muawiyyah (R.A.). But this time Amir Muawiyyah (Rad. A) took it as a threat and refused to recognize

Hadrat Ali (R.A.) as the Khalifah unless he avenged Hadrat Uthman's assassination. In this way the last attempt proved to be fruitless.

On the evening of the last day of Muharram, 37 A.H. Hadrat Ali (R.A.) gave orders to his army to attack the Syrian forces because they had been given enough time to think. The war started the following morning. Hadrat Ali (R.A.) gave strict orders that no person should be killed if he left the field or ran away. Women and old people would be secure. Hadrat Amir Muawiyyah (R.A.) also gave the same order to his army.

The war started on Tuesday Ist Safar, 37 A.H. On the first day a battalion of Hadrat Ali's army, led by Ushtar fought with the Syrians led by Ḥabib bin Muslimah. On the second day another battalion led by Hashim bin Utbah from Hadrat Ali's side fought with the Syrians led by Abul Awar Salama. On the third day the battalion from Hadrat Ali side was led by Hadrat Ammar bin Yasir and the Syrians were led by Amr bin As (R.A.). During the battle Hadrat Ammar bin Yasir (R.A.) was martyred but no result came out. The martyrdom of Hadrat Ammar bin Yasir, however, proved that Hadrat Ali (R.A.) was right because of the following Hadith mentioned in Bukhari, Muslim, Tirmidhi and other authentic books of Hadith: According to this Hadith the Holy "Prophet (Sallallahu 'alaihi wa Sallam) said, "Ammar bin Yasir would be killed by a group of rebels." Since Hadrat Ammar (R.A.) was fighting in favour of Hadrat Ali, and was killed by the army of Hadrat Amir Muawiyyah (R.A.) Hadrat Ali (R.A.) was in the right and his opponents were the rebels.

For seven days the battle continued in this way. A new battalion used to fight from each side under a new commander. On the 8th day the whole army of Hadrat Ali (R.A.) clashed with that of Amir Muawiyyah (R.A.). A fierce battle was fought but with no end in sight. According to most of the historians, Hadrat Ammar bin Yasir was martyred on that day. However no result came out till the evening. The death of Hadrat Ammar bin Yasir was a shock to Hadrat Ali (R.A.). The battle went on the whole night. At one time Hadrat Ali reached the tent of Hadrat Muawiyyah and challenged him to fight personally with him instead of shedding Muslim blood, the winner would be the Khalifah. But Hadrat Muawiyyah (R.A.) did not accept the challenge because Hadrat Ali was a noted warrior of Arabia.

On the second day of the battle Amir Muawiyyah (R.A.) was about to lose the battle. But, Amir Muawiyyah was a shrewd person and had been the governor of Syria from Hadrat Umar's time. He had with him Hadrat Amr bin As (R.A.), the conqueror of Egypt and a recognised statesman of Arabia. Seeing the impending defeat he consulted Hadrat Amr bin As (R.A.) who advised Amir Muawiyyah to give orders to the troops of the front ranks to fasten the Holy Quran to their lances as a sign that war would cease and that the decision would be referred to the Holy Book.

Seeing copies of the Holy Quran on lances, Hadrat Ali (R.A.) recognised it as a clever move of the enemy but a good many men of his army did not share his view and stopped fighting. Being helpless he ordered his troops to stop fighting.

The Arbitration : Hadrat' Ali (R.A.) sent his envoy to Hadrat Muawiyyah (R.A.) to find out what he meant by making the Holy Quran a judge. Hadrat Amir Muawiyyah told him that he wanted an arbitration through judges, one from his side and the other from Hadrat Ali's side, and that both the parties should abide by the decision of the judge. Hadrat Ali accepted it. He tried to make Hadrat Abdullah bin Abbas as the arbitrator from his side, but some of his followers objected to it on the ground that he was related to Hadrat Ali. They proposed the name of Hadrat Musa Ashari (R.A.). Hadrat Ali accepted their proposal and he was appointed as the arbitrator of Ali's (R.A.) side. Hadrat Muawiyyah appointed Amr bin As (R.A.) as the arbitrator from his side, and none of his followers questioned his choice although he was related to Amir Muawiyyah. This shows that the followers of Hadrat Muawiyyah were more united than the followers of Hadrat Ali. There were many Sabaites in Hadrat Ali's camp and they were the real cause of such differences. Whenever they saw the Muslims uniting they tried to create confusion with the aim of disuniting them.

In case the two arbitrators could not come to an agreement, the decision was to lie with eight hundred men (four hundred from Hadrat Ali's camp and four hundred from Hadrat Muawiyyah camp) and it would be settled by the majority. A place named Daumatul-Jandal, in between Syria and Iraq, was proposed for the talks. Both the judges with 800 would go there to finalise their award by the month of Ramadan, and to make it public. A temporary agreement was signed on 13th Safar, 37 A.H. between Hadrat Ali and Hadrat Muawiyyah. The two armies then left for their homes leaving about 90,000 men dead in the field of Siffin, which number exceeded the total Muslim casualties in all the Islamic battles against the non-Muslims by the time.

"Khawarij" or Dissenters : Hadrat Ali (R.A.) who was almost winning the battle against Amir Muawiyyah (R.A.) marched back from Siffin with a sense of loss. There was a tremendous loss of Muslim lives in Siffin. Never before in the history of Islam had the loss of Muslim blood been so heavy. Hadrat Ali after all wanted a peaceful solution, although the price was heavy.

When Hadrat Ali announced the agreement before his troops, formed of various tribes. Two brothers of the Tribe of Anza stood up and opposed appointment of Arbitrator ("Hakam" or Judge) between the two parties for Allah's commandments were with them in the form of the Holy Quran which is the best "Hakam". Other people also followed this example and a good many people were against the arbitration. According to them the Arbitration was against the spirit of Islam. Some of these men requested Hadrat Ali to throw away the agreement but he said, "I did not want any agreement at that stage but you forced me to do so. When I gave my word of honour, you are forcing me to give them up. I would never do it." The followers of Hadrat Ali split into two groups. One group stood by the agreement while for the other the arbitration was un-Islamic.

The second group, which was opposing arbitration, was known as Kharijites ("Khawarij" in Arabic). By the time Hadrat Ali returned to Kufa, their number reached 12,000. They did not stay with other Muslims in Kufa; instead, they encamped at Harorah and appointed Sheith bin Rabii as their commander-in-chief, and Abdullah bin Kawa as their Imam to lead Salats. They announced their policy which was as follows:

> "The Baiat (Pledge of Loyalty) is only for Allah, and He alone is to be obeyed. To spread good and forbid evil according to the Holy Quran and the Sunnah is our foremost duty. There exists neither a Khalifah nor an Amir. Both Ali and Muawiyyah are in error. Muawiyyah in error because he did not accept Ali while Ali is in error because he agreed on arbitration. After gaining power, we will set up a social order based on Allah's Book (i.e. the Holy Quran)."

After returning to Kufa Hadrat Ali sent Abdullah bin Abbas to remove the misunderstanding of the Khawarij (Dissenters). Instead of returning to the right belief, they started a lengthy argument with him. Seeing this Hadrat Ali himself went to them. He gave them all the assurances that the arbitration would only be accepted if it was based upon the Holy Quran and the Sunnah. He was successful in his efforts after a great difficulty, and the "Khawarij" joined him again temporarily.

Verdict of the Arbitrators : The two arbitrators thought over the matter for six months then met at the frontier town of Dumat-ul-Jandal in Shaban, 37 A.H. (Jan. 658). Each of them was having four hundred men with him. The commander of men from Hadrat Ali's side was Shuraih bin Hani, and the Imam Hadrat Abdullah bin Abbas. The four hundred men from Muawiyyah's camp were under Surjil bin Samah. Besides these some neutral Companions like Abdullah bin Umar, Abdullah bin Zubayr, and Sad bin Waqqas were also present there.

Hadrat Amr bin As, the judge appointed by Hadrat Muawiyyah, was a famous statesman and diplomat of Arabia. On the other hand Abu Musa Ashari, the judge from Hadrat Ali's side, was a simple Muslim, unacquainted with diplomatic tactics. In the beginning a discussion between the two judges took place. A scribe was ordered to write down the points of agreement during the discussion. They reached on the following agreement after a long discussion:

> "Ali and Muawiyyah both withdraw their right for the Khilafat. The Muslims should appoint a third person as their Khalifah."

According to some historians the discussion was not recorded and the agreement was reached verbally. However they could not reach an agreement on the choice of the most suitable person to be approved as the Khalifah in place of Hadrat Ali or Hadrat Muawiyyah.

After the agreement Hadrat Amr bin As asked Hadrat Abu. Musa Ashari to make it public by announcing it in the mosque before the Muslims. Hadrat Abu Musa (R.A.) announced: "We have agreed that neither Ali nor Muawiyyah would be considered as the Khalifah. You may elect any other man you think fit." After this Hadrat Amr bin As (R.A.) stood up and said, "I do not consider Ali fit for the Khilafat, but in my opinion Muawiyyah is fit for it." The statement of Hadrat Amr not only showed the split of opinion between the Arbitrators but also meant one sided decision according to which Hadrat Ali (R.A.) was supposed to lose his power but not Amir Muawiyyah (R.A.).

Hearing the statement of Amr ibn As (R.A.) there was a big uproar. The result of the arbitration was a mere confusion. In this way the arbitration proved to be a futile and the hopes of peace were gone. Both the parties left the place in great disgust. The acceptance of such arbitration, really proved to be disastrous to Ali. Hadrat Ali lost the case before it opened.

When Ali (R.A.) heard the result of the arbitration he said, "The judgement is not based upon the Holy Quran and the Sunnah which was the condition for arbitration. Therefore it cannot be accepted." He then delivered a lecture in the Jami' Masjid of Kufa and asked the Muslims to prepare to attack Syria.

Split in Community

As soon as the "Khawarij" knew the result of arbitration they again separated and this time rose in an open revolt. A new group was thus created in the history of Islam which proved to be more dangerous than any other group existing before then.

As it has been discussed in connection with the assassination of Hadrat Uthman (R.A.), the Muslim community was divided into four main groups viz, Uthmanis, Shian-i-Ali, Marhabah and Ahl al-Sunnah wal Jamaah. Marhab is were absorbed in other groups. The remaining three groups were still existing. Now the fourth group of Kharijites ("Khawarij") was formed. Before proceeding further let us see the main beliefs of these groups.

Uthmanis: They were now confined to Syria under the banner of Amir Muawiyyah (R.A.). They demanded that until the assassins of Hadrat Uthman were punished or handed over to them, they would not accept the Khilafat of Hadrat Ali. But after the so called judgment of the arbitrators, they totally rejected the Khilafat of Hadrat Ali and took Baiat (Pledge of Loyalty) at the hand of Amir Muawiyyah after declaring him as the Khalifah. It would be discussed in more detail later on.

Shian-i-Ali (or Shia's): They called themselves as the friends of Ali (R.A.) in the beginning but later on they developed their own beliefs and considered Hadrat Ali as "Wasi" i.e. Administrator of the Holy Prophet (Sallallahu 'alaihi wa Sallam), and the only fit person for the Khilafat. They not only criticised and condemned Amir Muawiyyah (R.A.) but also Umar, Abu Bakr, and Uthman (R.A.) and discarded the authority of the first three Khalifahs. However they did not criticise the first two Khalifahs openly during the time of Hadrat Aii (R.A.). As years passed this group became an exponent of a separate school of thought in Islamic Law and Jurisprudence and they wrote their own books of Hadith, History of Islam and Commentaries of the Holy Quran based upon their beliefs. They disagreed with most of the works produced by Sunni Scholars.

Ahl-i-Sunnah wal-Jamaah: The majority of the Companions, and Muslims at the time were not only in favour of Hadrat Ali but all the preceding Khalifahs i.e. Abu Bakr, Umar and Uthman (Rid. A.). They believed that the "Right Path" was to follow the Sunnah of the Holy Prophet (Sallallahu 'alaihi wa Sallam) and the traditions of his pious Jamaah (i.e. all the Companions), especially the first four Khalifahs who set examples to solve various problems according to the Holy Quran and the Sunnah. This group was in great majority not only at that time but in all the periods of Islamic History.

They fully supported Hadrat Ali (R.A.) during his Khilafat. According to them Amir Muawiyyah (R.A.) was not right in not accepting Hadrat Ali authority. But they considered that mistake based upon "Ijtihad". After all, he was a pious Companion and the sincerity of a Companion must not be questioned. Hadrat Shah Waliullah, in his famous book, halat-ul-Khafa writes: Amir Muawiyyah (R.A.) was an excellent Companion of the Holy Prophet (Sallallahu 'alaihi wa Sallam). Do not criticise or condemn him otherwise you would be committing a "Haram" (unlawful) act because in a Hadith the Holy Prophet (Sallallahu 'alaihi wa Sallam) said: Do not criticise and condemn my Companions. I swear by Allah, Who holds my life, gold equal to mountain Uhud, spent by you for the sake of Allah, cannot be equal even to the handful of grains spent by a Companion. (Abu Daud). According to a number of A Hadith, it is forbidden for a Muslim to criticise a Companion. In a number of A Hadith the virtues of Hadrat Muawiyyah (R.A.) have been mentioned. Once the Holy Prophet (Sallallahu 'alaihi wa Sallam) prayed for Amir Muawiyyah as follows: "O Allah!, make him a Muslim who would be on Your Guidance and such a Muslim who may guide others." Ibn Sad says that the Holy Prophet (Sallallahu 'alaihi wa Sallam) prayed for Amir Muawiyyah as follows: "O Allah!, give him the knowledge of the Book (i.e., the Holy Quran) and make him ruler (king) of the countries, and save him from the punishment (of the Hereafter)." Moreover Amir Muawiyyah (R.A.) was one of the scribes of the Revelation (i.e., the Holy Quran) during the time of the Holy Prophet. It is necessary, therefore, that we must not question his sincerity. Due to political conditions at that time, he was strict in his demand of chastisement of the assassins of Hadrat Uthman (R.A.). Most of the historians agree on this point that he did not declare himself a Khalifah during the life of Hadrat Ali although people took Baiat on his hand.

The "Khawarij", : The Khawarij were more a political group than theological. They accepted the authority of Hadrat Abu Bakr and Umar (R.A.) but denounced Hadrat Uthman, Ali, and Muawiyyah (Rid. A.). They said that the "Hakam" (Arbitrator or Judge for the dispute between Hadrat Ali and Muawiyyah) was against the principles of Islam. Only Allah! had to be obeyed through the Holy Quran and not the Hakam. They also formulated a number of other beliefs as well. In the later period of Islamic history this group became almost extinct.

Kharijite Trouble

The "Khawarij" set up their centre at Nahrwan and began to preach their cult. Many people gathered around them and they gained sufficient strength. They were very harsh to those who differed from them and regarded such muslims as rebels against Islam and murdered them. Loyalty to the Khalifah was a great crime in their eyes and they called it "the cult of personality".

The Kharijites seemed to be very pious as far as their appearance was concerned. They used to offer long Salats wore simple dress and were honest in their dealings. But they were misguided in beliefs and killed all those who said that they were the followers of the Khalifah.

After the failure of arbitration Hadrat Ali (R.A.) wanted to march to Syria but the Kharijite movement diverted his attention. It was a great danger not only to the Muslim-unity but to the Islamic beliefs and practices as a whole. It was an urgent need to wipe out such a movement in its early stage. Therefore he set out for Nahrwan, the centre of "Khawarij" instead of Syria.

Reaching there Hadrat Ali tried to negotiate with them peacefully. He sent some prominent Companions to persuade Khariji leaders but they did not listen to them. Then Hadrat Ali asked them to hand over such people who have murdered innocent Muslims. He told them that he would leave the rest if they handed over the murderers. To this he replied to the Khalifah, "All of us are murderers and we want to murder all of your followers. We would never stop from this."

The stage reached when there was no other way than to fight with them. Before declaring war against them Hadrat Ali declared that those who would be loyal to him or those who left Nahrwan and did not fight would be given amnesty. On his appeal 3000 Kharijites repented and again took Baiat at his hands. The rest did not move from their position.

The battle began. A fierce fight took place. Kharijites fought desperately but were defeated. Most of their leaders were slain. After the battle Hadrat Ali searched the slain body of the man about whom the Holy Prophet had prophesied, and had given some of the signs which were, really the forecast of Kharijite trouble. Hadrat Ali (R.A.) found the body with all the signs told by the Holy Prophet (Sallallahu 'alaihi wa Sallam) and remarked, "The Holy Prophet was very true in his prophecy."

Unwillingness to March to Syria : After the battle at Nahrwan Hadrat Ali (R.A.) wanted to march on to Syria but his men were in no mood for that. They asked for some rest when he was encamping at Nakhila, some miles away from the Capital. Hadrat Ali (R.A.) allowed them to take some rest over there but they started to slip away to their homes, and only a few of them were left with him. Seeing the situation Hadrat Ali was also forced to return to Kufa.

After some time Hadrat Ali again asked the Kufis to march on to Syria. He gave a stirring address in the Jami Masjid of the Capital but the leaders of Kufa did not show any inclination. Despite many efforts Hadrat Ali was not successful in raising another army against the Syrians.

Fall of Egypt : Hadrat Ali (R.A.) appointed Qais bin Sad (R.A.) as the governor of Egypt. He took pledge of loyalty from the Egyptians for Hadrat Ali (R.A.). The inhabitants of the town of Khartaba were not loyal to Hadrat Ali. He left them alone on the condition of a peaceful conduct. Some friends of Hadrat Ali, who were having an eye on the governorship of Egypt, started to doubt loyalty of Qais to Hadrat Ali. They told Hadrat Ali that Qais was more sympathetic to Hadrat Muawiyyah and must be sacked.

When Hadrat Muawiyyah noticed that ,the position of Qais was doubtful in the eyes of Hadrat Ali, he declared him as his man. Hearing this Hadrat Ali (R.A.) dismissed him and appointed Muhammad bin Abu Bakr as the governor of Egypt. Muhammad bin Abu Bakr was a young man and was not able to control the Egyptians in a tactful way. He forced the people of Khartaba to pledge loyalty for Hadrat Ali and remained busy with them for a long time. In the meantime the battle of Siffin took place but he was so busy with the internal affairs of Egypt that he could not send any army to help Hadrat Ali (R.A.).

After the battle of Siffin Hadrat Ali appointed Malik bin Ushtar as the governor of Egypt. Ibn Ushtar was a strong man, but he could not join his duty and passed away in the way. Muhammad bin Abu Bakr, therefore, continued as the governor of Egypt.

After the award of the arbitration, the Syrians declared Hadrat Muawiyyah as their Khalifah and took Baiat on his hands. According to a number of historians, Amir Muawiyyah did not declare himself as the Khalifah during the life of Hadrat Ali (R.A.).

However he tried to extend his control over the Islamic state after the award. The first step was to send his army under the command of Hadrat Amr ibn As to attack Egypt. Muhammad bin Abu Bakr, the governor of Egypt wrote to Hadrat Ali for help. But before he got any help Amr ibn As (R.A.) reached Egypt with six thousand men. Ten thousand inhabitants of Khartaba also joined his army. They easily beat back two thousand men of Muhammad bin Abu Bakr. He himself took shelter in a house but was caught and slain. In 38 A.H. Hadrat Amir Muawiyyah (R.A.) became the master of Egypt. He appointed Hadrat Amir ibn As as the governor.

Unrest in Basrah and Iran

Hadrat Abdullah ibn Abbas (R.A.) was the governor of Basrah controlling the whole of Persia and other parts of the Islamic State in the East. Basrites were pro-Ali but there were Uthman (pro-Muawiyyah) elements as well over there. In 38 A.H. Hadrat Abdullah ibn Abbas went to Kufa to pay a visit to the Khalifah. Abdullah ibn Hadrami, an Uthman (pro-Muawiyyah) was in Basrah in those days. In the absence of Ibn Abbas he saw his chance and incited the people to avenge the assassination of Hadrat Uthman. He got support and was able to raise an army which invaded Basrah. The governor's deputy, Ziyad ibn Abu Sufyan, could not face him and fled. Hearing the rising Hadrat Ali sent Jariah ibn Qudamah who belonged to Bani Tamim tribe. He went to Basrah with fifty people and negotiated with Basrites, most of whom were from Bani Tamim tribe. He was successful in his mission and the rebellion was put down. Ibn Hadrami and seventy of his followers shut themselves in a house which was burnt by pro-Ali Basrites.

When the people of Eastern Persia and Kirman heard the burning of Ibn Hadrami they refused to pay Kharaj Revenue in protest. However their rising was put down by police action.

After consulting with Abdullah ibn Abbas (R.A.), Hadrat Ali appointed Ziyad ibn Abu Sufyan as the governor of Basrah to control Persia and other Eastern parts of the State.

After the award, Uthmanis tried to create general unrest in the country. During the year 39 A.H. strong parties were set out from Syria. Hadrat Ali (R.A.) tried to stir his friends in Kufa but they would never come out at Ali's call. Neither they were prepared to fight the Syrians again nor they tried seriously to check the invading parties of Uthman is.

One of such parties went to Ain al-tamr under the command of Numan ibn Bashir but he was defeated by Ali's governor, Malik ibn Kaaba. Another party of six thousand men under Sufyan ibn Auf went to Ambar and Madain (Medina).

They killed the officer incharge of Ambar. Hadrat Ali sent Said ibn' Auf with an army but they ran away. Another party of three thousand men under Dahak ibn Qais came as far east as the neighbourhood of Basrah. Hadrat Ali sent four thousand men under Hajar ibn Adi. A fight took place in which 19 Syrians (Uthmanis) were killed. Rest of them ran away in the darkness of the night.

In the same year (i.e., 39 A.H.) Hadrat Ali sent his deputy ibn Abbas, to lead Hajj. Amir Muawiyyah also sent his deputy, Yazid ibn Sanjar to lead the Hajj. A tussle between the two men took place. At the end it was settled that a third person, Shaibah ibn Uthman ibn Abu Talha, would lead the Hajj. In this way Hadrat Ali lost this symbol of Khilafat as well.

Hadrat Ali's hold weakened day by day. His most effective and eloquent speeches could not arouse his friends to action. Each day that passed witnessed the Khalifah growing more and more helpless.

A number of other incidents between pro-Muawiyyans and pro-Alis also took place in the same year the details of which are ignored here.

Attacks on Hijaz and Yemen

Hijaz and Yemen were still under the control of Hadrat Ali (R.A.). In the year 40 A.H., Amir Muawiyyah sent Busr ibn Abu Artat with three thousand men to Hijaz. First of all he went to Medina. The governor of Medina, Abu Ayub was not able to check the Syrians and he left for Kufa. Busr took pledge of loyalty from the Medinites forcibly for Amir Muawiyyah (R.A.), and exclaimed, "Had Muawiyyah not forbidden me, I would not have left a single adult in Medina alive."

After taking over Medina, Busr reached Mecca and occupied it unopposed. There too he took the pledge of loyalty from the Meccans for Amir Muawiyyah forcibly.

From Mecca Busr went to Yemen : At that time Hadrat Ubaidullah ibn Abbas was the governor of Yemen. Hearing of the Syrian army he fled to Kufa. Busr occupied Sana, the capital of Yemen and killed two little sons of Ubaidullah. He also slew a number of Ali's supporters in Yemen.

Hearing the cruelty of Busr Hadrat Ali sent Jariah ibn Qudamah with two thousand men. But before he reached Yemen, Busr fled to Syria. He also sent Wahb ibn Masud with another two thousand men to Hijaz. Jariah ibn Qudamah, after establishing Ali's rule in Yemen, was advancing to Mecca. As soon as he reached the Holy city, he received the news of Hadrat Ali's assassination which ended his campaign.

According to Ibn Jarir at the end of the year 40 A.H. a treaty was signed between

Amir Muawiyyah and Hadrat Ali, on the request of Amir Muawiyyah to avoid blood shed among the Muslims. Under that treaty Syria and Egypt remained under the control of Amir Muawiyyah and the rest of the state under the control of Hadrat Ali. Thus the conflict between the two parties ended. This civil war which ended to the detriment of Hadrat Ali was the end of Islamic democratic rule.

But according to some other historians, no treaty took place between Hadrat Ali and Muawiyyah. While Hadrat Ali (R.A.) was preparing to attack Syria, (for which he had issued an ordinance compelling each and everyone under him to march to Syria) he was assassinated.

The Victories

The civil war did not allow Hadrat Ali (R.A.) to launch Jihad (Holy War) and the Islamic Empire saw no further extension. However some parts of Sistan (near Kabul) were conquered during this period. According to some histories Muslims made a naval attack on Kohan (near Bombay, India) in the year 38 A.H.

Tragic End

After the battle of Nahrwan the "Khwarij" had gone underground. As a matter of fact they were as much against Hadrat Ali (R.A.) as they were against Hadrat Muawiyyah (R.A.). They were still working against the Khilafat and they were greatly disgusted with the civil war that seemed endless.

To end this state of affairs, they worked out a dangerous plot. According to them Muslims were divided because of differences between Hadrat Ali and Amir Muawiyyah. They also disliked Amr ibn As and considered him as chief planner for Amir Muawiyyah. They decided, therefore, to assassinate-all the three of them. It was planned that the three personalities would be struck at the same time on the same day.

Three persons, appointed to assassinate Ali, Muawiyyah and Amr ibn As (R.A.) were Abdur Rahman Muljam Bark ibn Abdullah, and Amr ibn Bark respectively. Early hours of the 17th of Ramadan, 40 A.H., was fixed for the assassination.

After the Fajr Salat of the 17th Ramadan in the year 40 A.H. (661 A.D.) the three appointed Kharijis struck the men. Amir Muawiyyah escaped with a scratch, Hadrat Amr ibn As did not turn out for the Imamat because he was sick that day, thus was unhurt, but Hadrat Ali (R.A.) was mortally wounded with the poisoned sword of Ibn Muljam. He passed away in the evening of Ramadan 20, 40 A.H.

Ibn Muljam was caught by the people after he had struck Hadrat Ali. Hadrat Ali asked the Muslims to slay him if he died. At the same time of his death Hadrat Ali called his sons and advised them to serve Islam and to be good with the Muslims. When somebody asked him should the Muslims take pledge of loyalty at the hands of his elder son, Hadrat Hassan, he replied, "I leave this decision to the Muslims." He also advised people not to kill any person other than the assassin to avenge him.

He was sixty three years old at the time of his death and had ruled for four years and nine months as the Khalifah.

According to a number of historians his real grave is not known because his son Hadrat Hasan took out his body from the grave after he was buried because of the fear of Kharijis and buried him at an unknown place.

TEN

SERVANT OF ISLAM

The period of Hadrat Ali's Khilafat extending to four years and about nine months, was marked by civil war. His rule was characterised by a series of revolts for the first time in the history of Islam. He was elected as the Khalifah in the most critical period of Islamic history. The martyrdom of Hadrat Uthman was an extraordinary event about which the Holy Prophet (Sallallahu 'alaihi wa Sallam) had already prophesied. Hadrat Ali was in a very difficult situation. On the one hand the assassins and the insurgents were creating endless trouble for him, and on the other hand Banu Umayyah (Uthman's family) fled to Syria and incited Amir Muawiyyah to stick to his demand for avenging Hadrat Uthman's assassins. Hadrat Ali faced these problems and difficulties with extraordinary courage and presented before us an exemplary character. He never had full support even from his friends in Kufa but still remained firm in his position.

As it has been described before, he could never locate the real assassins of Hadrat Uthman and this could not be achieved until peace was established. Therefore his first task was to create an atmosphere of peace in the state. But the Sabaites (insurgents) never wanted peace. They worked on both sides. On the one side they made it difficult for Hadrat Ali to find out the assassins, and on the other hand they sent their agents to Syria to incite the people (especially Umayyads) against Hadrat Ali. Their main aim was to let the Muslims fight among themselves so that they might prosper. Although Hadrat Ali knew all this but he was unable to take any firm action because of the civil war.

The third problem faced by Hadrat Ali (R.A.) was the Kharijite movement. They were extremists and misled a number of innocent Muslims. They did not hesitate to use sword against persons who do not agree with them. They developed many beliefs foreign to Islam, although they appeared to be very pious but very politically, they were corrupt. Hadrat Ali dealt with them with an iron hand. He realised that if they were not wiped out in the beginning they would mislead future generations. He was successful in destroying their strong hold. However some of them, who escaped, went underground but they were never in a strong position.

Hadrat Ali (R.A.) tried his utmost to unite the Muslims and bring them back on one platform but he was not successful. The tragic death of Hadrat Uthman (R.A.) was a signal for bloodshed among the Muslims. The Companions were not to be blamed for it at all. This was caused by anti-Islamic elements in the form of Sabaites. (Abdullah ibn Saba and his followers). Historical facts bear it out that Abdullah ibn Saba became the greatest enemy of Islam. It was he who shattered the unity of Muslims forever. After completing their mission the Sabaites made a pretence of being Ali's friends but they never helped him nor the cause of Muslim Unity. No sooner had Hadrat Ali assumed Khilafat than a group of the same miscreant Sabaites who had brought about the cold-blooded assassination of Hadrat Uthman (R.A.) began to demand due retribution for the murder of the Khalifah and started to incite Muslims only to create division among them. Thus they played a double role. A group of them showed themselves as friends of Ali and another group (much smaller than the first) went to Syria and other parts of Islamic State to incite the Muslims against Hadrat Ali (R.A.).

Hadrat Ali (R.A.) faced all these problems with courage and never lost heart. He was a man of strong will power and determination and was quite right in his decisions.

Character, Piety and Excellence

Hadrat Ali (R.A.) was a model of simplicity and self denial. He led a simple life from the cradle to the grave, and was a true representative of the Holy Prophet (Sallallahu 'alaihi wa Sallam). Ali (R.A.) had neither a servant nor a maid when Fatima (R.A.) the most beloved daughter of the Holy Prophet was married to him. She would grind corn with her own hands. Purity of motives and selflessness were the keynote of his life. He was a wise counsellor, a true friend and a generous foe. He did not have a desire for the Khilafat after Hadrat Uthman's assassination, but when he was selected he tried his best to fulfil his responsibility.

He was very honest and trustworthy. His trustworthiness can well be imagined from the fact that the Holy Prophet entrusted to him all the cash and other things, he was having in his trust, at the time of his migration to Medina so that Ali (R.A.) would return them to the owners. Once some oranges came to Baitul Mal, Hadrat Hasan and Husain took one orange each. When Hadrat Ali saw them having the oranges he took the fruit away from them and distributed them among the poor. Whenever any booty came to be distributed according to the Islamic law, he distributed it very honestly. Once he distributed all the revenue of the Baitul Mal (Public Treasury), then broomed it and offered two rakat Salat in the room.

He did not leave his simplicity even though he was the Khalifah and the ruler of a vast state. Once a person named Abdullah ibn Zarir had an opportunity to take meals with him. The meal was very simple. Abdullah asked, "O Amirul-Muminin, don't you like the meat of birds?" Hadrat Ali replied, "The Khalifah has a right in Muslim (Public) property only to the extent sufficient for him and his family."

Hadrat Ali was a very generous Muslim. He never refused a beggar. Sometimes he gave all of his property to the poor and sold his arms to get food. Once he said during his lecture, "I went to sell my sword. I swear Allah, had I only that amount of money for which I could buy a "Sirwal" (i.e. a trousers), I would never have sold my sword." Hearing this one person stood up and said, "I give you a loan." There are many stories about his generosity which for lack of space are not being mentioned.

Hadrat Ali (R.A.) was a great worshipper and used to offer long Salats. He was Hafiz of the Holy Quran. He was so punctual for the "Tasbih" (the famous Tasbih-i-Fatima) i.e. remembrance of Allah that he never left it, even during battles. He was very kind to others. He showed his kindness even to his enemies. Once one of his enemies fell down naked because of his attack. Seeing his condition he did not kill him and left him so that he might not be ashamed of his nakedness. After the battle of "Jamal" against lady Aishah, he treated lady Aishah (R.A.) very respectfully. He himself went to see her and when she told him that she would like to go to Medina he asked her brother Muhammad bin Abu Bakr to escort her. He never mistreated his enemies. During the time of the Holy Prophet (Sallallahu 'alaihi wa Sallam) once he overcame a Jew in a fight, and sat on his chest to kill him. The Jew spat at his face. Hadrat Ali at once left him. Seeing this the Jew was very much surprised and asked the reason. Ali (R.A.) said, "I was killing you for Allah's sake but when you spat on my face, my sincerity was endangered because of the personal feelings." Hearing this the Jew immediately accepted Islam. His character and morals were so high that even Amir Muawiyyah praised them. Once Amir Muawiyyah asked Dirar Asadi, one of his friends, to tell some of Ali's high quality.

Dirar Asadi refused first but when Amir Muawiyyah insisted Dirar said, "He was a man of strong will power and determination. He always gave a just judgement, and was a fountain of knowledge. His speech was full of wisdom. He hated the pleasure of this world and loved the darkness of night to cry before Allah. His dress was most simple and he liked simple meals. He lived like a common man and when anybody put any question before him, he replied with outmost politeness. Whenever we asked him to wait for us he waited like a common man. Although he was very near to us because of his high morals, we were afraid of him sometimes of his grandeur and eminence due to his nearness to Allah. He always respected a pious man and a scholar. He was nearest to the poor. He never allowed a powerful man to take advantage of his power. The weak were never disappointed of his justice. I bear witness that in many battles he woke up during the night and took hold of his beard and started to cry and weep before Allah as though he was in a state of commotion and exclaimed: "O world! do not try to betray me. I have divorced (left) you long ago. Do not have any desire for me. I hate you. Your age is short and your end is despised. O! the provision is very little and the journey is too long (i.e., the journey to hereafter), and way is full of danger....." Hearing this Hadrat Amir Muawiyyah started to weep and cry and said, "May Allah bless Abul Hasan (i.e. Ali). I swear by Allah he was a person of the character, you described."

At this point it should be noted that the differences of the Companions were not like that of us. They differed with each other for the sake of Allah but always admired each other's good habits. Although Amir Muawiyyah was having differences with Hadrat Ali, he admired the excellence of Ali throughout his life and often said that he could never be equal to Ali (R.A.). As a matter of fact the degree of their sincerity could not be imagined. We think every thing in terms of wordily benefit, they considered every matter in terms of love with Allah, love with the Prophet of Allah and the success in the hereafter.

Tasawwuf and Hadrat Ali

The genealogical chain of "Sufis" (Islamic Mystics) ends at Hadrat Ali (R.A.) and through him it is linked to the Holy Prophet (Sallallahu 'alaihi was Sallam) in most of the orders. Thus Hadrat Ali (R.A.) has been considered as the great Imam of Tasawwuf (Spiritual Science or Mysticism).

As it has been mentioned in Urdu book, "Tasalsulat-i-Imdadiah", Hadrat Shah Waliullah of Delhi holds the view that the genealogical chain of the great "Sufis" is linked to the Holy Prophet through all the first four Caliphs among whom Hadrat Ali (R.A.) stands like a gateway between the "Sufis" on the one hand and the first three caliphs and the Holy Prophet on the other hand. Spiritual secrets were transferred by the Holy Prophet (Sallallahu 'alaihi wa Sallam) to Hadrat Abu Bakr. From Abu Bakr (R.A.) the secrets were transferred to Hadrat Umar; and from Umar (R.A.) to Hadrat Uthman; and from Hadrat Uthman (R.A.) to Hadrat Ali and from Hadrat Ali to "Sufis" through Imam Hasan Basri (R.A.) as it is believed in most of the Schools of Thoughts of Tasawwuf.

Historically there are not enough proofs that Hadrat Hasan Basri had only tutelage under Hadrat Ali. However it has been confirmed that Hasan Basri met Hadrat Ali at the age of 15. In the science of Tasawwuf training under the Sheikh ("Murshid" or "Pir" or Spiritual Guide) is not necessary and spiritual secrets can be transferred even in a single meeting from the "Sheikh" to the "Murid" (the spiritual disciple). Therefore the great "Sufis" do not doubt the fact that Hadrat Ali (R.A.) transferred spiritual secrets to Hasan Basri (R.A.), from whom they were passed on to the succeeding generations.

Therefore Hadrat Ali (R.A.) and Imam Hasan Basri are the most important links in the genealogical orders ("Shajrahs") of most of the Schools of Thought of Tasawwuf.

Gate of the City of Knowledge

The Holy Prophet (Sallallahu 'alaihi wa Sallam) said: "I am the City of Knowledge and Ali is its gate." No doubt Hadrat Ali (R.A.) was a great scholar and jurist of Islam. He had memorised whole of the Holy Quran during the time of the Holy Prophet (Sallallahu 'alaihi wa Sallam) and knew its commentary including the order of descent and the time of revelation of various verses. It is given in Tabaqat Ibn Sad that Hadrat Ali said, "I could tell for each and every verse of the Holy Quran why and when it was revealed." Hadrat Ali has been counted among the top most commentators of the Holy Quran. Nobody among the Companions with the exception of Abdullah ibn Abbas was so learned in the Holy Quran as Hadrat Ali (R.A.). His commentaries of various verses of the Holy Quran have been given in a number of books like "Ibn-i-Jarir," "Ibn Abu Hatim", "Ibn Kathir" etc. He had confined himself to his home for six months after the death of the Holy Prophet (Sallallahu 'alaihi wa Sallam) only to collect various parts of the Holy Quran. He was excellent in deducing law from the verses of the Holy Quran. When he argued with "Khawarij" on the question of Arbitration they could not stand before him. He was also very learned in the knowledge of "Nasikh" and "Mansukh" *i.e.* the knowledge of such verses of the Holy Quran out dating the laws given in other verses.

Hadrat Ali (R.A.) spent thirty years of his life with the Holy Prophet (Sallallahu 'alaihi wa Sallam) and knew all the manners and practices of the Holy Prophet (Sallallahu 'alaihi wa Sallam). He stood next to Abu Bakr (R.A.) as far as the knowledge of sayings, practices and orders of the Holy Prophet (Sallallahu 'alaihi wa Sallam) were concerned. During the period of the first three caliphs and also during his time he was the great Mufti (Jurist) of Islam. He performed this service for about thirty years after the death of the Holy Prophet (Sallallahu 'alaihi wa Sallam). In the narration of Hadith he was very cautious like three of his predecessors. For this reason only 586 Ahadith, narrated by Hadrat Ali (R.A.) have been mentioned in the books of Hadith. He has also mentioned a number of sayings of various Companions as well. Hadrat Shah Wali Allah of Delhi says: "Most of the Ahadith in connection with the appearance of the Holy Prophet, his method of offering Salat and praying to Allah etc. have been mentioned by Hadrat Ali (R.A.) because of the fact that he was with him not only in his public but also in the private life." Ali (R.A.) was one of the few Companions who were having collections of Hadith recorded during the time of the Holy Prophet (Sallallahu 'alaihi wa Sallam).

Hadrat Ali (R.A.) was not only a great scholar but a great Jurist as well. He was famous for giving correct verdicts of different problems very quickly which were based upon the Holy Quran and the Sunnah of the Holy Prophet (Sallallahu 'alaihi wa Sallam). Great Companions used to visit him for seeking solution of different problems of Islamic Law and Jurisprudence. Hadrat Umar remarked," 'Ali is the greatest jurist and judge among all of us". Hadrat Abdullah ibn Masud said," Ali's decision is the most authentic." Because of his vast knowledge of the Holy Quran and Hadith, he become the greatest jurist of his time, as Islamic Jurisprudence requires knowledge of the Holy Quran and Hadith to the fullest possible extent. On many occasions he corrected the decisions given by great Companions like Umar and Uthman (R.A.). Even though Amir Muawiyyah was having differences with Ali, he sometimes referred some of the complicated problems of Islamic Law to Hadrat Ali (R.A.) and admitted his profundity in this field.

Hadrat Ali (R.A.) was a great orator as well. On many occasions mobs of people were changed because of his effective speeches. Arabic knowing persons can note the beauty of his speeches. He was a wonderful master of the Arabic language. His writings were as effective as his speech. He had also composed a few poems as well. He also framed rules of Arabic syntax and appointed Abul Aswad to compose a book on the basis of the rules he framed.

No doubt Hadrat Ali was one of the greatest sons of Islam. Very few Companions equalled him in his closeness to the Holy Prophet (Sallallahu 'alaihi wa Sallam), which burrished qualities of head and heart. Muslims are forever indebted to him.

Wives and Children

(a) Hadrat Ali's first wife was the most beloved daughter of the Holy Prophet, Hadrat Fatima (R.A.). He got three sons (Hasan, Husain and Muhsin), and two daughters (Zainab and Umm-i-Kulthum) from her. The youngest son, Muhsin died in childhood.

After the death of Hadrat Fatima he married a number of wives from time to time:

(a) Umm al-Banin bint Hizam from whom he got Abbas, Jafar, Abdullah and Uthman. All of these except Abbas were martyred at Karbala.

(b) Laila bint Masud who gave birth to Ubaidullah and Abu Bakr. They were martyred at Karbala.

(c) Asma bint Umais who gave birth to Yahya and Muhammad Asghar.

(d) Sahba bint Rabia who gave birth to Umar and Ruqayya.

(e) Amamah bint Abul As: She was daughter of Zainab (R.A.). daughter of the Holy Prophet

(Sallallahu 'alaihi wa Sallam). Hadrat Ali got Muhammad Aswat from her.

(f) Khaulah bint Jafar who gave birth to Muhammad ibn Ali.

(g) Umm-i-Said who gave birth to Umm Hasan and Ramlah Kubra.

(h) Mahyah bint Ummul Qais she gave birth to a daughter who died in childhood.

He also had a number of slave girls from whom he bore the following daughters:

Umm-i-Hani, Maimunah, Zainab Sughra, Ramlah Sughra, Umm-i-Kulthum Sughra, Fatima, Umamah, Khadijah, Umm-i-Salama, Umm-i-Jafar, Jamanah and Nafisah, According to ibn-i-Jarir, Hadrat Ali had 17 daughters and 14 sons. His family continued through five sons: Imam Hasan, Imam Husain, Muhammad ibn Ali, Umar bin Ali, and Abbas ibn Ali.

ELEVEN

THE GEMS

WORDS OF WORTH

Hadrat Ali was an embodiment of knowledge and wisdom. Some of the sayings of Hadrat Ali which breathe wisdom and have attained the dimensions of aphorisms are on record. Some of these are quoted hereunder:

- Fear God and you will have no cause to fear anyone.
- Resignation to the Will of God is the cure of the disease of the heart.
- The word of God is the medicine of the heart.
- Lead such a life that when you die, the people may mourn you and while you are alive they long for your company.
- The days of life pass away like clouds, so do good while you are alive.
- Of all the follies the greatest is to love the world.
- Opportunity is swift of flight but slow to return.
- Pride, cowardice and miserliness are bad for men but good for woman.
- The most happy is he to whom God has given a good wife.
- He who knows himself knows God.
- Do not sell your conscience for anything but Heaven.
- The disease of the heart is worse than the disease of the body.
- To fight against one's desires is the greatest of all fights.

- The strongest amongst you is he who subdues his self.
- Wealth and greed are the roots of all evils.
- Riches without faith are the greatest poverty.
- A man's worth depends upon the nobility of his aspirations.
- Knowledge enlivens the soul.
- The learned lives, although he dies.
- The sum total of excellence is knowledge.
- To respect the learned is to respect God.
- Generosity hides shortcomings.
- The wealth of a miser is as useless as a pebble.
- Desire is one's most inveterate enemy.
- Those who walk on the surface of the earth shall one day be interned in it.
- Every breath of man brings him nearer to death.
- People are asleep as long they are alive, they are awakened when they die.
- Patience is the fruit of faith.
- Virtue never dies.
- A man's glory from his virtue is greater than the glory of his pedigree.
- No shelter is safer than piety.
- A man's behaviour is the index of his mind.
- Courtesy costs nothing but buys everything.
- Clemency graces power.
- Jealousy devours virtue as fire devour fuel.
- He that lends a listening ear to reproach is one of those that deserve reproach.
- Forgiveness is the crown of greatness.
- Carnal appetites are nets spread by the devil.
- Every arrow does not hit the mark, nor is every prayer granted.
- Ostentatiousness spoils prayers.
- Fear none but your sins.
- He who praises you murders you.
- A man who praises himself displays his deficiency of intellect.
- Honour your parents and your sons will honour you.

- A man is hid under his tongue.
- The tongue of a wise man lies behind his heart.
- The tongue pierces deeper than the spear.
- He who purifies his heart from doubt is a believer.
- The opinion of a wise man is an oracle.
- To seek counsel is to go to the fountain of guidance.
- Association with a fool is tyrannical to the soul.
- God hasten the fall of tyrants.
- Tyranny leads to moral cowardice.
- A tyrant's success is his moral defeat.
- It is better do die than to beg.
- When a man begs he loses his faith.
- Hajj is the Jihad of every believer in faith.
- A wise enemy is better than a foolish friend.
- Silence is the best reply to a fool.
- The best speech is one which is short and reasonable.
- Speech is like a medicine, a small dose of which cures but an excess of which kills.
- He that has no courage has no religion.
- His grief is long whose hope is short.
- The right of freedom of speech consists in speaking the truth.
- Repentance washes away sins.
- Folly is an incurable disease.
- To assist the wrong is to oppress the right.
- Sinning is a disease, repentance is its medicine and abstinence from it a sure cure.
- Sorrow makes a man old before his time.
- Pride impedes progress and mars greatness.
- To forgive is the crown of greatness.
- He who understands humanity seeks solitude.
- Right is the best argument.
- Misrepresentation spoils narration.
- As a man's wisdom increases, so his desire to speak decreases.

- He who seeks to do justice with men, let him desire for them what he desires for himself.
- The greatest sin is the sin which the sinner considers to be ordinary.
- Contentment is the asset which is never exhausted.
- Government is a trial for men.
- He who fights against the truth, the truth will defeat him.
- Finding fault in others is one's greatest fault.
- Haste is a species of madness.
- Greed is perpetual enslavement.
- He who does not know his own worth is doomed to destruction.
- The best investment is one with which duties are performed.
- Anger is a fire kindled, he who restrains anger extinguishes the fire, he who gives vent to it is the first to be consumed by such fire.
- Jihad is the highway of prosperity.
- None is more solitary than a miser.
- Knowledge is the ornament of the rich and the riches of the poor.
- Knowledge is the sum total of excellence.
- He who teaches you a letter binds you with a fetter of gratitude.
- As long as we do not hope, we do not fret.
- He who indulges in jokes and loose talk loses a part of his wisdom.
- Truth is bitter, but its result is sweet, falsehood appears to be sweet but it is poisonous in its effect.
- Miserliness is the root of many evils.
- Knowledge and practice are twins and both go together. There is no knowledge without practice and no practice without knowledge.
- He who dissembles plays with his honour.
- When God wants to humiliate a person he deprives him of knowledge.
- When your power increases, decrease your desires accordingly.
- He who listens to a back-bitter loses a friend.
- It is no justice to decide a case on mere conjecture.
- He who does not know his own worth is deemed to ignomy.
- He who practises thrift would never be in want.

- He who does not know should not be ashamed to learn.
- Patience is to faith, what head is to the body. When patience goes faith goes, when head goes, the body goes.
- The grace of God is the best guide.
- A good disposition is the best companion.
- Wisdom is the best friend.
- Good breeding is the best inheritance.
- There is nothing more hateful than pride.
- Be among men like bee among birds.
- Mix with the people with your tongue, but be separate from them in your deeds.
- Be generous but do not be a spendthrift.
- Do not run after the world, let the world run after you.
- A wise man is he who does not despair of the bounty and mercy of God.
- He who is aware of his own faults is oblivious of the fault of others.
- What the eye sees the heart preserves.
- The vision of the eye is limited; the vision of the heart transcends all barriers of time and space.
- Do not be misled by appearances for these are apt to be deceptive.
- Do not have too many irons in the fire; concentrate on one thing at a time.
- What you do not like for your self, do not like it for others.
- Contentment is the treasure which is never exhausted.
- The advice of old men is dearer than the bravery of young men.
- That knowledge is superficial which is merely on the tongue; that knowledge is real which demonstrates itself in your practice.
- Waste of time is one's greatest loss.
- He who knows to keep his secret knows the way to success.
- Foresight is the way to safety.
- No relationship is stronger than the relationship that exists between man and God.
- Enlighten the heart with prayers.
- Strengthen your heart with faith.
- Suppress all lust with piety.

- Do not sell the Hereafter for the world.
- Do not speak in a state of ignorance.
- Refrain from unnecessary talk.
- Do not tread the path from which you can apprehend the danger of running astray.
- In the affairs of God, do not be afraid of the accusations of the evil mongers.
- In all that you do seek the protection of God,.
- Do not covet what is undesirable.
- If you seek the truth neither stray from the right path, nor be assailed by doubts.
- Do not become a slave of your desires.
- That wealth is no wealth which brings dishonour.
- Whatever harm accrues of silence can be remedied but whatever harm is done because of speech cannot be remedied.
- It is better to restrain your desires than to stretch your hand before others.
- A little that is earned because of honest labour is better than a larger amount gained through dishonest means.
- Guard well your secret.
- He who seeks more than what is necessary indulges in error.
- To oppress the weak is the worst tyranny.
- Do not bank on false hopes for that is the capital of the dead.
- A wise man takes a lesson even from a minor lapse.
- Overpower desires and suspicions by patience and faith.
- He who does not take the middle course strays.
- A stranger is he who has no friends.
- When hopes are frustrated despair becomes the way of life.
- He who trusts the world, the world betrays him.

Concept of God : In his various sermons conspicuous for the depth of learning Hadrat Ali had dwelt on the various attributes of God in a most masterly way. Extracts from some of his sermons are given hereunder:

> "All praise is due to the Creator of the world whose wisdom is hidden. The various objects of nature openly confirm His existence. It is impossible to the physical eye to behold. His Majesty thus one who has not seen Him has no

right to deny. His existence; He surpasses in strength and superiority. He is nearest to us. No one can be nearer to us than He. His distant height has not segregated Him from His creation and His nearness has not established His equality with His creation. He is that sublime and matchless. Being in comprehending when the intellect cannot reach the bottom of his attributes, yet noting prevents a person from comprehending Him. He is that Being Whose existence even an atheist feels in his heart of hearts. Undoubtedly God is free and sublime and bears no comparison with anyone, then how can anyone have the audacity to deny Him."

"God is higher and superior to all things to such an extent that even the wildest imagination cannot have a definite idea about him. He is the beginning which has no end. He is Infinite. God is one. He has no partner. He is the first cause of everything. There was nothing before Him. He existed when nothing existed. He is Unique. We can have only glimpses of His greatness. His effulgence is so dazzling that we cannot face it. Our intellect is finite and He is Infinite. We cannot describe Him with any degree of exactitude. He is beyond description. He is Almighty. All things in the heavens and on earth are subject to His command."

"We thank God for what He has taken, for what He has given, for what kindness. He had done, and what tests He has taken. He is aware of all that is hidden. He knows every secret. Whatever is concealed in one's heart is known to Him. He is omnipotent and omniscient. None is to be worshipped except Him. He has no partner. He has no parallel. He is Unique. He is might, majesty and mercy. He is our Creator. We come from Him and we have to ultimately return to Him. His bounties are unlimited."

When did God Exist : A Jew once went to Hadrat Ali and asked him, when did God exist Hadrat Ali said that God is above considerations of time and space Creation was not and He was, He was while there was no being. He existed without cause. He has beginning and no end. He is subject to no limitations. He is Infinite. He is the end of all souls. The Jew next asked, "What is fate" Hadrat Ali said, "It is a gloomy road, tread it not". The Jew repeated the questions and Hadrat Ali said, "It is a deep sea, avoid it". The Jew repeated the question for the third time and Hadrat Ali said, "It is a mystery of God which is hidden from you, do not probe into it." The Jew insisted on a reply and Hadrat Ali asked him, "Has God created you for what? He has willed, or what you have willed?". The Jew said, "Indeed, for what. He has willed". Thereupon Hadrat Ali said, "Then He will do with you as He thinks fit and that is fate "This impressed the Jew and he was converted to Islam at the hands of Hadrat Ali.

Protection of God : Once a Jew came to Hadrat Ali with a view to ridiculing Islam. The Jew was very rich and he disparaged the Islamic way of austerity. He tried to enter into argument with Hadrat Ali and declared that if his questions were answered to his satisfaction he would accept Islam Hadrat Ali said that he would be glad to answer any question that was put to him. The Jew said, "Suppose you are standing on the roof of a high building at a dizzy height, who will protect you'?" Hadrat Ali said, "Of course, God will protect me". The Jew thereupon said, "Do you feel confident that God would really protect you" Hadrat Ali said, "Certainly, it is our faith that as long as we are ordained to live, God will protect us. "The Jew observed, "If you are sure of the protection of God, would you be prepared to climb to a high building and then jump therefrom in order to test how God protects you." Hadrat Ali said that he was not a fool to jump from a high building for nothing. The Jew said that he was not asking him to undertake the exercise for nothing, for if God actually protects him, he would thereby get a Jew converted to Islam. Hadrat Ali said that such stipulation was erroneous and fallacious. How was that? enquired the Jew. Hadrat Ali said that God is the master and man is His servant. It is open to the master to put the servant to test but it does not behove the servant to put the master to test Hadrat Ali added "If we put God to any test, that means our lack of faith and when faith is lost everything is lost."

The Jew said, "This means that you are afraid that if you take a jump, you will die and God will not protect you" Hadrat Ali said, "I am not afraid of death, but as a servant I cannot defy the Master. Everything in the universe is subject to the will of God. That will is the law and man has been endowed with reason and intelligence to discern such law. If knowing the law I choose to defy it, I will have to suffer for breaking the law. When I deliberately break down the law laid down by the Master, I lose the right of His protection Moreover. God protects us as long as we are ordained to live. If I take a jump and die, it would merely mean that I am ordained to die like that, it would not mean that God has withdrawn his protection."

The argument of Hadrat Ali impressed the Jew. He said "All you are right, we must observe the law and then seek the protection of the Master. We certainly lose the right of His protection when we break the law." Thereupon the Jew was converted to Islam and for the rest of his life he remained a true Muslim.

Counsels with Reference to God : Some of the counsels of Hadrat Ali with reference to God are:

(1) Fear God and you will have no cause to fear anyone else. Fear of God checks the soul from committing sins and restrains one from transgression. Shedding tears for the fear of God enlightens the heart and fortifies it against the repetition of sins. Fear of God purifies the heart.

(2) Resignation to God's will is the cure of the diseases of the heart. Resignation to the will of God makes the greatest affliction easy.

(3) Glorify God even for little blessings. If you are grateful to God for His blessings, He will increase them.

(4) The word of God is the medicine of heart. A believer is thankful to God in prosperity and patient in adversity. To repose ones trust in God is the believers, castle.

His Prayer to God : Hadrat Ali used to pray to God in the following terms.

> "O God, forgive my sins of which you know more than me. And if I commit these sins again, even then because of your munificence forgive me. If all the promises that I had made with myself to act according to your command have not been fulfilled, kindly pardon my lapse. Moreover if I sought your proximity through my tongue but my heart did not keep accord with my tongue even then forgive me. O God, forgive my acts of commission or omission, advertent or inadvertent."

Life in this World and Life in the World Hereafter : In one of his sermons, Hadrat Ali counselled the people about the life in this world and the life in the world Hereafter in the following terms:

> "O men of God' May God keep you happy, and shower His favours on you? You should prepare yourself for the long journey that awaits you. There are many difficulties that beset your path. Death is ever anxious to devour you. Renounce the riches of the world and catch hold of piety. Life in this world is short, whereas life after death will be everlasting. Buy those commodities here which will stand you in good stead in the other world. Do not demean yourself before God who is well acquainted with your innermost feelings. Do not allow your soul to be lost in this world before death may overtake you. O men' Cast a glance on this world from a wise man's point of view. She turns out her guests in a short pace of time. She harasses those with whom she fondles and prattles. Whatever part of life is wasted in idle pursuits can never be recalled. Its gratifications and enjoyments are soon changed into suffering and pain; its embellishment and decorations are changed into deformation and impoverishment. The days of this life are numbered. Death is inevitable and is bound to come soon. After having adorned your person with good deed, you should not pay any heed whether death catches you or you catch death. Many men buy clothes, which instead of being worn by them are used in their coffin. Many persons build houses which instead of becoming abodes

> become their graves. No one has lived forever in this world and no one has invented such a medicine which may make men immune from the clutches of death. Solomon the prophet reigned with great pomp and majesty but when his time came he had to depart leaving all such pomp and glory. The world was left without him and his places became a heap of ruins. Look to the case of those men who lived impregnable citadels on the top of mountains with the most powerful army and when their time came death ejected them from those fortified places and put them to eternal sleep in graves. One can hear the whisper of angels over their graves "Where are those stiff-necked people who boasted of their pelf and power and their crowns and thrones? Where are their royal robes? What became of those beauties whose radiance under veils dimmed the light of the sun? Where have gone those forts which were decorated with golden curtains, in front of which stood sentries for watch and ward? Do not they tell us how powerless they were? Have not the worms eaten those bodies, who a few days ago set a magnificent and sumptuous table with luxurious plates?. The vicissitudes of fortune have ruined their citadels, destroyed their royal robes and reduced to dust their crowns and thrones."

Evil of the World : In another sermon, Hadrat Ali dwelt on the evils of the world as follows:

> "Beware! The world stands on the threshold of decay and destruction. Its mouth sounds the farewell notes of annihilation. It is uncanny and uncharitable. With great rapidity it turns its back. Alas, the world drives its inhabitants into pitfalls of destruction Through the hands of death it drags its exasperated neighbours to annihilation. Its transparent water becomes bitter and its sparkling spring becomes opaque in the next world. It has nothing to offer except the leavings which stick to utensils after the meal or the wet piece of stone which is kept in the mouth to quench parching thirst. Whatever is in the world is superficial, mortal and perishable O followers of God'. Then get ready to leave this abode whose in-dweller are destined to taste death. Take heed lest the desires and lust should overwhelm you and this transitory life should appear a long one to you and its short sojourn be taken as a long one by you. By God, if you grumble and moan like the wretched camels of burden shed bitter tears like a pigeon and implore forgiveness of God like those monks who have renounced the world and having renounced your worldly goods and family, you come out to seek nearness to God so that. He may exalt your lot or forgive some of your sins which the angels have recorded in your book of deeds, all these things will have little value as compared with the

> reward which awaits you if you follow my instructions. By God, if for the love of God you melt your hearts away and for the love of His rewards and fear of His punishment your eyes shed blood instead of tears and you live in this condition till this world lasts, even then your indefatigable and untiring efforts can be of no match for the numerous blessings which God has so kindly and bountifully bestowed upon you. You can never return the thanks of the Almighty Lord for the guidance. He has so mercifully shown to us."

The World and the Hereafter : In another sermon, Hadrat Ali talked about the world and the Hereafter in the following terms:

> "The world has turned its face and given an indication of its impending end. The Hereafter is now becoming manifest. Beware, today is the day to activate your body, tomorrow is the day assigned for the race. Now either Paradise or. Hell lie ahead of you. Is there no one among you who should repent before his death and do some good deeds which would stand him in good stead in the Hereafter? You are living today in the worlds of hopes and desires, but beware that death lies in ambush. He who does good deeds before his death, such deeds would be a source of profit for him. His death will not harm in any way. He who falls into error before his death will be at loss and will come to grief. In the event of weal or woe you should act as one would act in the case of fear or terror. The truth is that there is no reward greater than Paradise and there is no punishment severer than Hell. Beware that whom the truth does not profit, falsehood will certainly harm him. He who is not guided is doomed to destruction. Beware that you have been given the command to march. The goods that you can carry with you on your march have also been indicated. I am worried about you in two things, firstly your subservience to your lust and secondly the excess of your longings March to the. Hereafter with such assets which can save you from punishment on the Doomsday."

Transitory Character of the World : In most of his sermons, Hadrat Ali has brought out the transitory character of the world in the following words:

> "All praise is for God. Do not despair of His mercy. His bounties are unlimited. There is no shame in His worship. He is God whose mercy is ever lasting and Whose bounties would never exhaust. Remember that the world is transitory in character and your life is a mere sojourn. The world is doomed to destruction. It is outwardly pleasant and attractive, but inwardly hollow. See that when you depart from this world you do so with good grace and carry with you assets which all stand you in good stead in the Hereafter. For this journey do

not overload yourself with unnecessary paraphernalia. Do not covet anything beyond what is necessary. Keep in mind that the world is a tavern where no one can stay for long. Do not be enamoured of the world. . Its attracts are a trap Those who are lured by its charms get involved into an ordeal You should keep in mind that you will have to be called to account for what you do in the world For the wise, the world is a shadow which may appear at one moment and soon disappear. Fear God and face death with a stock of good deeds. Purchase everlasting things for things which are perishable. An arduous journey awaits you. Prepare yourself for it. Be ever ready to face death, for it may come at any moments. Be receptive to words of advice God Almighty has not created you in vain nor has He left you free to run amok. Death separates you from this world and Paradise or Hell in the Hereafter. Remember that your life is diminishing every moment. You should hasten cheerfully to your real destination While alone, purchase such assets which would be a source of profit to you in the Hereafter. You should overpower your lusts. Know that desires are deceptive and death lies in ambush. Satan is after you. It is the game of Satan that death should catch you unaware. When you have not amassed the assets necessary for the journey to eternity, against the manoeuvres of Satan, seek the protection of God.

Other Sermons : Dwelling on the same theme, in the course of other sermons, Hadrat Ali said:

"The world is a tavern where no one can stay for long. Such is the lure of the world that none can escape from being involved therein. The world is an ordeal and a trial. Whatever you get out of the world will be of no avail to you. It is only that which helps you for the Hereafter that can be a source of profit for you. For the wise, the world is merely a shadow which may disappear any moment thus manifesting its unreality."

"O people, what should I say about the world which begins in grief and ends in destruction. Those who are rich and wealthy are involved in mischief and those who are poor and needy are grieved and distressed. The world eludes him who seeks it. It runs after him who runs away from it. He who sees it as a place of trial is enlightened, he who is lured by its charm is blinded."

Political Thoughts : Hadrat Ali was a political thinker. In his writings in Nahj-ul-Balagha we come across many passages which project his political thought in the context of Islam. It is surprising that such thoughts expressed fifteen hundred years ago have an air of his modernity about them. One marvels at the profoundity of his thought.

State and Government: Hadrat Ali defined the State as "Community in action". He defined Government as an instrument of the State charged with the responsibility of fulfilling the purpose of the State. He conceived Islamic Ummah as an organic entity capable of possessing moral and spiritual qualities. He held that an individual cannot lead his life in isolation and has to live as a part of the Ummah safeguarding the "Haqooq-ul-Abad" (duties of individuals towards his fellow men). This can be done by developing a sense of group solidarity and loyalty and by each person striving to live in harmony with his fellow men without encroaching upon or usurping the rights of others. Hadrat Ali held that mankind with all its faults and vices would survive by a corporate sense of responsibility. As such good government should not be merely regulative; it should be reformative as well in its character and application.

The Caliph: Hadrat Ali held that the Caliph is the agent of the community charged with the responsibility to administer the affairs of the community in accordance with the injunctions of Islam. He should strive to follow in the footsteps of the Holy Prophet. He should be a pious and staunch Muslim who should follow the Shanah himself and should enforce it for others. He should be a man of knowledge and should not be ignorant. He should not be covetous or ambitious. He should be concerned more with Hereafter than the world. He should be sympathetic. He should not be cruel and should not oppress the people. He should have a firm hold on authority and should see that the functionaries of the State perform their duties honestly and efficiently. He should be just and should administer justice without fear or favour. He should promote the welfare of the people. He should enforce law and order with a strong hand. He should be a source of strength for the weak and a matter of terror for those who usurp the rights of others. He should defend the country against foreign aggression. He should maintain law and order within the country. He should keep a strict watch on the functionaries of the State. He should be sympathetic and should solve the problems of the people. The people should have easy access to him and he should command their confidence. He should regard government as a trail and should take steps to ensure that when weighed in the balance he is not found wanting.

The People: Hadrat Ali held that the people are the main power and they have the right to criticise the Government. The Government should work for the welfare of the people and should keep them satisfied. Hadrat Ali was particular that the minorities should be well cared for and their rights should be safeguarded. The minorities should have the freedom of worship and they should enjoy autonomy in the administration of their own affairs. Hadrat Ali held that it was the obligation of the State to look after the destitute and the distressed. He attached particular importance to the care of the widows and orphans.

Taxation: Hadrat Ali held that the people should be taxed according to their capacity. There should be no hardship or coercion in the collection of taxes. The system of taxation should be such that the people pay the taxes voluntarily as a religious obligation. The Collectors should bot indulge in any act which is not liked by the people. They should not collect anything beyond what is enjoined by law. Taxes should be remitted in the case of famine, failure of crops or any other calamity.

Functionaries of the State: Hadrat Ali held that only such persons should be appointed as the functionaries of the State who spoke the truth, however unpalatable it might be. The functionaries of the State should fear God and they should perform their duties with pious intensions, good faith and fear of God. They should be scrupulously honest. They should be paid reasonable remuneration so that they are not beguiled into monetary temptations. There should be a good system of espionage to watch the working of the functionaries of the State at various levels. Hadrat Ali held that good care should be taken of the soldiers. They should be respected and treated kindly. Only pious and holy men with fear of God should be appointed as Qadis and they should administer justice without fear or favour in accordance with the commandments of God. They should not be greedy and should not make errors in their judgements. The businessmen and traders should be protected and proper facilities should be provided for the development of trade and industry Hadrat Ali laid down that the Government was under an obligation to ensure that prices of commodities were kept at a reasonable level and the businessmen were not allowed to make exorbitant profit. The functionaries of the State had to take steps to ensure that there was no hoarding or black marketing. Hadrat Ali enjoined that public funds were to be administered as a trust. Liberal allowances were to be paid to the people. The State should avoid ostentation. Public funds should not be wasted. Only as much should be spent as was absolutely necessary.

Foreign Policy: Hadrat Ali held that in the matter of foreign policy, the State should take steps to ensure peace with other states. War should be avoided as far as possible. The Government should, however, remain alert and be prepared to meet any emergency. If war is resorted to it should be only in the cause of God and for the vindication of the truth Hadrat Ali held that in the case of war, let the first shot to be fired by the enemy. Bloodshed was to be avoided as far as possible. In the enemy land the fields were not to be harmed and the fruit trees were not to be cut. The aged and the women were not to be made the victims of vengeance.

Social and Ethical Thought : Hadrat Ali was a great thinker. In his sermons, addresses and other writings, which have come down to us in the shape of his book Nahl-ul-Balagha, we come across many a gem of precious thoughts. Some of these thoughts characterised by great depth are given hereunder.

Friends of Allah: Friends of. Allah are those who look to its inward aspect when the ordinary people look to the outward aspect of the world and when the other people are engrossed in the affairs of the world they get anxious about the Hereafter.

Momins and Hypocrites: A Momin is he whose neck if placed under my sword, would not think ill of me. A hypocrite is he whom even if I load with gold and silver he would not think good of me.

Faqih: A Faqih is one who would not make the people despair of the mercy of God.

Justice and Mercy: The purpose of justice is to give a person what is due to him. Mercy goes a step further and it gives a person something more than what is due to him.

The World and the Hereafter: He who seeks the world, death runs after him, he who seeks the Hereafter the world runs after him.

Momin and Infidel: He who tells of his want to a Momin is as if has requested God. He who seeks his want from an infidel is making a complaint against God.

Proximity to the Ruler: He who is in proximity to the ruler is like a person riding on a lion and there can be no knowing when the lion might overturn and devour him.

Haste: Haste is a kind of madness. One who does things in haste has to face shame and if he is not ashamed his madness is confirmed.

Faith and Faithlessness: Faith with the faithless is faithlessness before God and faithlessness with the faithless is faith.

Philosophy: If what the philosopher says is correct, it is a cure, if what he says is incorrect it is a disease.

Forgiveness: Forgiveness is the Zakat of success. If you wish to succeed in life, learn to forgive others.

Secret of Success: Success depends on self-confidence. Self-confidence depends on due deliberation. Deliberation depends on protecting ones secrets. He who cannot keep his secret cannot succeed.

Kinds of Patience: Patience is of two kinds, firstly patience at a thing which one does not like, and secondly patience at not getting a thing one desires.

Wealth and Poverty: Wealth provides one with the facilities of home country while travelling in a foreign land. Poverty make a person a stranger even in his home land.

Faith: Faith lies in preferring truth to falsehood even when the truth might lead to any harm and falsehood might lead to any advantage. An evidence of your faith is that what you say is in accordance with what you practise.

Momin: A Momin is he whose face wears a smiling look even though his heart is distressed.

Perfection: Perfection consists in three things: patience in affliction moderation in pursuit and offer of assistance to a supplicant.

Heresy: Heresay has four aspects namely concealment of truth, waging of war against truth, going astray from the path of truth and adoption of an inimical attitude to truth.

Seven Things of the Devil: There are seven things of the devil namely: excessive anger, excessive sneezing, excessive yawning, vomiting, bleeding of the nose, clandestine discourse and sleeping during devotional exercise.

Generosity: Generosity lies in affording relief to the needy without his asking for it. When the supplicant is assisted when he asks for it, that is liberality and munificence and not generosity.

Tauhid: Tauhid is a conviction of the heart which is above doubt.

Justice: Justice is determination against which there can be no accusation.

Broad-mindedness: Learning and good disposition go together and lead to broad-mindedness.

Wealth and Health: One cannot trust two things namely wealth and health. One does not know when they might forsake him.

Two Types of Subsistence: There are two types of subsistence, one after which you run and the other which runs after you.

Truth and Falsehood: There is distance of four fingers between truth and falsehood. Falsehood is that you say that you heard it from someone else. The truth is that you say that you saw it with your own eyes.

Things that are the Best: Resignation to the will of God is the best policy. Knowledge is the best inheritance. Good conduct is the best ornament. The best wealth is the suppression of desires. The middle course is the best course.

Things to which Nothing is Better: No honour is more respectable than sword. No religion is better than Islam. No citadel is stronger than piety. No one is better interceder than repentance. No treasure is richer than contentment.

Success and Failure: When you succeed do not feel proud. When you fail do not lose patience.

Persons Doomed to Ignominy: Two persons are deemed to ignominy, firstly he who creates dissensions and secondly he who levies false accusations.

Three Friends: Your three friends are: your friend, a friend of your friend and an enemy of your enemy.

Three Foes: Your three foes are: your foe, the foe of your friend and the friend of your foe.

Two Types of Men: There are two types of men in the world–one who sells himself to the world and the world destroys him, the other is the one who ransomed himself for the world and has released himself from its captivity.

Greetings and Favours: If somebody greets you, greet him in better terms. If somebody favours you, confer a greater favour on him.

Humiliation: Accept death, but do not accept humiliation.

Two Hungry Persons: There are two hungry persons whose hunger is never satisfied, firstly he who seeks knowledge and secondly he who seeks the world.

Miser: A miser lives in the world as an indigent and he will be called for in the Hereafter to give account as a capitalist.

Offshoots of Patience: Desires, fear and piety are the offshoots of patience.

Miserliness, Patience, Piety and Cowardice: Miserliness is dishonour. Patience is bravery. Piety is shield against hell. Cowardice is inferiority complex.

The Greatest and the Vilest: Wisdom is the greatest treasure. Folly is the greatest poverty. Of all thing pride, is the vilest. The greatest excellence is good disposition.

Companies to be Avoided: Avoid the company of a fool for he will harm you while trying to benefit you. Avoid the company of a liar for he will bring you near what is undesirable and remove you from what is desirable. Avoid the company of a miser for he would withhold from you what you stand in need of. Avoid the company of a libertine for he will sell you for a trifle.

Two Things to be Afraid of: Two things of which you should be afraid of are firstly giving way to your lust, and secondly harbouring high and far-fetched hopes.

The Worst Enemies: Before God two persons are the worst enemies, firstly the man who makes innovations, and secondly the man who creates dissensions.

Things that are Worse: There is no distress worse than ignorance. There is no enemy worse than self-adulation. There is no worse companion than bad conduct.

The Similes : Hadrat Ali had the peculiar skill to explain things by giving appropriate similes In his various addresses and sermons we come across many instances of the brilliance of his expression in bringing home the truth through interesting examples.

The World: He likened the world to a serpent which was outwardly very soft skinned but poisonous from within.

Falsehood: Hadrat Ali held that like the feathers of a peacock, falsehood might look very attractive, but was as ugly as the feet of the peacock. Falsehood has no legs to stand upon.

The Unbelievers: Hadrat Ali compared the unbelievers to a bat which can see when it is dark, but which is blind and cannot see anything when it is daylight.

People who did not Respond to His Call: When Hadrat Ali exhorted the people of Iraq to respond to his call for war against Muawiyyah, they did not respond to his call. He said, "You are like a pregnant woman who undergoes the ordeal of childbirth, but gives birth to a dead child."

The Tree and the Fruit: When after the death of the Holy Prophet, the Quraish based their claim to the caliphate on the ground that they belonged to the same tree as the Holy Prophet, Hadrat Ali said, "It is strange that they look to the tree, but neglect its fruit."

People of Basra: When the people of Basra who had originally taken the oath of allegiance to him, but later chose to fight against him, Hadrat Ali said that these people were near the water but far from the sky.

People of the Age of Ignorance: Referring to the people of the age of ignorance in the pre-Islamic era, Hadrat Ali said that they were like an egg which is broken in the nest.

People of Kufa: Addressing the people of Kufa, Hadrat Ali said: "When I invite you to fight, your eyes begin to move in your sockets as if you are in the agony of death. You are like the camels whose herdsmen have disappeared and when these animals are collected on one side, they scatter on the other side."

Mughira b Shuaba: Mughira was regarded by the Quraish as a wise man. When Mughira favoured Muawiyyah, Hadrat Ali said, "Mughira has profited from Islam only to the extent seeking worldly end. He is obvious of the Hereafter."

People who Run after the World: About the people who run after the world, Hadrat Ali said: "Those people who run after the world are like beasts who fall at one another, with the strong oppressing the weak."

People who are not Deceived by the World: About the people who are not deceived by the world, Hadrat Ali said, "Those who have understood the deceptive character of the world do not feel distressed on death. They are like the people who migrate from a famine-struck land to a land of plenty."

Complaint against the Umayyads: During the caliphate of Hadrat Uthman, Hadrat Ali had a complaint that the Umayyads were withholding from him what was due to him. He said, "The Umayyads are withholding what is due to me as the camelman, when milking the she-camel, withholds the milk from the young one of the camel"

Falsehood of Muawiyyah: Referring to the falsehood of Muawiyyah, Hadrat Ali said that falsehood had appeared in his case as the horns on the head of a young one of a goat.

Shedding of Sins through Prayer: In a sermon, Hadrat Ali said that through prayer the sins of a man are shed as a tree sheds it leaves.

Cleanliness and Prayers: In another sermon, Hadrat Ali said "Prayer is like a hot spring of water which flows at your door and provides you the wherewithal for cleanliness."

Crumbs after the Meals: In a sermon, Hadrat Ali said that the world had run its cause and nothing had been left of it except the crumbs after the meals.

People who did not Respond to His Call: In an address, Hadrat Ali compared the people who did not respond to his call to a camel who ran away from the herd shrieking with the pain of belly.

Heart of the People: In a sermon Hadrat Ali prayed for the heart of the people to melt at the mention of the Word of God as salt dissolves in the water.

Ignorant Persons: In an address, Hadrat Ali said that the ignorant persons were like a person riding on a beast of burden which could not see. He deplored that such ignorant persons dealt with the injunctions of Islam as air scatters the straw.

Ashas b Qais: Hadrat Ali said that among his companions. Ashas b Qais was what. Abdullah b. Abi Sahl was in the time of the Holy Prophet.

Patience and Faith: Hadrat Ali held that patience and faith bear the same relations as in the case of a human being the head bears to the body. There can be nobody without head, and there can be no faith without patience.

Disease and Sins: Hadrat Ali held that disease sheds sins as the tree sheds the dead leaves.

Death of the Virtuous: Hadrat Ali compared the death of the virtuous to the migration journey of the people from a famine-struck land to a land of plenty.

Days of Life: Hadrat Ali held that the days of life pass as the passing of clouds in the sky.

Devotion to the World: Hadrat Ali held that those who are devoted to the world are like barking dogs and ferocious animals who fall at one another and the strong devour the weak.

Seekers of the World: Hadrat Ali compared the men seeking the world to camels which are let loose and which roam about causing mischief.

Virtue of Silence: Hadrat Ali advocated the virtue of silence by advancing the simile that water can be preserved in a water skin only when its mouth is tied.

Thirsty Camels on a Water Pond: When the people flocked to him and urged him to accept their allegiance, Hadrat Ali compared them to thirsty camels who flock to the water pond when their strings are untied.

Caliphate of Hadrat Umar: When Hadrat. Abu Bakr died and still ignoring his claims, Hadrat Umar became the Caliph, Hadrat Ali held that the second Caliph was like a person riding a camel whose reins if tightened would injure the camel and if loosened would endanger the rider.

Umayyad Use of the Baitul Mal: Referring to the appropriation of the funds of the Baitul-Mal by Umayyads for personal ends during the caliphate of Hadrat Uthman, Hadrat Ali held that they ate away the public funds as the camel eats away the grass.

Withholding the Milk of the She-camel from its Young One: Hadrat Ali had the complaint that during the caliphate of Hadrat Uthman the Umayyads withheld from him what was his right like the camelman who, while milking the she-camel, withholds its milk from its young one.

Handle of the Grinding Stone: When Hadrat. Abu Bakr became the Caliph, Hadrat Ali held that Hadrat. Abu Bakr had assumed the mantle of the caliphate forcibly while he knew that he (Hadrat Ali) was as essential for the caliphate as the handle is necessary for moving the grinding stone.

The Simile of a Sinner: Hadrat Ali held that a sinner is like a person riding on an animal over which he has no control and which is running fast to hurl him into precipice.

Drops of Rain: Hadrat Ali held that the injunctions of God descend like the drops of rain.

The Summer Clouds: When the people of Kufa did not respond to the call of Hadrat Ali to rise to meet the challenge of Muawiyyah, Hadrat Ali said that he longed for warriors who in their action and speed should be like the summer clouds.

Goat and the Lion: Addressing the people of Kufa, Hadrat Ali said, "I want you to tread the path of the truth, but you run from it as the goat runs away on hearing the roar of a lion."

Taking the Thorn out of the Foot with a Thorn: On another occasion Hadrat Ali said that the people of Kufa were like a person who picked out the thorn from his foot with a thorn.

Solution of Salt in Water: With reference to the people of Kufa, Hadrat Ali prayed "O God melt their hearts as the salt is dissolved in water."

Bull with Crooked Horns: When Talha defected after taking the oath of allegiance to him, Hadrat Ali likened Talha to a bull with crooked horns.

Shaking of Plants: Referring to the piety of the Companions of the Holy Prophet, Hadrat Ali said that they shuddered at the mention of the. Hereafter as the plants shake when a strong wind blows.

Pregnant Woman Separating from the Child: Addressing the people of Kufa, Hadrat Ali said that they were not dependable and they were likely to leave him, as the pregnant woman on childbirth is separated from the child bred in her womb.

Household of the Holy Prophet: Hadrat Ali said that the simile of the household of the Holy Prophet was like stars which if one star sets another star rises.

Foaming Waves of the Sea: While addressing Hadrat Uthman, Hadrat Ali said that treason was likely to wage like the foaming waves of the sea.

Anecdotes

He Decried Flattery: Once a person flattered Hadrat Ali. Hadrat Ali said:

> "Do not flatter me. I am not what you say, but I am more than what you think of me in your heart."

He Denounced Praise: One day Hadrat Ali delivered a sermon which was most impressive and eloquent. Some one praised him for his sermon. He said:

> "Do not praise me. That would mislead me and beguile me into vainglory. Remember that all praise is for God alone."

He would Carry his Own Burden: One day Hadrat Ali purchased some provisions in the market. It was a heavy load and he carried it himself. Many persons offered to carry the load for him. He refused the offer saying that everyone should carry his burden himself.

He did not Want the People to Follow in his Retinue: One day Hadrat Ali was riding a horse. Some people followed him and began to walk in his train. He asked them why they were following him. They said that they felt elated to walk in his retinue. He said:

> "Go back to your business By walking behind me you will breed feelings of inferiority in yourselves and infect me with arrogance."

He Prayed for Patience to Bear Suffering: At the battle of Uhud, Hadrat Ali received over a hundred wounds. In spite of these wounds he continued fighting and said:

> "May God grant me patience to bear this suffering. It is a favour of God that he gave me the courage to stand and fight and not to leave the battlefield."

His Complaint against his People: One night Hadrat Ali saw the Holy Prophet in a dream. He complained to the Holy Prophet that he had received much trouble from his people. The Holy Prophet said that he might invoke the curse of God on them. When it was day, he lifted his hands after the morning prayer and said:

> "O God, give me a better people and give these people a worse ruler than me."

He Rode on a Mule instead of a Horse: When going to battle, Hadrat Ali used to ride on a mule instead of a horse. He was asked why he preferred a mule to a horse when the horse would carry him faster. He said that it was so he did not wish to fly from the battlefield.

He would Never Turn his Back to the Enemy: Hadrat Ali always wore the armour on the front part of his body. He was asked why he did not wear the armour on his back. He said that it was so because he did not want to turn his back to the enemy.

He would not Seek a Concession: Once Hadrat Ali went to the market to purchase some cloth. He went to a shop and a shopkeeper recognising him offered the cloth at a concessional rate. Hadrat Ali refused to make the purchase.

He Preferred his Slave to himself: Once Hadrat Ali went to the bazar to purchase some cloth for himself and his slave. One piece was purchased at a higher price and the other at a lower price. He gave the costlier piece of cloth to his slave and kept the cloth of inferior quality for himself.

He had no Ambition for the Caliphate: It is related that when on the way to Basra, Hadrat Ali and his troops were camping at Rabda, Ibn. Abbas came to see him. At that time Hadrat Ali was mending his shoe. Hadrat Ali asked Ibn. Abbas as to what would be the value of the shoe. Ibn. Abbas said that the old shoe had hardly any value and its value would at the most not exceed quarter of a dirham. Hadrat Ali thereupon said, "By God, this shoe is more valuable to me than the caliphate. I have no ambition to rule."

He Freed the Slave who did not Respond to his Call: Once Hadrat Ali called his slave, but the slave did not respond to his call. He called him thrice, but the slave kept silent. Thereafter, Hadrat Ali went to the slave and said, "Did you not hear my call?". He said that he had listened to his call, but was at that time calling upon God Who had subjected him to the humiliation of slavery". Thereupon Hadrat Ali said, "I release you from slavery forthwith in the name of God. "

He Saw God with Inward Eyes: Once Hadrat Ali was asked whether he had seen God. He said that verily he had seen God because he could not worship Him without knowing Him. He was asked how he had seen Him and he said that. He had seen him with the inward eyes of the heart.

He Lost Consciousness while Praying: Once an arrow stuck in the feet of Hadrat Ali. It could not be taken out because of the intensity of the pain felt. When Hadrat Ali stood up in prayers, he was so much absorbed in the devotional exercise that the surgeon pulled out the arrow without Hadrat Ali feeling any pain.

He would not Pay the Enemy on its Own Coin: At the battlefield of Siffin, the forces of Muawiyyah had the control over the source of water supply and they would not allow, thereto, the troops of Hadrat Ali. When the troops of Hadrat Ali overpowered the enemy and got control over the source of water supply, Hadrat Ali was advised that he should deny access of water to the enemy. He repudiated the advice saying that he would not pay the enemy in its own coin, but in the coin of Islam.

He Preferred his Men to Himself: During the water shortage in Siffin he refused to quench his own thirst saying that the water should be given to those of his men who were more thirsty than him

Two Wrongs cannot Make a Right: When, after the battle of Siffin, Muawiyyah began harassing the people by making raids into the territory adjoining Syria, the Governor of Hadrat Ali, Kameel b Ziyad, suggested that he should be authorised to lead retributive expeditions into Syria. Hadrat Ali turned down the suggestion saying, "Two wrongs cannot make a right. Let Muawiyyah take pleasure in harassing innocent people I cannot resort to such measures."

He was Dispirited because he had no Guest: One day Hadrat Ali felt unusually dispirited and dejected. When asked about the reason for his unusual dejection he said that he was feeling dispirited because he had received no guest for a week.

He wore Dress of Coarse Cloth: Hadrat Ali always wore dress of coarse cloth. When asked why did he wear such shabby dress when he was the head of the State, he said that it was so because coarse cloth softened the heart while fine cloth hardened the heart.

He Wanted to Travel Light: The house of Hadrat Ali was bereft of the usual furniture. When asked why he deprived himself of such necessities when he was the ruler of a State he said, "This life is a journey and while on a journey one should travel light. I have booked my luggage for the destination—the Hereafter."

He would not Break Open the Lock of the Shop of God: Once. Aqueel, a brother of Hadrat Ali, asked him to provide some relief for him as he was feeling sore. Hadrat Ali said that when he got his usual allowance from the Baitul Mal, he would give something out of it to him. That did not satisfy Aqueel. Hadrat Ali thereupon said, "Then you may break open the locks of the shops in the market. Aqueel said, "Do you want me to become a thief. " Hadrat Ali retorted "Then do you want me to break open the lock of the shop of God and become a brigand instead of the custodian of the Baitul Mal."

He was not Afraid of Death: In the battle of Siffin, Hadrat Ali penetrated into the front ranks of the Syrian forces without any protective armour. One after another his assailants fell before the onslaught of his sword. His son Imam Hassan objected to such neglect to protect himself. Hadrat Ali said. "It is immaterial to me whether I fall to death or death falls on me. I love death as much as a suckling loves the milk of its mother."

He did not Care for the Booty: In a battle Hadrat Ali killed a wealthy Quraish chief Umar b Uqba, but contrary to the Arab custom he did not mutilate his body, nor took off his costly coat of mail. When asked why he had not taken his valuable coat of mail, Hadrat Ali said, "The lion who enters the battlefield either kills himself or is killed. He does not brother about the booty."

He would not Own the Treasure in the Land that He had Purchased: Once Hadrat Ali purchased a plot of land from a person in Medina. When the plot was dug a treasure was found therein. Hadrat Ali would not accept the treasure as it did not form a part of his transaction with the original owner. He offered the treasure to the original owner, but he too did not accept it. Thereupon Hadrat Ali distributed the entire treasure in charity.

He undertook to Clear the Debt of a Dead Muslim: Once the Holy Prophet attended the funeral of a dead Muslim. Before leading the funeral prayer, the Holy Prophet enquired whether the dead man had to clear any debt. He was informed that the dead man had to pay the debt of a dinar. The Holy Prophet said that before he could lead the funeral prayer someone should undertake the responsibility of clearing the debt of the dead Muslim. It was Hadrat Ali who stepped forward to undertake the responsibility for clearing the debt.

He would not Accept the Allegiance from whom he had Released: Marwan, a cousin of Muawiyyah, was a bitter enemy of Hadrat Ali. He had played a great part in inciting revolt against the caliphate of Hadrat Ali. He was taken captive in the battle of the Camel at Basra and when brought before Hadrat Ali he asked for mercy. Hadrat Ali released him unconditionally. Thereupon, Marwan offered to pay allegiance to him, but Hadrat Ali said, "I did not want his allegiance I released him for the sake of God and not for securing allegiance to me."

He did not Believe in the Prognostications of the Astrologer: When Hadrat Ali led his troops against the Kharijites at the battle of Nahrawan, an astrologer advised him not to proceed to battle as the time was not propitious. Hadrat Ali refused to act on the advice saying, all knowledge of the unknown belongs to God I cannot accept any person as a partner in the knowledge of God."

He would Take no Precaution to Protect Himself: During the last days of his life, when Hadrat Ali was asked to take protective measures against any murderous attack, he said, "The shield of God is around my body, and nobody can harm me against the will of God. And if God wills me to be martyred, no protective measures will avail."

People Stood in the Way of his Right: At Basra, someone said to Hadrat Ali that he was ambitious for the caliphate Hadrat Ali said, "I am not ambitious, what has happened is that there are people who stand in the way of my right. To strive for the right is no ambition."

Spacious House: At Basra, Hadrat Ali went to the house of one of his companions A ala b Ziyad. He had constructed a spacious house. Hadrat Ali was critical of the spaciousness of the house. He said, "Aala what have you gained by constructing a spacious house in this world. You should have built a spacious house for yourself in the world Hereafter."

Renunciation, not the Way of Islam: It was complained to Hadrat Ali that one of his Companions. Ibne Ziyad was undergoing devotional exercise to such an extent that he had neglected and disregarded his obligations to his wife and children. Hadrat Ali reprimanded him and said that renunciation was not the way of Islam. He asked him to maintain a proper balance between his duties to God and his duties to the people.

Hosting Dinners: When it was brought to the notice of Hadrat Ali that one of his Governors had hosted a big dinner Hadrat Ali wrote him a letter expressing his disapproval and said "What have you gained by hosting such dinner where the wealthy are fed extravagantly and the poor are turned out."

He could Still Wield the Sword: Writing to Muawiyyah, Hadrat Ali said in one of his letters, "I wield the same sword with which I severed the head of your maternal grandfather, maternal uncle and brother with the same stroke."

BIBLIOGRAPHY

Abbas, Nadwi Abdullah : *Learn the Language of the Holy Quran,* Kitab Bhavan, New Delhi, 2002.

Abdali, M.R. : *Scientific Thought in Islam,* Pious Publications, Hyderabad, 2001.

Abdul, Hamid Siddiqui : *The Life of Muhammad (PBUH),* Islamic Pub., New Delhi,1997.

Abdullah, Muhammad : *Islamic Prayers,* Idara Ishaat-e-Diniyat Pvt. Ltd, New Delhi, 1999.

Acquinas, St. Thomas : *The Political Ideas of Islam,* Hafner Publishing Company, New York, 1953.

Adair and Yazbeck Haddad : *Islamic Values in the United States,* Oxford, New York, 1997.

Adams, C.C. : *Islam and Modernism in Egypt,* Oxford University Press, New York, 1953.

Adil, H. M. : *Letters of Hadrat Usman Ghani (R.A.A.),* Kitab Bhavan, New Delhi, 1992

Affifi : *The Mystical Philosophy of Ibn Arabi,* Cambridge, New York, 1979.

Aghanides, N.P. : *Mohammedan Theories of Finance,* Oxford, New York, 1916.

Ahmad, Aziz : *Islamic Modernism in India and Pakistan,* Oxford University Press, 1970.

———— : *Studies in Islamic Culture in the Indian Environment,* Oxford, New York, 1964.

Ahmed, Hasanuddin : *A Handbook of Muslim Belief,* Goodword Books Pvt. Ltd., New Delhi, 1995.

———— : *Islamic Economics,* Goodword Books Pvt. Ltd., New Delhi, 1991.

———— : *Principles of Islamic Culture,* Goodword Books Pvt. Ltd., New Delhi, 1989.

———— : *Social Justice in Islam,* Goodword Books Pvt. Ltd., New Delhi, 1990.

———— : *A Brief History of Islam,* Goodword Books Pvt. Ltd., New Delhi, 1998.

———— : *Islamic Business Ethics,* Goodword Books Pvt. Ltd., New Delhi, 1998.

Ahmad, Ilyas : *Social Contract and the Islamic State,* Urdu Publishing House, Allahabad, 1940.

——— : *Sovereignty, Islamic and Modern,* Allies Book Corporation, Karachi, 1965.

Ahmad, Imtiaz : *Divorce and Remarriage among Muslims in India,* Manohar Publishers, New Delhi, 2003.

——— : *Ritual and Religion among Muslims in India,* Manohar Publishers, New Delhi, 1984.

Ahmad, K. N. : *Muslim Law of Divorce,* Kitab Bhavan, New Delhi, 1988.

Ahmad, Khurshid : *Islam : its Meaning and Message,* Islamic Council of Europe, London, 1976.

Ahmad, Manzooruddin : *Pakistan : the Emerging Islamic State,* Allies Book Corporation, Karachi, 1966.

Ahmad, Moinuddin : *Religions of Mankind,* Kitab Bhavan, New Delhi, 1994.

Ahmad, M.M.Z. : *Mystical Tendencies in Islam in the Light of the Quran and Traditions,* Daya Publishing House, Delhi, 1986.

Ahmad, Naseem : *Liberation of Muslim Women,* Gyan Books Pvt., Ltd., New Delhi, 2001.

Ahmad, Zubaid : *The Contribution of Indo-Pak to Arabi Literature,* Royal Pub., Lahore, 1968.

Akhtar, Hakeem M. : *Remedies to Spiritual Maladies,* Idara Ishaat-e-Diniyat Pvt. Ltd, New Delhi, 1991.

Akhtar, Wazir : *Economics in Islamic Law,* Kitab Bhavan, New Delhi, 1992.

Alfieri, Binaca Maria : *Islamic Architecture of the Indian Subcontinent,* Lawrence King, New York, 1989.

Al-Hujwiri : *The Kashf al Mahjub,* Luzac and Co. Ltd., London, 1976.

Ali, Akhtar : *Israel and Prophesies of Islam,* Raj & Co., New Delhi, 1997.

Ali, Kattani : *Muslim Minorities in the World Today,* Ashish Publishing House, New Delhi, 2001.

Ali, Adil : *Presidential Addresses on Arab Islamic Studies,* Kitab Bhavan, New Delhi, 2002.

Ali, A. Yusuf : *Message of Islam,* Kitab Bhavan, New Delhi, 2000.

Ali, Mansur : *Guide to Dargah Sharif,* Bismillah Pub., Lucknow, 1985.

Ali, S. Ameer : *Muhammadan Law,* Kitab Bhavan, New Delhi, 1986.

Ali, Syed Ameer : *Islam,* Kitab Bhavan, New Delhi, 1992.

Allchin, Bridget : *The Rise of Civilization in India and Pakistan,* Cambridge University Press, New Delhi, 1989.

Allman, G. J. : *Greek Geometry from Thales to Euclid,* Dublin, 1889.

Altaf, Hussain Ahanger : *Customary Succession among Muslims,* Uppal Publishibng House, New Delhi, 1997.

Amery, Reeves : *The Anatomy of Peace,* Oxford, New York, 2001.

Amini, Mualana Taqi : *Fundamentals of Ijtihad,* Idaara-I-Adabiyat, Delhi, 1986.

Anawati, G.C. and Gardet Louis : *Mystique Musulmane,* Allen & Co., Paris, 1961.

Andre, Beaufre : *General Introduction to Strategy,* Oxford, New York, 2001.

Andre, Mauris : *History of England,* Britain Pub., England, 2001.

Antonio, Cassese : *The Self-determination of Peoples,* Columbia University, Columbia, 1981.

Antony, G.N. Flew : *Wants or Needs : Choices or Commands,* Allen & Co., Paris, 1953.

Anwarullah : *The Islamic Law of Evidence,* Kitab Bhavan, New Delhi, 2000.

Arberry, A. J. : *The Doctrine of the Sufis,* Kitab Bhavan, New Delhi, 2000.

Arbery : *Sufism,* George Allen & Unwin Ltd., London, 1996.

Arnold and Guillaume : *The Legacy of Islam,* Oxford University Press, London, 1949.

Arnold, Toynbee : *The World and the West,* Macmillan, London, 2000.

Arnold, Sir Thomas : *The Caliphate,* MacMillan, London, 1965.

Arnold, T. W. : *Preaching of Islam,* Luzac & Co., London, 1913.

——— : *The Caliphate,* Routledge & Kegan Paul Ltd., London,1965.

Arnold, Thomas : *The Legacy of Islam,* Oxford University Press, New York, 2000.

Arvind, Sharma : *Women in World Religion,* New York Press, New York, 1990.

Asad, Majda : *Indian Muslims : Festivals and Customs,* Publication Division, New Delhi, 1989.

Asad, Muhammad : *The Principles of State and Government in Islam,* University of California Press, California, 1961.

Asborn, Eide : *Human Rights in World Society,* New Millennium Pub., Oslo, 1977.

Athar, Ali : *Mughal Nobility under Aurangzeb,* Pupular Prakashan, Bombay, 1968.

Atta, Mohiuddin : *Abu Bakr,* Feroz Pub., Lahore, 1999.

Aurobindo, Sri : *The Foundations of Islamic Culture,* New York, 1973.

Azad, G. Murtaza : *Judicial System of Islam,* Kitab Bhavan, New Delhi, 1994.

Aziz, Noomi Kurtha : *Prisoners of War and War Crimes,* Deep Publications, Lacknow, 1980.

Azmi, Majaz : *Muslim Wife,* Idara Ishaat-e-Diniyat Pvt. Ltd, New Delhi, 1991.

Bagby, Philip : *Culture and History,* University of California Press, California, 1991.

Bagley, R.R.C. : *Ghazzali's Book of Counsel for Kings,* Oxford, New York, 1964.

Bahedur, Kalim : *The Jamaat-i-Islami of Pakistan,* Progressive Books, Lahore, 1978.

Baksh, S. K. : *Politics in Islam,* Kitab Bhavan, New Delhi, 2003.

Ballard, Robert D. : *Exploring our Living Planet,* National Geographic Society, Washington, 1989.

Baloch, N. A. : *Great Books of Islamic Civilization,* Kitab Bhavan, New Delhi, 2001.

Baral, Lok Raj : *Regional Migrations : Ethnicity and Security,* Popular Prakashan, Bombay, 1995.

Barkatullah, M. : *Khilafat,* MacMillan, London,1924.

Basham, A. L. : *A Cultural History of India,* Oxford, New York, 1975.

Basil, King : *The Conquest of Fearm,* Illias Pub., Islamabad, 2000.

Batty and Morgan : *War its Conduct and Legal Results,* Feroz Pub., Lahore, 2000.

Bawer, Raymond : *The New Man in Soviet Social Psychology,* Oxford, New York, 1990.

Beckett, Katharine Scarfe : *Perception of the Islamic Word,* Cambridge University Press, New Delhi, 1992.

Berger, M. : *Islam in Egypt Today : Social and Political Aspects of Popular Religion,* MacMillan, London, 1970.

Berkes, N. : *Turkish Nationalism and Western Civilization,* Allen & Unwin, London, 1959.

Berkey, Jonothan P. : *The Formation of Islam : Religion and Society in the Near East,* Cambridge University Press, New Delhi, 1990.

Bertram, Thomas : *Arabia Felix,* Oxford, New York, 2003.

Bevan, E. R. : *House of Seleucus,* Allen & Unwin, London, 2001.

Bhatia, H. S. : *Studies in Islamic law, Religion and Society,* Deep & Deep Publications, New Delhi, 1997.

Bhawany : *Revolutionary Study of National Development,* Allen & Unwin, London, 2001.

Binder, L. : *Religion and Politics in Pakistan,* University Press, Berkeley, 1961.

Boland, B.J. : *The Struggle of Islam in Modern Indonesia,*The Hague, Nijhoff, 1971.

Boyle, J. A. : *The Cambridge History of Iran,* Cambridge, London, 1968.

Brett, M. : *Northern Africa : Islam and Modernization,* Allen & Unwin, London, 1973.

Brigadier, Gulzar Ahmed : *The Battles of the Prophet of Allah (PBUH),* Aziz Pub., Islamabad, 2001.

——— : *The Prophets (PBUH) Concept of War,* Aziz Pub., Islamabad, 2000.

Briffault, Robert : *The Making of Humanity,* Islamic Book Foundation, Lahore, 1980.

Brockelman, C. : *History of the Islamic People,* G.P. Putnam's Sons, New York, 1947.

Broun, Daniel : *A New Introduction to Islam,* Atlantic Publishers, New Delhi, 2004.

Brow, John R. : *Islam, Law, and Equality in Indonesia : an Anthropology of Public,* Cambridge University Press, New Delhi, 1997.

Browne, G. Edward : *Islamic Medicine,* Goodword Books Pvt. Ltd., New Delhi, 1996.

Browne, E. G. : *History of Arabian Medicine,* Cambridge, New Delhi, 1921.

——— : *History of Arabian Polity,* Cambridge, New Delhi, 1922.

Bucaille, Maurice : *The Bibal, Quran and Science,* Kitab Bhavan, New Delhi, 2004.

Bukhsh, S. K. : *Contribution to the History of Islamic Civilization,* Kitab Bhavan, New Delhi, 2000.

Burges, James : *The Muhammadan Architecture of Ahmadabad,* Bernard Quaritch, London,1900.

Burton, Sir Richard : *Sind and Races that Inhabit the Valley of the Indus,* Allen & Unwin, London, 1851.

Cajori, F. : *A History of Muslims,* Oxford, New York, 1954.

——— : *A History of Mathematics,* Oxford, New York, 1924.

Calverley, Edwin Elliot : *Worship in Islam,* University of Madras, Madras, 1925.

Campbell, Arnold : *Arabian Medicine,* Oxford, New York, 2002.

Carl, Bockleman : *History of Islamic Peoples,* Oxford, New York, 2003.

Carra, De Vaux : *Penseurs d' Islam,* A. & B. Pub., Paris, 1921.

Carre, Olivier : *Islam and the State in the World Today,* Manohar Publisher, New Delhi, 1989.

Chaghatai, M. A. : *Muslim Monuments of Ahmadabad through their Inscriptions,* Deccan College Research Institute, Pune, 1942.

Chiragh, Ali : *The Proposed Political Legal and Social Reform under Muslim Rule,* Popular Prakashan, Bombay, 1883.

Clothey, W. : *Images of Man : Religious and Historical Process in South Asia,* New Era Publications, Madras, 1984.

Commissariat, M. S. : *A History of Gujarat,* Longman's Green & Co., Bombay, 1938.

Cook, Michael : *Forbiding Wrong in Islam : an Introduction,* Cambridge University Press, New Delhi, 1985.

Corbin, H. : *Avicenna and the Visionary Recital,* MacMillan, London, 1960.

Crone, Patricia : *Themes in Islamic History,* Cambridge University Press, New Delhi, 2000.

Daniel, N.A. : *Islam : Europe and Empire,* University Press, Edinburgh, 1966.

——— : *Islam and the West : the Making of an Image,* University Press, Edinburgh, 1962.

Dawud, Rahbar : *God of Justice,* Mac & Jac Pub., Leiden, 1960.

De, Laet : *Description of India and Fragment of Indian History,* Oxford, New York, 1963.

——— : *The Political Systems of Empire,* Oxford, New York, 1963.

Desai, A. : *Hind Islami : Tarz-e-Tameer,* Publication Division, New Delhi, 1993.

Dhagamwar, Vasudha : *Law, Power and Justice : Protection of Personal Rights under Islam,* Popular Prakashan, Bombay, 2001.

Dhaul, Laxmi : *The Sufi Shrine of Ajmer,* Rupa & Co., New Delhi, 1987.

Dieterici, F. : *Alfarabi's Philosophische Abhandlungen,* Mac & Jac Pub., Leiden, 1890.

Dinet and Salman : *Life of Muhammad (PBUH),* Feroz Pub., Lahore, 2003.

Divine, Epiphany : *Man and Transformation,* MacMillan, London, 1964.

Dorothy, Vaugham : *Europe and the Turks,* Oxford, New York, 2004.

Doughty, C.M. : *Travels in Arabia Deserta,* MacMillan, London, 1923.

Drfyer, J. L. E. : *History of the Planetary Systems,* Cambridge, New York, 1903.

Duchesne, L. : *Early History of the Christian Church,* Luzac & Co., London, 1914.

Durrani, F.K.K. : *Muhammad (PBUH) the Prophet,* Oxford, New York, 2001.

Edward, Mortimer : *Faith and Power, the Politics of Islam,* Oxford, New York, 2002.

Edwards, Beverly Milton : *Islam and Politics in the Contemporary World,* Blackwell, New York, 1987.

Elliot and Dowson : *History of India,* Ali & Co., Aligarh, 1952.

Emil, Brunner : *Justice and the Social Order,* Oxford, New York, 2000.

Engineer, Asghar Ali : *Islam : Challenge in Twenty-first Century,* Gyan Books Pvt. Ltd., New Delhi, 2004.

——— : *Islam : Women and Gender Justice,* Gyan Books Pvt. Ltd., New Delhi, 2001.

——— : *A Rational Approach to Islam,* Gyan Books Pvt. Ltd., New Delhi, 2001.

——— : *The Islamic State,* Vikas Publishing House, New Delhi, 1987.

Ernst, Carl W. : *Teaching of Sufism,* Deep & Deep, New Delhi, 2000.

Faris, Nabith A. : *The Foundations of the Articles of Faith,* Feroz Pub., Lahore, 1963.

——— : *The Book of Knowledge,* Feroz Pub., Lahore, 1962.

Faruqi, Bherhan Ahmad : *The Mujaddid's Conception of Tauhid,* Feroz Pub., Lahore, 1940.

Faruqi, Ziya-ul Hasan : *The Deoband School and the Demand for Pakistan,* Popular Prakashan, Bombay, 1963.

Fatima, T. : *Islamic Law and Judiciary,* Deep & Deep Publications, New Delhi, 2001.

Fazal, Abul : *Akbar Namah,* Kitab Bhavan, New Delhi, 1977.

Field, Cland H. : *Al-Ghazali : the Alchemy of Happiness,*Macmillan, London, 1910.

Flynn, V.J.A. : *Fathepur-Sikri,* Popular Prakashan, Bombay, 1975.

Fordon, S. : *Preliminary Statement on a General Theory of the Islamization of the Malay-Indonesian Archipelago,* Kuala Lumpur, 1969.

——— : *The Origin of Malay Shair,* Kuala Lumpur, 1968.

Foster, W. : *The English Factories in India,* Oxford, New Delhi, 1906.

Francois, Bernier : *Travels in the Mogul Empire,* MacMillan, London, 1916.

Friedmann, Yahanan : *Tolerance and Coercion in Islam : Interfaith Relations in the Muslims Traditions,* Cambridge, New York, 1990.

Frykenberg, R.E. : *Land Control and Social Structure in Indian History,* University Press, Wisconsin, 1969.

Fuller, J.F.C. : *Decisive Battles of the Western World,* Oxford, New York, 2000.

Herklots G. A. and Jafar Sharif : *Islam in India,* Atlantic Publishers, New Delhi, 1999.

Gaborieau, M. : *The Cult of Saints among Muslims in Nepal and North India,* Cambridge University, Press, Cambridge, 1983.

Gairdner, W.H. Temple : *Al-Ghazzali's Mishkatul-Anwar : the Niche for Lights,* Oxford, London, 1915.

Gare, Frederic : *Political Islam in the Indian Subcontinent : the Jannat-i-Islam,* Manohar Publishers, New Delhi, 2001.

Gauba, K.L. : *The Prophet of the Desert (PBUH),* Feroz Pub., Lahore, 2000.

Gellner, E. : *Doctor and Saint,* University of California Press, Berkeley, 1972

———— : *Post-Traditional Forms in Islam : the Turf and Trade,* Oxford, New York, 1982.

Gerges : *American and Political Islam : Clash of Cultures or Claush of Interest?,* New Academic Publishers, New Delhi, 1992.

Gibb, H.A.R : *Islamic Society and the West,* Luzac & Co., London, 1960.

———— : *Studies in the Civilization of Islam,* Beacon Press, Boston,1962.

———— : *Modern Tends in Islam,* University Press, Chicago, 1950.

Gibbon, Edward : *History of the Decline and Fall of Roman Empire,* Oxford, New York, 2000.

Gibran, Khalil : *The Prophet,* Jaico Publishing House, New Delhi, 1995.

Gillispie, Charles Coulston : *Dictionary of Scientific Biography,* Charles Scribner's Sons, New York, 1981.

Gilsenam, Michael : *Recognizing Islam,* MacMillan, London, 2001.

———— : *Saint and Sufi in Modern Egypt : an Essay in the Sociology of Religion,* Oxford, New York, 1973.

Gins Berg, M. : *Evolution and Progress,* William Heinemann Ltd., London, 1982.

Glubb : *The Great Arab Conquests,* Feroz Pub., Lahore, 2001.

———— : *The Story of Arab Legion,* Feroz Pub., Lahore, 2000.

Goldziher, J. : *Muhammedanische Studien,* University Press, Halle, 1889.

Gonda, J. : *History of Indian Literature,* University Press, Wiesbaden, 1973.

Grunebaum, G.E. : *Islam : Essays in the Nature and Growth of a Cultural Tradition,* American Anthropological Association, 1955.

Grunebaum, Gustave Edmund Von : *Modern Islam,* University Press, Los Angeles, 1952.

———— : *Unity and Variety in Muslim Civilization,* University of Chicago Press, Chicago, 1955.

Guillaume, A. : *The Traditions of Islam,* Khayats, Beirut, 1966.

Gustav, E. Von Grunebaum : *Unity and Variety in Muslim World,* Oxford, New York, 2003.

Hafiz, Ghulam Sarwar : *Muhammad (PBUH) the Holy Prophet,* Dar-ul Ishaat, Karachi, 1997.

Haji, Khalifah : *Kashf-al-Zunan,* Faiz-a-Islam Pub., Istanbul, 1943.

Halepota, A.J. : *Philosophy of Shah Waliullah,* Feroz Pub., Lahore, 1986.

Hamid, Enayat : *Islam in the Political Process,* Cambridge University Press, Cambridge, 1993.

Hamidullah, M. : *Battlefields of the Prophet Muhammad,* Kitab Bhavan, New Delhi, 2003.

——— : *Rasul-i-Akram Ki Siyas : Zindagi,* Dar-ul Ishaat, Karachi, 1961.

——— : *The Muslim Conduct of State,* Feroz Pub., Lahore, 1943.

Hans, Morgenthu : *Politics : Among Nations,* Oxford New York, 1954.

Haq, M. Anwarul : *The Faith Movement of Mawlana Muhammad Ilyas,* Country Pub., London, 1972.

Haqq, Enamul : *Muslim Bengali Literature,* Dar-ul Ishaat, Karachi, 1957.

Hardy, P. : *The Muslims of British India,* Cambridge University Press, New Delhi.

Harrison : *India and Pakistan : the First Fifty Years,* New Academic Publishers, New Delhi, 1992.

Harun, Yahya : *Islam : the Religion of Ease,* Goodword Books Pvt. Ltd., New Delhi, 1993.

——— : *Allah is Known through Reason,* Goodword Books Pvt. Ltd., New Delhi, 1989.

Hasan, Ehteshamul : *Fundamentals of Islam,* Idara Ishaat-e-Diniyat Pvt. Ltd, New Delhi, 1990.

Hasan, Mushirul : *Islam, Communities and the Nation : Muslim Identities in South Asia and Beyond,* Manohar Publishers , New Delhi, 1998.

Hasan, M. : *Hadrat Ali Murtada (R.A.A.),* Kitab Bhavan, New Delhi, 2003.

Hasan, S. Badrul : *Muslim Behaviour,* Kitab Bhavan, New Delhi, 1991.

Hasan, Ibn : *The Central Structure of the Mughal Empire,* Adam Pub., New Delhi, 1980.

Hasan, Mushirul : *Islam and Indian Nationalism : Refection on Abdul Kalam Azad,* Manohar Publishers, New Delhi, 1992.

Haskins, C.H. : *Arabic Science in Western Europe,* R. Lal & Co., New Delhi, 1987.

Hasrat, B.J. : *Dara Shikoh: Life and Works,* Madan Lal & Co., New Delhi, 1982.

Hassan, M. : *Hadrat Abu Bakr Siddique (R.A.A.),* Kitab Bhavan, New Delhi, 2004.

Haykel, Bewnard : *Revival and Reform in Islam : the Legacy of Muhammad al-Shawkani,* Cambridge University Press, New Delhi, 1963.

Heath, T. L. : *Aristarchus of Samos,* Oxford, New York, 1913.

Helminski : *Women of Sufism : a Hidden Treasure,* New Academic Publishers, New Delhi, 1990.

Henderson, J.J. Craik : *Parliament : a Survey,* George Allen & Unwin, London, 1965.

Herbert, Friedman : *The Amazing Universe,* National Geographic Society, Washington D.C., 1980.

Heyd, U. : *Foundations of Turkish Nationalism,* Oxford, London, 1950.

Heyworth-Dunne : *Religious and Political Trends in Modern Egypt,* Washington,1950.

Hodgson, G.S : *The Order of Assassin,* Oxford, New York, 1955.

Hogarth, D. G. : *The Nearer East,* Royal Book Co., London, 1905.

Holt, P.M. Lambton : *The Cambridge History of Islam,* Cambridge, New York, 1970.

Hourani : *Islam in European Thought,* New Academic Publishing House, New Delhi, 1989.

Hourani, Albert : *Thought in the Liberal Age,* Oxford, New York, 1962.

Houtsma, T. and Others : *Encyclopaedia of Islam,* Macmillan, London, 1934.

Huart, C. : *Histoire des Arabes,* Routledge & Kegal Paul Ltd., Paris, 1911.

Hughes, T.P. : *Dictionary of Islam,* Allen & Co., London, 1935,

Hurgronje, C. Snouck : *Mohammedanism,* Oxford, New York, 1916.

——— : *Selected Works,* Allen & Co., Leiden, 1957.

Husain, Wahed : *Administration of Justice during the Muslim Rule in India,* Kitab Ghar, New Delhi, 1977.

Husaini, Waqar : *Islamic Thought,* Goodword Books Pvt. Ltd., New Delhi, 1999.

Husaini, H.A. : *The Religious thought of Mir Syed Ali Hamadani,* Al-Hamra Publishers, Srinagar, 1979.

Husaini, S.A.Q : *The Constitution of the Arab Empire,* Feroz Pub., Lahore, 1954.

——— : *The Pantheistic Monism of Ibn al-Arabi,* Feroz Pub., Lahore, 1970.

Hussain, M. Hadi : *Imam Abu Hanifah : Life and Work,* Kitab Bhavan, New Delhi, 2001.

Hussain, S. Saukat, : *Human Rights in Islam,* Kitab Bhavan, New Delhi, 2001.

Ibn, Jubair : *Rihlat Ibn Jubair,* University Press, Cairo, 1955.

Ibn, Sina : *Al-Qanun fil-Tibb,* University Press, Lukhnow, 1905.

Ikram, S.M. : *Muslim Civilization in India,* Oxford, New York, 1981.

——— : *The Cultural Heritage of Pakistan,* Royal Pub., Karachi, 1955.

Imamuddin, S. M. : *Arab Muslim Administration,* Kitab Bhavan, New Delhi, 1984.

Imtiaz Ahmed, Helmut Reifeld : *Islam in South Asia : Adaptation, Accommodation and Conflict,* Social Science Press, New Delhi, 1999.

Inge, R. : *Philosophy of Plotinus,* MacMillan, London, 1918.

Inostranzev : *Iranian influences on Moslem literature,* Popular Prakashan, Bombay, 1918.

Iqbal, Muhammad : *Six Lectures on the Reconstruction of Religious Thought in Islam,* Royal Pub., Lahore, 1930.

——— : *The Development of Metaphysics in Persia,* Royal Pub., Lahore, 1964.

———: *The Reconstruction of Religious thought in Islam,* Oriental Publishers, Delhi, 1980.

Iran, Society : *Al-Biruni,* University Press, Calcutta, 1951.

Irfan, Habib : *The Agrarian System of Mughal India*, Popular Prakashan, Bombay, 1963.

Irvine, W. : *Later Mughals*, Deep & Deep Pub., New Delhi, 1971.

Isaac, Asimove : *Exploring the Earth & the Cosmos*, Crown Publishers, New York, 1989.

Izutsu, Toshihdo : *A Comprehensive Study of the Key Philosophical Concepts of Sufism and Taoism*, University Press, Tokyo, 1966.

Jabir, Ibn Hayyan : *Musannafat em-al-Kimiya*, A. B. C., & Co., Paris, 1928.

Jafar, Sharif : *Islam in India*, Oxford, New Delhi, 1972.

Jalbani, G. N. : *Teachings of Hazrat Shah Waliyullah*, Kitab Bhavan, New Delhi, 1997.

——— : *Teachings of Shah Waliyullah of Delhi*, Royal Pub., Lahore, 1983.

James, Conrnell and John Surowiecki : *The Pulse of the Planet*, Crown Publishers, U.S.A. 1972.

James, Piscarton : *Islam in the World of National States*, Macmillan, New York, 1982.

Jamil, Jalbi and Qazi A. Qadir : *The Changing World of Islam*, Royal Pub., Lahore, 1992.

Jamila, Khatun : *The Face of God*, Adam Pub., New Delhi, 1996.

Jansen, G.H. : *Militant Islam*, Pan Books, London, 1979.

Jaspers, Karl : *Man in the Modern Age*, Routledge & Kegan Paul Ltd., London, 1997.

John, J. Hue and John L. Esposite : *Islam in Transition*, Oxford, New York, 1969.

Joshua : *The Chronicle of Joshua the Stylite*, Cambridge, New York, 1882.

Jotwani, Motilal : *Sufis of Sindh*, Publications Division, New Delhi, 1991.

Kalerji : *From War to Peace*, Oxford, New York, 1991.

Kalim, M. Siddiq : *Studies in Pakistan Culture : an International Perspective*, Manohar Publications, New Delhi, 1993.

Karnal, A. Faruqui : *Islam : Today and Tomorrow*, Deep & Deep Pub., New Delhi, 1989.

Karpinski, L.C. : *Algebra of al-Khwarizmi*, Oxford, New York, 1915.

Kaur, R. : *Islamic Co-operation and Unity*, Deep & Deep Publications, New Delhi, 1993.

Keddie, Nikki, R. : *Saints and Sufis, Muslim Religious Institutions since 1500*, University of California Press, California, 1972.

Kernig, C.D. : *Marxism Communism and Western Society*, Oxford, New York, 1972.

Khab, Qamaruddin : *The Political Thought of Ibn Taimiyah*, Islamic Book Foundation, Lahore, 1983.

Khaduri, M. : *War and Peace in the Law of Islam*, Hopkins Press, Baltimore, 1955.

Khaja, Khan : *Studies in Tasawwuf*, University of Madras, Madras, 1923.

Khalifa, Abdul Hakim : *The Islamic Ideology*, Fortune Books,London, 1993.

Khalifa, Abdul Hakim : *The Prophet (PBUH) and His Message*, Islamic Pub., Lahore, 1996.

Khan, Inayat : *Mysticism of Sound*, Pilgrims Book House, New Delhi, 1997.

Khan, Wahiduddin : *The True Jihad*, Goodword Books Pvt. Ltd., New Delhi, 1995.

——— : *Islam Activism,* Goodword Books Pvt. Ltd., New Delhi, 1994.

——— : *Polygamy and Islam,* Goodword Books Pvt. Ltd., New Delhi, 1996.

——— : *Introducing Islam,* Goodword Books Pvt. Ltd., New Delhi, 1995.

——— : *Islam and Peace,* Goodword Books Pvt. Ltd., New Delhi, 1996.

——— : *Muhammad : a Prophet for all Humanity,* Goodword Books Pvt. Ltd., New Delhi, 1996.

Khan, M. Ishaq : *Kashmir's Transition to Islam : the Role of Muslim Rishis,* Manohar Publishers , New Delhi, 2002.

Khan, Mumtaz Ali : *Planning Process and Muslims Responses to Rural Development in India,* Uppal Publishing House, New Delhi, 1996.

Khan, N. M. Yamin : *God Soul and Universe in Science and Islam,* Kitab Bhavan, New Delhi, 1993.

Khan, Qamaruddin : *Political Concepts in the Quran,* Islamic Book Foundation, Lahore, 1982.

——— : *The Methodology of Islamic Research,* Institute of Islamic Studies, Karachi, 1973.

King, L.W. and Thompson, H.R. : *Sculptures and Inscriptions of Darius the Great on the Rock of Behistan,* Oxford, London, 1907.

Lambton, A.K.S. : *Islam and Russia,* Oxford, New York, 1956.

Landau, R. : *The Philosophy of the Ibn Arabi,* Century Pub., London, 1959.

Laroui, Abdullah : *The Crisis of the Arab Intellectual,* University of California Press, California, 1976.

Le, Strange E. : *Palestine under the Moslem,* Century Pub., London, 1890.

Leclerc, L. : *Histoire de la Medicine Arabe,* Millennium Pub., Paris, 1876.

Lee, Yerhune : *The Indian Muslims,* Rupa & Co., New Delhi, 1990.

Les, Motifis : *Zoroastriens dans la philosophie de Sohrawardi,* University Press, Tehran, 1946.

Levantin : *The Myth of International Security,* Oxford, New York, 1967.

Levonian, L. : *Studies in the Relationship between Islam and Christianity,* University Press, Millennium Pub., London, 1940.

Levy, Reuben : *The Social Structure of Islam,* Cambridge University Press, New York, 1993.

Lewin, Roger : *In the Age of Mankind,* Simithsonian Books, Washington, D.C., 1956.

Lewis, Bernard : *The Emergence of Modern Turkey,* Millennium Pub., London, 1961.

——— : *Islam,* Oxford, New York, 1974.

——— : *The Middle East and the West,* Century Pub., London, 1964.

Lewis, Richards : *Universe,* Harmony Books, New York, 1973.

Lings, Martin : *A Sufi Saint of the Twentieth Century,* Century Pub., London, 1971.

Litvak, Strart : *Sufism : The Sufi Path to Seeking Wisdom,* Jaico Publishing House, New Delhi, 1987.

Lorus and Margery Milne : *The Nature of Life,* Crown Publishers, New York, 1995.

Ludwig, Renn : *The Relation of War to Society,* Oxford, New York, 1989.

Lyde, L.W. : *The Continent of Asia,* New Century Pub., London, 1923.

Mac, Closky : *Pacts for Peace,* New Century Pub., London, 1980.

MacDonald, D.B. : *Development of Muslim Theology,* New Century Pub., London, 1903.

———— : *The Religious Attitude and Life in Islam,* Modern Pub., Beirut, 1965.

Madhavan, A. : *What is Sufism ?,* Rupa & Co., New Delhi, 1981.

Mahmood, Tahir : *Hayat-i Mahmud,* A. M. U., Aligarh, 1977.

Malik, Jamal : *Colonization of Islam : Dissolution of Traditional Institutions in Pakistan,* Manohar Publication, New Delhi, 2000.

Maneckji, Nusservanji D. : *Zoroastrian Civilization,* Oxford, New York, 1922.

Manzuruddin, Ahmad : *Islamic Political System,* Kitab Bhavan, New Delhi, 1991.

Mardin, Serif : *The Genesis of Young Ottoman Thought,* Princeton, New York, 1962.

Masabih, Mishkatul : *Selection from Muhammadan Traditions : Being a Carefully Choren and Thoroughly,* Atlantic Publishers, New Delhi, 1998.

Masudi : *Muruj adh-Dhab,* de Courteille, Paris, 1861.

Mathew, Thomas : *Political Economy of Etimic Conflict,* School of International Studies, Jawaharlal Nehru University, New Delhi, 2003.

Maudoodi, S.A.A. : *Islami Riyasat,* Islamic Book Foundation, New Delhi, 1999.

May, L. S. : *The Evolution of Indo Muslim Thought from 1857 to Present,* Uppal Publishing House, New Delhi, 1991.

Mayer, A. C. : *Caste and Kinship in Muslim India,* University of California Press, Berkeley, 1970.

———— : *Pir and Murshid : an Aspect of Religious Leadership in West Pakistan,* Royal Pub., Lahore,1967.

Mayne, P. : *Saints of Sind,* New Century Pub., London, 1965.

McIver, R.M. and Oage, Charles H. : *The Society,* Macmillan & Co., London, 1959.

McIver, R.M. : *The Community,* Macmillan & Co., London, 1928.

Mcllwain, Charles Howard : *The Constitutionalism,* Great Seal Books, New York, 1947.

Meer, Hassan Ali : *Observations on the Musulmauns of India,* Macmillan & Co., London, 1832.

Meherhof, H. : *New Light on Hunayn ibn Ishaq,* Oxford, New York, 1926.

Menon, M. Indu : *Status of Muslims Women in India,* Uppal Publishing House, New Delhi, 1993.

Merivale, C. : *History of the Romans under the Empire,* MacMillan & Co., London, 1896.

Michael, Williams : *Outlines of World Military History,* Oxford, New York, 1996.

Miller : *Current International Treaties,* Oxford, New York, 1991.

Mir, Valiuddin : *Love of God,* Amit Pub., Hyderabad, 1968.

Mirza, Waheed : *The Life and Works of Amir Khusrau,* University of Calcutta, Calcutta, 1935.

Misra, Neeru : *Sufis and Sufism : Some Reflections,* Manohar Publisher , New Delhi, 2004.

Mohaghegh, Mahdi and Landolt, *Collected Papers on Islamic Philosophy and Mysticism,* Tehran, 1971.

Mohiuddin, Ahmad : *Saiyid Ahmad Shahid,* Modern Pub., Lucknow, 1975.

Mōle, Marigan : *Les Mystiques Musulmans,* MacMillan & Co., Paris, 1965.

Mommsen, T. : *Provinces of the Roman Empire,* MacMillan & Co., London, 1909.

Montgomery, Watt : *Muhammad (PBUH) at Medina,* Oxford, New York, 1973.

——— : *The Majesty that was Islam,* Oxford, New York, 1973.

Moreland, W.H. : *From Akbar to Aurangzeb,* MacMillan & Co., London, 1923.

——— : *India at the Death of Akbar,* MacMillan & Co., London, 1920.

Muhammad, Asad : *Islam at the Crossroads,* Kitab Bhavan, New Delhi, 2003.

Muhammad, Abdullah Enan : *Decisive Moments in the History of Islam,* Islamic Book Company, Delhi, 1996.

Muhammad, Ayub : *The Politics of Islamic Revolution,* Royal Pub., Lahore, 1991.

Muhammad, Kazim Munishi : *Alamgir-Nama,* A.B.C. & Co., Calcutta, 1865.

Muhammad, Latif : *Auliya -i-Lahore,* Royal Pub., Lahore, 1962.

Muhammed, Ataur-Rahim : *Jesus a Prophet of Islam,* Idara Ishaat-e-Diniyat Pvt. Ltd, New Delhi, 1995.

Muir, Sir William : *The Caliphate, its Rise, Decline and Fall,* Oxford, Edinburgh, 1915.

Muir, William : *Early Caliphate,* Oxford, New York, 1970.

Muni, S.D. and Kalim Bahadur : *Domestic Conflicts in South Asia,* South Asia Publishers, New Delhi, 1986.

Murata, S. and Others : *The Vision of Islam,* Ashish Publishing House, New Delhi, 1991.

Murthy, T.S. : *Muslim : the Difficult Years,* Himalayan Books, Chandigarh, 1983.

Musil, A. : *The Manners and Customs of the Rwala Bedounis,* Oxford, New York, 1928.

Muslehuddin, M. : *Banking and Islamic Law,* Idara Ishaat-e-Diniyat Pvt. Ltd, New Delhi, 1990.

——— : *Islam : its Political System,* Kitab Bhavan, New Delhi, 1999.

Myron, Weiner : *Sons of the Soil : Migration and Ethnic Conflict in India,* University Press, Prineton, 1978.

Najjar, Fauzi M. : *The Islamic State : a Study in Traditional Politics,* Oxford, New York, 1967.

Narayan : *Pan Islamism,* MacMillan, New York, 1953.

Nasr, Syed Husain : *Three Muslim Sages,* Cambridge, New York, 1959.

Nasr, Seyyed H. : *An Introduction to Islamic Cosmological Doctrines,* Cambridge, 1964.

——— : *Ideas and Realities of Islam,* MacMillan & Co., London, 1966.

——— : *Ismailli contributions to Islamic Culture,* Adam Pub., Tehran, 1977.

——— : *Science and Civilization in Islam,* Cambridge, New York, 1966.

——— : *Sufi Essays,* MacMillan, London, 1972.

Nicholson, R.A. : *Literary History of the Arabs,* Kitab Bhavan, New Delhi, 1994.

——— : *A Literary History of the Arabs,* Cambridge, New York, 1930.

——— : *History of the Muslims,* MacMillan & Co., London, 1922.

——— : *Rumi, Poet and Mystic,* MacMillan, London, 1950.

——— : *Studies in Islamic Mysticism,* Cambridge, New York, 1967.

——— : *Tales of Mystic Meaning,* MacMillan & Co., London, 1931.

——— : *The Idea of Personality in Sufism,* Cambridge, New York, 1923.

——— : *The Mysteries of Islam,* MacMillan & Co., London, 1914.

Noorani, A.G. : *Islam and Jihad,* Manohar Publishers, New Delhi, 2002.

Nusaibah, Azam Zaki : *The Ideas of Arab Nationalism,* Cornell University Press, New York,1956.

Oman K.R. : *The Art of War,* Oxford, New York, 1993.

Oudha, Abdul Qadir : *Criminal Law of Islam,* Kitab Bhavan, New Delhi, 1999.

Padwick, C.E. : *Muslim Devotions,* MacMillan & Co., London, 1960.

Palamer, E.H. : *Oriental Mysticism: a Treatise on the Sufistic and Unitian Theosophy of the Persians,* Lozac & Co., London, 1969.

——— : *The Quran,* Atlantic Publishers, New Delhi, 1996.

Pandit, Sneh : *Perspectives in the Fhilosophy of Culture,* S. Chand & Company Ltd., New Delhi, 1990

Pearson, M. M. : *Pious Passengers : the Hajj in Earlier Times,* Sterling Publishers Pvt. Ltd., New Delhi, 1999.

Philips, E.C. : *Politics and Society in India,* MacMillan & Co., London, 1963.

Phillips, O. Hood : *Reform of the Constitution,* MacMillan & Co., London, 1970.

Pickthall, M. M. : *Cultural Side of Islam,* Idara Ishaat-e-Diniyat Pvt. Ltd, New Delhi, 1999.

——— : *Islamic Culture,* Feroz Sons Publishers, Lahore, 1992.

Pierce, R.A.: *Russia in Central Asia, 1867-1917,* University of California, Berkeley, 1960.

Poole, Lane, S. : *The Mohammedan Dynasties,* MacMillan & Co., London, 1895.

Qanungo, K.R. : *Dara Shikoh*, Modern Book Co., Calcutta, 1935.

Qureshi, A. Iqbal : *Islam and the Theory of Interest*, Kitab Bhavan, New Delhi, 1994.

Qureshi, W. : *Selections from the Iqbal Review*, Iqbal Academy Pakistan, Lahore, 1983.

Qureshi, I.H. : *The Administration of the Mughul Empire*, Feroz Pub., Karachi, 1966.

——— : *The Administration of the Sultanate of Delhi*, Adam Pub., New Delhi, 1971.

——— : *The Muslim Community of the Indo-Pakistan Subcontinent*, The Hague, New York, 1962.

——— : *The Administration of the Sultanate of Delhi*, Royal Pub., Karachi, 1944.

Rabi, Muhammad Mahmud : *The Political Theory of Ibn Khaldun*, MacMillan & Co., London, 1967.

Rabnson, Chave F. : *Islamic Histroriography*, Cambridge University press, New York, 1990.

Rafiqi, A. Q. : *Sufism in Kashmir*, Ashish Pub., Delhi, 1977.

Rahim, Abdur : *Principles of Islamic Jurisprudence*, Kitab Bhavan, New Delhi, 1994.

Rahman, F.: *Islam*, Weidenfeld and Nicolson, London, 1966.

Raverty, H. G : *Selections from the Poetry of the Afghans*, MacMillan & Co., London, 1862.

Ray, Samirendra : *Judicial Review and Fundamantal Rights*, Eastern Law House, Kolkata, 2002.

Riazul, Islam : *Indo-Persian Relations*, University of Tehran, Tehran, 1970.

Richard, Rowan : *The Story of Secret Service*, Oxford, New York, 1980.

Richards, J.F. : *Mughal Administration in Golkonda*, Oxford, New York, 1975.

Rizvi, Hasan Askari : *Islami Reassertion : a Socio Political Study*, Progressive Publishers, Lahore, 1981.

Rizvi, S.A.A. : *A History of Sufism in India*, Ashish Pub., Delhi, 1978.

——— : *Muslim Revivalist Movements in Northern India in the Sixteenth and Seventeenth Centuries*, Neeru Pub., Agra, 1965.

——— : *Religious and Intellectual History of the Muslims in Akbar's Reign*, Deep & Deep Pub., Delhi, 1975.

——— : *Muslim Revivalist Movements in Northern India in the Sixteenth and Seventeenth Centuries*, Neeru Pub., Agra, 1965.

Roberts, Robert : *The Social Laws of Islam*, Williams and Morgate, Ltd., London, 1925.

Rodinson, Maxime : *Islam and Capitalism*, Penguin, London,1974.

Rosenthal, E.I.J. : *Political Thought in Medieval Islam*, Cambridge, New York, 1962.

——— : *Islam in the Modern National State*, University Press, Cambridge,1965.

——— : *Political Thought in Medieval Islam*, University Press, Cambridge, 1958.

Rumi, Jalaludin : *The Masnavi*, Gyan Books Pvt. Ltd., New Delhi, 2000.

Ruthven, Malise : *Islam : a Very Short Introduction*, Oxford, New York, 1990.
Sabiruddin : *Muslim Husband and Wife : Right and Duties*, Kitab Bhavan, New Delhi, 2000.
Sadiq, M. : *A History of Urdu Poetry*, MacMillan & Co., London, 1964.
Sahai, Surendra : *Indian Architecture : Islamic Period (1192-1857)*, Prakash Books, New Delhi, 1967.
Said, Edward W. : *Orientalism*, Pantheon Books, New York, 1978.
Saksena, B.P. : *History of Shahjahan of Dehli*, Vora Pub., Allahabad, 1958.
Saksena, R.B. : *A History of Urdu Literature*, Vora Pub., Allahabad, 1927.
Saran, P. : *Mystical Dimensions of Islam*, Chape Hill, New York, 1975.
——— : *Provincial Government of the Mughals*, Aman Pub., Allahabad, 1941.
——— : *Studies in Medieval Indian History*, Deep & Deep Pub., Delhi, 1952.
——— : *The Religious Policy of the Mughal Emperors*, MacMillan & Co., London, 1962.
——— : *Provincial Government of the Mughals*, Deep & Deep Pub., Allahabad, 1941.
Sardar, Ziauddin : *The Future of Muslim Civilization*, Croom Helm, London, 1979.
Sarton, George : *Introduction to the History of Science*, Carnegie Institute, Washington, 1950
Saxena, V. K. : *Muslims and the Indian National Congress*, Discovery Publishing House, New Delhi, 1985.
Saxena, K.P. : *Human Rights: Perspective and Challenges*, Lancers Books, New Delhi, 1996.
Scarman, Leslie : *Law : the New Dimensions*, Stevens and Sons, London, 1974.
Schacht, J. : *The Origins of Muhammadan Jurisprudence*, Clarendon Press, Oxford, 1953.
Schacht, Joseph, and Bosworth, C.E. : *The Legacy of Islam*, Oxford University Press, New York, 1979.
Schimmel, A. : *Gabriel's Wing*, MacMillan & Co., London, 1963.
Schwartz, E. : *Science and Civilization in Islam*, Cambridge, London, 1966.
Seervai, H. : *Constitutional Law of India*, N.M. Tripathi & Co., Bombay, 1967.
Sergeant : *Constitution of Madina*, Feroz Pub., Lahore, 1992.
——— : *The Sunnah Jamia*, Feroz Pub., Lahore, 1992.
Setalvad : *War and Civil Liberties*, Feroz Pub., Lahore, 1992.
Shad, Abdur Rehman : *Duties of an Imam*, Idara Ishaat-e-Diniyat Pvt. Ltd, New Delhi, 1990.
——— : *Muslim Etiquettes*, Idara Ishaat-e-Diniyat Pvt. Ltd, New Delhi, 1999.
Shah, Sirdar Ikbal Ali : *Islamic Sufism*, Idarah-I-Adbiyat-I-Delhi, Delhi, 1979.
Shaheed, A. Q. A. : *Islamic System of Justice*, Kitab Bhavan, New Delhi, 1994.
Shaikh, N. M. : *Women in Muslim Society*, Kitab Bhavan, New Delhi, 1991.
Sharib, Zahurul Hasan : *Tarikb-i-Sufiya-i-Gujarat*, Jamil Academy, Ahmadabad, 1981.
Sharif, M. Raihan : *Islamic Social Framework*, Islamic Book Foundation, Dacca, 1980.

Sharif, M.M. : *A History of Muslim Philosophy*, Feroz Pub., Lahore, 1993.

Sharma, R.S. and Jha, V. : *Indian Society: Historical Probings*, Rawat Pub., Delhi, 1974.

Sharma, S.R. : *Mughal Government and Administration*, Popular Prakashan, Bombay, 1951.

———— : *Women's Education in Ancient and Muslim Period*, Discovery Publishing House, New Delhi, 1996.

Shaukat, Ali : *Masters of Muslim Thought*, Deep & Deep Pub., New Delhi, 1992.

Shehadi, F. : *Ghazzali's Unique Unknowable God*, MacMillan & Co., London, 1964.

Shemesh, A.B. : *Taxation in Islam*, MacMillan & Co., London, 1965.

Sherfuddin, Mohd. : *Muslim Faith and Practice*, Kitab Bhavan, New Delhi, 1982.

Sherwani, H.K. : *Cultural Trends in Medieval India*, Popular Prakashan, Bombay, 1968.

———— : *Muhammad Quli Qutb Shah*, Popular Prakashan, Bombay, 1968.

Sherwani, H.R.K. : *Studies in Muslim Thought and Administration*, University of Hyderbad, Hyderabad, 1945.

Shibli, Numani : *Al-Mamun*, University of Agra, Agra, 1894.

Siddiqi, M.Z. : *Hadith Literature*, Deepali Pub., Calcutta, 1961.

Siddiqi, M.Z. : *Six Lectures on the Reconstruction of Religious Thought in Islam*, Feroz Pub., Lahore, 1930.

Siddiqui, M.A. : *History of Muslims*, Atlantic Publisher, New Delhi, 1996.

Sikandar, bin Manjhu : *Mirat-i Sikandari*, Department of History, Faculty of Arts, M. S. University, Baroda, 1961.

Singh, Nagendar : *Human Rights and International Cooperation*, S. Chand & Co., New Delhi, 1969.

Smith, Vincent : *The Oxford History of India*, Oxford, New York, 1987.

Smith, W. C. : *Modern Islam in India : a Social Analysis*, Manohar Publishers, New Delhi, 1985.

Smith, D.E. : *History of Iran and Turkey*, Oxford, New York, 1950.

Smith, M. : *Al-Ghazzali : the Mystic*, MacMillan & Co., London, 1944.

———— : *An Early Mystic of Baghdad*, Cambridge, New York, 1920.

———— : *Readings from the Mystics of Islam*, MacMillan & Co., London, 1950.

———— : *Studies in Early Mysticism in the Near and Middle East*, MacMillan & Co., London, 1931.

Smith, M., Rabia : *The Mystic and her Fellow Saints in Islam*, Cambridge, London, 1929.

Smith, V.A : *Early History of India*, Oxford, New York, 1914.

Smith, W. Cantwell : *Islam in Modern History*, Princeton University Press, New Jersey, 1957.

———— : *The Cambridge History* of *Islam*, Cambridge University Press, New York, 1970.

Som, Tamarci : *A Brief History of Islam,* Blackwell, New York, 1992.

Spear, P. : *Twilight of the Mughals,* Cambridge, London, 1969.

Stanton : *Teaching of the Quran,* Discovery Publishing House, New Delhi, 1989.

Stern, S.M. : *Fatimid Decrees,* Faber and Faber, London, 1964.

Stobart, J.W. H. : *Islam and its Founders,* Uppal Publishing House, New Dlehi, 1974.

Storey, C.A. : *Persian Literature : a Bibliographical Survey,* Lozac & Co., London, 1927.

Subhan, J.A. : *Sufism : its Saints and Shrines,* Kitabiyat Pub., Lucknow, 1960.

Suhrawardi, Umar : *Awarif al Maarif bin Muhammad,* Sheikh Ghulam Shahabuddin Ali & Sons, Lahore, 1964.

Syed, Amir Ali : *The Spirit of Islam,* Royal Pub.,Lahore, 1979.

Syed, M. H. : *Islamic Terrorism : Myth or Reality,* Gyan Books Pvt. Ltd., New Delhi, 2002.

——— : *Islam and the Modern Age,* Anmol Publications, New Delhi, 2003.

——— : *Human Rights in Islam,* Anmol Publications, New Delhi, 2004.

——— : *Islam and Science,* Anmol Publications, New Delhi, 2003.

——— : *Status of Women in Islamic Society,* Anmol Publications, New Delhi, 2003.

——— : *Impact of Islam,* Anmol Publications, New Delhi, 2003.

——— : *History of Muslims in India,* Anmol Publications, New Delhi, 2003.

Syed, Nageeb al-Attas : *Raniri and the Wajudiyyah of 17th Century Acheh,* Century Books, Singapore, 1966.

——— : *The Mysticism of Hazmali Fansuri,* A. Pub., Kuala Lumpur, 1970.

Tarachand : *Influence of Islam on Indian Culture,* Adam Pub., Allahabad, 1963.

——— : *Society and State in the Mughal Period,* S. Chand, & Co., Delhi, 1961.

Tarn, W. W. : *The Greeks in Bactria and India,* Cambridge, London, 1938.

Tavernier, Jean-Baptiste : *Travels in India,* W.Crooke, London, 1925.

Temple, R.C. : *The Administration of the Mughal Empire,* Feroz Pub., Karachi, 1966.

——— : *The Religious Policy of the Mughal Emperors,* MacMillan & Co., London, 1962.

——— : *The Sufi Path of Love,* MacMillan & Co., London, 1954.

Thomas, W.F. : *Mutual Influence of Muhammedans and Hindus in India,* Cambridge, London, 1892.

Titus, M. : *Indian Islam,* Milford, New Delhi, 1979.

Tod, J. : *Annals and Antiquities of Rajasthan,* Oxford, New York, 1920.

Trimingham, J.S. : *The Sufi Orders in Islam,* Oxford, New York, 1920.

Tripathi, R.P. : *Some Aspects of Muslim Administration,* Vora Pub., Allahabad, 1959.

Tritton, A.S. : *The Caliphs and their Non-Muslim Subjects,* Oxford, New York, 1930.

Tutsch, Hans E. : *Facets of Arab Nationalism,* Wayne State University Press, Detroit, 1965.

Ulama, Majlisul : *Islamic Hijaab,* Idara Ishaat-e-Diniyat Pvt. Ltd, New Delhi, 1997.

Ullah, M. : *Administration of Justice in Islam,* Kitab Bhavan, New Delhi, 1990.

Umaruddin, M. : *The Ethical Philosophy of al-Ghazzali,* Adam Publishers, New Delhi, 1996

Underhill, E. : *Mysticism : a Study in the Nature and Development of Man's Spiritual Consciousness,* Oxford, New York, 1956.

Usmani, J.M. Tariq : *The Authority of Sunnah,* Kitab Bhavan, New Delhi, 1998.

Usmani, Taqi Muhammad : *An Introduction to Islamic Finance,* Idara Ishaat-e-Diniyat Pvt. Ltd., New Delhi, 1999.

Valliuddin, Mir : *The Quranic Sufism,* Motilal Banarsi Das Publishers, New Delhi, 1989.

Vaudeville : *Charlotte Kabir,* Oxford, New York, 1974.

Wahed, Husain : *Administration of Justice during the Muslim Rule in India,* Ashish Publishing House, New Delhi, 1977.

Waheed, Akhtar : *Sufi Approach to the Problem of Alienation,* Wilson & Co., New Delhi, 1975.

——— : *The Early Imamiya Shiite Thinkers,* Ashish Publishing House, New Delhi, 1995.

Waheed, Mirza : *The Life and Works of Amir Khusrau,* Kaveri Pub., Calcutta, 1935.

Waines, Davids : *A Introduction to Islam,* Cambridge University Press, New Delhi, 1995.

Walker, Benjamin : *Foundation of Islam : the Making of World Faith,* Rupa & Co., New Delhi, 2001.

Wang, Gungwu : *Self and Biography,* Allen & Co., Sydney, 1974.

Warmington, E.H. : *The Commerce between the Roman Empire and Arabs,* Faber & Faber Co., New York, 1939.

Wasiti, Hakim Nayyar : *Muslim Contribution to Medicine,* Deep & Deep pub., New Delhi, 1993.

Watt, M. : *Muslim Intellectual : a Study of al-Ghazzali,* Edinburgh University Press, Edinburgh, 1959.

——— : *The Faith and Practice of Al-Ghazzali,* MacMillan & Co., London, 1953.

Watt, W.M. : *Islamic Surveys,* Edinburgh University Press, Edinburgh, 1999.

——— : *Islam and the Integration of Society,* Routledge, London, 1961.

——— : *Muhammad at Mecca,* Oxford University Press, New York, 1953.

——— : *Muhammad at Medina,* Oxford University Press, New York, 1956.

Weeramanthy, G. G.: *Islamic Jurisprudence—an International Perspective,* Vishwa Lekha, Culcutta, 1980.

Wensick, A.E. : *A Handbook of Early Muhammadan Traditions,* Luzac & Co., Leiden, 1960.

Whitting, C.E.J. : *Al-Fakhri*, Oxford, London, 1947.

Wilfred, Seamen Blunt : *The Future of Islam,* Macmillan, London, 1991.

Willoughby, W. : *Principles of the Constitutional Law of the United States,* Baker Voorthis & Company, New York, 1938.

Winer, L. : *Contributions towards a History of Arabico-Gothic Culture,* Oxford, New York, 1917.

Wolfson, H.A. : *Glimpses of Medieval Indian Culture,* Popular Pub., Bombay, 1959.

———— : *The Philosophy of the Kalam,* Oxford, London, 1976.

Yeome, Yezbeck Haddad : *Islamic Values in the United States,* Oxford, New York, 1999.

Yousuf, Abbas Hashmi : *Rasul (PBUH),* Adam Pub., New Delhi, 2001.

Yusuf, Iblish and Peter Lambron Wilson : *Traditional Modes of Contemplation and Action,* University Press, Tehran, 1977.

Yusuf, S.M. : *Economic Justice in Islam,* Kitab Bhavan, New Delhi, 1988.

Zaehner, R.C. : *Hindu and Muslim Mysticism,* Oxford, London, 1960.

Zafeeruddin, M.M. : *System of Modesty and Chastity in Islam,* Idara Ishaat-e-Diniyat Pvt. Ltd, New Delhi, 1995.

Zahid, Malik : *Subjects of Quran,* Kitab Bhavan, New Delhi, 1998.

Zartman, I.W. : *Man, State and Society in the Contemporary Muslim World,* Lozac & Co., London, 1973.

Zaydan, Jurji : *History of Islamic Civilization,* Kitab Bhavan, New Delhi, 1994.

———— : *Umayyads and Abbasides,* Luzac & Co., London,1907.

Ziadah, N.A. : *Sanusiyah : a Study of a Revivalist Movement in Islam,* Poul & Co., Leiden, 1958.

REFERENCES

Arabic Books

Al-Kamil fi al-Tarikh Ibn al-Athir Jazri, published in Idara al-Tabaat al-Muniryya, Egypt records the life of Prophet Muhammad.

Ansab al-Ashraf : Abu al-'Abbas Ahmad ibn Yaha ibn Jabir Baladhuri. Edited by Dr. Hamid-Ullah. Egypt, 1959.

Insanul 'Uyun fi Sirat al-Amin al-Mamun, popularly known as Al-Sirat al-Halbiyyah by Ali, b. Burbanuddin Halabi, al-Shafai.

Jami-al-bayan an Tawil al-Quran, popularly known as Tafsir al-Tabari, by Abu Jafar Muhammad ibn Jarir Tabari. Published by Matba Mustafa Albabi al-Halbi. (Egypt, 1954.)

Kitab al-Tabaqat al-Kabir : Muhammad Ibn Saad, (845 A.H.) Katib al-Waqidi. Edited by E. Miltwoch and E. Sachau, Leiden 1904-1918. (Only the first two volumes deal with the life of the Holy Prophet.)

Kitab Fuluh al-Buldan by Abu al-Abbas Ahmad Ibn Yahya ibn Jabir al-Baladhuri, edited by M. J. de Goeje, Leiden, 1866.

Kitab-al-Maghazi by Ali Abd Allah b. Omar al-Waqidi. Edited by A. Von Kremer., Published by Asiatic Society Bengal (Calcutta) in 1855.

Muhammad by Muhammad Rida, Cairo, 1368 A.H.

Tanwir-ul-Miqyas min Tafslr Ibn 'Abbas, edited by Abu Tahir b. Muhammad b. Ya'qub al-Ferozeabadi Al-Shafi'i. Published by ('Abdul Hamid Ahmad Hanifi, Egypt).

Z'ad al-Ma'ad fi. Hadyi Khair-al-'Ibad by Hafiz Abu 'Abdallah Muhammad b. Abu Bakr, popularly known as Hafiz Ibn Qayyim. Edited by Muhammad Hamid al-Fiqi, published in Cairo in October 1953.

Abd al-Karim, Fathi : *Al-d-Daulah wa al-Siyadah Fi'l Fiqh al-Islami, Dirasah Miqarnah,* Maktabah Wahbah, Cairo, 1977.

Abd al-Raziq Ali : *Al-Islam wa* Usul *al-Hukm,* Matba' Misr, Cairo, 1925.

Abdullah Yusuf Ali : *The Holy Quran—English translation and commentary*

Abul Hassan Nadvi : *Nabi-e-Rahmat* (PBUH).

Al-Biruni : *Kitab-al-Tafhim,* Cairo, 1318 A.H.

Al-Biruni, Abu-al-Raihan Muhammad Ibn Ahmad : *Al-Qanun-al-Masudi,* Hyderabad Deccan, 1954.

Al-Farisi Karnal-al-Din Abul-Hasan : *Tanqih-al-Manazir,* Hyderabad Deccan, 1850.

Ali`Mansur : *Mukhtasar Sawanih Hadrat Saiyid Salar Masud Ghazi,* Bahraich, 1968.

Al-Idrisi, Sharif : *Nuzhat-al-Mushtaq fi Ikhtirag-al-Afaq.*

Al-Istakhri : *Kitab-al-Masalik wal-Mamalik,* Leiden, 1927.

Al-Kalabadhi : *Kitab-al-Tasawwuf Li, Madhab ahl'al Tasawwuf* , The Doctrines of the Sufis, English translation A.J. Arbery, Cambridge University Press, Cambridge, 1979.

Al-Khawarizmi, Muhammad Ibn Musa : *Kitab-al-Jabr wal-Muqabalah,* Cairo, 1939.

Al-Qifti, Jamal-al-Din Abul-Hasan : *Tarikh-al-Hukama,* Leipzig, 1320 A.H.

Al-Sufi, Abdal-Rahman : *Sarwaral-Kawakib,* Hyderabad Deccan, 1954.

Al-Sufi, Abd-al-Rahman Ibn Umar : *Al-'Amal bil Asturlab,* Hyderabad Deccan, 1962.

Hayat-i Shaikh : *Abdul-Haqq Muhaddis Dihlawi,* Delhi, 1953.

Kahhalah, Muhammad Rida : *Mujam-al-Mullifin,* Demascus, 1961.

Khallaf, Abd al-Wahab : *Khulasah Tarikh al-Tashri al-Islami,* 1968.

Holy Quran

Abdullah Yusuf Ali : *The Holy Quran*: An Interpretation in English Sh. Muhammad Ashraf, Lahore, 1934.

M. Abdul Majid Daryabadi : *Translation & Commentary,* Taj Company, Lahore.

Marmaduke Pickthall: *The Meaning of the Glorious Quran,* Hyderabad-Deccan, 1938.

Sale's Preliminary : Discourse to the Translation of the Koran prefixed as *Introduction to Wherry Commentary on the Kuran,* Trubner, London.

Holy Tradition

Al-Adab al-Mufrad, compiled by Imam Bokhari (trans-lated into Urdu by M. Khalil-ur-Rahman Nu'mani), Published in Karachi.

At-taliq-us-Sxbih 'ala Mishkat-il-Masabih. Muhammad Idris Kandhalvi, Damascus.

Commentary on Sahih Muslim : Abu Zakriya, Yahya al-Nawwi. It is appended: to the original Text, published by Karkhana Tajarit-Kutab, Delhi, in 1930.

Fath al- Bari (commentary on Sahih al-Bokhari), Hafiz Ibn Hajar 'Asqalani (852 A.H.), Cairo 1959.

Jami-al-Tirmidhi : Abu Isa Muhammad b. Isa Delhi.

Kitab-al-Sunan of Abu Bakr Ahmad ibn al-Husain, commonly known as Baihaqi.

Muslim, Abul-Husain, al-Hajjaj al-Quishairi : *Sahih Muslim,* Islamic Books, Beirut, 1978.

Musnad : al-Imam Abu Abd Allah Ahmad b. Muhammad Ibn Hanbal, Ed. by Ahmad Shakir, Cairo, 1949.

Nail-ul-Autar by Imam Muhammad b. Abu b. Muhammad al-Shaukani (1255 A.H.), Cairo 1357 A.H.

Shamail Tirmidhi : Abu Isa Muhammad b. Isa Tirmidhi with explanatory notes in Urdu by M. Muhammad Zakriya Karachi.

Tuhfat-al-Ahwadhi by Abd al-Rahman Mubarakpuri. Delhi 1353 A.H.,

Persian Books

Abdul-Karim Khwaja : *Bayan-i Waqi,* Lahore, 1970.

Abdul-Qadir Khan Jaisi : *Tarikh Imad al-Mulk,* Bankipur, 1915.

Abu Talib al-Makki : *Qut al-Qulab,* Cairo, 1306/1888-89.

Ansari, Muhammad Riza : *Bani-i dars-i Nizami,* Lucknow, 1973.

Aqil Khan Razi : *Waqi 'at-i 'Alamgiri,* Aligarh, 1946.

Asad Beg Qazwini : *Halat-i Asad Beg,* Rieu, III.

Azad, Mawlana Abui-Kalam, *Tazkira,* Lahore, n.d. Azar, Hajji Lutf Ali Beg, Atash-Kada, Bombay, 1277/1860.

Badakhshi, Haji Muhammad Amin : *Manoqib-i Hazrat,* Author's Personal Collection.

Bayazid Biyat : *Tazkira-i Humayuna wa Akbar,* Calcutta, 1941.

Chekhovich, O.D. : *Samarqand Documents,* Moscow, 1974.

Danishmand Khan : *Ni 'm'at Khan-i 'Ali, Ruz-nama-i Waqa 't' Ayyami-darjuljihad,* Haydarabad, 1901.

Farid, B. Shaikh Ma'ruf Bhakkari : *Zakhiratu'l-khawanin,* 3 vols, Karachi, 1961-74.

Ghulam Husain B. Hidayat Ali Khan : *Tarikh-i Muhammad-Shahi.* Asafiya MS.

Ghulam Husain Khan Jawhar : *Gulzar-i Asafiya,* Bombay, 1891.

Gulbadan Begam : *Humaun-nama,* London, 1902.

Hasan Beg Rumlu : *Ahsanu 't-Tawarikh,* Baroda, 1931.

Haydar Malik : *Tarikh-i Kashmir,* Ethe.

Ikram, Shaikh Muhammad : *Ab -i kawsar,* Lahore, 1975.

Ishwar Das Nagar : *Futuhat-i'Alamgiri,* Rieu, I.

Jawhar Aftabchi : *Tazkiratu'i-waqi'at,* Rieu, I.

Karl Jahn : *Rashid u 'd-Din 's History of India,* The Hague, 1965.

Khafi Khan, Muhammad Hashim : *Muntakhabu'l-Lubab,* Calcutta, 1850-1874.

Lutf, Ali, Mirza : *Gulshan-i Hind,* Delhi, 1960.

Mihr, Ghulam Rasul : *Saiyid Ahmad Shahid,* Lahore.

Mir, M. Amin Bukhari : *Ubaydullah-nama,* Tashkent MS.

Mirza, Haydar Dughlat : *Tarıkh-i Rashidi,* Riew, I, English tr. by E. Denison Ross, London, 1898.

Mirza Ali Lutf : *Gulshan-i Hind,* Hyderabad-Deccan, 1906.

Muhammad Latif : *Auliya'-i Lahore,* Lahore, 1962.

Muhammad Miyan : *Ulama-i Hind ka Shandar Mazi,* 4 vols., Delhi, 1957-60.

Muhammad Qasim : *Nanawtawi, Qibla-nama',* Deoband, 1969.

Murtaza Husain : *Hadiqat al-Aqalim,* Lucknow, 1881.

Nawwab Dargah Quli Khan Salarjang : *Muraqqa'i Delhi,* Hydera-bad-Deccan.

Nimatullah B. Habibullah al-Harawi : *Tarikh-i Khan-Jahani wa Makhzan-i Afghani,* Dacca, 1960.

Qazwini, Mirza Muhammad Amin : *Badshah-nama,* Rieu, I.

Quddusi, Fijazu'l-Haqq : *Tazkira-i Sufiya' i-Sind,* Karachi, 1959.

Rashidud-Din Fazlullah : *Jamit'u't-tawarikh,* Tehran, 1970, English tr. by J.E. Boyle, New York and London, 1971.

Sadiq Sadiqi, Mirza Muhammad : *Subh-i-Sadiq,* Bankipur.

Shahid, Muhammad Isma'il : *Taqwiyat al-Iman wa Tazkirat al-Ikhwan***,** Lucknow.

Sikandar, B.M. Manjhu : *Mir'at-i Sikandari,* Bombay, 1890.

Thaneswari, Muhammad Jafar : *Hayat-i Saiyid Ahmad Shahid,* Karachi, 1968.

Wali, Mir Abu Turab : *Tarikh-Gujarat,* Calcutta, 1909.

Yusuf Salim Chishti : *Anwar, Mujaddidi,* Lahore, 1961.

Zahiru'd-Din, Saiyid Ahmad : *Kamalat-i 'Aiizi,* Karachi, 1972.

Zaidpuri, Ghulam Husain Khan Salim : *Riyazu's -Salatin,* Calcutta, 1902-1904.

Zawwar Husain Shah, Saiyid : *Hazrat Mujaddidi Alf-i Sani,* Karachi 1972.

Urdu Books

Abul Hassan Nadvi : *Nabi-e-Rahmat* (PBUH).

Abul Kalam Azad : *Rasul-e-Rehmat* (PBUH)

Al-Zahrawi, Abul-Qasim Khalf Ibn Abbas : *Al-Tasrif,* Bismillah Pub., Lakhnow, 1908.

Amin, Ahmad Razi : *Haft Iqlim,* A. & B. Pub., Dacca, 1999.

Jalaluddin Jaffery : *Khatimun Nabiyeen* (PBUH).

Khalid Alvi : *Insan-e-Kamil* (PBUH).

Maulana Abdul Majid Daryabadi: *Tafsir-i-Majidi.* (Taj Company, Lahore).

Maulana Ashraf Ali Thanvi : *Bayan-ul-Quran* (Taj Company, Lahore).

Misbahuddin Ahmad : *Seerat-e-Ahmad-e-Mujtaba* (PBUH).

Naeem Siddiqui : *Mohsin-e-Insaniyyat* (PBUH).

Nurani, Muhammad Abd al-Rashid : *Lughat al-Quran,* Modern Islamic Pub., Delhi, 1945.

Qazi Sulaiman Mansurpuri : *Rahmat-ul-Ul-Aalamin* (PBUH).

Raza, Muhammad Ashraf : *Hayat-e-Risalat Maab* (PBUH).

INDEX

A

I

J

K

L

M

❑❑❑